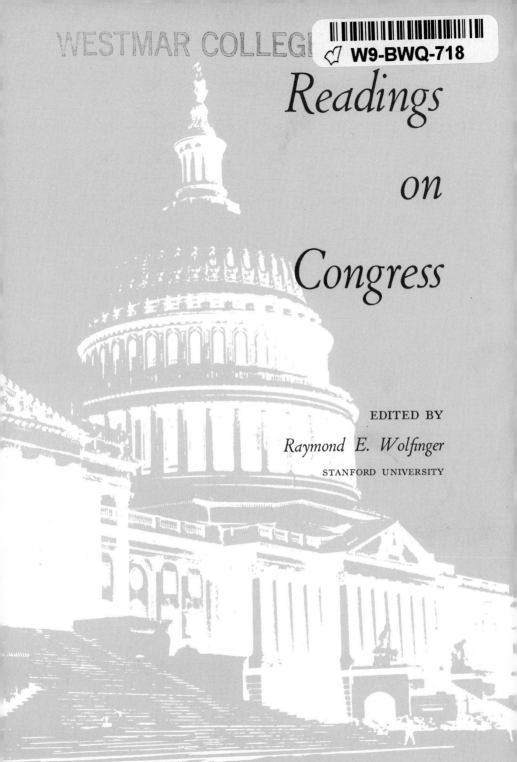

Readings

on

Congress

EDITED BY

Raymond E. Wolfinger

STANFORD UNIVERSITY

PRENTICE-HALL, INC., ENGLEWOOD CLIFFS, N.J.

C: 13–761262–1   P: 13–761254–0

Library of Congress Catalog Card Number: 75–123082

Current printing (last digit):

10 9 8 7 6 5 4 3 2 1

PRENTICE-HALL INTERNATIONAL, INC., *London*
PRENTICE-HALL OF AUSTRALIA PTY. LTD., *Sydney*
PRENTICE-HALL OF CANADA LTD., *Toronto*
PRENTICE-HALL OF INDIA PRIVATE LIMITED, *New Delhi*
PRENTICE-HALL OF JAPAN, INC., *Tokyo*

Printed in the United States of America

Preface

This is a collection of 23 pieces chosen for their usefulness in describing
and explaining the workings of Congress to undergraduate students.
These articles are the best available empirical material on the principal
aspects of Congress, ranging from how its members are elected to
the ways they influence administration of the laws. With the exception
of the newest selections, these readings are ones that I have found most
useful in an undergraduate course on Congress over the past six years.
This book can, however, be used in any course in which students have
had additional textbook exposure, however slight, to Congress.

The selections are all substantive. In other words, I have included
no methodological material nor abstract conceptual approaches to the
study of Congress, e.g., mathematical models or simulations. With the
exception of the first article, which reports survey research on the electorate,
this book is based on extensive first-hand observation of Congress.
A third of these articles, in fact, were written by people with practical
working experience on Capitol Hill.

All of these selections are concerned with Congress as it is and are not
aimed at prescribing the ideal legislature. This is a far cry, however,
from saying that they do not help students understand how Congress can
be improved. Rather, what they do is to show how present practices serve
real political and organizational needs, and they will therefore further
understanding of the possibilities and limitations of congressional reform.

RAYMOND E. WOLFINGER

Contents

The Electoral Base

Voters are the base from which each congressman and senator builds his power in Washington, and just as congressional careers begin with the electorate, so should an understanding of Congress. This section examines public opinion and voting on Congress, some of the principal features of campaign organization, and the distribution of competitive seats between the two parties. Each of the three selections is based on data on the House, but each is almost equally pertinent to the Senate.

In the past fifteen years survey research has become a precise and reliable instrument for the study of individual voters' opinions, knowledge, and interests, and therefore we can be fairly confident about certain aspects of public opinion toward Congress. Ignorance of Congress and disinterest in its activities are widespread. As the first article shows, most voters do not know even the name of their representative, much less the name of the man who runs against him. Scarcely a majority of voters even know whether the Democrats or Republicans control Congress, and hence much of the electorate is not in a very good position to hold either party accountable for its performance on Capitol Hill. It goes without saying that the great mass of voters is unaware of the voting records of their representatives, and even less aware of more refined aspects of legislative behavior.

Lacking information about either the candidates for Congress or the issues upon which they may be running, voters typically rely upon the great fixed principle of American political decision-making: party identification. Most Americans consider themselves Republicans or Democrats.

Such identifications are both durable and loosely related to opinions on particular issues. It should not be surprising, then, that the election outcome is scarcely in doubt in most congressional districts, which are consistently won by one party or the other, year after year, decade after decade.

Two main factors introduce a dynamic element into congressional elections. One is the ability of some candidates to establish themselves as political personalities in their own right, or to raise issues so compelling that the voters will have some reference point other than party identification upon which they can base their votes. This is more likely to occur in the Senate than in the House, if only because of the Senate's greater visibility. The second source of change in congressional elections is the shifting images of the two parties, which affect chiefly that fraction of the electorate not firmly committed to one or the other of the parties. Such shifts reflect perceptions of the presidential candidates and the public image of the president, however, and thus are almost wholly beyond the control of congressional candidates. When disaster strikes during a Republican administration, as was the case with the Depression during Herbert Hoover's term of office, the wrath of the voters falls with a fine lack of discrimination upon Republican presidential and congressional candidates alike. More recently, the widespread sense of disillusion with President Johnson that resulted from our involvement in Vietnam and from the continued exposure of Johnson's rather exotic personality was reflected in the defeat of fifty-two Democratic representatives in the 1966 elections. Changes in the outcome of congressional elections are affected predominantly by the tides of national politics, rather than by local conditions. Thus in 1966 only five Republican congressmen were unseated. In short, when it comes to the decisions made by voters, congressional candidates are vulnerable to national trends upon which they can have only a peripheral influence.

The first step toward Capitol Hill is not winning a general election, but gaining the nomination of one party or the other, and here the important influences are almost entirely local rather than national. Neither party has anything remotely resembling a national "machine" that can bestow and deny congressional nominations; indeed, most attempts by national figures to intervene in nominations have backfired spectacularly. Because the nominating process is so decentralized, the nominee owes little if anything to his party's national leaders in the White House or Congress.

By the same token, the candidate is on his own during the campaign. While some money and expert help are given by national party organizations, the vast bulk of the funds and work are provided through the efforts of the candidate, his local supporters, and party organizations in the constituency. A winning candidate, then, seldom feels that he owes his seat to what the national party has done for him; obligations are owed chiefly to local people. Thus the first call on a congressman's loyalties is from his constituents, not his party's leaders or the White House. The independence of each congressman's campaign efforts is the theme of the second selection, which is based on round-table discussions with a number of congressmen of both parties. In other words, the national importance of the two parties in congressional elections is reflected in the dominant influence of party identification on individual voters. But parties *as organizations* for securing nomination and conducting campaigns are almost wholly local in character. Thus while the most important determinant of voting decisions is the national party image, this factor is largely beyond the control of anyone, and those things that politicians can do to affect the outcome of the election are done mostly at the local level.

The third selection is concerned with southern influence in the House. In pursuit of this topic it traces relationships between constituency characteristics, the geographical allocation of noncompetitive seats, and the distribution of institutional power positions. This article also demonstrates how the number of safe Democratic seats has decreased in the South while growing in the North, thus altering the locus of congressional power and enhancing Democratic cohesion as the era of southern dominance on Capitol Hill draws to a close.

The number of representatives and senators who are relatively sure of reelection means that legislators have far longer Washington careers than the leading political figures in the Executive Branch. The more senior congressmen have been in government while a procession of presidents has come and gone. The younger ones, beginning their careers, look forward to remaining in office long after the current wielders of presidential power have departed. One consequence is that legislators have a longer time perspective than the president. Among other things, this means that most of them do not feel so impelled to make an immediate impact, knowing that they will have a far longer time to leave their mark on the world. A second consequence is that congressmen make common cause with those other durable figures on the Washington scene, the career bureaucrats and the interest groups. And third, Congress is organized by and for men who expect to be there for a long time, and therefore can afford to wait their turn for the most desirable positions, access to which is governed in considerable (but not exclusive) degree by precedence. These themes will recur in many of the selections throughout this book.

1

DONALD E. STOKES / WARREN E. MILLER

Party Government and the
Saliency of Congress

Any mid-term congressional election raises pointed questions about party
government in America. With the personality of the President removed
from the ballot by at least a coattail, the public is free to pass judgment
on the legislative record of the parties. So the civics texts would have
us believe. In fact, however, an off-year election can be regarded as an
assessment of the parties' record in Congress only if the electorate possesses
certain minimal information about what that record is. The fact of
possession needs to be demonstrated, not assumed, and the low visibility
of congressional affairs to many citizens suggests that the electorate's actual
information should be examined with care.

How much the people know is an important, if somewhat hidden,
problem of the normative theory of representation. Implicitly at least
the information the public is thought to have is one of the points on
which various classical conceptions of representation divide. Edmund
Burke and the liberal philosophers, for example—to say nothing of Hamilton
and Jefferson—had very different views about the information the public

The research from which this report is drawn was supported by grants of the
Rockefeller Foundation and the Social Science Research Council. The authors also
gratefully acknowledge the skilled assistance of Ralph Bisco, Jon Faily, Julie Crowder,
and Arthur Wolfe.

Reprinted from *The Public Opinion Quarterly,* 26 (Winter 1962), 531–46,
by permission of the publisher. Copyright © 1962 by *The Public Opinion Quarterly.*
Messrs. Stokes and Miller are Professors of Political Science at the University of
Michigan.

could get or use in assessing its government. And the periods of flood tide in American democracy, especially the Jacksonian and Progressive eras, have been marked by the most optimistic assumptions as to what the people could or did know about their government. To put the matter another way: any set of representative institutions will work very differently according to the amount and quality of information the electorate has. This is certainly true of the institutional forms we associate with government by responsible parties. A necessary condition of party responsibility to the people is that the public have basic information about the parties and their legislative record. Without it, no institutional devices can make responsibility a fact.

To explore the information possessed by those who play the legislative and constituent roles in American government, the Survey Research Center of the University of Michigan undertook an interview study of Congressmen and their districts during the mid-term election of Eisenhower's second term. Immediately after the 1958 campaign the Center interviewed a nationwide sample of the electorate, clustered in 116 congressional districts, as well as the incumbent Congressmen and other major-party candidates for the House from the same collection of districts.[1] Through these direct interviews with the persons playing the reciprocal roles of representative government, this research has sought careful evidence about the perceptual ties that bind, or fail to bind, the Congressman to his party and district. We will review some of this evidence here for the light that it throws on the problem of party cohesion and responsibility in Congress.

The Responsible-Party Model and the American Case

What the conception of government by responsible parties requires of the general public has received much less attention than what it requires of the legislative and electoral parties.[2] The notion of responsibility generally

---

[1] The 116 districts are a probability sample of all constituencies, although the fact that the study was piggy-backed onto a four-year panel study of the electorate extending over the elections of 1956, 1958, and 1960 made the design of the 1958 representation sample unusually complex. In particular, since metropolitan areas and non-metropolitan counties or groups of counties, rather than congressional districts, were used as primary sampling units when the panel sample was originated in 1956, the districts represented in our 1958 sample did not have equal probability of selection and the efficiency of the sample of districts was somewhat less than that of a simple random sample of equal size. Descriptions of the sample design may be obtained from the Survey Research Center.

[2] For example, the 1950 report of the American Political Science Association's Committee on Political Parties, the closest approach to an official statement of the responsible-party view as applied to American politics, concentrates on the organiza-

is understood to mean that the parties play a mediating role between the public and its government, making popular control effective by developing rival programs of government action that are presented to the electorate for its choice. The party whose program gains the greater support takes possession of the government and is held accountable to the public in later elections for its success in giving its program effect.

Two assumptions about the role of the public can be extracted from these ideas. *First,* in a system of party government the electorate's attitude toward the parties is based on what the party programs are and how well the parties have delivered on them. The public, in a word, gives the parties *programmatic* support. And, in view of the importance that legislative action is likely to have in any program, such support is formed largely out of public reaction to the legislative performance of the parties, especially the party in power.

Second, under a system of party government the voters' response to the local legislative candidates is based on the candidates' identification with party programs. These programs are the substance of their appeals to the constituency, which will act on the basis of its information about the proposals and legislative record of the parties. Since the party programs are of dominant importance, the candidates are deprived of any independent basis of support. They will not be able to build in their home districts an electoral redoubt from which to challenge the leadership of their parties.[3]

How well do these assumptions fit the behavior of the American public

---

tion of Congress and the national parties and deals only very obliquely with the role of the public. See American Political Science Association, *Toward a More Responsible Two-party System* (New York: Holt, Rinehart & Winston, Inc., 1950). In general, theoretical and empirical treatments of party government have focused more on the nature of party *appeals*—especially the question of whether the parties present a real "choice"—than on the cognitive and motivational elements that should be found in the *response* of an electorate that is playing its correct role in a system of responsible-party government. For example, see the excellent discussion in Austin Ranney and Willmoore Kendall, *Democracy and the American Party System* (New York: Harcourt, Brace & World, Inc., 1956), pp. 151–52, 384–85, 525–27.

It should be clear that the data of this report are taken from a particular election of a particular electoral era. We would expect our principal findings to apply to most recent off-year elections, but they are of course subject to modification for earlier or later periods.

[3] This assumption does not imply that pressures toward party cohesion come *only* from the mass public. Other sanctions against party irregularity are of equal or greater importance, especially those available in the nominating process and within the legislative parties themselves. To cite the most celebrated empirical case, the cohesiveness of the British parliamentary parties is not enforced primarily, if at all, by the British electorate. Nevertheless, the public ought not to give aid and comfort to the legislative party irregular; the idea of the candidate building a local bastion of strength from which he can challenge the party leadership is clearly contradictory to the party-government model.

as it reaches a choice in the off-year congressional elections? A first glance at the relation of partisan identifications to the vote might give the impression that the mid-term election is a triumph of party government. Popular allegiance to the parties is of immense importance in all our national elections, including those in which a President is chosen, but its potency in the mid-term congressional election is especially pronounced. This fact is plain—even stark—in the entries of Table 1, which break down the vote for Congress in 1958 into its component party elements. The table makes clear, first of all, how astonishingly small a proportion of the mid-term vote is cast by political independents. Repeated electoral studies in the United States have indicated that somewhat fewer than 1 American in 10 thinks of himself as altogether independent of the two parties.[4] But in the off-year race for Congress only about a twentieth part of the vote is cast by independents, owing to their greater drop-out rate when the drama and stakes of the presidential contest are missing.

**Table 1   1958 Vote for House Candidates,
by Party Identification**

	Party Identification*			
	Democratic	*Independent*	*Republican*	*Total*
Voted Democratic	53%†	2%	6%	61%
Voted Republican	5	3	31	39
Total	58%	5%	37%	100%

* The Democratic and Republican party identification groups include all persons who classify themselves as having some degree of party loyalty.
† Each entry of the table gives the per cent of the total sample of voters having the specified combination of party identification and vote for the House in 1958.

Table 1 also makes clear how little deviation from party there is among Republicans and Democrats voting in a mid-term year. The role of party identification in the congressional election might still be slight, whatever the size of the party followings, if partisan allegiance sat more lightly on the voting act. But almost 9 out of every 10 partisans voting in the off-year race support their parties. Indeed, something like 84 per cent of *all* the votes for the House in 1958 were cast by party identifiers supporting their parties. The remaining 16 per cent is not a trivial fraction of the whole— standing, as it did in this case, for 8 million people, quite enough to make and unmake a good many legislative careers. Nevertheless, the low frequency of deviation from party, together with the low frequency of indepen-

[4] See Angus Campbell, Philip E. Converse, Warren E. Miller, and Donald E. Stokes, *The American Voter* (New York: John Wiley & Sons, Inc., 1960), p. 124.

dent voting, indicates that the meaning of the mid-term vote depends in large part on the nature of party voting.

The Saliency of the Parties' Legislative Records

If American party voting were to fit the responsible-party model it would be *programmatic* voting, that is, the giving of electoral support according to the parties' past or prospective action on programs that consist (mainly) of legislative measures. There is little question that partisan voting is one of the very few things at the bottom of our two-party system; every serious third-party movement in a hundred years has foundered on the reef of traditional Republican and Democratic loyalties. But there is also little question that this voting is largely nonprogrammatic in nature. A growing body of evidence indicates that party loyalties are typically learned early in life, free of ideological or issue content, with the family as the main socializing agency. Certainly the findings of adult interview studies show that such loyalties are extremely long-lived and, summed across the population, give rise to extraordinarily stable distributions.[5] The very persistence of party identification raises suspicion as to whether the country is responding to the parties' current legislative actions when it votes its party loyalties.

That this suspicion is fully warranted in the mid-term election is indicated by several kinds of evidence from this research. To begin with, the electorate's perceptions of the parties betray very little information about current policy issues. For the past ten years the Survey Research Center has opened its electoral interviews with a series of free-answer questions designed to gather in the positive and negative ideas that the public has about the parties. The answers, requiring on the average nearly ten minutes of conversation, are only very secondarily couched in terms of policy issues. In 1958, for example, more than six thousand distinct positive or negative comments about the parties were made by a sample of 1,700 persons. Of these, less than 12 per cent by the most generous count had to do with contemporary legislative issues. As this sample of Americans pictured the reasons it liked and disliked the parties, the modern battlefields of the legislative wars—aid-to-education, farm policy, foreign aid, housing, aid to the unemployed, tariff and trade policy, social security, medical care, labor laws, civil rights, and other issues—rarely came to mind. The main themes in the public's image of the parties are not totally cut off from current legislative events; the political activist could take the group-benefit and prosperity-depression ideas that saturate the party images and connect

[5] For evidence on this point, see *ibid.*, pp. 120–67.

them fairly easily with issues before Congress. The point is that the public itself rarely does so.

How little awareness of current issues is embodied in the congressional vote also is attested by the reasons people give for voting Republican or Democratic for the House. In view of the capacity of survey respondents to rationalize their acts, direct explanations of behavior should be treated with some reserve. However, rationalization is likely to increase, rather than decrease, the policy content of reasons for voting. It is therefore especially noteworthy how few of the reasons our respondents gave for their House votes in 1958 had any discernible issue content. The proportion that had—about 7 per cent—was less even than the proportion of party-image references touching current issues.

Perhaps the most compelling demonstration of how hazardous it is to interpret party voting as a judgment of the parties' legislative records is furnished by the evidence about the public's knowledge of party control of Congress. When our 1958 sample was asked whether the Democrats or the Republicans had had more Congressmen in Washington during the two preceding years, a third confessed they had no idea, and an additional fifth gave control of the Eighty-fifth Congress to the Republicans. Only 47 per cent correctly attributed control to the Democrats. These figures improve somewhat when nonvoters are excluded. Of those who voted in 1958, a fifth did not know which party had controlled Congress, another fifth thought the Republicans had, and the remainder (61 per cent) correctly gave control to the Democrats. However, when a discount is made for guessing, the proportion of voters who really *knew* which party had control of the Eighty-fifth Congress probably is still not more than half.[6]

It would be difficult to overstate the significance of these figures for the problem of party government. The information at issue here is not a sophisticated judgment as to what sort of coalition had *effective* control of Congress. It is simply the question of whether the country had a Democratic or a Republican Congress from 1956 to 1958. This elementary fact of

[6] Plainly, some deduction has to be made for guessing. One model of the situation would be to think of the sample as composed of three types of people: those who knew, those who didn't know and said so, and those who didn't know but guessed. Assuming that for those who guessed $p = q = \frac{1}{2}$, where p is the probability of guessing Republican, we would deduct from the Democratic answers a percentage equal to the 18 per cent who guessed Republican incorrectly, hence reducing the proportion of voters who really knew which party controlled Congress to 43 per cent. This model may be too severe, however, in view of the presence of the Republican President. It may be more reasonable to admit a fourth type of person, those who did not guess but were misled by Republican control of the White House. Or we might think of the guessers as following a probability law in which $p > \frac{1}{2} > q$. In either of these cases something less than 18 per cent would be deducted from the Democratic answers; hence, the proportion of voters who *knew* which party controlled Congress would lie somewhere between 43 and 61 per cent.

political life, which any pundit would take completely for granted as he interpreted the popular vote in terms of party accountability, was unknown to something like half the people who went to the polls in 1958.

It is of equal significance to note that the parties' legislative record was no more salient to those who *deviated* from party than it was to those who voted their traditional party loyalty. It might be plausible to suppose that a floating portion of the electorate gives the parties programmatic support, even though most voters follow their traditional allegiances. If true, this difference would give the responsible-party model some factual basis, whether or not the greater part of the electorate lived in darkness. But such a theory finds very little support in these data. In 1958 neither the issue reasons given for the congressional vote nor the awareness of party control of the Eighty-fifth Congress was any higher among those who voted *against* their party identification than it was among those who voted *for* their party, as the entries of Table 2 demonstrate. If anything, correcting perceived party control for guessing suggests that voters who deviated from their party in 1958 had poorer information about the course of political events over the preceding two years.

Table 2   Issue Responses and Awareness of Which Party Controlled Eighty-fifth Congress among Party Supporters and Voters Who Deviated from Party

	Of Party Identifiers Who	
	Voted for Own Party	Voted for Other Party
Aware of party control:		
Uncorrected	61%	60%
Corrected for guessing*	44	35
Giving issue reasons for House vote	6	7

* This correction deducts from the proportion attributing control to the Democrats a percentage equal to the proportion attributing control to the Republicans. See footnote 6.

Nor do the perceptions of party control of Congress that *are* found supply a key to understanding the congressional vote. Whatever awareness of control the electorate had in 1958 was remarkably unrelated to its support of candidates for the House. To make this point, Table 3 analyzes deviations from party according to three perceptions held by party identifiers voting in 1958: *first,* whether they thought the country's recent domestic affairs had gone well or badly; *second* (to allow for the complication of divided government), whether they thought Congress or President had the greater influence over what the government did; and, *third,* whether they thought the Democrats or Republicans had controlled Congress. To

Table 3   Percentage of Party Identifiers Voting against Party in 1958, by Perception of Party Control of Government and Course of Domestic Affairs

Thought That Domestic Affairs	*Thought That More Effective Branch of Government Was Controlled by*	
	Own Party	*Other Party*
	I	II
Had gone well	16	22
	(N = 43)	(N = 46)
	III	IV
Had gone badly	14	13
	(N = 152)	(N = 122)

recreate the basis on which the voter might assign credit or blame to the parties, the second and third of these perceptions may be combined; that is, partisans may be classified according to whether they thought their own party or the opposite party had controlled the more effective branch of government. Crossing this classification with perceptions of whether domestic affairs had gone well yields four groups for analysis, two of which (I and IV) might be expected to show little deviation from party, the other two (II and III) substantially more. In fact, however, the differences between these groups are almost trifling. According to the familiar lore, the groups that thought affairs had gone badly (III and IV) are the ones that should provide the clearest test of whether perceptions of party control are relevant to voting for the House. Moreover, with a recession in the immediate background, most people who could be classified into this table in 1958 fell into one of these two groups, as the frequencies indicate. But when the two groups that felt there had been domestic difficulties are compared, it seems not to make a particle of difference whether the Democrats or Republicans were thought to have controlled the actions of government. And when the two groups (I and II) that felt things had gone well are compared, only a slight (and statistically insignificant) difference appears. Interestingly, even this small rise in the rate of deviation from party (in cell II) is contributed mainly by Democratic identifiers who wrongly supposed that the Congress had been in Republican hands.

The conclusion to be drawn from all this certainly is not that national political forces are without *any* influence on deviations from party in the mid-term year. Clearly these forces do have an influence. Although the fluctuations of the mid-term party vote, charted over half a century or more, are very much smaller than fluctuations in the presidential vote or of the congressional vote in presidential years, there is *some* variation, and these moderate swings must be attributed to forces that have their focus at the national level.[7] Even in 1958 one party received a larger share of deviating votes than the other. Our main point is rather that the deviations that *do* result from national forces are not in the main produced by the parties' legislative records and that, in any case, the proportion of deviating votes that can be attributed to national politics is likely to be a small part of the total votes cast by persons deviating from party in a mid-term year. This was specifically true in 1958.

If the motives for deviations from party are not to be found primarily at the national level, the search moves naturally to the local congressional campaign. A third possibility—that deviations are by-products of state-wide races—can be discounted with some confidence. Despite the popular lore on the subject, evidence both from interview studies and from aggregate election statistics can be used to show that the influence of contests for Governor and Senator on the outcome of House races is slight in mid-term elections, although these contests can have an immense influence on turn-out for the House.[8] In our 1958 sample, a majority of those who deviated from party in voting for the House *failed* to deviate also at the state level; more often than not, what had moved them into the other party's column at the House level was dissociated from the contests for Governor or Senator in which they voted. Moreover, the fact that an elector deviates from his party in voting both for the House and some office contested on a state-wide basis is not conclusive evidence that the state race has influenced his choice for the House, rather than the other way round. When the possibility of *reverse* coattail effects is allowed for, the reasons for believing that the state-wide race is a potent force on the House vote seem faint indeed.[9]

7 A simple but persuasive comparison is this: from 1892 to 1960 the standard deviation of the two-party division of the mid-term congressional vote was 3.9 per cent; of the presidential-year congressional vote, 5.5 per cent; of the presidential vote, 8.2 per cent. Moreover, if the realignment of party loyalties that occurred in the early 1930's is taken into account by computing deviations from pre- and post-1932 means, rather than from a grand mean for the whole period, the standard deviation of the mid-term congressional vote is found to have been 2.4 per cent, compared with a standard deviation of 7.5 per cent for the presidential vote. Some of the remaining variability of the mid-term vote may be due to fluctuations of turnout that do not involve deviations from party. Yet, even ignoring this possibility, the bounds within which national political forces can have influenced the off-year vote by inducing deviations from party appear narrow indeed.

8 A remarkable fact is that while the total vote for the House increased by 3 million between 1954 and 1958, more than 2 million of this increase was contributed by New York, where Rockefeller sought the governorship; by Ohio, where a fierce referendum battle was fought over the issue of "right-to-work"; and by California, where the fantastic Knight-Knowland-Brown free-for-all was held.

9 This conclusion is fully supported by an analysis of the variance of turnout and party vote in the mid-term congressional elections of the 1950's. If state-wide races have a major influence on local House races, the election results for the several con-

As we search for the motives for deviation from party, analysis of the local congressional race pays greater dividends.

The Saliency of Congressional Candidates

By the standards of the civics text, what the public knows about the candidates for Congress is as meager as what it knows about the parties' legislative records. Of the people who lived in districts where the House seat was contested in 1958, 59 per cent—well over half—said that they had neither read nor heard anything about either candidate for Congress, and less than 1 in 5 felt that they knew something about both candidates. What is more, these remarkable proportions are only marginally improved by excluding nonvoters from the calculations. Of people who went to the polls and cast a vote between rival House candidates in 1958, fully 46 per cent conceded that they did so without having read or heard anything about either man. What the other half *had* read or heard is illuminating; we will deal with its policy content presently. Many of our respondents said they knew something about the people contesting the House seat on the basis of very slender information indeed.

The incumbent candidate is by far the better known. In districts where an incumbent was opposed for reelection in 1958, 39 per cent of our respondents knew something about the Congressman, whereas only 20 per cent said they knew anything at all about his nonincumbent opponent. The incumbent's advantage of repeated exposure to the electorate is plain enough. In fact, owing to the greater seniority and longer exposure of Congressmen from safe districts, the public's awareness of incumbents who were unopposed for reelection in 1958 was as great as its awareness of incumbents who had had to conduct an election campaign that year.

The saliency of a candidate is of critical importance if he is to attract support from the opposite party. However little the public may know of those seeking office, any information at all about the rival party's candidate creates the possibility of a choice deviating from party. That such a choice occurs with some frequency is shown by the entries of Table 4, whose

---

gressional districts of a state should vary together; similar changes of turnout and party division should be seen in the districts that are influenced by the same state-wide contests. An analysis of the variance of the differences between the 1954 and 1958 turnout level and partisan division for all congressional districts in states having at least two districts indicates that state races have a large effect on turnout; the intraclass correlation expressing the ratio of the between-state variance to the total variance of turnout was more than .45. But this analysis shows, too, that state-wide races have almost no effect whatever on the party division of the House vote; the intraclass correlation expressing the ratio of the between-state variance to the total variance of the party division was not more than .02.

Table 4   Percentage Voting for Own Party Candidate and
Other Party Candidate for House in 1958, by Saliency of Candidates
in Contested Districts

Voted for Candidate	Voter Was Aware of			
	Both Candidates (N = 196)	Own Party Candidate Only (N = 166)	Other Party Candidate Only (N = 68)	Neither Candidate (N = 368)
Of own party	83%	98%	60%	92%
Of other party	17	2	40	8
Total	100%	100%	100%	100%

columns separate party identifiers in contested districts in 1958 according
to whether they were aware of both candidates, the candidate of their own
party or the other party only, or neither candidate. The condition of no
information leads to fairly unrelieved party-line voting, and so to an even
greater degree does the condition of information only about the candidate
of the voter's own party. But if partisan voters know something about the
opposition's man, substantial deviations from party appear. In fact, if such
voters know *only* the opposition candidate, almost half can be induced to
cast a vote contrary to their party identification. In the main, recognition
carries a positive valence; to be perceived at all is to be perceived favorably.
However, some *negative* perceptions are found in our interviews, and when
these are taken into account the explanation of deviation from party becomes surer still. For example, if we return to Table 4 and select from the
third column only the voters who perceived the candidate of the other
party *favorably*, a clear majority is found to have deviated from party allegiance in casting their votes. And if we select from the first column only
the handful of voters who perceived the candidate of their own party
negatively and of the opposite party *positively*, almost three-quarters are
found to have deviated from their party loyalty in voting for the House.

What our constituent interviews show about the increment of support
that accrues to the salient candidate is closely aligned to what the candidates themselves see as the roots of their electoral strength. Our interviews
with incumbent and nonincumbent candidates seeking election to the House
explored at length their understanding of factors aiding—or damaging—
their electoral appeal. In particular, these interviews probed the candidates'
assessment of four possible influences on the result: traditional party loyalties, national issues, state and local contests, and the candidates' own record
and personal standing in the district. Caution is in order in dealing with
answers to questions that touch the respondent's self-image as closely as
these. Specifically, we may expect some overstatement of the candidate's

own importance, particularly from the victors, and we may expect, too, that too large a discount will be applied to party allegiance, since this "inert" factor, having little to do with increments of strength, is so easily taken for granted.

After these allowances are made, it is still impressive how heavy a weight the incumbent assigns his personal record and standing. The Congressman's ranking of this and the other factors in the election is shown in Table 5. As the entries of the table indicate, more than four-fifths of the incumbents reelected in 1958 felt that the niche they carved out in the awareness of their constituents had substantial impact on the race, a proportion that exceeds by half the percentage who gave as much weight to any of the three other factors. This difference is more than sheer puffing in the interview situation, and the perceptual facts it reveals deserve close attention. Among the forces the Representative feels may enhance his strength at the polls, he gives his personal standing with the district front rank.

Table 5   Relative Importance of Factors in Reelection as Seen by Incumbent Candidates in 1958

Perceived as	Personal Record and Standing	National Issues	Traditional Party Loyalties	State and Local Races
Very important	57%	26%	25%	14%
Quite important	28	20	21	19
Somewhat important	9	20	24	27
Not very important	3	27	18	19
Not important at all	3	7	12	21
Total	100%	100%	100%	100%

In view of the way the saliency of candidates can move the electorate across party lines, great stress should be laid on the fact that the public sees individual candidates for Congress in terms of party programs scarcely at all. Our constituent interviews indicate that the popular image of the Congressman is almost barren of policy content. A long series of open-ended questions asked of those who said they had any information about the Representative produced mainly a collection of diffuse evaluative judgments: he is a good man, he is experienced, he knows the problems, he has done a good job, and the like. Beyond this, the Congressman's image consisted of a mixed bag of impressions, some of them wildly improbable, about ethnicity, the attractiveness of family, specific services to the district, and other facts in the candidate's background. By the most reasonable count, references to current legislative issues comprised not more than a thirtieth part of what the constituents had to say about their Congressmen.

The irrelevance of legislative issues to the public's knowledge of Representatives is underscored by the nature of some primary *determinants* of saliency. A full analysis of the causes of constituent awareness of candidates goes beyond the scope of this paper. Although our investigation has given a good deal of attention to communication factors and to characteristics of Congressmen and constituents themselves that determine the probability a given Congressman will be known to a given constituent, this interplay of causes cannot be explored very deeply here. However, it *is* noteworthy in the present discussion that many factors increasing the saliency of candidates are unlikely to enhance what the public knows about their stands on issues. An excellent example is sex. Both for incumbents and nonincumbents, a candidate property that is related to saliency is gender; one of the best ways for a Representative to be known is to be a Congress*woman*. How irrelevant to policy issues this property is depends on what we make of the causal relation between sex and salience. The fact of being a woman may make a candidate more visible, but a woman may have to be unusually visible (like a Congressman's widow, say) before she can be elected to the House, or even become a serious candidate. If the first of these inferences is even partially right, the salience of the candidate is not likely to be in terms of positions taken on legislative issues.

Given the number of women who run for Congress, the role of sex may seem a trivial example to demonstrate the irrelevance of issue stands to saliency. However, the same point can be made for a much wider set of districts by the greater saliency of candidates who live in the constituents' home community. Just as there is enormous variety in the communities that make up the American nation, so there is the widest possible variation in how well a congressional district coincides with a natural community, and the goodness of this fit is a fundamental way of typing districts. At one extreme is the constituency whose area is lost within one of the country's great metropolitan centers, comprising at best a small fraction of the whole community. At the middle of the range is the district that is itself a natural community, consisting of a single medium-sized city and its environs. At the other extreme is the district whose territory includes a great number of small communities, as well as surrounding open country that goes on, in some cases, for hundreds of miles. In all but the metropolitan districts the salience of the candidate for the voter differs markedly according to whether candidate and voter live in the community. The fact of common residence— of being "friends and neighbors"—stands for important facts of communication and community identification. Candidates will be joined by formal and informal communication networks to many of the voters living in the same community, and they may also be objects of considerable community pride.

The reality of this local effect is demonstrated by Table 6. As the entries of the table show, dividing a nationwide sample of constituents according to whether they live in the same community as their Congressman or his opponent produces marked differences of saliency. The "friends and neighbors" effect made familiar by studies of primary voting in one-party areas has a counterpart in voting for Representatives throughout the country, apart from the large metropolitan areas.[10] And despite the fact that localism is found here in the context of as tightly party-determined an election as any in American politics, the irrelevance of local appeal to legislative issues is probably as great as it is in the wide-open, one-party primary.

Table 6   Influence of "Friends and Neighbors" Factor on Saliency of Candidates for Voters*

	Incumbent Candidate Lives in		Non-incumbent Candidate Lives in	
	Same Community as Voter	Other Community than Voter	Same Community as Voter	Other Community than Voter
Voter Is	(N = 269)	(N = 414)	(N = 304)	(N = 447)
Aware of candidate	67%	45%	47%	22%
Not aware of candidate	33	55	53	78
Total	100%	100%	100%	100%

* Metropolitan and large urban districts, for which the notion of the candidate living outside the voter's community has no clear meaning, are excluded from the analysis.

Conclusion

What the public knows about the legislative records of the parties and of individual congressional candidates is a principal reason for the departure of American practice from an idealized conception of party government. On the surface the legislative elections occurring in the middle of the President's term appear to be dominated by two national parties asking public support for their alternative programs. Certainly the electorate whose votes they seek responds to individual legislative candidates overwhelmingly on the basis of their party labels. Despite our kaleidoscopic electoral laws, the candidate's party is the one piece of information every voter is guaranteed. For many, it is the only information they ever get.

[10] See V. O. Key, Jr., *Southern Politics* (New York: Alfred A. Knopf, Inc., 1949), pp. 37ff. We have demonstrated the "friends and neighbors" effect in terms of candidate salience because of our interest in the policy content of candidate perceptions. However, owing to the impact of salience on the vote, living in the same community with the candidate has a clear effect on voting as well.

However, the legislative events that follow these elections diverge widely from the responsible-party model. The candidates who have presented themselves to the country under two party symbols immediately break ranks. The legislative parties speak not as two voices but as a cacophony of blocs and individuals fulfilling their own definitions of the public good. Party cohesion by no means vanishes, but it is deeply eroded by the pressures external to party to which the Congressman is subject.

The public's information about the legislative record of the parties and of members of Congress goes far toward reconciling these seemingly con-tradictory facts. In the congressional election, to be sure, the country votes overwhelmingly for party symbols, but the symbols have limited meaning in terms of legislative policy. The eddies and crosscurrents in Congress do not interrupt a flow of legislation that the public expects but fails to see. The electorate sees very little altogether of what goes on in the national legislature. Few judgments of legislative performance are associated with the parties, and much of the public is unaware even of which party has control of Congress. As a result, the absence of party discipline or legislative results is unlikely to bring down electoral sanctions on the ineffective party or the errant Congressman.

What the public's response to the parties lacks in programmatic support is not made up by its response to local congressional candidates. Although perceptions of individual candidates account for most of the votes cast by partisans against their parties, these perceptions are almost untouched by information about the policy stands of the men contesting the House seat. The increment of strength that some candidates, especially incumbents, acquire by being known to their constituents is almost entirely free of policy content. Were such content present, the Congressman's solidarity with his legislative party would by no means be assured. If the local constituency possessed far greater resources of information than it has, it might use the ballot to pry the Congressman away from his party quite as well as to unite him with it. Yet the fact is that, by plying his campaigning and servicing arts over the years, the Congressman is able to develop electoral strength that is almost totally dissociated from what his party wants in Congress and what he himself has done about it. The relevance of all this to the problem of cohesion and responsibility in the legislative party can scarcely be doubted.

The description of party irresponsibility in Amerca should not be over-drawn. The American system *has* elements of party accountability to the public, although the issues on which an accounting is given are relatively few and the accounting is more often rendered by those who hold or seek the Presidency than by the parties' congressional delegations. Especially on the broad problem of government action to secure social and economic welfare it can be argued that the parties have real differences and that these have penetrated the party images to which the electorate responds at the polls.

Nevertheless, American practice does diverge widely from the model of party government, and the factors underlying the departure deserve close analysis. An implication of the analysis reported here is that the public's contribution to party irregularity in Congress is not so much a matter of encouraging or requiring its Representatives to deviate from their parties as it is of the public having so little information that the irregularity of Congressmen and ineffectiveness of the congressional parties have scant impact at the polls. Many of those who have commented on the lack of party discipline in Congress have assumed that the Congressman votes against his party because he is forced to by the demands of one of several hundred constituencies of a superlatively heterogeneous nation. In some cases, the Representative may subvert the proposals of his party because his constituency demands it. But a more reasonable interpretation over a broader range of issues is that the Congressman fails to see these proposals as part of a program on which the party—and he himself—will be judged at the polls, because he knows the constituency isn't looking.

2

CHARLES L. CLAPP

The Problem of Being Returned

Financing the Campaign

Sources of Funds

Campaigns are expensive and raising the money is not always an easy task. Some congressmen are fortunate in that the party organization handles fund-raising problems. But those members are few in number. There are problems involved in heavy dependence on the official organization, as the following comment illustrates: "I've never had a finance committee before, having relied on the local organization. But I am thinking about organizing one because of all the criticism back home from the party about my vote on the labor bill." If the organization disapproves of an incumbent's voting record, it may be reluctant to provide him with adequate funds. Even if it is sympathetic, it may not be able to allocate an amount the congressman regards as minimal.

Party committees—from national to local levels—generally are less generous than candidates feel they should be. Said one congressman:

> The whole matter of financing says a great deal about the attitude of American party organizations toward members of Congress. They just don't think we amount to very much. The sheriff in my county has seventy or eighty jobs to pass out, and everyone is interested in who is sheriff. No one cares about us.

Reprinted from *The Congressman: His Work as He Sees It* (Washington, D. C.: The Brookings Institution, 1963), pp. 344–48, 351–61, 366–69, by permission of the publisher. Copyright © 1963 by The Brookings Institution. Mr. Clapp has been a senior staff member of The Brookings Institution and legislative assistant to Senator Leverett Saltonstall, and is now a Special Assistant to the President.

An aggressive candidate, it is true, may succeed in wresting from the national or congressional committee a sum in excess of that provided to colleagues in his particular category of need (as established by the committee involved), but that is not an easy task. In those rare instances, it is more than likely that the committee, rather than supplementing its original contribution from the treasury, will suggest to a potential contributor that his contribution be sent directly to the candidate. In that way other candidates may not realize their colleague is receiving extra assistance.

Inadequate support from the party organization emphasizes the importance of enlisting the aid of a vigorous finance committee; in many instances, despite such support, a congressman will be required to become —some of them choose to become—his own chief fund-raiser. This is a time-consuming and difficult task. Complained one congressman:

> In a district where I have half a dozen radio stations, three TV stations, and about thirty-five weekly papers, I can run a pretty good campaign on about $15,000, which is not a lot of money. But I have to spend so much of my own time the first couple of months as a fund-raiser—time which I could far more effectively put into straightforward politicking.

Another disadvantage is that if a legislator solicits funds for his own cause, he may find it difficult later to deny a contributor's request for help. And, in view of the laws regarding ceilings on campaign expenditures, it may be preferable for him to remain apart from the fund-raising ventures.

As the earlier discussion of campaign costs illustrates [see original source], many candidates are required to contribute generously to their own campaigns, and must turn to relatives for help, too. A surprising number of congressmen appear to have decided to run for the office without the encouragement of party leaders in their district and thus in early contests are more likely to have depended on personal funds than on organizational support. Veteran legislators are more likely to begrudge personal expenditures.

Often congressional candidates appoint finance committees, composed whenever possible of respected bankers, lawyers, businessmen, and union officials, and rely on them to tap available sources in the district.[1] It is not uncommon for these committees to incur the wrath and resentment of

---

[1] One Democrat from California, where politics remains somewhat unorthodox, found Republicans to be much better fund-raisers than Democrats and now selects Republican dominated finance committees to raise his money. Says he:

"I have never had a campaign successfully financed by my Democratic workers. I find that my Democratic group will tell me money can't be raised, and they won't try. But my Republican groups have an entirely different attitude. They will go out and try. They have been primarily responsible for financing my last three campaigns, not with big contributions but with a lot of effort."

county and local party leaders since the official organization is often seeking funds from the same sources.

Other independent groups supporting the candidate are encouraged to be self-sustaining and, where possible, to provide financial support for some of the candidate's campaign activities. "Friendly" national organizations may be of appreciable assistance by providing fees and honoraria for speeches and talks. The head of one such group interested in congressional elections views this form of indirect financial assistance as of nearly as great significance as the direct campaign contributions made by his organization.

Representatives of both parties seem to agree that of the organized nonparty groups, labor helps the most. Republicans who receive relatively little labor support frequently mention that labor not only contributes substantial sums to Democratic coffers but provides paid election day workers in support of Democratic candidates. And one Democratic legislator expressed the view of many Democrats when he said: "Labor is the only group I am aware of that is conscious of congressional elections and looks upon them as important." One of his liberal colleagues expressed the view that labor's financial support, while appreciated by candidates, has not always been favorably regarded by party officials. "In some northern urban districts," he said, "labor contributions have created tensions between them and the party people. Some party people are beginning to say that if they don't provide financial assistance to candidates and labor does, allegiance may turn to labor rather than party. In some areas, it has resulted in more financial assistance from the party."

While labor union support for Democratic congressional candidates is widespread, its recipients state that much, if not the bulk of their financial support, comes from small business and professional people. Nor are all of them entirely satisfied with what they receive. Three liberal Democrats, one representing an eastern urban area, another a sparsely settled western district, and the third a midwestern industrial area, gave their views:

I've heard that the unions have made contributions to pro-labor men in marginal districts. I thought some of you on the labor committee would benefit from that since I know of contributions of $1,000 and better to some candidates. One labor leader told me they couldn't make a contribution to me but suggested that I give them my printing bill, and they would take care of it. The bill came to a little more than $3,000 and I submitted it to them. Then they said they had run out of funds, so I had to pay it myself. I had another bad experience. I had an argument with a labor leader. Labor had offered to contribute $1,000 to my campaign and had the check ready when a labor leader from whom I wouldn't take any guff called the union and told them not to give it to me. The union official showed me the check and said he had been told to countermand it. I couldn't get the money because another labor union not in my district said, "We don't want you to give it to him."

I got a contribution from labor last time, the only contribution I have ever received from them. But when Senator Goldwater was kind enough to put all the labor reports in the *Congressional Record,* I went down the list and discovered that even though I was a member of the labor committee and from a marginal district, the contribution to me was small in comparison to some sent to anti-labor congressmen—some even Republicans—in other areas. In my state at least, contributions of the labor people to their own political organization, COPE, don't come back to the state. They are used elsewhere.

I have found it important to build up a close personal link with the top labor people in my area so they feel a sense of personal responsibility to raise funds for my campaign. They feel they are letting me down unless they go out and push the right button here in the capital to take care of me back home. I think it is a splendid attitude for them to have.

One freshman Democrat interviewed at the time a controversial labor bill was before the House spoke out sharply against the charge that he was a "labor" congressman. Said he:

Some people say those of us who oppose this legislation are controlled by labor. That is nonsense. Labor made a contribution to my campaign last time and I appreciated it. I got $3,100 from them. That was helpful, but it amounted to only 12 percent of my campaign budget. That means, relatively speaking, it was not much noticed. Who is going to sell out for $3,100?

As the following discussion indicates, leading industries of a state or congressional district do not always contribute heavily, or as anticipated, to congressional campaigns.

There is no rule of thumb you can apply to where funds will come from once you have counted the labor group. There is no industry in our state that has more reason to be interested in what happens in Congress than the oil industry. Yet they are tight as far as contributing to a congressional campaign is concerned. Individual oilmen who should be interested in what kind of legislation is passed with respect to depletion allowance or imports are notorious in their refusal to get interested in congressional campaigns in a financial way—and that goes for contributions to either party. On the other hand, you will find small businessmen or lawyers or dentists taking a pretty substantial financial interest, generally on the grounds that they know the man and are interested in seeing him go to Congress.

Is this an unkind suggestion to make: It is pretty difficult for congressmen from certain states to vote against the predominant industry in their states, so there is no need for the industry to use any leverage.

That is true if you are going to put it only on the basis of votes, but everyone here knows that your vote is not the point at which you exert the most influence for something that is of interest to your district or state. If you confined your activities in behalf of your district to voting, you would not be much of a factor in Congress.

There is a large lumbering industry in my state and year after year they give money to the Republican candidate. My predecessor voted against every housing bill that came along, and yet they consistently supported him because he was a Republican. I could do a lot more for them. . . .

The Role of Official Party Organizations

Congressional recognition that perhaps the best way to woo many voters is by means of activities not directly related to the election campaign does not result in minimizing campaign efforts. Waging an effective campaign is, understandably, a major concern of congressmen, and they are constantly searching for new techniques. Many informal discussions are held with colleagues on the matter, and there is much adapting of undertakings which have been used successfully in other districts. Countless hours are spent reviewing campaign ads and literature, posters, automobile bumper stickers, and billboard suggestions in the search for effective materials; additional time is spent with layout artists and editorial assistants worrying about wording and position placement problems. Where an election is concerned, no task seems too small, no detail too insignificant to attract the attention and concern of some of the campaigners.

For some members campaigning is an ordeal; for others it is strenuous but enjoyable. A few even approach the contest with enthusiasm and relish. But whatever the attitude toward running for office, there is considerable congressional sentiment that members are required too often to "go it alone" in the endeavor.

The feeling is strong that local, state, and national party organizations are indifferent and/or ineffective in lending support. Said one Republican, "If we depended on the party organization to get elected, none of us would be here. Because the organization is not too helpful, it doesn't have very much influence with us." Except for the rare member who is the beneficiary of a strong city organization, the statement appears to reflect general House opinion. There are indications that in some areas congressional contests are becoming more fully integrated into state and local campaigns, but even there the effort is unlikely to be sufficient to alter congressional views appreciably. As one politically experienced Democrat observed philosophically:

I don't think there is any element of the party that is particularly interested in or concerned with the election of members of Congress. The National Committee is preoccupied with the White House. The state committee has its eyes on the state house and the county committee is interested only in the court house. The congressman is just sort of a fifth wheel on the whole wagon.

A colleague agreed:

That is the experience in my state, too—congressmen are just orphans. The past election was the first time in memory that congressional candidates had their names on state billboards of the party. It was also the first time we were mentioned in radio and television spot advertising done in behalf of the party—and that was an afterthought.

State and Local Organization

For the most part, state party organizations are relatively unimportant in the campaign plans of members of Congress, though it appears that the congressional races are receiving somewhat more attention than formerly from state chairmen and state central committees. In a few states, central finance committees are beginning to contribute funds to congressional campaigns, and, as noted, there are areas where the local organization is so strong that they select the congressional candidate and conduct and bear the expenses of the major part of the campaign effort.

But more often one hears congressmen maintain that not only is it unusual to receive financial assistance from local official party organizations, but, indeed, congressional candidates may be expected to contribute to the support of such groups. Representative of this situation are the following comments:

I was rather amused by the question about support from county and district organizations because we always contribute to the county organizations and help subsidize them in our district. In our state their activities are pretty well confined to getting out the vote on election day.

In my state the state committee asks for contributions from the candidates and the congressional candidate is expected to contribute approximately $300.

I have to subsidize my county organization. Our state had a $100 dinner in the last campaign and raised $700,000 in one evening, and I didn't get a penny of it. When I asked the national and congressional campaign committees for help, they said they were having trouble raising money, and if they could raise it, they couldn't send it to my state. "You raise $700,000 there in one evening," they said. "We don't even think about that kind of money down here." So I get nothing from the national, nothing from the state, and have to give some to each of my three county organizations.

On the other hand, there was some testimony of this kind: "As far as fund-raising is concerned in my own district, the county committee had a fund-raising subcommittee which does a large portion of the fund-raising for the district."

Criticism that state and local groups do not concern themselves with congressional elections is widespread. A frequently expressed comment is that of a first term Republican:

There wasn't one congressional candidate in my section of our state who had even one inquiry from headquarters as to how we were doing in our campaign. Even ____, who was having the fight of his life, heard nothing from the state committee. Most of us felt we were operating in a complete vacuum as far as any liaison with the state campaign committee went.

In some areas the local group is hostile rather than indifferent. Said one Democrat, "My county committee is never any problem because it is so inactive it is difficult to find. When I have found it, it usually has opposed me." Added another Democrat from a section of the country where strong party organization is much more customary: "When I first ran for the House, our district leader favored my opponent. In order to be protected back home, I had to become district leader the next time around. Thus I have to double in brass. I am the congressman and the district leader." While examples of such hostility seem relatively rare, the different goals of incumbent congressmen and state and local party leaders tend to promote a working relationship which, though often pleasant, is loose and informal and perhaps a little distant. It is especially difficult for congressmen whose districts are geographically distant from Washington to maintain the close associations with local officials that promote full confidence.

A few states are organized on congressional district lines, but this is not common practice. As one representative indicates, this fact points up a problem that is likely to cause some degree of continuing difficulty:

One reason we have to do so much ourselves is that most of us do not represent a natural political subdivision. Our districts may cut across city or county lines. Few states are organized along congressional district lines. To representatives of other political entities congressmen are boobs who think only of their district's political problems rather than local or state or over-all national problems. Before I came to Congress I was active in politics at the county and state committee level, and I couldn't understand why congressmen were so hard to get along with. But after being elected to Congress, I attended a state central committee meeting and I could see what was wrong. The party is not organized to be of maximum benefit to us, and we are forced to rely on our own organizations.

One reflection of the lack of interest on the part of state party leaders in things congressional is the fact that they seldom seek to exert influence on House members, especially with respect to legislation. In the experience of one House leader: "Our national committeeman and the state chairman have called me occasionally about something, but I suspect they were calling because the White House had asked them to do so. They have never been too effective because they didn't know too much about the subject of their call."

The National Party Organizations

Although it is suggested occasionally that the national and congressional campaign committees of both parties should exert a more positive role in the selection of congressional candidates, few congressmen regard such a proposal as feasible or realistic. Even where genuine concern is expressed regarding the ability of local party groups to designate high caliber candidates, hope for improvement is directed toward the state rather than the national party leaders. The legislators are sensitive to local pride and prejudice and are convinced that national intervention would be resented. As one member of Congress said: "These committees just can't be more active in seeking candidates for congressional seats. Even though they might do a better job than some of the people at the local level, they are in no position to do it. You know the old saying—he's an SOB, but he's our SOB." Nor does one solon who headed his state party organization for a time believe it generally desirable to draft candidates. Says he:

Unless the candidate is sufficiently interested to seek the job himself, it may not work out well. I am inclined to feel some of the people who are drafted are not particularly interested or effective. Local pressure on potential candidates is to be preferred to national pressure, but the best procedure is to have good candidates seek office on their own initiative.

While reluctant for the national party to participate directly in the selection of congressional candidates, many congressmen believe the national groups have a positive obligation to provide direct assistance in the form of money, materials, and practical advice once the candidate has been chosen. An obligation exists too, it is felt, to stimulate interest in the contest and to arouse and maintain local enthusiasm for the candidate and the importance of the race. As one member stated:

I think the national and congressional campaign committees can and should perform valuable services in a congressional race. They shouldn't attempt to select the candidate, but once he is selected, they can give a great deal of assistance from an organizational point of view and can also provide tips with regard to publicity.

You have to go slowly in terms of interfering in the local district. We may all worship the same God, but we want to do it in our own way.

Another legislator believes it is the function of the national and congressional committees to develop an organization "to get at the grass roots and provide for the screening of candidates. Of course they can't select candidates for local areas, but they could help set up machinery and in other ways make it more likely better candidates would be forthcoming." Evidence is slight that, at the House level, national party groups do much more. Occasionally, one hears that overtures are made to attractive prospective candidates, but for the most part reliance seems to be placed on attempting to impress local organizations with the necessity of obtaining high quality nominees.

The national committee is relied upon by very few members of Congress for contributions—financial, informational, or services. Contacts between the individual legislator and the national committee are infrequent and, regardless of which party acts as initiator, tend to consist of requests for assistance of some sort. Republicans tend to be somewhat more critical of their national committee than Democrats, but little enthusiasm is evident anywhere in Congress for the top party committee.

Republicans have the benefit of a well-developed congressional campaign committee created specifically to meet their needs and focused directly on ensuring as large a Republican congressional representation as possible. Since in the absence of a strong congressional committee, these functions would be performed by the national committee, their transfer to the congressional scene deprives the parent body of an important means of strengthening its relationship with congressmen. Democratic legislators, lacking a congressional service organization of the magnitude of their Republican counterparts—marked differences exist in budget, staffing, and activities— are somewhat more dependent on their national committee. Though they are not happy with the services they receive from party headquarters or the attention they believe is given there to problems at the congressional level, they are more likely to be critical of the inadequacies of their congressional committee, which many contrast unfavorably with the Republican committee.

The Republican tendency to downgrade their national committee is no doubt influenced in part by the natural rivalry and antagonism which exists between the congressional committee, whose services to them are many and tangible, and the national committee itself. What is often forgotten, however, is that the congressional campaign committee is almost entirely dependent for operating funds on the national committee. Campaign committee personnel criticize the national committee for failing to provide them with sufficient funds to do an effective job,[2] and since the congressional committee budget determines in part how helpful the committee can be to individual legislators, it is not difficult to convince congressmen of the correctness of this position. This somewhat uneasy relationship increases the reluctance of national committee officials and staff to approach congressmen directly since such action might be regarded as an attempt to usurp congressional committee prerogatives. Thus, the natural affinity of the legislator for his benefactor, the congressional committee, is increased by the aloofness of the national committee, which creates an impression of lack of interest.

Both national committees are negligent about providing legislators with information regarding their activities as well as the nature of their potential services. Thus, one Republican, the only member of his party holding a statewide office in his state, was irate when the Republican national chairman entered the state on a speaking tour without informing the congressman that such a trip was contemplated. To politicians, alert to the political implications of such a visit and the prestige factors attached to participating in the arrangements, negligence of that kind is unpardonable.

One legislator who has also seen extended service as a national committee member discussed the uneasy situation existing between Republican congressmen and their national committee:

As a member of Congress and at the same time a member of the Republican National Committee I've been a little disturbed about the tensions and frictions which exist between the National Committee and the Congress. I think much of it is unnecessary, although some of it is understandable when you consider the personalities involved at both levels. The National Committee has not done an adequate job of publicizing the services they can perform for members of Congress. As a result many congressmen think they do nothing over there. I think each group unnecessarily antagonizes the other. It just never crosses people's minds to use the National Committee for many things. They have a fine research division, and there are any number of ways they could help.

At that point, another legislator commented, "They don't take the trouble to tell us what they can do for us." To that statement, the lawmaker with service in both bodies replied:

I have suggested that to them. Someone from the National Committee should come up at the beginning of the session and call on all congressmen, establish a relationship, and tell them what the committee has to offer, and of its interest. Also, the Congressional and Senatorial Campaign Committees are saying, "We

2 In 1962 the National Committee made this distribution of its receipts: national committee 56 percent; senatorial committee 11 percent; congressional committee 33 percent. In 1963, its $2,980,000 budgeted included $850,000 for the congressional committee and $200,000 for the senatorial committee.

are the boys who do things for you and they won't give us enough money." It is the National Committee which raises the money for the national party. The Congressional Committee couldn't perform any services if the National Committee didn't get the money and make it available.

But running through discussions of the National Committee were comments such as these: "What I would like to know is what they do. Does anyone get any benefit from them in his district?" "We are all agreed the National Committee should be abolished, aren't we?" "It does more harm than good."

To criticism that the National Committee should be doing far more for the party, one defender responded:

Their activity depends on how much money is available. If they had the money they would expand their services. If they don't raise enough, then they have to telescope down and do the best they can with what they have. They have done a pretty good job of keeping the party alive, of sending out materials and information. They ought to get "E" for effort.

Though legislators are agreed that the National Committee performs important and necessary functions during presidential campaigns, some think they should maintain only skeleton staffs between those contests, as the following discussion points up:

The two Congressional Committees have not been operating very long. When you get three committees you will have a certain amount of rivalry.

There ought to be very close liaison among the three groups. Other than that, the National Committee ought to become almost dormant between presidential elections.

They are!

They sure spend a lot of money for a dormant organization!

A knowledgeable Democrat, in summarizing the major differences between the Democratic Congressional Campaign Committee and the Democratic National Committee, makes an important point about the nature of prepared materials distributed by such groups, which is often missed by congressmen and their staffs: no matter how high the quality of materials emanating from the committees, to be most useful to a congressman they should be adapted to the local situation. Some releases, speeches, fact books, or suggested advertising, can be used with little or no change; others are valuable primarily in suggesting ideas or possible approaches. Said the congressman:

The services of the National Committee are greater [than those of the Congressional Committee]. They are more likely to send you research material and information sheets. They have a larger staff than the Congressional Committee and are in a much better position to help, but they must necessarily prepare things of a general nature. Then the material has to be adapted if it is to be used effectively in an individual district. The committee is doing a fair job in an important situation. It sends you a great deal of stuff you cannot use, but on the positive side it does give you ideas.

In constrasting the two Democratic committees another congressman said:

The National Committee has been helpful, at least in my kind of district, in coming up with useful research material. The fact books they publish, and other material of that nature, contain much good ammunition. The Congressional Campaign Committee has come up with a moderate amount of money for me every time I've run. It has been my impression that there is more sound and fury coming out of that Congressional Campaign Committee than valuable material.

On the other hand, one influential congressman dryly described his relationship with the Democratic National Committee: "The national party organization has never provided any services to me. It has never provided any funds for me. After I get nominated each time, however, it does send me a telegram of congratulations which I am very happy to have."

There is evidence that at least occasionally the committee is lax in meeting its commitments about money. Said one legislator:

When I came to Congress—even before—I went to the National Committee and offered to be of assistance to the Democratic party. During a recent presidential campaign, they sent me out to make 26 speeches in five or six states, in the course of which I expended $680. After the campaign I decided it was reasonable to ask the committee to reimburse me for these expenses since it had insisted in the beginning that I would be reimbursed. I sent in my statement and said, "I am $680 in arrears," and they replied, "Well, what about it? We are $1,500,000 in arrears." Finally, after I raised a row I received a reply from an employee of the committee saying. "Congressman, don't you know that you should have collected your expenses from each place that you spoke?" Now, that was ridiculous. In the final days of the campaign I spoke in as many as five or six places some days. Usually I knew no one in the community.

There is general recognition that the chairman of the National Committee serves an important and necessary function in acting as a party spokesman and in offsetting and countering the claims of the opposition. Individual members of the National Committee are sometimes singled out for special praise also. Said one congresswoman: "In our state we have a national committeewoman who is a catalytic influence throughout the whole state. I couldn't get along without her during the period between elections. She solves every problem. We never could have accomplished what we did in our state without that kind of personality." Another House member attributes increased interest within the state organization in the fate of congressional candidates to the activities of his national committeeman:

> In my state we decided to bring life into the party by getting a new national committeeman. He makes special trips down here with the state chairman and vice chairman and committeewoman and we have conferences. It has been very, very helpful. The relationship has been so good that the state organization has set up a special committee to help congressmen, financially and otherwise. This last campaign is the first time we had any real help from them.

But such testimonials are relatively rare. Members of Congress tend to be negative or, at best, neutral when speaking of their National Committee.

Criticism may rest partly on congressional belief that the more national orientation of the National Committee and the national party are not always especially consistent with the more parochial interests of the individual congressman and his district. In 1959 the chairman of the Republican Congressional Committee underscored this point by openly advising Republican congressmen to disassociate themselves from those policies of the Republican President with which they disagreed. He emphasized they were running in their own districts on their own platforms, and he made it clear that his committee would not discriminate in any way against congressmen with antiadministration records. His statement served to explain the legislators' preference for their own congressional committee as opposed to the national committee.

At the same time that one notes congressional grumbling that neither the National Committee nor the Congressional Committee helps sufficiently in the campaign itself, it should be pointed out that many congressmen really do not want committee representatives in their districts. They want money, but they do not care about advice. The following discussion touches on this point:

> I didn't get any help from the National Committee, nor did I get much from the Congressional Committee. They had a coordinator for several states, but he didn't do much for me, and they sent me less money than ever before—practically none, in fact. You can understand that in a presidential year, but last year with no president to elect, all the focus was on the congressional race. Here is _____ with what he means to the party, in a very close race. Why wouldn't they be in there working like mad?

> Did you call on the committees for help? Maybe they figured if you needed any help you would let them know.

> Frankly I wouldn't want the Congressional Committee or the National Committee playing around in my district. They could not influence any voters in my

favor. [This statement by a congressman in a district where the opposition party has a heavy majority.]

They have been thrown out of so many districts they don't go in unless there is some indication they are wanted. . . .

Volunteers and Personal Committees

In some areas, where the formal organization is not strong or has not been as helpful to the congressman as he feels it should be, legislators have developed rather effective personal organizations. These groups may function with a minimum of coordination and consultation with the official organization, or they may work with them harmoniously, adding important dimensions to the necessarily limited activities which the party conducts in behalf of its congressional candidate. The bulk of the volunteers and draftees are not sophisticated politically, but enthusiasm and a willingness to perform the everyday chores compensate, in part at least, for the lack of political acumen. Often, however, they include some remarkably skillful people. This type of organization shares with others problems of attrition, and faces too frequently the problem of what to do with the well-meaning but ineffective volunteer. On balance, however, congressmen find these amateur groups a source of tremendous assistance, without which the campaign effort would be greatly reduced. To many congressmen they are indispensable. Said one:

> Our sense of warm appreciation for the many good citizens who can't possibly get anything back from us for what they have done, except hope we will give them the best government of which we are capable is a note that we probably don't vocalize on very much. But at the end of each campaign, win or lose, I am sure we all have a tremendously warm feeling toward all the people in our own areas who have involved themselves so intimately in shaping our lives.

In one southern state where traditionally state and local party organization has been notoriously weak, the clusters of groups which gather around the congressional nominee are achieving significance. As the state has moved toward a two party system, the weak official organizations have sought to rally party standards around the more powerful independent structures. Reported one congressman, "Our state committee has found that by working through the congressman they can help build up their county organizations. Our organization gives us leverage, and we are beginning to get money and cooperation from the state group. They are finding we can help them in providing key people and getting good people interested in party organization and help build a party unit through our individual organizations."

Nonparty Groups

The role of nonparty groups in congressional elections is often substantial. Organizations such as the League of Women Voters do not endorse candidates or contribute financially to campaigns except as their membership may do so in an individual way. But by sponsoring nonpartisan forums for a discussion of the issues, they may be said to exercise some degree of influence.

Far more important—to congressional candidates at least—are the organizations that provide campaign funds and workers and endorse or "rate" candidates on the basis of their voting records. Some of these are well-established, continuing organizations. Others are temporary groups that are dissolved once an election is over, perhaps to be re-created when the next election approaches. The names of some groups provide no information as to the identity of their backers or the purpose for which contributions are made.[3] Of all the groups that regularly participate in election campaigns, those associated with labor are the best known and the most controversial.

---

[3] Thus the *Congressional Quarterly* found that in 1962 a Committee on American Leadership was closely connected with the coal industry; the Committee for Economic Growth was established by restaurant owners to aid members of Congress who supported their position on the 1962 tax bill; the Nonpartisan Committee for National Betterment was identified with the lumber industry; and all contributors to "James H. Lum, a political committee for the November 6, 1962 elections," were executives of Monsanto Chemical Company. *Congressional Quarterly* Special Reports, July 26, 1963, p. 1193.

3

RAYMOND E. WOLFINGER /
JOAN HEIFETZ HOLLINGER

Safe Seats, Seniority, and
Power in Congress

The president's difficulties in inducing Congress to pass his legislative program are usually ascribed to the different constituencies of the two institutions. This difference would make for disharmony under any circumstances, but it is said to be particularly important because the seniority system bestows the most power on congressmen whose constituencies are most unlike the president's. His policy commitments are responses to the needs of a heterogeneous, industrialized, urban society. The occupants of the most influential congressional positions come from districts that reelect them regardless of national political trends. The representative from such a district "views with alarm the great issues that sweep the nation and threaten to disrupt the familiar and comfortable politics of his district,"[1] which is usually characterized as a rural backwater.

The authors were aided in gathering data by Milton C. Cummings and Richard Scammon. Many helpful comments on an earlier draft of this article were made by Richard F. Fenno, Jr., Fred I. Greenstein, Duncan MacRae, Jr., Donald R. Matthews, Nelson W. Polsby, Randall B. Ripley, Alan Rosenthal, Stephen Smith, Leo M. Snowiss, Aaron B. Wildavsky, and Barbara Kaye Wolfinger. We are grateful for financial support from the Edgar Stern Family Fund, the John Simon Guggenheim Memorial Foundation, and the Committee on Political Behavior of the Social Science Research Council, and to the Brookings Institution for use of its facilities.

[1] James MacGregor Burns, *The Deadlock of Democracy,* rev. ed. (Englewood Cliffs, N.J.; 1963), p. 244.

Reprinted from the *American Political Science Review,* 59 (June 1965), 337–49, by permission of the publisher. Part V was revised in 1969. Mrs. Hollinger is a doctoral candidate in history at the University of California at Berkeley.

Both political parties are described this way. Because the Democrats have controlled Congress for all but four of the past 36 years, most illustrations of this thesis are drawn from conflicts between Democratic presidents and Democratic congresses. More specifically, the focus of attention is usually on the refusal of southern Democratic congressional leaders to support presidential legislative requests. In this article we will be concerned with this phenomenon in the House of Representatives. The thesis we examine may be restated as follows: lack of responsibility in the Democratic party is due to control of Congress by Southerners. Their influence is due to their seniority, which is a result of the lack of party competition in the South. Most academic descriptions of American politics include this thesis.[2] It is particularly common in textbooks. We will call it the "textbook theory."

Another interpretation of congressional behavior, that might be called the "insiders' theory," has a good deal of currency in Washington circles close to Congress.[3] The insiders concede both the one-party South and southern congressional power, but they say that the former is not a sufficient cause of the latter, and introduce other considerations to explain it. Southern influence in Congress, according to the insiders, is not due just to the lack of party competition in the South, since there are many safe Democratic seats in the North. The men in these northern seats allegedly do not, however, make use of their "potential seniority." They are less interested in congressional careers and tend to "committee hop," thus losing the benefit of whatever seniority they have accrued. Many of these congressmen come from machine-dominated big cities where command of local patronage and contracts is the real sign of status and power. When an opportunity for such a position opens up back home, they desert the House for state or local government.

In the insiders' view, Southerners value a career in the House of Representatives more highly than do Northerners. One presumed reason is that the South, less developed industrially than the rest of the country, offers fewer alternate careers to ambitious young men. A second explanation is that the plantation owners' traditional *noblesse oblige* has made politics a more highly valued activity in the South, attracting some of the most able men from all walks of life. In the North politics has been not so much a gentleman's calling as a channel of social mobility for underprivileged ethnic groups.

---

2 Burns is probably the best-known contemporary advocate of this point of view.

3 While the insiders' theory is probably the prevailing one among Washington *cognoscenti,* it has not been given the literary circulation of the textbook theory. Hints and scraps of it may be found in the writings of William S. White; see particularly *Citadel* (New York, 1956).

The central proposition of the insiders' theory is that the level of southern influence in Congress is due to more than the "natural" consequences of the lack of party competition in the South. More generally, the insiders' theory raises a number of questions about the relationship between types of party systems and effective legislative representation, and between career alternatives and types of legislative behavior. It suggests that the constituent environment may influence not only the direction of congressional behavior (for example, votes pro or con), but also the roles played by legislators from different types of party systems.[4]

Most of the empirical propositions and assumptions in the two theories are readily verifiable. Yet published evidence on them is surprisingly scarce. Their evaluation involves answering the following questions:

1. Do congressmen in southern safe seats have more congressional seniority than those in northern safe seats?
2. Do the career patterns of the Northerners indicate any greater willingness to leave the House?
3. Do congressmen from southern safe districts have more committee seniority than safe Northerners?
4. Do the Southerners have more chairmanships than they are "entitled to" by their seniority?
5. Do members of the House have more prestige in the South than in the North?

If these questions can be answered affirmatively, the insiders' explanation is a crucial modification of the textbook theory. If not, the insiders' theory is superfluous. If the insiders are right, then the growing northern Democratic representation in Congress will be partly vitiated by members who do not take full advantage of their opportunities to accrue seniority. Our purpose in this article is twofold: to examine the available data in an attempt to answer these five questions; and to explore the implications of recent shifts in the distribution of safe House seats.

I. The Regional Distribution of Influential Positions in the House

As a prelude to examination of the relevant evidence, it is useful to review the familiar topic of alleged southern and rural dominance in the House of Representatives. There were 255 Democratic representatives on January 7,

[4] For an extensive treatment of this subject at the state level see John Wahlke *et al., The Legislative System* (New York, 1962). See also James Q. Wilson, "Two Negro Politicians: An Interpretation," *Midwest Journal of Political Science,* 4 (November 1960), 346–69.

1964.[5] Of these, 38 per cent were from southern districts.[6] Table 1 shows the representation of congressmen from different types of district (urban-rural, North-South) in influential positions. Contrary to some impressions, the Southerners did not have a disproportionate share of appointments to the Appropriations, Rules, and Ways and Means Committees, generally considered the top three committees in the House.[7] But they are significantly overrepresented in other powerful posts. They account for 53 per cent of

[5] Since minor changes in the composition of the House occur frequently, it is necessary to choose a date for any analysis of House membership. We chose January 7, 1964 because a House roster for that date was published in the *Congressional Quarterly Weekly Report,* January 10, 1964.

[6] Throughout this article the South is defined as the eleven states of the Confederacy: Alabama, Arkansas, Florida, Georgia, Louisiana, Mississippi, North Carolina, South Carolina, Tennessee, Texas, and Virginia.

We have included the five border states (Kentucky, Maryland, Missouri, Oklahoma, and West Virginia) in the North. Some observers of Congress classify some or all of these states as southern, or put them in a separate category. We saw no reason to do this, since the voting record of the 28 Democratic representatives from these states is similar to that of northern congressmen, and very different from the Southerners'. In 1963, for instance, the border congressmen had a Presidential Support score of 80, compared to 59 for the Southerners and 82 for congressmen from the northeastern states. The Presidential Opposition scores of the three groups were 9, 27, and 5, respectively. (These scores are based on individual voting records for 71 House roll calls during 1963 on proposals on which President Kennedy took a position. The support score is the percentage of the 71 roll calls on which the member supported the president. Since failure to vote lowers a member's support score, we also present the opposition scores. The individual scores are in *Congressional Quarterly Weekly Report,* March 13, 1964.)

Congressional Quarterly defines as "urban" any central city with at least 50,000 population and any suburban city with 100,000 or more people. "Suburban" areas are those "closely settled areas contiguous to central cities," with the exception of cities over 100,000 in population. All other areas are classified as rural. See *CQ Census Analysis: Congressional Districts of the United States* (Washington: Congressional Quarterly, Inc., 1964), pp. 1786, 1792. We have combined *CQ's* "urban" and "suburban" classifications for the purpose of testing the propositions stated in the text. We have classified districts as "rural" if they are 50 per cent or more rural according to *CQ,* and "urban" if they are less than 50 per cent rural.

[7] The absence of southern overrepresentation on the top three committees is due partly to the recent appointment of four Northerners to the Appropriations Committee. During most of the period from 1947 to 1963 every southern state had a representative on that committee. (We are indebted to Richard F. Fenno, Jr. for this information.) If one splits the Appropriations Committee's 30 Democratic members on the basis of seniority, the former southern advantage becomes apparent. Eight of the top-ranking 15 members are Southerners, compared to only one of the 15 most recent appointees.

Appointments to the Ways and Means Committee are made on the basis of regional zones, but it should not be thought that this guarantees equitable representation on the committee to all parts of the country. The zones are not redrawn after every election to take account of changes in state delegations, and, perhaps for this reason, there is considerable variation in the number of representatives assigned to each zone. The range was from 14 to 24 in the 86th Congress. See Nicholas A. Masters, "Committee Assignments in the House of Representatives," *American Political Science Review,* 55 (June 1961), 347.

Table 1   Distribution of Democratic Congressmen in Influential
Committee Positions, by Region—January, 1964

	North Urban %	North Rural %	South Urban %	South Rural %	Total No.	Total %
All Democratic congressmen	42	21	9	29	255	101*
Membership on top three committees	40	24	5	31	55	100
Major committee chairmanships	29	18	0	53	17	100
Subcommittee chairmanships	29	17	6	47	109	99*
Holding first three positions	37	14	4	45	51	100

* Does not sum to 100 because of rounding.

the chairmanships of the 17 major standing committees;[8] 53 per cent of the chairmen of all these 17 committees' subcommittees; and 49 per cent of all the representatives who hold the first three positions (chairman and first and second ranking majority members) on each of the 17 committees. For a variety of reasons this last measure may be the best index of committee seniority. The number of chairmanships is so small that the death or retirement of a single chairman produces a sizeable percentage change, and subcommittee chairmen are not appointed solely on the basis of seniority. The top-ranking majority members are next in line for the chairmanship. Together with the chairman and the two ranking minority members, they are usually appointed to conference committees on bills the committee has handled.[9] Among their various other advantages is first preference in questioning witnesses at hearings.

II. The Distribution and Characteristics of
Democratic Safe Seats

For the purposes of our study we defined safe Democratic seats as those which met all three of the following criteria:

1. Won by a Democrat in every special[10] and general election since 1940.
2. Won by an average of 60 per cent or more of the two-party vote since 1944.

8 There are 20 standing committees. Members generally consider three of them unimportant: the District of Columbia, House Administration, and Un-American Activities Committees. The first of these—important to permanent residents of the District—is in effect Washington's city council, the second is occupied with housekeeping, and the third (renamed the Committee on Internal Security in 1969) reports virtually no legislation. Membership on one of these three committees does not preclude assignment to another standing committee.
9 This practice is not required by the rules, but is usually followed.
10 Two seats, one each in the North and South, were omitted because they were won by Republicans at the special election following the death of the incumbents.

3. Won by not less than 55 per cent of the two-party vote in every election since 1946.

Changes in district boundaries proved not much of a problem in our efforts to identify safe districts. We were usually able to "follow" the incumbent. Where a change in incumbent coincided with redistricting, we used maps to trace the district's lineage. Our definition of safety turned out to be rather stringent. It excluded the seats held by three major committee chairman: Wayne Aspinall of Colorado, Interior and Insular Affairs; George P. Miller of California, Science and Astronautics; and Clarence Cannon of Missouri, Appropriations. Cannon's winning percentage dipped below 55 per cent on two occasions, while the first two seats were held by Republicans in the 1940s. Also excluded were a number of seats which, because of redistricting or population movement, now seem to be completely safe. But the inclusion of such newly safe seats would not contribute much to our analysis of members' responses to the opportunity to accrue seniority. Implicit in our definition is the assumption that the key aspect of safety is the incumbent's belief that he can stay in his seat as long as he wants.

By our definition we counted a total of 122 safe Democratic seats in the 88th Congress, 45 in the North and 77 in the South. Table 2 shows how these were distributed between urban and rural constituencies: 72 are rural and a bare majority of them are both southern and rural. More than a third of the safe seats are northern. There are four urban safe seats for every rural one in the North; in the South this ratio is reversed. Seven of the nine northern rural safe seats are from the border states of Kentucky, Missouri, Oklahoma, and West Virginia. The urban seats include five from Chicago, three from Detroit, eleven from New York, and three from the Los Angeles area. The boundaries of most of these Democratic city districts were drawn by Republican legislatures.

Table 2   Distribution of Democratic Safe Seats by Region and Type of Constituency

	North		South		Totals	
	Urban %	*Rural* %	*Urban* %	*Rural* %	*No.*	%
Safe Seats	30	7	11	52	122	100
All Democratic Seats	42	21	9	29	255	101*

* Does not sum to 100 because of rounding.

Compared to northern non-safe seats held by Democrats in 1964, the safe districts included a somewhat higher proportion of low-income families, of Negroes, and of first- and second-generation Americans, as Table 3 shows. These differences are not large, however, and the safe seats are no

Table 3   A Socioeconomic Profile of Northern Safe and Non-Safe
Democratic Districts—1964

	Northern Safe Democratic %	Northern Non-Safe Democratic %
1959 median family income:*		
Per cent of districts in:		
first quartile†	18	31
second quartile	36	35
third quartile	31	24
fourth quartile‡	16	10
	101‖	100
N	(45)	(115)
Per cent Negro:		
0–4.9%	31	64
5–9.9%	27	13
10–19.9%	13	12
20–29.9%	9	4
30% and over	20	6
	100	99‖
N	(45)	(115)
Per cent first- and second-generation:§		
0–9.9%	20	17
10–19.9%	9	25
20–39.9%	36	44
40% and over	36	13
	101‖	99‖
N	(45)	(115)
Type of constituency:		
urban	80	61
rural	20	39
	100	100
N	(45)	(115)

Sources: 1960 Census data reported in U. S. Bureau of the Census,
Congressional District Data Book (*Districts of the 88th Congress*)
(Washington, 1963); and *CQ Census Analysis.*
* The average median family income for the safe seats was $5,506,
compared to $5,921 for the non-safe districts. If rural districts from
the border states are eliminated from both groups, the figures are $5,811
and $6,099, respectively.
† Quartiles are based on nationwide ranking.
‡ All but one of the northern safe seats in the 4th quartile are from rural
border districts.
§ Includes all persons born abroad (except of American parents)
or with at least one foreign-born parent.
‖ Does not sum to 100 because of rounding.

less diverse in their socioeconomic characteristics than the others. The higher level of ethnicity in the safe seats is the greatest difference. Half of the safe districts in the first income quartile and 43 per cent of those in the second quartile had 40 per cent or more first- and second-generation residents. Twenty-seven of the 45 safe constituencies had 40 per cent or more foreign-stock residents or 20 per cent Negroes, or both.

We explored the textbook theory proposition that congressmen in safe seats are less likely to support their president, presumably because they are subject to different constituency pressures.[11] Tables 4 and 5 show the Presidential Support and Opposition scores for congressmen in safe and non-safe seats with region and type of constituency controlled. Table 4 suggests that

Table 4   Presidential Support Scores of Democratic Congressmen in Safe and Non-Safe Seats, by Region—1963

	North		South	
	Urban	*Rural*	*Urban*	*Rural*
Safe Seats	76	77	75	55
Non-Safe Seats	83	82	61	55

Table 5   Presidential Opposition Scores of Democratic Congressmen in Safe and Non-Safe Seats, by Region—1963

	North		South	
	Urban	*Rural*	*Urban*	*Rural*
Safe Seats	5	8	14	28
Non-Safe Seats	4	8	31	36

Northerners in safe seats gave slightly less support than those from non-safe districts. Since failure to vote lowers a member's support score and many New York City congressmen are notorious absentees, Table 5 may be a better indicator of presidential support.[12] It shows no differences between safe and non-safe northern congressmen. The extremely spotty attendance records of two members from rural safe districts account for most of the difference in the support scores of rural Northerners. The lower support by non-safe Southerners may result from Republican competition forcing these incumbents to adopt a more conservative position. In short, the level of

[11] See, *e.g.,* Burns, pp. 242–44. Lewis A. Froman, Jr., discusses several other propositions about relationships between competition and party loyalty at both state and national levels. See his *Congressmen and their Constituencies* (Chicago: Rand McNally & Co., 1963), Chap. 9; and the works cited there.

[12] Of course, failure to vote also lowers the Presidential Opposition score, but the rate of opposition in all northern cells is so low that 100 per cent voting participation would not change the opposition scores significantly.

party competition does not appear to be a useful general explanation of voting patterns among Democratic congressmen.[13]

III. Career Patterns of Safe Seat Holders

We come now to our major concern: the different levels of interest in a congressional career by members from different sides of the Mason-Dixon line. Years of consecutive service is one index of this interest. If northern congressmen in safe seats were less intersted in House service, then, taken as a group, they should have less congressional seniority. But as Table 6 indicates, this does not appear to be the case. There were no important differences in length of consecutive service between northern and southern representatives.

Table 6   Years of Consecutive Service by Democratic Congressmen in Safe Seats, by Region—1964

Years of Consecutive Service	Northerners %	Southerners %
0–9	38	32
10–19	33	38
20–29	25	23
30 and over	4	6
	100	99*
N	(45)	(77)

* Does not sum to 100 because of rounding.

According to the insiders' theory, many congressmen from urban machines are only serving time in the House until they can get a more highly prized post. The principal example offered is a tendency for New York City congressmen to quit the House abruptly when a judgeship becomes available. (These are usually elective offices, but access to them has been effectively controlled by the regular Democratic organization in New York.) By extension other northern big-city congressmen are alleged to have the same preference for careers in state and local government. In contrast, a seat in Congress is said to be the high ambition of almost any southern politician. Those fortunate few who attain this goal are content to stay in the House (unless an opportunity for the Senate presents itself),

[13] After examining voting records for the 87th Congress, Froman came to the same conclusion (*ibid.*, p. 114). Other recent findings indicate that when region is controlled, length of service is not strongly related to the support that congressmen of either party give to their president. See Judson Mitchell and George Spink, "Presidential Support and Length of Service in the House of Representatives" (unpublished paper, Stanford University).

patiently going along and working their way up the ladder of seniority to a position of real influence in national affairs.

We tested this proposition by examining the circumstances under which safe seat incumbents left their seats from January 1947 to the beginning of 1964. In all but a few cases the reasons for leaving were either stated by the incumbent or were obvious enough, *e.g.*, death in office, defeat in a primary, retirement. In a few instances we inferred the reason from the man's subsequent occupation. These data, classified by region, are presented in Table 7.

Table 7   Safe Seat Holders' Reasons for Leaving Congress, by Region—1947–1964

Reasons for Leaving	*Northerners* %	*Southerners* %
Death in office*	37	22
Retirement due to health or age	5	12
Defeat in primary	11	26
Run for Senate	16	12
Run for state or local office	21	2
Go into business or law	3	22
Appointed to government position	8	5
	101†	101†
N	*(38)*	*(59)*

Sources: Congressional Quarterly Weekly Reports; Biographical Directory of the American Congress, 1774–1961 (Washington: Government Printing Office, 1961); and various issues of *Congressional Directory* (Washington: Government Printing Office).
* See below, p. 51, for a discussion of this regional difference.
† Does not sum to 100 because of rounding.

The insiders' theory is confirmed on one point: 21 per cent of the Northerners who left the House did so to run for a state or local office, in contrast to only one Southerner. Almost all of these Northerners were from New York City and most of the offices sought were state or county judgeships. Quitting one's seat to go into business also is an indication of lack of interest in a House career, and here the regional ratio is reversed. Twenty-two per cent of the Southerners who left Congress went into private business or law practice, compared to just one Northerner. Since preferences for local public office or for private business to continuing congressional service are both examples of voluntary departure, the two categories can be combined to provide an overall measure of low interest in a House career. When so combined, these categories account for an identical proportion of northern and southern quitters: 24 per cent.

Fear of losing a primary may cause a member to quit in favor of another job. Rumors have it that several congressmen, from both North and South, have done this in the past decade. There is no reason to believe, however, that this fear is any more prevalent among Northerners than Southerners, or *vice versa*. One could argue that, everything considered, primary defeat may be less of a hazard for Northerners because of the strong political organizations in many cities. The data in Table 7 support this proposition; more than twice as many Southerners were defeated in primaries.

The data presented thus far do not support the insiders' claim that Northerners evince less interest in Congress. Table 7 indicates that, in fact, Northerners who leave Congress are more likely to remain in public service than Southerners. This may reflect fewer opportunities for rewarding government posts in the largely rural South. It may also be a result of the unstructured southern political parties. There appears to be much less articulation between congressional politics and state and local politics in the South.[14]

We have seen that incumbents in northern safe seats have as much seniority as their opposite numbers from the South. Seniority in Congress is useful chiefly to secure desirable committee assignments. Since committee rank is a result of consecutive service on the committee, the northern safe seat holders conceivably could dissipate their congressional seniority by "committee hopping."

The data do not support this speculation. Twenty-nine per cent of the southern safe seat holders and 31 per cent of the Northerners were in one of the top three positions on the 17 major standing committees. Of the 14 major chairmanships held by members from safe districts, Southerners held nine and Northerners five; 12 per cent of the Southerners were major committee chairman, and 11 per cent of the Northerners.[15] The southern advantage in total chairmanships appears to be a result of their greater number of safe seats, and nothing else.

Finally, we examined the proportions of the two groups of safe seat holders who were chairmen of subcommittees. Here there is a southern advantage; 36 per cent of the Northerners were subcommittee chairmen, compared to 45 per cent of the Southerners. Subcommittee chairmen are chosen by the committee chairmen, who need not make their selections solely on the basis of seniority. Favoritism by the predominantly southern committee chairmen might account for the disparity in subcommittee chairmanships. We tested this proposition by counting, on each of the 17 major committees, those committee members who were not subcommittee chairmen

---

[14] See V. O. Key, *Southern Politics* (New York, 1949), Chap. 18 and *passim*.

[15] The figure for the Southerners would be 13 per cent if we took account of George Mahon's accession to the chairmanship of the Appropriations Committee on the death of Clarence Cannon in May 1964.

themselves but who had more seniority than the lowest ranking subcommittee chairman. A total of 28 congressmen were in this position, 18 Northerners and 10 Southerners.[16] On committees chaired by Southerners, nine Northerners and three Southerners were by-passed. With northern chairmen, the proportion was more even: nine Northerners and seven Southerners.

Favoritism may not be the only reason for setting aside seniority in appointing subcommittee chairmen. Someone with special expertise may receive such an appointment out of turn. An uninterested or hopelessly incompetent member may be passed over. Some members may be reluctant to accept the chairmanship of an undesirable subcommittee in hopes of being chosen eventually to head a more powerful one. There is no reason to believe, however, that any of these considerations would apply disproportionately more to southern than northern members. Thus while the data in the preceding paragraph cannot be considered conclusive evidence of southern favoritism, they provide at least some basis for an explanation of the disproportionate number of subcommittee chairmanships held by Southerners.

The data presented up to this point indicate that the insiders' theory is wrong on every count:

1. Congressmen in southern safe seats do not have more congressional seniority than those in northern safe seats.
2. The post-congressional career patterns of the two groups do not indicate any greater northern inclination to leave the House for another career.
3. The safe Southerners do not have more committee seniority than safe Northerners.
4. Safe Southerners have more chairmanships than they are "entitled to" only at the subcommittee level, where considerations other than seniority affect the selection process.

The final element in the insiders' theory, concerning differences in the prestige of congressmen, will be discussed in the following section.

IV. Other Regional Differences

The finding that northern safe seat holders do not quit congress any more readily than their southern counterparts does not by itself dispose of the proposition that Southerners are more effective legislators. Is it possible to examine the proposition that while the Northerners are no less likely to

---

[16] It might be thought that the larger number of by-passed Northerners results from the fact that there are more of them in the House. But Southerners comprise 44 per cent of the membership of the highest-ranking half of the 17 major committees, and it is from this group that subcommittee chairmen are chosen.

leave Congress, they do not use their House positions as effectively as the Southerners? Are the Northerners, as a group, less able men? Some fragments of data can be considered.

In the first place, the role of United States Representative does not appear to be any more prestigious among the mass of southern citizens than among those in the North. In a survey conducted in 1947 the National Opinion Research Center studied a national sample's assessment of the "general standing" of 90 occupations, one of which was "United States Representative in Congress."[17] Each of the 2920 respondents was asked to rate each occupation's "general standing" on the following scale: "excellent," "good," "average," "somewhat below average," and "poor." When tabulated by region, with southern Negro respondents removed, the results do not indicate any significant regional differences in congressional prestige. Eighty-eight per cent of the white southern respondents gave "excellent" or "good" ratings to the job of congressman, compared to 92 per cent in the Midwest and 94 per cent in Northeast and West. When all occupations were ranked, congressmen were sixth in the West and Midwest and seventh in the South and Northeast.[18]

The office of representative may be accorded as much respect by the mass electorate in the North, as in every section, and yet not be as highly regarded in the specialized political milieu in which politicians are socialized. Urban political organizations control Democratic congressional nominations in many northern one-party areas. Since these machines typically are based on the tangible rewards that can be drawn from control of local government, status in them generally goes to those who distribute jobs and contracts. Positions that have a share in this distribution process are the most desirable that the machine can bestow. In such cities many people see politics as a way to make money through the exercise of discretion.

Congressmen have hardly any patronage of their own[19] and, when there is a party organization of any consequence back home, federal appointments are cleared with its leader. In any event, federal patronage is negligible compared to the jobs and contracts that any machine-influenced local government can dispense. For most politicians who have worked their way up in an urban machine, being a congressman has little appeal. Some local

[17] For a full description of this study see Albert J. Reiss, Jr., *Occupations and Social Status* (New York, 1961).

[18] *Ibid.*, pp. 6, 19, 200, 220. Data on white Southerners were obtained from the National Opinion Research Center through the Inter-University Consortium for Political Research. We are grateful to Ralph L. Bisco of the Consortium and Patrick Bova of NORC for their kind help.

[19] In addition to nominations to the service academies (which usually are heavily dependent on objective examination scores), the average congressman is lucky if he can name a Capitol policeman, elevator operator, or page. It takes a number of terms to acquire enough seniority to have much more appointment power.

bosses have also been congressmen, *e.g.*, the late William Green of Philadelphia or Charles Buckley of the Bronx, but their political power was not a result of their congressional seats. In his study of the Chicago congressional delegation, Leo M. Snowiss found that in that city's powerful Democratic organization the job of congressman was not as highly prized as any of a number of party and local governmental positions. Consequently, at least some congressional nominations go to less highly regarded organization figures, tired mediocrities in late middle age.[20] Most regular machine politicians in New York City seem to have a similarly low evaluation of congressmen. Richard H. Rovere's description of Peter J. McGuinness, an old-time boss in Brooklyn, includes an interesting example of this point of view:

> Like most politicians of his school, McGuinness considers congressmen members of an inferior class. To him, the local party bosses, who pick the legislators and tell them what to do, are the elite of politics and congressmen are men who, unable to make the grade themselves, must serve as legislative secretaries to men who have made the grade. He cannot understand the tendency, comparatively recent in this city, of political bosses to take congressional nominations for themselves. "I've sent plenty of them to Albany and Washington," he says, "but I'd never be such a damn fool as to send meself. Believe me, I'm glad I was never in a fix where anyone else could send me. If a man's a leader in New York, what the hell business has he got in Washington?"[21]

One of the authors of this article, engaged in research that provided many opportunities to observe status relations in a very cohesive traditional northeastern urban organization, noted that the local congressional candidate seemed to get very little deference from most members of the organization.

This is not to say that all big-city congressmen are incompetent. The candidate just mentioned, for instance, has become a congressman with a considerable reputation for ability and effectiveness. Many other able representatives have come to Washington from the machines. In fact, given the low value generally placed on House seats in such political *milieux,* some ambitious men probably realize that the competition for such positions is less than for more lucrative posts at home. Nevertheless, politicians, like everyone else, are partly products of their environment, and there are indications that machine-controlled districts in the North produce more than their share of ineffective congressmen.

The New York City delegation is a case in point. Its members make up the core of the "Tuesday-to-Thursday club": congressmen who are in Washington only from Tuesday morning through Thursday afternoon and

---

[20] Leo M. Snowiss, "Congressional Recruitment and Representation," *American Political Science Review,* 60 (September 1966), 629–31.

[21] Richard H. Rovere, "The Big Hello," in *The American Establishment* (New York, 1962), pp. 45–46.

spend the rest of their time back home in more congenial and profitable pursuits. This habit is so prevalent that the decision of a second-term Democratic congressman from Queens to live in Washington evoked quasi-anthropological awe from *The New York Times:* "Mr. Rosenthal is the first New York City Democrat to take this step, as far as anyone in the state delegation can recall."[22]

The best available measure of attendance is *CQ's* voting participation score, which gives the percentage of roll calls (119 in 1963) at which each member was present.[23] A serious disadvantage of this score as a measure of interest in legislation is that the leadership, aware of the members' habits, tries to schedule roll calls when most congressmen are in Washington. Since the House has been in Democratic hands for the past ten years, votes are seldom held when many Democrats are absent. As a practical matter, this means that there is little voting except on Tuesday, Wednesday, and Thursday. If a member's score is low, his attendance must be very spotty indeed. Table 8 contains voting participation scores for safe and non-safe congressmen, with region controlled. Although a safe congressman should not have

Table 8   Voting Participation by Democratic Congressmen in Safe and Non-Safe Seats, by Region—1963

Type of District	*Voting Participation Score*
Northern Safe	79
Northern Non-Safe	86
Southern Safe	83
Southern Non-Safe	87

to spend as much time mending fences at home, the northern safe group scored somewhat lower than the non-safe Northerners. The New York City delegation accounts for most of this difference. When they are excluded, the northern safe group's score rises from 79 to 82, virtually the same as the southern safe score.

Since a number of Southerners also have unimpressive attendance records (although no southern delegation can match the New Yorkers), it is difficult to derive marked regional differences from these data. The complaints about the New York and Chicago delegations come chiefly from people who would usually like to be able to count on their votes. Possibly conservative spokesmen are equally bitter about southern absenteeism, but do not exhibit their disappointments in print.

Another bit of evidence may be useful in determining whether there are regional differences in legislative effectiveness. Despite the intentions of the

22 *The New York Times,* March 16, 1964, p. 37.
23 *Congressional Quarterly Weekly Report,* January 31, 1964.

spirit, the flesh may be weak. Some congressmen might not be physically capable of working as hard as they want. Representatives in northern safe seats are more likely than their southern counterparts to begin their congressional careers at fairly advanced ages. As Table 9 shows, a quarter of the present northern safe seat holders entered the House when they were fifty or older, compared to 11 per cent of the Southerners. This explains the finding in Table 7 that more Northerners than Southerners die in office.

Table 9   Age Distribution at Beginning of Current Term of Service of Incumbents in Safe Seats, by Region—1964

Age at Entry	Northerners %	Southerners %
25–34	13	17
35–39	33	32
40–44	18	29
45–49	11	10
50–54	16	10
55 and over	8	1
	99*	99*
N	(45)	(77)

* Does not sum to 100 because of rounding.

The machine-dominated recruitment patterns discussed earlier may account for the regional age difference. Like other rewards for faithful service, congressional nominations are not given to neophytes. The leaders of urban machines typically are older men who have put in decades of work for the party and do not regard upstarts highly. On the other hand, nominations for available seats in most southern districts are more often fought over by a number of ambitious young men.[24] Since this prize is seldom one that can be bestowed by a cohesive organization, precedence has less to do with who gets it.

On the basis of these scattered data, it appears that Northerners in safe seats may be somewhat less vigorous than Southerners. This difference cannot be established as either large or conclusive.

V. Trends in the Competitiveness of Congressional Districts

Our definition of safe seats is static and does not take account of districts that have become noncompetitive since 1946. As Charles O. Jones has shown, the trend since then has been an increase in the number of non-

24 The classic description of the unstructured politics of most southern states is Key's book, *op. cit.* See also Julius Turner, "Primary Elections as the Alternative to Party Competition in 'Safe' Districts," *Journal of Politics,* 15 (May 1953), 197–210.

competitive seats. The proportion of districts represented by the same party for five consecutive elections climbed from 70 per cent in the 1930s to 78 per cent in 1952–60, when fully 340 districts were represented by the same party.[25] Yet even these figures exaggerate the risks faced by congressmen running for reelection. The proportion of incumbents who won in each election varied from 91 per cent to 96.5 per cent in the fifties.[26] This trend has continued in the 1960s. The worst year for incumbents was 1964, when Senator Goldwater's generally unpopular views, combined with his strong appeal in the South, brought about many voting shifts. Even so, 89 per cent of incumbents won; in 1964 a challenger had one chance in nine of beating a sitting congressman. The odds were a bit worse for challengers in 1966, while in 1968—a year of considerable political upheaval—only nine incumbents were deposed, and four of these defeats were by other congressmen in districts where reapportionment had matched two incumbents against each other. (Incumbent Senators enjoy about the same degree of invulnerability. Three lost in the 1964 general election,[27] one in 1966, and four in 1968.) What effect is this trend away from competition likely to have on the distribution of political power in the House Democratic party? Does it modify the picture of safe districts painted by Burns and other spokesmen of the textbook theory?

To explore these questions we traced the number of noncompetitive Democratic districts in every election from 1946 through 1968. 1946 is a good starting point for two reasons: it was the first postwar election and it marks the low point of Democratic congressional votes in the past 40 years. For purposes of this discussion we will define a noncompetitive election as one in which the Democratic candidate received at least 65 per cent of the major party vote. This is an arbitrary criterion, designed only to put uncontested southern seats in a comparative framework with northern noncompetitive districts.

Table 10 shows the distribution of noncompetitive districts in every election since the war. The number of southern districts in this category remained almost constant through 1958, with the exception of 1956, and has declined since then. The number of northern noncompetitive districts has increased and now is larger than the number of southern noncompetitive seats. Since 1956 northern districts have never comprised less than 44 per cent of all seats won by 65 per cent or more. At least as great a proportion of noncompetitive districts has been urban since 1956. It is no longer

[25] Charles O. Jones, "Inter-Party Competition for Congressional Seats," *Western Political Quarterly,* 17 (September 1964), pp. 461–76.

[26] Charles O. Jones, "The Role of the Campaign in Congressional Politics," in M. Kent Jennings and L. Harmon Zeigler, eds., *The Electoral Process* (Englewood Cliffs, N.J.: Prentice-Hall, Inc., 1966), pp. 23–24.

[27] This does not count Pierre Salinger of California, who lost the seat to which he was appointed during the campaign.

Table 10   Congressional Seats Won by Democrats by at Least
65 Per Cent of the Two-Party Vote, by Year
and Region—1946 through 1968

	North				South				Total Seats Won by 65%		Total Democratic Seats Won
	Urban		Rural		Urban		Rural				
Year	No.	%	No.	%	No.	%	No.	%	No.	%	
1946	16	15	7	6	11	10	76	69	110	100	188
1948	31	23	14	10	12	9	78	58	135	100	263
1950	25	19	13	10	12	9	79	61	129	99*	235
1952	24	20	4	3	12	10	78	66	118	99*	213
1954	40	28	14	10	9	6	79	56	142	100	232
1956	32	26	8	7	13	11	68	56	121	100	234
1958	61	35	20	11	20	11	75	43	176	100	283
1960	57	36	12	8	19	12	70	44	158	100	260
1962	53	39	10	7	10	7	64	47	137	100	259
1964	81	49	25	15	12	7	48	29	166	100	294

	All Northern		All Southern				
	No.	%	No.	%			
1966	66	53	59	47	125	100	248
1968	61	52	57	48	118	100	243

Sources: for election returns, various editions of Richard Scammon, ed., *America Votes* (Pittsburgh: University of Pittsburgh Press); several editions of the *Congressional Directory;* various editions of Clerk, U.S. House of Representatives, *Statistics of the Congressional and Presidential Elections* (Washington: Government Printing Office); *Complete Returns of the 1964 Elections by Congressional District* (Washington: Congressional Quarterly, Inc., 1965); *Congressional Quarterly Weekly Report,* November 11, 1966, Part I; and *ibid.,* June 6, 1969, Part I. The task of classifying congressional districts as urban or rural proved to be rather complicated and was not done for elections after 1964. For the 1962 and 1964 elections we used *CQ Census Analysis,* and for 1956 through 1960 similar data in *Congressional Quarterly Weekly Report,* February 2, 1962. In an earlier classification published in 1956, *CQ* used a completely different four-point classification scheme; see *Congressional Quarterly Almanac, 1956* (Washington: Congressional Quarterly, Inc., 1956), pp. 788–92. We adapted this scheme to the urban-rural one on the basis of apparent similarities in the two taxonomies. For the elections from 1946 through 1950 we used the 1956 data, modified by examination of congressional district maps.
* Does not sum to 100 because of rounding.

true that noncompetitive districts "have a heavily rural bias," as Burns said in 1963.[28]

The increase in Democratic strength in the North is due in part to population growth and movement. Better-off urban residents have been moving to the suburbs. The remaining city dwellers include higher proportions of Negroes, ethnic groups, and the poor. The growing number of non-

[28] Burns, *op. cit.,* p. 242.

competitive districts may also result from reapportionment after the 1950 and 1960 Censuses and from the Supreme Court decision (*Wesberry v. Sanders*) requiring that congressional districts be of equal size.[29] Republican state legislatures often follow a strategy of concentrating Democratic voting strength in a few districts.[30]

The increase in northern noncompetitive seats has been accompanied by a considerable weakening in the South's former Democratic solidity. In 1947 there were 103 Democratic representatives from the South and only two Republicans. By 1963 there were eleven southern Republican seats; and in 1969 there were 26, and 80 Democratic ones. Primary losses and redistricting have also eroded southern power in the House. From 1947 through 1964 eight southern congressmen lost their seats through redistricting and 15 more were deposed in primaries. Other southern states have gained the redistricted seats, but the new incumbents in these 23 districts could not inherit the seniority of the supplanted congressmen.

These trends mark an important shift in the distribution of power in the Democratic party. The northern wing of the congressional party is just now recovering the ground lost in the Republican sweep of 1946. The enormous Democratic losses in that election were confined almost entirely to the North. One of the long-term consequences of the Republican landslide was the creation of a "seniority generation" dominated by Southerners. In 1965, when this article was written, the trend depicted in Table 10 suggested that "northern Democrats with useful amounts of seniority will soon be as numerous as the weakened southern contingent. Within a few years the North should begin to realize in its turn the fruits of the seniority system." This prediction has come true more thoroughly than we expected. In 1969 there were 118 Democratic congressmen with ten or more years of consecutive service. Thirty-six were Southerners and 82, more than twice as many, were from the North. The consequences of this development for power in the House can be seen in Table 11, which compares the southern

---

[29] The wholesale reapportionment resulting from *Wesberry v. Sanders* has notably increased urban and suburban representation in the South, with the result that both Republicans and liberal Democrats have been elected at the expense of old-style conservative Democrats. The most conspicuous victim of this development was Howard W. Smith of Virginia, former Chairman of the Rules Committee and leader of the southern bloc in the House. His district, formerly far below the state average in population, gained many suburban residents when it was brought up to its proper size. "Judge" Smith's new constituents were not very amenable to his brand of politics and were responsible for his astonishing defeat by a young liberal in the 1966 Democratic primary. Smith, stunned by his defeat, backed the Republican nominee, who won the general election and was handily reelected in 1968.

[30] This is an example of how a rational strategy for Republican parties at the state level—conceding a minimum number of seats to the Democrats—is harmful to the party's interests on the national level because it enables these Democrats to build up seniority in Congress.

share of influential committee positions in 1964 and 1969. There has been a 5 per cent drop in the proportion of Southerners in the total Democratic membership, of which they now comprise just a third. No change has occurred in their share of membership on the top three committees, an area where they were not overrepresented earlier. But there has been a sharp decline in the proportion of Southerners who are committee and sub-committee chairman and who hold the top three positions on the 17 major committees. There is now very little southern overrepresentation in these various measures of institutional power. The biggest change has come in subcommittee chairmanships, appointments where the committee chairman's discretion is important. The drop in the southern share of these positions seems to reflect a "multiplier effect" of the southern loss of committee chairmanships.[31]

Table 11   Trend in Southern Share of Influential Committee Positions—1964 and 1969

	Per Cent Held by Southerners		*Number*	
	1964	*1969*	*1964*	*1969*
All Democratic congressmen	38	33	255	243
Membership on top three committees	36	36	55	55
Major committee chairmanships	53	41	17	17
Subcommittee chairmanships	53	37	109	119
Holding first three positions	49	34	51	51

The familiar debate over "party responsibility" often leads to rejoinders that lack of central coordination is inevitable in American political parties. Some fragmentation is unavoidable, but it is one thing to say that we cannot (or should not) have cohesive parties on the English model, and quite another to claim that any particular existing level of fragmentation is immutable. As the changes in House rules at the beginning of the 1965 session demonstrate,[32] arrangements to make the process more or less responsive to majorities can occur within the basic framework of dispersed

[31] Trends in the Senate similar to those described in this paragraph are reported in Randall B. Ripley, "Power in the Post-World War II Senate," *Journal of Politics,* 31 (May 1969), 465–92. These developments suggest that Capitol Hill is becoming much less of a southern bastion than it was in the postwar generation, and that various interpretations of Congress pointing to disproportionate southern power there need to be reevaluated in light of present conditions.

[32] Procedures were changed to reduce the Rules Committee's power to prevent floor consideration of legislation and to avoid appointing conference committees. Most Southerners resisted these decisions, which were reversed after Democratic losses in the 1966 election. The point of this example is that the rules changes made a difference, and that with them or without them, the House was still a "bargaining system."

centers of power. A "bargaining system" can be any of a variety of political orders, from just short of anarchy to something like what happens in Great Britain when one party does not have a decisive majority. All systems characterized by bargaining do not assign similar resources to the principal actors. If the effective power of the president and the majority leadership were enhanced by any of half a dozen procedural changes, *e.g.*, an item veto, it would still be necessary for the actors to bargain with each other. The change would be in the cards dealt to the players, not in the game. This is a simple point, but it seems to be overlooked by some of the more enthusiastic academic apologists for antimajoritarian aspects of our political system.

Dissension in the congressional Democratic party is due largely to Southerners.[33] As the relative strength of the South decreases, the cohesive potential of the party as a whole will increase, for there is little reason to expect that the northern wing of the party will become proportionately more divided as it grows in strength.[34] To put it another way, the decline of the Southerners will be accompanied by a Democratic president's greater ability to get his way with Congress, and by more support for liberal legislation when a Republican is in the White House. It appears, then, that present trends are in the direction of greater cohesion and "responsibility" in the Democratic party.

[33] There are, of course, many Southerners, including powerful committee chairmen, who are loyal to Democratic presidents all or most of the time. (And there are likely to be more of them as more congressmen are elected from southern big cities.) One cannot validly label all southern congressmen as invariably dissident from the mainstream of their party. Nevertheless, there is also no doubt that the southern wing of the party is the major source of deviance on Capitol Hill.

[34] Some political scientists have argued that large legislative majorities are less responsive to the president, because they lead to factionalism. It is unclear whether this proposition refers simply to a majority for the president's party, or an effective majority for his policies. Even if it refers to the latter, there are some difficulties. Most important, it would seem that the smaller the majority, the easier it is for a potential defector to impede the president's program, since he needs to win fewer other dissidents to destroy the majority. As the majority grows, so does the size of the splinter group necessary to make an impact, and hence so does the magnitude of the defector's task. For discussions of this "law of economy" see E. E. Schattschneider, *Party Government* (New York, 1942), pp. 85–96. William H. Riker, who is cited on this point, actually discusses the weakness of big majorities only when they are so big that they become "a coalition of the whole." See his *A Theory of Political Coalitions* (New Haven: Yale University Press, 1962), p. 56.

Statements of this proposition are usually accompanied by reminders that President Roosevelt, having won enormous congressional majorities in 1936, found his legislative program bogged down soon thereafter. This appears to be the major item of evidence to support the proposition. It does *not* appear that presidents have restrained their efforts to elect friendly congresses for fear of suffering Roosevelt's fate. A systematic examination of the historical record found that, if anything, big majorities are better than little ones. See Jay Goodman, "Legislative Majorities and Presidential Success" (unpublished paper, Brown University).

VI. Summary

We have presented data to test two theories about southern influence in the Democratic party in the House of Representatives. The central question is whether southern power can be explained solely by the lack of party competition in the South, or whether it is due also to regional differences which result in more dedication to legislative careers on the part of Southerners. We approached this problem by comparing northern and southern occupants of safe Democratic seats. There were no regional differences in congressional or committee seniority, or in forsaking Congress for other careers. Lack of party competition, aided perhaps by southern favoritism in appointment of subcommittee chairmen—and in the wake of the northern Republican sweep in 1946—seems to be an adequate explanation for the disproportionate number of Southerners in influential positions in the House. The textbook theory, accordingly, appears to be correct on this point.

The Southerners may be more vigorous in the use they make of the positions they have. If age is any indication, Northerners, while they remain in the House, may be less able and energetic than Southerners. We could find no evidence of regional differences in the prestige of congressmen among electorates. The Northerners did tend to include more absentees and more members who first entered Congress at age 50 or older. These differences are not great, however, and must be interpreted with caution.

The number and share of noncompetitive seats held by the North have increased markedly in the past twenty years. The textbook theory is increasingly invalid in its description of the characteristics of noncompetitive districts. Unless this trend is reversed, which appears most unlikely, northern Democrats will continue to be more influential in the House, since the other findings of this article do not indicate that they are any less likely to accrue seniority. The effect of these trends—already evident—will be a decrease in the power of the deviant wing of the Democratic party and therefore an increase in party cohesion.

Congress as a Place
to Work

People who have spent much time on Capital Hill invariably are
impressed by how much Congress is a special place, with its own mood and
style. The three articles in this section are concerned with the "sociology
of work" on the Hill, and they all reflect its special tone. The authors have
extensive experience in one or both houses of Congress. The first selection,
by Lewis A. Froman, Jr., is based in large measure on the author's observations
and interviews while working in the Senate and House. Each of the latter
two selections is drawn from numerous interviews with legislators, staff
members, and lobbyists.

Froman's article is an important guide to much of the remainder of
this book, since, in describing how the House differs from the Senate,
he provides a useful key to interpreting and applying later selections that
describe only a single chamber. Froman attributes the differences between
the chambers to two elementary facts: the House is almost four and a half
times as large as the Senate, and its members represent constituencies
which usually are smaller and more homogeneous. From these two basic
distinctions he develops a series of important propositions about how the
procedures, rules, and conditions of work differ between the two chambers,
and then demonstrates the truth of his propositions. The House,
being so much bigger, is more impersonal, hierarchical, and specialized
than the rather easygoing Senate. It is something of a truism in Washington
that freshman representatives count for little in the scheme of things,
either socially or politically. The Senate is a far different story; every
senator is an important personage from the date of his election.

The rules and "folkways" of the Senate reflect this fact, which is of considerable importance with respect both to procedures and to the outcome of legislation.

The general distinctions drawn by Froman are useful in considering Lewis Anthony Dexter's more general treatment of the job situation confronting congressmen. As Dexter shows, the challenge facing both representatives and senators is the tremendous amount of work to be done. There are so many things to consider and think about that each man must make careful choices about what tasks his staff will work on and where he will invest his own limited resources of attention and energy. Dexter observes, "Congress is not a temporary convocation. It is an ongoing social system which must preserve itself intact and which deals with problems on a long-run, rather than a one-shot basis." Proceeding from this basic assumption, Dexter demonstrates the various ways congressmen have devised for meeting the demands of their jobs, and argues that this diversity in fact helps to relieve some of the pressures on legislators because of their freedom to choose how they will spend their time.

Thinking of Congress as a social system reminds us that all established, more or less stable social groups have habits, customs, and norms which guide the behavior of their members. The Senate is no exception to this generalization. Furthermore, the members of the Senate are unusually able, experienced, and determined men whose interaction is continuous and intense, while their activities are of great consequence, both to themselves and to society. Donald R. Matthews describes the principal "folkways" that characterize the behavior of most senators as they deal with each other. He shows that over the years a body of expectations has been built up about how senators should behave, and that indeed almost all members do behave in this way. This is not to say that the senators who ignore the folkways are cast into outer darkness, nor that they play no useful recognized role in the Senate or in the larger context of American government. These are questions that are still a subject of controversy. But the more limited problem under investigation, the expectations about proper senatorial behavior, are convincingly demonstrated by Matthews.

4

LEWIS A. FROMAN, JR.

Differences between the House and Senate

A...general characteristic of Congress is that the House and the Senate, while similar in some respects, are actually quite different political bodies. The important similarities are two: First, both are relatively decentralized political institutions with a high degree of division of labor through the committee system. Second, both are equal in power. Except for the constitutional provisions which give to the Senate (but not to the House) the power to ratify treaties and advise and consent in political appointments, and which give to the House the privilege of originating all revenue bills (and, by practice, appropriation bills), actions of Congress require the consent of both houses. And, unlike many other legislative systems, neither house can legally force the other body to act, nor can bills become law without the concurrence of both houses.

It is the differences, however, between the House and the Senate (listed in Table 1) which prove most interesting.

Probably the two most important differences between the House and the Senate, and the two from which most of the others are derived, are that the House is more than four times as large as the Senate, and that senators represent sovereign states in a federal system whereas most congressmen represent smaller and sometimes shifting parts of states.

The fact that the House of Representatives is relatively large and

Reprinted from *The Congressional Process: Strategies, Rules, and Procedures* (Boston: Little, Brown and Company, 1967), pp. 6–15, by permission of the publisher. Copyright © 1967 by Little, Brown and Company, Inc. Mr. Froman is Professor of Political Science at the University of California at Irvine.

Table 1   **Major Differences between House and Senate**

House	*Senate*
Larger (435 members)	Smaller (100 members)
More formal	Less formal
More hierarchically organized	Less hierarchically organized
Acts more quickly	Acts more slowly
Rules more rigid	Rules more flexible
Power less evenly distributed	Power more evenly distributed
Longer apprentice period	Shorter apprentice period
More impersonal	More personal
Less "important" constituencies	More "important" constituencies
Less prestige	More prestige
More "conservative"	More "liberal"

the Senate relatively small affects the operation of the two houses in a number of ways. Perhaps the most striking difference noticed by most visitors to the Capitol is the apparent confusion and impersonality in the House chamber as contrasted with the relatively more informal and friendly atmosphere in the Senate. House members are less well known than Senate members. This is further accentuated by the fact that senators have fixed desks and visitors are allowed to take into the galleries a seating chart available at the office of the Sergeant-at-Arms which aids in identifying less well-known senators. There is more "electricity" in the galleries when Senator Dirksen or Senator Mansfield strides into the Senate chamber than when Carl Albert or Gerald Ford walks into the House chamber. Not only are the senators more visible (in a smaller chamber), they are also a good deal more "visible" in the sense that more people know approximately what they look like.

Furthermore, microphones are used in the House and not in the Senate. This adds to the impersonality and formality of the House proceedings as compared with the Senate.

The larger size of the House also requires a more hierarchical structure and organization if it is to work efficiently. Since it is unable to carry on elaborate clearing procedures as in the Senate because of the large number of people involved, the leadership in the House is more powerful *vis-à-vis* the members than is true in the Senate. The Speaker of the House, with the majority leader and whip, find it less practical to schedule legislation to the convenience of all the members. Only the principal parties are usually consulted (e.g., committee and subcommittee chairmen). It is not unusual in the Senate, on the other hand, to re-schedule a piece of legislation or even a vote to suit the convenience of any single member. Leadership activities in the House, then, are more isolated from the lives and activities of the average member.

Also because of size, House members are less likely to know, even by sight, all other House members, especially those on the other side of the aisle. The larger size of the House and the pursuant greater anonymity produce situations in which individual members violate the spirit of comity which is essential to the smooth functioning of any organization. Such situations undoubtedly occur in the Senate also, but probably with less frequency since it is smaller. After final passage of the Senate-amended 1964 Civil Rights Bill in the House, for example, Representative John Bell Williams from Mississippi tied up the House for an hour by objecting to routine unanimous consent requests before finally being persuaded to cooperate. The day following the passage of the Cotton-Wheat Bill in April 1964, several Republicans monopolized the House with four hours of various procedural delays, essentially in retribution for the Democrats having kept the House in session until nearly one A.M. the previous day. One can also find, in the House, a member's words being taken down because he has allegedly violated the rules by engaging in name-calling on the House floor.

This somewhat less frequent observance of comity in the House means that fewer things are accomplished in the House by unanimous consent. Action by unanimous consent is widely practiced in both houses, but in the House, relatively speaking, fewer unanimous consent motions are offered than in the Senate. When they are offered, and there is an objection, it causes more havoc in the House than in the Senate. The House can literally come to a standstill if all motions to proceed in order are forced to roll-call votes. It takes an average of twenty-five minutes to call the roll in the House, and five or six of these can take a goodly portion of the afternoon. Furthermore, some actions, like dispensing with the full reading of the *Journal* each day, require unanimous consent. Any member may object to this procedure with the consequence that further time is lost.

Another result of the larger size of the House and its concomitant greater formality and hierarchical organization, is that the House is able to dispense with its business more rapidly than the Senate. Procedural delays like those mentioned above are the exception rather than the rule, and the "normal" business of the House proceeds quickly. Table 2 shows the relative number of hours spent on the floor in the House and Senate during the Eighty-eighth Congress (1963–64).

It is rare, for example, for any but major bills in the House to take longer than one day for consideration. Time is strictly limited, usually by a rule from the Rules Committee (most rules provide for one or two hours of general debate[1]). Debate in Committee of the Whole (in which most

---

1 James A. Robinson, *The House Rules Committee* (Indianapolis: Bobbs-Merrill Company, Inc., 1963), p. 54.

Table 2   Days and Hours in Session, Eighty-eighth Congress

	First Session Jan. 9–Dec. 30, 1963		Second Session Jan. 7–Oct. 3, 1964	
	Senate	House	Senate	House
Days in session	189	186	186	148
Time in session	1,044 hours 43 minutes	626 hours 14 minutes	1,350 hours 25 minutes	624 hours 33 minutes

Source: Congressional Record, Daily Digest, D821, October 23, 1964.

important pieces of legislation are considered) may be limited by majority vote (usually by a motion to end discussion at a certain time). Only under unusual circumstances will debate extend longer than one day. The 1964 Civil Rights Bill was discussed for nine days; the President's 1964 anti-poverty program took three days. In both cases the leadership planned for such extensive debate, given the controversial nature of these bills.

The Senate, on the other hand, is a much more leisurely body. The Senate often finds itself juggling two, three, or even four bills at the same time, shifting from one to another as it suits the convenience of the members. It is literally unheard of for the House, however, to have more than one measure before it at any time (excluding Conference Reports, which are privileged, and may interrupt pending business). Consequently, action is more fluid and less predictable in the Senate. Debate on one measure can extend for days, weeks, and sometimes months, even without a filibuster.

This brings us to the differences in rules and procedures between the two bodies. It may simply be pointed out here that the informal and more congenial Senate is able to function with quite lax and flexible rules. The two rules which make it most difficult to foresee when action will end on a bill in the Senate are the rules which provide for unlimited debate (requiring two-thirds of those present and voting for cloture), and a very weakly enforced germaneness rule which, although requiring germane debate for three hours each day, is violated at will, either by asking unanimous consent to waive the rule (and the informal rules of comity honor such a request under normal circumstances) or simply by ignoring the rule. In addition, except for appropriation bills, the Senate has no rule of germaneness regarding amendments. Thus, any matter may be discussed on the floor simply by moving an amendment to the pending business.

The House would find it next to impossible to function under such procedures. The size of the membership and the difficulty of clearing with all interested parties would effectively preclude such seemingly cavalier and casual action. The smaller size and the greater importance of comity in the Senate make such flexibility possible and in most cases workable.

Another consequence of the size difference between the House and Senate is the distribution of power within each body. Since the House...has only four more legislative committees than does the Senate (20 as compared with 16), but over four times as many members, each senator is appointed to more committees than each House member (usually three or four as compared with one or two in the House). Also, each senator is usually on at least one and more likely two of the more important committees. Each individual senator, then, can have influence over more issues, and over more important issues, than can each individual congressman.

Power is dispersed even further in the Senate in that a proportionately smaller number of House members usually assume positions of leadership than senators. There is a greater likelihood, for example, of a senator of the majority party assuming a committee or subcommittee chairmanship than for a congressman to do so. Table 3 provides data to support this point.

Table 3   Distribution of Committee and Subcommittee Chairmanships among Democrats in the House and Senate, Eighty-eighth Congress, Second Session (1964)

Number of Committees and Subcommittees Chaired by Each Member	*Senate*	*% of Democrats*	*House*	*% of Democrats*
5	1	1.5	0	0
4	5	7.5	1	0
3	12	18.0	5	2.0
2	16	24.0	25	10.0
1	18	27.0	73	28.0
0	15	22.0	154	60.0

As Table 3 shows, 78 percent of Senate Democrats have at least one committee or subcommittee chairmanship, while in the House the comparable figure is 40 percent. Also, in the Senate over 50 percent of the Democratic senators have two or more committee or subcommittee chairmanships, while again the comparable figure in the House is only 12 percent. To the extent that holding positions of importance is an index of power, these figures confirm the notion that power is more widely dispersed in the Senate than it is in the House.

It is also the case in the Senate as compared with the House that the time it takes to assume a position of leadership is shorter. This is true both for the party leadership positions and the committee and subcommittee chairmanships. For example, Speaker McCormack was in his thirty-third year as a member of the House before he assumed the office of Speaker. Carl Albert was in his fourteenth year before becoming majority leader. Mike Mansfield, on the other hand, was in office for eight years before receiving the Senate's major party position, although it took Hubert Humphrey twelve years to become assistant majority leader. Lyndon Johnson became Democratic leader after only four years in the Senate.

Senators may also attain committee chairmanships more quickly. House Chairmen in the Eighty-eighth Congress (1963–64) took an average of 16.35 years after entering the House to attain committee chairmanships and an average of 13.3 years after gaining a seat on the committee. The comparable figures for the Senate are 12.56 years after entering the Senate and 11.4 years after gaining a seat on the committee. It is even possible, in the Senate, for a member to become a subcommittee chairman in his first year, a happening unheard of in the House. Birch Bayh of Indiana, for example, became chairman of the Constitutional Amendments Subcommittee of the Judiciary Committee in the Senate in his freshman year.

The longer apprenticeship period in the House, plus the fact that serving a long period in the House is not as much of a guarantee, as it is in the Senate, of an eventual position of leadership, means that House members find it more difficult to develop a base of power from which they may operate. A senator will become more powerful earlier than will a House member. This is directly attributable to the fact that the Senate is a smaller body.

The second major factor which causes a number of differences between the House and the Senate is the kind of constituencies which senators and congressmen represent. Senators, of course, represent sovereign states in a political system which places some emphasis on a federal structure. Members of the House, on the other hand, normally represent only parts of states. This difference in base of support has a number of important consequences.

First, senators have more prestige than do House members. This is also a result of the fact that there are only two from each state. Senators get more press coverage and generally are more visible than members of the House.

More importantly, the fact that senators represent states rather than parts of states makes the Senate a more liberal body on most legislation. For example, it was the House of Representatives in the Eighty-eighth Congress (1963–64) that failed to pass an extension of the Area Redevelopment Administration, the Appalachia program, and Hospital Care for the Aged. The Senate passed all three of these top priority, liberal programs. Also, the Senate has often passed federal aid to primary and secondary schools education bills. Prior to 1965 the House passed the bill once (1960) only to have the Committee on Rules refuse to grant a rule to send the bill to conference with the more liberal Senate-passed version.

Findings also indicate that of 322 pieces of legislation which President

Kennedy submitted to Congress in the First Session of the Eighty-seventh Congress (1961) they were, as a whole, more likely to get by Senate committees and the Senate floor than they were in the House of Representatives. Table 4 presents data on this point.

Table 4   Favorable and Unfavorable Committee and Floor Actions
in the House and Senate on 322 Pieces of Legislation
Submitted by President Kennedy, Eighty-seventh Congress,
1st Session (1961)

	Actions on Kennedy Legislation					
	Committee			Floor		
House of	*Favorable*	*Unfavorable*	*No Action*	*Favorable*	*Unfavorable*	*No Action*
Congress	N %	N %	N %	N %	N %	N %
House	192 (59.6)	56 (17.4)	74 (23.0)	166 (51.5)	66 (20.5)	90 (28.0)
Senate	207 (64.3)	44 (13.6)	71 (22.1)	185 (57.4)	51 (15.8)	86 (26.8)

Source: Data from the *Congressional Quarterly Almanac* (Washington, D.C.: Congressional Quarterly, Inc., 1951), Vol. XVII. Reprinted from Lewis A. Froman, Jr., *Congressmen and Their Constituencies* (Chicago: Rand McNally & Co., 1963), p. 73.

The data in Table 4 confirm the generalization, at least for the First Session of the Eighty-seventh Congress (1961), that the Senate usually acts more favorably on the President's program than the House. The Senate also will act on more bills than the House, as indicated by the greater percentage of "no action" for the House at both the committee and floor stages.

It is also true that when the two bodies do pass different versions of the same legislation, the Senate version is often more liberal, the House version more conservative. Although this, of course, is not true for all bills (Civil Rights is probably the most notable exception), it is true in general. For example, again during the First Session of the Eighty-seventh Congress, it was found that on ten bills which were considered to be major parts of President Kennedy's domestic program, and which passed both Houses, of the 58 differing provisions which reached the conference committee, 33, or 57 percent, were liberalizing Senate amendments.[2] The Senate is also, for a number of reasons, likely to pass appropriation bills more nearly approximating what the administration requests than is the House.

The greater support for liberal legislation shown by the Senate is directly attributable to the differences in constituencies represented by senators and congressmen. Population characteristics of constituencies, for example, are

[2] See Lewis A. Froman, Jr., *Congressmen and Their Constituencies* (Chicago: Rand McNally & Co., 1963), p. 79.

associated with liberal-conservative voting. Members of Congress from urban districts with large numbers of voters who are blue-collar workers, who are economically less well-to-do, or who are first- or second-generation immigrants are more likely to support liberal legislation than are members of Congress representing districts with opposite population characteristics. But, voters with population characteristics associated with liberalism are not randomly distributed throughout the state. For example, large numbers of Negroes are often located in only a few congressional districts within a state. Hence most House members have few Negro constituents. Senate members, however, have all the Negroes in the state as constituents. The same is true for such factors as urbanism. There are more congressional districts below the state average on urbanism than above it. Since senators represent the state average, House members are by and large more conservative.[3]

The two factors of size and basis of representation, and the consequences of these factors, produce two quite different legislative bodies. Because the House and the Senate are so different from one another, they will be considered separately in this book. Each body has its own traditions, procedures, precedents, and rules, and it is more useful to keep each separate in an analysis of how the rules function.

[3] *Ibid.,* Chap. 6.

5

LEWIS ANTHONY DEXTER

The Job of the Congressman

The Job of the Congressman

Choosing a Job

It is a cliché that the main job of a Congressman is to be reelected.
There is much truth to it, but there are various ways of getting reelected.
Somehow, the Congressman must do things which will secure for him
the esteem and/or support of significant elements of his constituency. This
he can achieve in many ways. He can seek for himself a reputation as
a national leader, which may sometimes impress his constituents.
He can work at press relations, creating and stimulating news stories and
an image of activity. He can be a local civic leader, attending and speaking
at community functions. He can make a reputation for himself in the field
of legislation. In some states, he can be a party wheel horse and rely
on the organization to back him. He can get people jobs and do social
work and favors. He can become a promoter of certain local industries.
He can conduct investigations and set himself up as a defender of public
morals. He can take well-publicized trips to international hot spots. He can
befriend moneyed interests to assure himself a well-financed campaign.

Reprinted from Raymond A. Bauer, Ithiel de Sola Pool, and Lewis Anthony
Dexter, *American Business and Public Policy: The Politics of Foreign Trade*
(New York: Atherton Press, Inc., 1963), pp. 406–32, by permission of the
publisher. Copyright © 1963 by Atherton Press, Inc. All rights reserved. Mr.
Dexter, who has taught at a number of universities, is currently Canada Council
Visiting Professor of Political Science at Dalhousie University.

He can befriend labor unions, veterans' organizations, or other groups with a numerous clientele and many votes. The one thing he cannot do is much of all these things. He must choose among them; he has to be a certain kind of Congressman.

The reason he must choose is the scarcity of resources. Resources are various; they include time, money, energy, staff, information, and good will. All these have one common characteristic—there is never enough. They must all be budgeted and used with discretion. Opportunity is striking constantly or at least standing outside the door, but it is only occasionally that one has the wherewithal to capitalize on it. The skill of a Congressman is to make the choices which, with the resources at hand, will get him the greatest results in doing the kind of congressional job he has chosen to do. . . .

For these reasons, a rational Congressman who has decided what kind of Congressman he wants to be would then use his resources according to strategies consisting of whole packages of related acts. His stand on a particular issue would be far less dependent on what was specifically involved in that issue than on its role in a general policy or strategy on which he was working. . . .

A skillful Congressman also takes account of the strategies of the other players in the Capitol arena and the rules of the game there. He is part of a multiperson game in which the goals of the different players vary and in which each defines them for himself; in which the pieces are the scarce resources which can be allocated; and in which the optimal strategies depend on the coalitions which can be formed, the procedural rules of the House in which the game is being played, and the power and the goals of the other players. Voting strategies depend on many things besides the pros and cons of issues. A senior Senator, for example, can seek for himself the mantle of statesman with some chance of success, thanks to unlimited debate and his ability to balance special interests in one part of the state against those in another. A Representative has far less chance of playing that particular kind of game. Again, a Congressman can afford to vote the popular position in his constituency although he believes it wrong when he knows that there will be enough congressional votes to defeat him anyway. He may have to vote his principles with courage when he thinks his vote is going to count. But, even then, he may, if skilled at parliamentary procedure, satisfy his constituents by dramatic votes and gestures at moments when they cannot succeed.

How a Congressman defines his job, the importance of choice in the use of his time and resources, the continuing character of Congress as a social system, and the constraints of procedure and interaction form the substance of this section. The Congressman is typically thrust unprepared into a specialized milieu and confronted with a massive volume of highly technical legislation, with most of which he can deal only superficially. Counting on the assistance of a modest staff, he must work within the framework of a committee structure and is burdened with the additional task of servicing myriad personal requests from his constituents. These pressures combine to make time one of the Congressman's most critical resources and the study of its allocation and husbanding a key to the legislative process.

Allocating Time

The scholar tends to approach his problem as though it had equal salience in the minds of men dealing with it on a practical basis. But we have already observed, in our study of the business community, that foreign-trade policy was only one of many issues crying for the American businessman's attention and not one of the most pressing [see original source]. What has been said of the businessman must be said doubly of the Congressman. There are infinite demands on him, which he must meet with finite means. Both the scholar and the newsman often miss this point in their assumption that Congressmen can pay attention to all issues of national policy. We began our study with two major interests: legislation and communication. We wanted to know what Congressmen did about tariff legislation, and we wanted to know what and who influenced them in what they did. We tended to assume that the issues of public policy which were crucial to us were as crucial to the men with whom we were talking. Yet, few Congressmen viewed tariff legislation as their primary concern, and the way in which many of them noticed what they read and heard about reciprocal trade was in large part a consequence of the fact that tariff legislation was simply one of several competing interests for them.

The low priority assigned tariff matters and the effect of that on what Congressmen heard and did may be examined by considering their allocation of time. . . . A Congressman is a member of what sociologists call a free profession, in that he makes his working schedule for himself. His job is undefined and free, not only in schedule, but also in content and in standards of achievement. As a result, he lives under a heavy burden of multiple choices, and, what is more, the choices he has to make are far more fateful than those most citizens make. The citizen may conceive of the Congressman tackling his highly responsible choices with the same care and awe with which the citizen imagines himself tackling the few really responsible choices which he makes. But, by the very nature of their busy lives, Congressmen cannot do this.

Let us consider the ways in which a Congressman may occupy his time. He may concentrate on any of the following aspects of his job:

1. Legislative planning—the working out of legislation in committee.
2. Legislative criticism—an unpopular role in the House, but one common in the Senate.

3. Parliamentary procedure—specializing in rules and regulations for the conduct of congressional business.
4. Legislative tactics—like Lyndon Johnson when he was majority leader, or James Byrnes in an even earlier period.
5. Investigation.
6. Public education—rallying support for causes through forums, speeches, articles.
7. Personal advertisement and campaigning—birthday and condolence letters to constituents, congratulations to graduating high school seniors, newsletters, press releases, trips back home.
8. Seeing visitors and shaking hands.
9. Personal service—rectification of bureaucratic injustices; facilitating immigration of relatives of constituents; arranging military leaves, transfers, and hardship releases; helping confused constituents to route their inquiries to the right administrative office; providing information on social security rights, etc.
10. Representation of local or state interests—Senator Wiley (R., Wis.), ranking Republican on the Foreign Relations Committee, reported: "In 1939 on the occasion of the 75th anniversary of the Wisconsin cheese industry, it was my pleasure to preside over an appropriate celebration in Washington. It featured the world's largest cheese. . . . The cheese was eventually cut up and distributed . . . to Senators, Representatives, congressional employees, newspapermen and others. . . . I am satisfied that advancing the interests of one of the foremost food industries of my state. . . is one of the jobs for which I was sent to Washington. . . ."[1]
11. Participating in national political organization or campaigning—for example, Senator A. S. Mike Monroney (D., Okla.) has been chairman of the Speakers Division of the Democratic National Committee.
12. Development of local political organization and leadership—many Senators are state political bosses, for example, the late Senator Pat McCarran in Nevada.

A Congressman might decide that his chief responsibility is, after all, legislation. Even so, there is far too much legislation for any particular legislator to attend to all of it. During the Eighty-third Congress, 1953–1955 . . . the following legislative issues were among those considered:

1. Reciprocal Trade Extension acts of 1953 and 1954
2. Customs simplification bills
3. Cargo Preference Act of 1954
4. Excise tax
5. Complete overhauling of federal tax system
6. Social security revision

[1] A. Wiley, *Laughing with Congress* (New York: Crown Publishers, Inc., 1947), pp. 136–41. This book probably has the best treatment of the congressional work load. It is one of the indispensable books about Congress for anybody trying to find out what Congress does. Especially valuable is Chap. 6, "The Office Inferno," particularly pp. 90–96.

7. Unemployment compensation measures
8. Appropriations measures
9. Amendment to the Constitution[2]
10. Civil service pay raises
11. The lease-purchase bill
12. Revision of health-welfare-grant formulas
13. Flexible price supports
14. Reduction of wheat acreage
15. Reduction of the Air Force
16. Establishment of an Air Academy
17. Building of twenty merchant ships
18. Upper Colorado development
19. Niagara Falls development
20. Highway aid
21. Commercial use of atomic-energy patents
22. Range improvement by private interests on public lands
23. Alaskan statehood
24. Hawaiian statehood
25. End of price controls
26. Revision of the Taft-Hartley Act
27. New health insurance law
28. Windfall profits
29. The Bricker amendment
30. Wiretap bills
31. Suffrage for eighteen-year-olds
32. Raising the federal debt ceiling
33. Tidelands oil
34. Sale of government rubber plants
35. Abolition of the Reconstruction Finance Corporation
36. The St. Lawrence Seaway
37. Special Refugee Immigration Law
38. Interest rate rise for Federal Housing Administration
39. Excess profits tax
40. Bill for twenty-six new judgeships
41. Witness immunity measures
42. Ten plans for government reorganization
43. Rise in postal rates.

In addition, during the Eighty-third Congress members of the Senate were confronted with a number of other time-consuming issues which were not properly legislative but were more important than many laws in terms of policy. Prominent among these were the censuring of Senator Joseph McCarthy (R., Wis.), the proposal to unseat Senator Dennis Chavez (D., N.M.), and the confirmation of appointments to major commissions,

---

[2] A resolution providing for the replacement of House members killed in a national emergency.

cabinet and diplomatic posts, and judgeships. Some appointments were highly controversial. . . .

In the same session, the Senate and House conducted at least sixty-five investigations, some of which had specific legislative purposes. Finally, it should be considered that interested members of the House and Senate may and do devote long hours of work to legislative proposals that never reach the floor or achieve serious consideration in committee.

Only painstaking and continuous study can give a legislator command of the often complex details of any one of the many proposed pieces of legislation. Few Congressmen can or do master more than a handful of them. A Congressman with years of service may in time develop expertness in a particular field of legislation, but the best-informed of our lawmakers are fully acquainted with only a fraction of the bills that come before each session.

Furthermore, even if some particular legislation is the major focus of interest of a given Congressman, usually, if he is to be reelected, he cannot completely ignore other aspects of his job.[3] Said one administrative assistant:

> You know this business; it is like trying to deal with a great immovable beast or cleanse the Augean stables . . . you just cannot do much. . . . The Senator is now a member of fourteen important subcommittees, and he just cannot split up his time. . . . Now there is the [particular] subcommittee— . . . and all those questions are tremendous and vital questions. . . . Yet, you try to get these Senators [members of the subcommittee] even to agree to meet at any one time and you cannot even do that . . . they are so independent and rushed and all doing things their own way.[4]

---

[3] For a variety of reasons, House members, if they are so minded, are freer to "take it easy" than members of the upper body. They represent a smaller constituency. Crucial decisions in the House are usually made by the leadership. Also, each member of the larger House is on fewer committees.

[4] A senatorial assistant rejected the idea of having an intern from the American Political Science Association in his office because "the intern has lots of ideas—mostly good—but every single one of them means more work." We should note that among the duties of a Congressman is running his own office and staff. By 1959, House members received approximately $40,000 a year for the maintenance of staffs. They were permitted to employ as many as eight persons. In addition, members were allowed $1,200 per session for stationery, 2,700 minutes of telephone service, 12,000 words of telegraph service, $600 a year for official office expenses in the district, and $200 a year for airmail and special-delivery stamps. Very few members employ as many as eight persons or spend quite the maximum. Few Congressmen receive office space adequate for that number, and the use of a staff that large is likely to involve the personal financing of some office expenses.

The amount available to Senators for staff purposes varies from state to state. The average expense appeared to be more than $50,000 a year. This usually permits the Senator to employ two or three professional persons as legislative and administrative assistants and two or three clerks. [By 1965, even Senators from the smallest states had staffs twice this size—Ed.]

Not only is the Congressman himself overcommitted, but he is surrounded by similarly busy men. A salient fact about the Congressman's job is that what he does is invariably accomplished through other people, most of whom are as busy as himself. He becomes involved in a complex web of inter-dependence with colleagues and constituents as a result of the fact that each must work through the other to get what he wants, whether it be reelection, the passage of a piece of legislation, or service from a Congress-man. To anticipate a point which we shall develop later, it is highly naïve to think of a Congressman as being under pressure from one direction or even as being under cross-pressure from two opposing directions. More typically, he is under simultaneous influence and demands from many directions, a large number of which are relevant to the issue with which the scholar or interest group is concerned only in that they compete with that issue for the Congressman's time and energies.

However, our purpose is not to argue that Congressmen are busy people but to show specifically that their busyness affected their reaction to the reciprocal-trade extension.

Busyness blocked effective communication of constituents' views to their Congressmen. A Congressman can seldom readily inform himself as to how his constituents feel about any issue. A sense of acting in the dark about public opinion plagued many of the legislators we interviewed. On the simplest level, communications with respect to foreign-trade policy had to compete with, and frequently were lost in, the welter of other communica-tions. This is particularly true of conversations which Congressmen and their assistants had with other people. In 1955, a Senator's assistant commented:

You know, so many people have come into the office in the last two weeks on all these things—rubber disposal, stock market, reciprocal-trade extensions, and taxes—I just haven't been able to keep in mind which was which; and I think it is pretty difficult for the Senator to keep track, too.

One Representative who was very much concerned with the Reciprocal Trade Act complained about his impossible work load. He had recently been back to his district; he could remember vaguely that a number of people had talked to him about tariff and foreign-trade policy, but he could not recall who had wanted what.

Both these men belonged to the committees which handled reciprocal-trade extension. Yet, even for them, it was but one issue among many. They had no time to give more than a hurried glance to communications about it. As a result, they, too, had only the haziest notion of what public opinion in their constituency really was. The communications they received were poorly remembered and ill-understood. Most messages left only the impression that something had been said, not a clear recollection of what was said. We find that the net effect of communication was to heighten attention to an issue, rather than to convey specific content about it.

Some Areas of Initiative

Congressmen feel much freer than most outsiders think. They need not be unduly constrained by demands from constituents, interest groups, or party. Their freedom is secured by a number of conditions. For one thing, constituents and pressure groups are often satisfied with a fair hearing, not insisting on a specific conclusion. For another thing, American political parties seldom impose discipline in regard to issues.

Among all the conditions that make Congressmen free, there is one that deserves special attention; that is the fact that a Congressman's own decisions largely determine what pressures will be communicated to him. Paradoxical as it may seem, their "freedom" comes from the excessive demands made on them. The complexity of their environment which seems to Congressmen to rob them of initiative thrusts initiative back on them, for, when the demands on a man's resources clearly exceed his capacity to respond, he *must* select the problems and pressures to which to respond.

A Congressman Determines What He Will Hear

There are additional ways in which a Congressman largely determines for himself what he hears from the public. Several mechanisms converge to place a Congressman in a closed communication circuit. For one thing, like anyone else, a Congressman indulges in selective perception and recall of what he hears. Most messages received by a Congressman change saliency more than they change his attitudes on the subject with which they deal. They raise its saliency so that he thinks about it more and becomes more prone to express whatever predispositions he has regarding it. Beset by competing stimuli, he perceives the original message hurriedly, seeing in it what he expects is there. The effect of the stimulus is thus that he reacts more, but reacts in terms of his own accumulated predispositions, not in terms of the content of the communication. Messages serve more as triggers than as persuaders.[5]

Second, a Congressman must select those persons within his constituency on whom he is going to build his following; he cannot react to all equally.

[5] See Raymond A. Bauer, "The Communicator and the Audience," *Journal of Conflict Resolution*, 2 (March 1958), 67–77.

Third, a Congressman must discount as phony much of the material he receives, and the discounting process can lead to a variation of readings. Last, and perhaps most significant, the attitudes of a Congressman in large measure control what messages will be sent to him, because they determine, often overdetermine, the image people have of him.

Of course, Congressmen do get mail of all kinds, including some with which they are bound to disagree. Although the large bulk of issue mail is supportive, there are exceptions, and sometimes there may be large sacks of mail demanding that a Congressman take a difficult or unpalatable stand. When that happens, the Congressman wants to know how seriously to take those demands on him. Do they represent his constituents' deep feelings or are they the product of a slick promotion? He wants to know something of the degree of spontaneity, sincerity, and urgency of these communications. The Congressman's experience with other communications on the same and other issues is his touchstone for assessing the degree to which his mail is stimulated or spontaneous. Thus, a Senate mail clerk commented on one set of letters: "This mail is surprisingly unstereotyped; ... although the stationery may have been given out, the message was not. It is quite different from other heavy pressure mail."

... In general, experienced Congressmen and their staffs are quite tough-minded and skilled at assessing their mail. They are unlikely to feel pressure from the mere existence of numerous demands on them. That being the case, the demands that seem compelling to Congressmen are apt to be those which fit their own psychic needs and their images of the world.

One way or another, the Congressman must simplify the complex world. We interviewed two Congressmen from the vicinity of New Anglia. [New Anglia is a fictitious name.] It will be remembered that there was considerable unemployment in the textile industry around New Anglia. Northern textile unemployment may be interpreted in a variety of ways—as a result of technological obsolescence, foreign competition, Southern competition, and so on. Congressman Second, in virtually these words, said: "Unemployment and the need for protection are the same issue." He saw textile unemployment as the result of foreign competition. But Congressman First, when asked about foreign-trade policy, began immediately to talk about Southern competition and about the failure of the administration to grant defense contracts to the distressed New Anglia area. Rather than seeking relief via tariffs, he was trying to get from the Office of Defense Mobilization a "certificate of necessity" for a steel mill in New Anglia. He commented: "By and large, on...the tariff...New Anglia businesses feel it is New Anglia against the South, and New Anglia is getting a raw deal every time."

... In the Senate Office Building, the mail rooms were in the basement, a long walk from the Senators' offices. That fact, added to the volume of mail a Senator receives, made it far less likely for him to be aware of what was in his mail than was a Representative, whose mail clerk was right in his office. In one senatorial office, the Senator's administrative assistant was under the impression that they had received no mail on foreign-trade policy. One of us took a walk over to the Senator's mail room. The mail clerk said that the mail on foreign-trade policy was first or second in volume of mail on any issue. However, the Senator and his assistants were heavily involved in several other issues, and the mail clerk had not forwarded the reciprocal-trade mail, since, in her judgment, there was nothing that the Senator could do about the issue at the moment. . . .

We add another point that reinforces the notion that Congressmen interpret the pressures on them. Many communications to Congressmen leave the recipient in the dark as to precisely what is wanted of him. Communications to Congress are frequently ambiguous, and it is not surprising if the ambiguities are resolved in consonance with the Congressman's other interests and activities. A letter reporting industrial distress might be seen as a plea for tariff protection by Congressman Second and as a plea for selective allocation of defense contracts by Congressman First. Yet, both would regard themselves as truly and effectively expressing the plea of the constituent.

The work load of the Congressman and his staff reduces the precision with which Congressmen interpret that high proportion of mail which is only partially on target. For example, a large volume of protectionist mail was received from employees of the Westinghouse Corporation in protest against U.S. government purchase of foreign electrical installations. Although the mail was ostensibly directed against the extension of the Reciprocal Trade Act, it is probable that the issue confronting Westinghouse—government purchasing of foreign electrical equipment—should have called for mail asking an administrative tightening-up of the Buy-American Act, not for tariff legislation. But few Congressmen had the time or staff resources to investigate this problem. Our impression was that many Congressmen were not clear as to what was wanted of them by the Westinghouse Corporation. The mail might have had some effect on trade-legislation votes, but the effect, if any, may have been quite unrelated to the specific situation affecting Westinghouse.

The fact that a large part of the mail, and other communications, too, are only partly on target is one which cannot be too strongly emphasized. Sometimes it makes action to meet the request impossible, for many writers ask for something that is procedurally or otherwise impracticable. They may ask a Congressman to support a bill which is still in a committee of which he is not a member and where he has little influence with any member. For him to comply in any way other than by a polite reply to the correspondent would require a major investment of effort and good will. He would have to go out of his way to testify or to approach some of his better-placed colleagues.

On the other hand, the fact that petitioners are vague about what they want also helps make political action possible. Political action requires the formation of coalitions. Coalitions are held together by the glue of ambiguity which enables persons to perceive diverse goals as somehow akin. There are not enough people with an interest in the Buy-American regulations, for example, to produce congressional action. Nor are there enough who care about oil quotas to get such action. Nor are there enough who care about specific tariff rates as such. The only way any of them could achieve legislative effectiveness was to mobilize all of them as a coalition around some issue which might serve at least as a wedge for those whom it did not serve directly. . . .

Indeed, it happens more often than not in public-policy debates that the issues around which mass opinion is mobilized are not the crucial ones in the minds of those who frame legislative policy. This happens often enough so that Congressmen are well attuned to grievances as an index to the sources of public alarm, rather than as specific guidance on legislative drafting. A Congressman is concerned to allay the discontent of those who appeal to him. The complaint is a signal to him to do something, not a command as to what to do. Like a doctor, having made a diagnosis, he often has a range of choices of treatment open to him.

We consider now another range of alternatives among which a Congressman must choose. Almost every district is composed of a complex of interests, and Congressmen are faced with the task of deciding just whom they represent. They cannot give attention and energy equally to all. They must select some for whom they can become valued allies and from whom they can command more than passive support. They must find groups which have money, votes, media of communication, influence, and political desires which a Congressman can further. A Congressman must seek to make himself an important figure to some such groups within his constituency. These may change over time. A Congressman elected by labor votes may throw off this harness by turning to business support. But, at any one moment, a Congressman must relate to some key groups within his constituency, for a constituency is a social structure, not an amorphous mass. Thus, Representative Henderson Lanham (D., Ga.) came from a district with both farming and business interests. He had associated himself with the business group. Their protectionist interests, rather than the farmers' stake in international trade, were communicated to him, for people write and talk more to a Congressman whom they know, and he listens more to them.

Although a Congressman's established relationship to a particular group may increase the probability of its members communicating with him, this established relationship does not necessarily make him more compliant to their interests on a specific issue. This is a point so important and so over-looked in the pressure-group model of the democratic process that it deserves emphasis.

In the first place, the direction of influence is as apt to be from the Congressman to his closer constituents as the other way around. Citizens value a relation to a Congressman and are apt to be guided by him.

Second, established favorable relationships between Congressmen and groups in the constituency are invariably based on a range of issues. It is rare that any one of these is of such paramount importance that a group would renounce its allegiance to a Congressman who had pleased them on many other issues. . . . A Congressman wins the allegiance of multipurpose interest groups through both legislation and services. This allegiance, then, can buy him freedom from pressure on almost any individual issue on which he has firm personal convictions.

We may thus enunciate the general principle that whether a group will communicate with a Congressman and whether the Congressman will respond to the interests of that group are functions of the relationship between the group and the Congressman on a *range* of issues. . . .

Belief that a Congressman is busy with other matters will dry up the flow of communication to him on a given subject. The late Senator Joseph McCarthy had twice succeeded in getting the Reciprocal Trade Act amended to place a quota on the importation of foreign furs. But this was before he became involved in the investigation of communism. In 1954, an informed source commented: "None of the Wisconsin dairy or fur people would go see Joe. He's too busy and out of that world. They'd go see Wiley or Thye or Humphrey's assistant, but not Joe—he doesn't follow that sort of thing any more." The image of Senator McCarthy had become that of investigator of communism rather than that of representative of local and state interests.

In making that assertion, we take leave of the traditional theory of pres-sure politics as expounded both by the politician and the political scientist. The political scientist observing Congress gives too much credence to the way the Congressman himself describes the situation. The Congressman often sees himself as buffeted by a torrent of inexorable demands on his time and effort. Like any busy executive, he sees himself responding to stimuli that come to him from without. What he does not realize is that the nature of these forces on him is largely self-made. . . . One Congressman with an eye on issues will listen with concern to arguments put forward by constituents, whereas another Congressman with an eye on local social groups will feel no pressure from pompous statements about issues as he tries to keep track of births, marriages, and deaths. The Representative who is known to have arranged for the nonquota entrance of relatives of members of a given ethnic group will receive similar requests from other such persons. The Congressman who establishes his home office in a working-class section, where his secretary gives advice on social-security cases, will get such cases, which perhaps take more time than any other service. The Congressman who has interested himself in taxes will hear about taxes, and the one who has cultivated groups interested in foreign trade will hear about tariffs. . . .

A Congressman Is Relatively Free

One implication of the fact that the Congressman makes his own job and hears what he chooses to hear is that he can be a relatively free man, not the unwilling captive of interest groups or parties. There may seem to be a conflict between the two pictures we paint of the Congressman harassed by many demands and of the Congressman relatively free. But, as suggested above, it is precisely because the demands on him are excessive that he must be selective, and therein lies his relative freedom.

Early in our study we talked with a veteran Congressman who said:

You know, I am sure you will find out a Congressman can do pretty much what he decides to do, and he doesn't have to bother too much about criticism. I've been up here where a guy will hold one economic or political position and get along all right; and then he'll die or resign, and a guy comes in (from the same district) who holds quite a different economic or political position, and he gets along all right, too. That's the fact of the matter.

The reasons for this are many. In American political practice, neither the party nor the executive branch exercises more than slight control over a member of Congress. . . .

The sanction that counts much more than party or executive leadership in the congressional picture is that of reelection by the voters of one's district. But in that regard, too, the Congressman is quite free. There are limits on what is morally or sociologically conceivable. Few, if any, Congressmen could announce adherence to communism and be reelected. But the latitude is wide and of course wider on any one given issue than on all issues put together. A Congressman creates an image on the full range of issues which affects his chances of reelection, although even over the full range his freedom is much more substantial than is often realized.

A Congressman is free, as we have already noted, because each district is ordinarily a complex and he can choose the elements out of which he wishes to build his coalition. As Congressman Stubborn said about his district: "It is a good district, because, if the farmers are mad at you, the cities won't be; and, if the cities are, the farmers won't be; so you can be free."

He is freed from a slavish dependence on the elements in his coalition, not only because he can change it, but, even more, because, once he has built a coalition, he tends to lead it. His closest supporters, who may originally have rallied around him because they wanted him to take certain stands, come to be his men. Within very broad limits, when he shifts, they shift. They gain prestige by being close to a Congressman, and they fear to break a relationship which may some day be useful for important purposes. Once the leader has committed himself, his supporters are inclined to go along.

He is free also because the voters seldom know just what they want. Mostly they want evidence that he is concerned with their problem and is addressing himself effectively to it. Often he is viewed as the doctor who should recommend the appropriate cure. The larger number of constituents, and the ones the Congressman likes, are the ones who come in to say, "Congressman, this is my problem." Those, such as the League of Women Voters, who come in with a list of recommended votes are, fortunately for the comfort of the Congressman, fewer.

Indeed, even where the constituent frames his appeal to his Congressman as a highly specific demand, the Congressman is quite free to disregard it. Few constituents deny their vote to a Congressman who generally listens to them just because he differs on any one issue. Furthermore, for every demand on one side, there is a demand on the other. The Congressman who saw his job in no more imaginative light than doing what his constituents or large groups of them wanted would not only face impossible problems of doing that job, but would also soon find himself offending enough other constituents to undermine his chances of remaining in office.[6] He must view the demands with a more creative eye, seeking to invent formulas that will catch the imagination of constituents rather than taking all requests at face value.

Finally, a Congressman is free also because, as we shall see in the sections to come, the procedure of Congress is so complex that it is easy for him to obfuscate where he stands on any issue and what he has done about it.

Congress as a Social System

We have confined our attention to the way in which the context of other activities affects incoming information and the way in which the Congressman perceives and interprets it. The action which he takes on the basis of

6 *Cf.* Anthony Downs, *An Economic Theory of Democracy* (New York: Harper & Row, Publishers, 1957), for a demonstration of the proposition that, by following the majority on each issue, a legislator is likely to court defeat by a coalition of passionate minorities.

such information must also be placed in the context of his other activities. Though it is easy enough for the scholar to abstract one vote on one issue, Congressmen act on a complex of issues, rather than on a single one. The typical Congressman acts, not as if some bill were the only one to be decided, but as if it must be disposed of in such a way as simultaneously to facilitate desired actions on other issues, too.

In the first place, any one bill compounds many issues. Thus, one Congressman who indicated general support for the Reciprocal Trade Act voted against it in the House. In his district, there was considerable unemployment related to foreign imports. He was disgruntled that the Ways and Means Committee had not given him something he could represent as a token of his concern for the problems of business in his district. Then he added: "...and then there is another thing, that damn Eisenhower. I just cannot see why we should give him more power, can you? He...is so incapable." Where some people might see one issue, he saw three: national interest in a liberal-trade policy, his district's interest in protection from foreign imports (which he wanted to acknowledge on a token basis), and the delegation of powers to the president.

In the second place, action on any one bill affects action on other bills, too. The single enduring issue that complicates the consideration of all individual issues is the necessity for the Congressman to maintain effective working relationships with other Congressmen. In the words of Speaker Sam Rayburn, you have to "go along" to "get along.". . .

Few issues present themselves as a clear legislative black and white, and there are few uncompromising fighters on any issue. In an interview with Stewart Alsop, then Vice President Nixon stated forcefully the requirement for compromise in politics: "You know, you come to Washington, you have great ideas and there you are in the committees or on the floor of the House, and you have an inability to implement your ideas. . . . You've got to learn how to play the game."[7]

The complication of other issues, role conflict, and the realization that there are infinite demands on Congress' finite time result in Congressmen usually being interested in a viable, rather than in a definitive, solution to the problems with which they are faced. . . .

A legislative enactment is seldom a clean decision of important issues. It is normally a verbal formula which the majority of Congressmen find adequate as a basis for their continuing a policy struggle. It sets up new ground rules within which the issue may be fought out. The ground rules will reflect the balance of forces, but the minority is seldom so weak on a major issue that it has to accept a once-and-for-all decision. The formula must usually offer them the chance of later reversal, keeping the big issue

[7] "Nixon on Nixon," *Saturday Evening Post*, July 12, 1958, p. 26.

alive. The trade bills were just such formulas. They only authorized executive consideration of trade policy, leaving it open to further politics and propaganda to influence what administrative action would actually be and whether it would be liberal or protectionist. They allowed the Congressmen and their followers on both sides to continue their efforts on behalf of the policies about which they cared. The large majority of Congressmen of all tendencies agreed that some bill had to be passed. The old bill was about to expire, and having no bill at all would have created the worst possible situation in the eyes of all but a handful of protectionist extremists. Some bill was required, if only for the sake of having a functioning escape clause. Failure to pass some act would also have harmed the congressional system in ways having nothing to do with foreign trade. It would have damaged the public image of Congress, as similar failures to act have hurt in such countries as France. It would have brought the congressional leadership into bitter conflict with the White House. It would have injured American prestige abroad and thus have had severe consequences for foreign policy and defense spending. It would have tied up other bills in a legislative log jam. There was agreement on the need for action, but none on what action to take. Thus, the framers of the bill had to get some bill out so that the system could continue to function, but a bill that would force Congress as little as possible to make determinations on the issues which divided it the most. Once such a bill had been hammered out, it was helped through by members on both sides of the main issue, for example, Senator Eugene Millikin (R., Colo.) and Representative Robert Kean (R., N.J.). Each had other business to get on with, to which he could proceed on the basis of the text adopted.[8] Not the least of these goals was achievement of an effective, smooth-running congressional system, a goal far more important than almost any one bill and one to which we now turn our attention.

Congress is not a temporary convocation. It is an ongoing social system which must preserve itself intact and which deals with problems on a long-run, rather than a one-shot, basis.

Because Congress is a social system, what comes out in the form of legislation often, and probably usually, differs from what one would predict from an enumeration of the opinions of individual Congressmen.

---

[8] In the interviews, a recurrent theme by partisans of each side was that their struggle, though unsuccessful, was justified by the effect it would have at the next renewal. The protectionist theme in 1955 was: this is the last time "they" will be able to get through a tariff-cutting bill; the corner has been turned. The administration theme was: this is the last gasp of protectionism; "we have laid the basis for a liberal-trade policy." Judging by the ease of the 1958 renewal, the administration may have been right in 1955. Failure to resolve issues in 1954 and 1955 may have bought the time needed for public opinion to mature.

Suppose that, in the elections of 1954, a voter wished to cast a ballot to facilitate protectionist legislation by Congress. Suppose that, in his district, he faced the choice between a protectionist Democrat and a free-trading Republican, either of whom would be a freshman.[9] He would probably have been ill-advised to vote for the protectionist Democrat. The Democrat might have added one protectionist vote in the House. We say *might* have because, being a freshman, he might also have given in to the persuasive efforts of Sam Rayburn *et al.* and gone along with a liberal-trade policy in the hope of digging himself in with the Democratic leadership. But, in the House in particular, legislation is written mainly in the committees, and our freshman, a protectionist Democrat, would certainly have not got on the cherished Ways and Means Committee, where tariff legislation is written. The free-trading Republican, however, might have contributed to a Republican majority in the House. Had a Republican majority organized the House, the Ways and Means Committee would have been chaired by a Republican and dominated by a majority of Republicans ranging from mildly to militantly protectionist. Considering the composition of that committee in that period and the protectionist inclinations of Republican Congressmen James Utt (Calif.) and Victor Knox (Mich.), who were in fact displaced from their committee positions by the Democratic victory in 1954, the chances of a protectionist bill being fashioned by the Ways and Means Committee would have been greater with a Republican House. Thus, our hypothetical voter might have been well-advised to vote for a free-trade Republican if he wanted a protectionist law to come out of the House.

Of course, there is no logical reason why tariff legislation should at present be considered by the Ways and Means Committee of the House. Historically, it made sense, since the tariff was an important source of revenue. In the present, tariff legislation could just as reasonably, and perhaps more reasonably, be considered by the Foreign Affairs Committee, which, incidentally, is burdened with far less work. However, to make this shift would raise very delicate questions. If some members of the Ways and Means Committee who are more interested in foreign-trade policy than in taxation wanted to shift to the Foreign Affairs Committee, problems of seniority would arise. All in all, such a shift could cause considerable dis-equilibrium in the social organization of the House of Representatives, and it is not likely.

9 We present this as a hypothetical case. It has, however, some similarities to the 1954 New Jersey election of Clifford Case (R.) to the Senate. The public-relations firm which organized the right-wing campaign against Case on the grounds of his affiliation with the Fund for the Republic also represented some protectionist business groups. Had they won their fight against the Republican liberal trader, Case, they might have hurt the interests of their protectionist clients.

But it made a good deal of difference that tariff legislation was considered, not by the Foreign Affairs Committee, but by the Ways and Means Committee, if only because of its heavy work load, let alone the difference in committee memberships on the Republican side. The deferment of a decision in 1954 was to a large part due to the fact that the Ways and Means Committee was occupied with tax reform and other legislation dear to the heart of Chairman Daniel Reed (R., N.Y.) and did not have sufficient time for hearings. In 1955, additional legislation was introduced which might have taken much of the steam out of protectionist arguments. But, because of the work load, Ways and Means never got around to considering this legislation.

The fact that Congress is an organized body with its own institutions and procedures was far from a self-evident proposition to the people who were trying to influence Congress on foreign-trade policy in 1953–1955.

We have commented on the importance of committees for the passage of legislation. In the House, this is especially true, since bills are often reported out of committee under the closed rule, which makes it impossible to amend the bill on the floor. A member can vote either for or against the bill as presented. There are two principles which can be deduced from this simple circumstance. First, committee members on Ways and Means are much more important on foreign-trade measures than are other representatives. However, so far as we could ascertain, Ways and Means members received but little extra mail on the issue by virtue of their committee membership. The picture is slightly complicated,[10] but there was by no means the concentration of mail one would expect, were this simple principle grasped. Second, there was little or no point in writing the average Congressman advocating amendments to the Reciprocal Trade Act for specific products. (In 1955, there was a brief possibility that the bill would be opened to amendments from the floor, but this was an unusual circumstance.) Nevertheless, Congressmen from Michigan, for example, were confronted with mail which asked them to vote for the Reciprocal Trade Act, but to except cherries by giving them a protective tariff. Many other Congressmen were petitioned for protection for specific products and industries. Given the way in which legislation is passed in the House, these instructions constituted something less than a clearcut mandate to the Congressmen. They could not vote for reciprocal trade and for protection for the cherry industry or any other interest. They had to vote for or against HR 1 as reported out of committee.

---

[10] It looks as though committee members received a disproportionate number of press releases and other canned communications. This suggests that some interest groups were thinking at least in part of the importance of the committee. However, such canned communications are precisely the type of communication that is least effective with most Congressmen.

Congressmen specialize according to their committee assignments far more than most laymen realize. Most legislative work is done in committee. A Congressman can therefore ordinarily be effective in drafting and pushing legislation only in a field covered by his committee. Over the years, members of committees become experts in their subjects. Other Congressmen follow the lead of committee members in whose general point of view they have confidence. Thus, a generally protectionist Representative who was not on Ways and Means might not do anything about tariff legislation, except that when it got on the floor he would vote for those amendments supported by Dan Reed. Most creative work in framing amendments and strategy and congressional in-fighting would have been done by committee members.

That the pressure groups were not fully alert to exactly how Congress functions may also be demonstrated by their inattention to the conference committee. The Senate and House versions of HR 1 were referred to a joint conference committee, as happens when the bills passed by the two houses do not agree. That committee had a good deal of leeway. For example, it could have settled on substantially the original House bill and dropped most or all of the senatorial amendments. Would this, then, not have resulted in a bill which the Senate would reject? Not necessarily. In the interests of keeping the system moving, there is a strong congressional bias against rejecting a conference committee report. Amendments which a large majority of either House has inserted as an absolute condition for passing a bill may be quietly dropped if the conference committee has not accepted them. Congressmen, knowing that, will often propose and/or vote for some measure with the intent of demonstrating that they are alert to their constituents' needs, tacitly understanding that it will be amended in conference. Oregon's Senator Wayne Morse (D.) inserted into the Senate bill such an amendment to protect the cherry- and nut-growers.

The opportunity for modifying the bill in conference existed not only in the abstract. It was known that Jere Cooper (D., Tenn.) and Wilbur Mills (D., Ark.), the major House conferees, were dissatisfied with the Senate version and were apparently ready to fight for a substantial revision. This was an attractive opportunity for pressure groups to converge on a small group of men, the Senate-House conferees. But nothing of the sort happened. Perhaps the pro-reciprocal-trade groups were simply tired and had in effect disbanded their effort when the amended bill passed the Senate. Perhaps they were guilty of neglect or a political blunder, although they certainly knew the basic facts. In any event, they seem to have been inadequately sensitive to established institutions and procedures of Congress.

There are many other examples of how communications with Congress fail because the public has too simple a notion of what goes on there. Congressman Amiable, commenting on his wide experience in a state legislature and in Congress, complained, "You always hear from business too late."

Businessmen and their representatives respond to the news. They write to protest a bill when their newspaper or magazine reports it, and that is when it is reported out of committee for general debate. But, by that time, especially in the House, it is difficult to amend. If a communication arrives while the committee is still meeting, a member may feel free to work for the adoption of an amendment. But once he has voted, he is under obligation to go along with other members of the committee. He can scarcely afford to sacrifice his long-term working arrangements with the other Congressmen for this one issue. The very petitioners from his district have many interests. If he wants to serve his district, not only at the moment, but over the years, he must preserve his colleagues' respect.

Sometimes an alert trade-association secretary warns his members to write soon enough. In practice, we found relatively few who did so. However, what such a trade association gains in superior tactics it may lose in the appearance of being organized in its efforts.

When mail does come in time to influence the decision on a bill, subsequent amendments to the original bill may make it irrelevant. A communication which was initially clear in its intentions may become unclear in its implications as the congressional process wends its way. A note which said simply, "Vote for free trade," was presumably in favor of HR 1 as originally reported out, a reasonably liberal trade measure. But what about HR 1 as amended by the Senate? At least one Representative voted against it as a protectionist measure! Would our hypothetical Congressman make his free-trade correspondent happy by voting for or against the amended version?

There is one more relevant point which bears directly on the workings of Congress. Its established procedures are sufficiently complicated to make it often hard to tell exactly what stand a Congressman did take on a particular issue. In many instances, a Congressman will cast a record vote for a proposal only when he is sure it will be defeated, or against it when he is sure it will pass. The reason for this may be twofold. The leadership may release him if his vote does not matter, recognizing his need to impress his constituents. He may in fact be opposed to the measure, but want to get a vote in favor of it on his record. If he has guessed wrongly on how the votes divide, he can usually change his vote when the count is toted up. On the crucial votes in the House in 1955, the leadership in fact won by one vote, according to *The Congressional Record*. But at one time, members report, it had lost by seven votes. The leadership usually has enough of a reservoir of political credit to have a few votes switched if it would otherwise lose by a narrow margin.

A particular measure may involve a complex of issues. For example, the open-rule proposal was defended on grounds that the House should not be gagged. Certainly, whether in good conscience or not, a Congressman could have voted for debate under an open rule and claimed that he was nonethe-less for HR 1. Such things happen, and they happen regularly. We cannot help but remember the bemused comment of a trade-association representa-tive who said, "I don't know what the hell happened with 'em," referring to several Senators who promised to vote "his way" but apparently did not. Aware of the complexities of the congressional process, he knew that he could not take their apparent reneging on a promise as deception on their part, for they may have been hoping to serve him later.

If pressure is to be effective, there must be some clear criterion of yield-ing to the pressure. In view of the complexity of the congressional process, we suspect that an adroit Congressman could confuse the issue in a majority of instances. A look at the voting pattern of HR 1 suggests that a con-siderable number of Congressmen were doing just that. That is one reason why, after the open rule and the protectionist Reed amendment were beaten by the narrowest of squeaks, HR 1 went through with a considerable margin. How can one account for the Representatives who first voted to kill the bill and then to pass it? Among other things, they were putting themselves on record on both sides of the issue. To protectionists, they could say that they voted to have the bill changed, but when they were beaten they had no choice but to vote for it, rather than have no bill at all. To freer traders they could say that they voted for the bill. If challenged on their earlier votes, they could defend these in terms of desiring freer debate and improve-ments in the law.

The complexity of the organization and procedures of Congress reduces the effect of external voices on it. Its social organization exerts constraints on what any single Congressman can do. It also enables him to confuse the issue as to what he has in fact done and why he did it. Clearly, influencing Congress is more than a matter of pressuring individual Congressmen. The job is to approach the right Congressman at the right time and in the right way.

6

DONALD R. MATTHEWS

The Folkways of the Senate

The Senate of the United States, just as any other group of human beings, has its unwritten rules of the game, its norms of conduct, its approved manner of behavior. Some things are just not done; others are met with widespread approval. "There is great pressure for conformity in the Senate," one of its influential members said. "It's just like living in a small town."

What are the standards to which the senators are expected to conform? What, specifically, do these unwritten rules of behavior say? Why do they exist? In what ways do they influence the senators? How, concretely, are they enforced? What kinds of senators obey the folkways? Which ones do not, and why?

These are difficult questions for an outsider to analyze. Only those who have served in the Senate, and perhaps not even all of them, are likely to grasp its folkways in all their complexity.[1] Yet, if we are to understand why senators behave as they do, we must try to understand them.

[1] Significantly, the only major work on the Senate which gives much attention to these questions is W. S. White, *Citadel: The Story of the United States Senate* (New York: Harper & Row, Publishers, Inc., 1956). At the time he wrote this book, Mr. White was chief Congressional correspondent for *The New York Times* and very much an "insider." White's book both gains and suffers from the intimate position from which he viewed the Senate.

Reprinted from *U.S. Senators and Their World* (Chapel Hill: University of North Carolina Press, 1960), pp. 92–104, 109, 116–17, by permission of the publisher. Mr. Matthews is Senior Fellow in Governmental Studies at The Brookings Institution.

Apprenticeship

The first rule of Senate behavior, and the one most widely recognized off the Hill, is that new members are expected to serve a proper apprenticeship.

The freshman senator's subordinate status is impressed upon him in many ways. He receives the committee assignments the other senators do not want. The same is true of his office suite and his seat in the chamber. In committee rooms he is assigned to the end of the table. He is expected to do more than his share of the thankless and boring tasks of the Senate, such as presiding over the floor debate or serving on his party's Calendar Committee. According to the folkways of the Senate, the freshman is expected to accept such treatment as a matter of course.

Moreover, the new senator is expected to keep his mouth shut, not to take the lead in floor fights, to listen and to learn. "Like children," one freshman said, "we should be seen and not heard." Just how long this often painful silence must be maintained is not clear, but it is certainly wiser for a freshman to postpone his maiden efforts on the floor too long than to appear overly aggressive. Perhaps, ideally, he should wait until pushed reluctantly to the fore. "I attended the floor debates and voted for a year without giving a single speech," a senior senator said with pride. "Finally, one day, a matter came up with which I had had considerable experience in the House. My part in it had gotten some publicity. ——— leaned over to me and said, '———, are you going to speak on this?' I said, 'No.' 'You know a great deal about this,' he replied. 'I think you should speak.' I answered that I had not prepared a speech and that I would rather not speak on the bill. 'Look,' he said, 'I am going to get up on the floor and ask you a question about this bill. Then you will *have* to speak!' And that's how I made my first speech in the Senate."

Freshmen are also expected to show respect for their elders ("You may think you are smarter than the older fellows, but after a time you find that this is not true") and to seek their advice. (" 'Keep on asking for advice, boy,' the committee chairman told me. 'That's the way to get ahead around here.' ") They are encouraged to concentrate on developing an acquaintanceship in the Senate. ("Young senators should make a point of getting to know the other senators. This isn't very hard: there are only ninety-nine of them. And if the other senators know and like you, it increases your effectiveness.")

The freshman who does not accept his lot as a temporary but very real second-class senator is met with thinly veiled hostility. For instance, one old-timer tells this story: "When I came to the Senate, I sat next to Senator Borah. A few months later, he had a birthday. A number of the older men got up and made brief, laudatory speeches about it. Borah was pleased.

Then a freshman senator—one who had only been in the chamber three or four months—got to his feet and started on a similar eulogy. He was an excellent speaker. But between each of his laudatory references to Borah, Borah loudly whispered, 'That son-of-a-bitch, that son-of-a-bitch.' He didn't dislike the speaker, personally. He just didn't feel that he should speak so soon."

Even so, the veterans in the Senate remark, rather wistfully, that the practice of serving an apprenticeship is on the way out, and, to some extent, they are undoubtedly correct. The practice seems to have begun well before the popular election of senators and the exigencies of the popularly elected official have placed it under considerable strain. As one very senior senator, whose service extends back almost to the days before popular election, ruefully explained: "A new senator today represents millions of people. He feels that he has to *do* something to make a record from the start."

This judgment is also colored by the tendency in any group for the old-timers to feel that the younger generation is going to hell in a handbasket. To the present-day freshmen in the Senate, the period of apprenticeship is very real and very confining. As one of them put it, "It reminds me a little of Hell Week in college." Indeed, the nostalgic talk of the older senators regarding the unhappy lot of the freshman in the good old days is one way the senior senators keep the younger men in their place. One freshman Democrat, for example, after completing a floor speech found himself sitting next to Senator George, then the dean of the Senate. Thinking that he should make polite conversation, the freshman asked the Georgia patriarch what major changes had taken place in the Senate during his long service. Senator George replied, "Freshmen didn't use to talk so much."

Legislative Work

"There are two kinds of Congressmen—show horses and work horses. If you want to get your name in the papers, be a show horse. If you want to gain the respect of your colleagues, keep quiet and be a work horse."[2] Senator Carl Hayden of Arizona remembers being told this when he first came to the Congress many years ago. It is still true.

The great bulk of the Senate's work is highly detailed, dull, and politically unrewarding. According to the folkways of the Senate, it is to those tasks that a senator *ought* to devote a major share of his time, energy, and thought. Those who follow this rule are the senators most respected by their colleagues. Those who do not carry their share of the legislative burden or

2 *Washington Post and Times Herald,* February 19, 1956.

who appear to subordinate this responsibility to a quest for publicity and personal advancement are held in disdain.

This results, at first, in a puzzling disparity between the prestige of senators inside and outside the Senate. Some of the men most highly respected by their colleagues are quite unknown except on the Hill and in their own states; others whose names are household words are thought to be second-raters and slackers.[3] The words used to describe those senators who seem to slight their legislative duties are harsh—"grandstanders," "demagogues," "headline hunters," "publicity seekers," "messiahs." They are said to do nothing but "play to the galleries," to suffer from "laziness" and "verbal diarrhea," and not to be "team players." It is even occasionally hinted that they are mentally or emotionally deranged.

But this does not mean that all publicity is undesirable. It takes publicity to get, and stay, elected. This publicity, as long as it does not interfere with the performance of legislative duties, is considered necessary and desirable. Nor is there any objection to publicity calculated to further the cause of a program or policy or to publicity which flows from a senator's position or performance. But the Senate folkways do prescribe that a senator give first priority to being a legislator. Everything else, including his understandable desire for personal and political publicity, must be secondary to this aspect of his job.

Specialization

According to the folkways of the Senate, a senator should not try to know something about every bill that comes before the chamber nor try to be active on a wide variety of measures. Rather, he ought to specialize, to focus his energy and attention on the relatively few matters that come before his committees or that directly and immediately affect his state. "When you come to the Senate," one administrative assistant said, "you have to decide which street corner you are going to fight on."

In part, at least, senators ought to specialize because they must: "Thousands of bills come before the Senate each Congress. If some senator knows the fine details of more than half a dozen of them, I've never heard of him." Even when a senator restricts his attention to his committee work, the job

3 Cf. Harry S. Truman's comments. "I learned [upon entering the Senate] . . . that the estimates of the various members which I formed in advance were not always accurate. I soon found that, among my ninety-five colleagues the real business of the Senate was carried on by unassuming and conscientious men, not by those who managed to get the most publicity." *New York Times,* October 3, 1955.

is more than one man can do. "I belong to twelve or thirteen committees and subcommittees," a leading senator says. "It's physically impossible to give them all the attention I should. So I have picked out two or three subcommittees in which I am especially interested and have concentrated on them. I believe that this is the usual practice around here."

The relatively few senators who have refused to specialize agree. One of these, a relatively young man of awesome energy, says, "I'll be perfectly frank with you. Being active on as wide a range of issues as I have been is a man-killing job. In a few years I suspect that I will be active on many fewer issues. I came down here a young man and I'm gradually petering out." The limit of human endurance is not, however, the only reason for a senator to specialize. By restricting his attention to matters concerning his committee work and his home state, the senator is concentrating on the two things he should know best. Only through specialization can he know more about a subject than his colleagues and thus make a positive contribution to the operation of the chamber.

Moreover, speaking too much tends to decrease a senator's legislative impact. "Look at ————," one of them said. "He came in here with his mouth open and he hasn't closed it yet. After a while, people stop listening." Furthermore, a senator who is too active outside his specialty may destroy his influence within his area of special competence. "When ————, one of my best friends in the Senate, came here he was known as an expert on ————, and they used to listen to him as such. But then he began talking on many other issues as well. As a result, he lost some of his effectiveness on ———— matters as well as on the other issues to which he addressed himself."

Almost all the senators are agreed that: "The really effective senators are those who speak only on the subjects they have been dealing with at close quarters, not those who are on their feet on almost every subject all the time."[4] Why this pressure for specialization? Why does this folkway exist? There would seem to be a number of reasons.

The formal rules of the Senate provide for what amounts to unlimited debate. Even with the folkways limiting the activity of freshmen, discouraging "playing to the galleries," and encouraging specialization, the Senate moves with glacial speed. If many more senators took full advantage of their opportunities for debate and discussion, the tempo of action would be further slowed. The specialization folkway helps make it possible for the Senate to devote less time to talking and more to action.

Moreover, modern legislation is complex and technical, and it comes before the Senate in a crushing quantity. The committee system and specialization—in a word, a division of labor within the chamber—increase skill

4 *Providence* (R.I.) *Evening Journal,* February 8, 1956.

and decrease the average senator's work load to something approaching manageable proportions. When a senator refuses to "go along" with specialization, he not only challenges the existing power structure but also decreases the expert attention which legislative measures receive.

Courtesy

The Senate of the United States exists to solve problems, to grapple with conflicts. Sooner or later, the hot, emotion-laden issues of our time come before it. Senators as a group are ambitious and egocentric men, chosen through an electoral battle in which a talent for invective, righteous indignation, "mud-slinging," and "engaging in personalities" [is] often [an] asset. Under these circumstances, one might reasonably expect a great deal of manifest conflict and competition in the Senate. Such conflict does exist, but its sharp edges are blunted by the felt need—expressed in the Senate folkways—for courtesy.

A cardinal rule of Senate behavior is that political disagreements should not influence personal feelings. This is not an easy task; for, as one senator said, "It's hard not to call a man a liar when you know that he is one."

Fortunately, a number of the chamber's formal rules and conventions make it possible for him to approximate this ideal—at least so far as overt behavior is concerned. The selection of committee members and chairmen on the basis of their seniority neatly by-passes a potential cause of grave dissension in the Senate. The rules prohibit the questioning of a colleague's motives or the criticism of another state. All remarks made on the floor are, technically, addressed to the presiding officer, and this formality serves as a psychological barrier between antagonists. Senators are expected to address each other not by name but by title—Earle C. Clements does not disagree with Irving M. Ives, but rather the Senior Senator from Kentucky disagrees with the Senior Senator from New York.

Sometimes the senators' efforts to achieve verbal impersonality become ludicrous in their stilted formality. For example:

MR. JOHNSON of Texas. The Senator from Texas does not have any objection, and the Senator from Texas wishes the Senator from California to know that the Senator from Texas knew the Senator from California did not criticise him....[5]

Few opportunities to praise publicly a colleague are missed in the Senate. Senators habitually refer to each other as "The distinguished Senator from ———" or "The able Senator from ———." Birthdays, anniversaries, re-election or retirement from the Senate, and the approach of adjournment

---

[5] *Congressional Record* (Daily Edition), April 24, 1956, p. 6148.

are seized as opportunities for the swapping of praise. Sometimes, on these occasions, the sentiment is as thick as Senate bean soup. For example, the following recently took place on the Senate floor and was duly printed in the *Record:*

> MR. JOHNSON of Texas. Mr. President, if the Senate will indulge me, I should like the attention of members of both sides of the aisle for a bipartisan announce-ment of considerable importance. It involves the minority leader, the distinguished Senator from California (MR. KNOWLAND).
>
> For many years, I have been closely associated with the Senator from California. Like every member of this chamber—on either side of the aisle—I have found him to be able, patriotic, courteous, and thoughtful.
>
> But I wonder how many of my colleagues know that he is also a five-time winner in the contest for the proudest granddaddy in the Senate?
>
> His fifth victory was chalked up last Monday when Harold Jewett II discovered America. Anybody who has found buttons lying on the floor in front of the minority leader's desk in the past few days can know now that they popped right off BILL KNOWLAND's shirt.[6]

This kind of behavior—avoiding personal attacks on colleagues, striving for impersonality by divorcing the self from the office, "buttering-up" the opposition by extending unsolicited compliments—is thought by the senators to pay off in legislative results.[7] Personal attacks, unnecessary unpleasantness, and pursuing a line of thought or action that might embarrass a colleague needlessly are all thought to be self-defeating—"After all, your enemies on one issue may be your friends on the next." Similar considerations also suggest the undesirability of excessive partisanship. "I want to be able to pick up votes from the other side of the aisle," one Republican said. "I hope that a majority of the Republicans will vote for anything I sponsor. But always some of them are going to have special problems that impel them to vote against the party." They also suggest, despite partisan differences, that one senator should hesitate to campaign against another. "The fellows who go around the country demagoguing and calling their fellow senators names are likely to be ineffective senators. It's just human nature that the other senators will not cooperate with them unless they have to."

In private, senators are frequently cynical regarding this courtesy. They say that "it doesn't mean a thing," that it is "every man for himself in the Senate," that some of their colleagues "no more should be senators than I should be Pope," that it is "just custom." Senator Barkley's advice to the

---

6 *Congressional Record* (Daily Edition), June 13, 1956, pp. 9147–48.

7 For example, witness the following exchange from the *Congressional Record* (Daily Edition), June 11, 1956, p. 8990.
MR. HILL. Mr. President, although I greatly love the Senator from Illinois and al-though he has been very generous toward me in his remarks on the bill, —
MR. DOUGLAS. I had hoped I would soften up the Senator from Alabama. (Laughter).

freshman senator—if you think a colleague stupid, refer to him as "the able, learned and distinguished senator," but if you *know* he is stupid, refer to him as "the *very* able, learned and distinguished senator"—is often quoted.[8] Despite its blatant hypocrisy, the practice persists, and after serving in the Senate for a period of years most senators grow to appreciate it. "You discover that political self-preservation dictates at least a semblance of friendship. And then before you know it, you really *are* friends. It is rather like the friendships that might develop within a band of outlaws. You all hang together or you will hang separately."

Courtesy, far from being a meaningless custom as some senators seem to think it is, permits competitors to cooperate. The chaos which ensues when this folkway is ignored testifies to its vital function.

Reciprocity

Every senator, at one time or another, is in a position to help out a colleague. The folkways of the Senate hold that a senator should provide this assistance and that he be repaid in kind. The most important aspect of this pattern of reciprocity is, no doubt, the trading of votes. Occasionally this is done quite openly in the course of public debate. The following exchange, for example, took place during the 1956 debate on acreage allotments for burley tobacco:

MR. LANGER [North Dakota]. We don't raise any tobacco in North Dakota, but we are interested in the tobacco situation in Kentucky, and I hope the Senator will support us in securing assistance for the wheat growers in our State.

MR. CLEMENTS [Kentucky]. I think the Senator will find that my support will be 100 per cent.

MR. BARKLEY [Kentucky]. Mr. President, will my colleague from Kentucky yield?

MR. CLEMENTS. I yield.

MR. BARKLEY. The colloquy just had confirms and justifies the Woodrow Wilsonian doctrine of open covenants openly arrived at. (Laughter).[9]

Usually, however, this kind of bargain is either made by implication or in private. Senator Douglas of Illinois, who tried unsuccessfully to combat this system, has analyzed the way in which a public works appropriation bill is passed.

. . . This bill is built up out of a whole system of mutual accomodations in which the favors are widely distributed, with the implicit promise that no one will kick over the applecart; that if Senators do not object to the bill as a whole, they will "get theirs." It is a process, if I may use an inelegant expression, of mutual back-scratching and mutual logrolling.

8 Alben W. Barkley, *That Reminds Me* (Garden City, N. Y.: Doubleday & Company, Inc., 1954), p. 255.
9 *Congressional Record* (Daily Edition), February 16, 1956, pp. 2300–2301.

Any member who tries to buck the system is only confronted with an impossible amount of work in trying to ascertain the relative merits of a given project; and any member who does ascertain them, and who feels convinced that he is correct, is unable to get an individual project turned down because the senators from the State in which the project is located, and thus is benefiting, naturally will oppose any objection to the project; and the other members of the Senate will feel that they must support the Senators in question, because if they do not do so, similar appropriations for their own States at some time likely will be called into question.[10]

Of course, *all* bills are not passed as the result of such implicit or explicit "deals."

On the other hand, this kind of bargaining (or "logrolling" or "back-scratching" or "trading off," phrases whose invidious connotations indicate the public's attitude toward these practices) is not confined just to the trading of votes. Indeed, it is not an exaggeration to say that reciprocity is a way of life in the Senate. "My boss," one highly experienced administrative assistant says, "will—if it doesn't mean anything to him—do a favor for any other Senator. It doesn't matter *who* he is. It's not a matter of friendship, it's just a matter of I won't be an S.O.B. if you won't be one."

It is this implicit bargaining that explains much of the behavior of senators. Each of them has vast power under the chamber's rules. A single senator, for example, can slow the Senate almost to a halt by systematically objecting to all unanimous consent requests. A few, by exercising their right to filibuster, can block the passage of all bills. Or a single senator could sneak almost any piece of legislation through the chamber by acting when floor attendance is sparse and by taking advantage of the looseness of the chamber rules. While these and other similar powers always exist as a potential threat, the amazing thing is that they are rarely utilized. The spirit of reciprocity results in much, if not most, of the senators' actual power not being exercised. If a senator *does* push his formal powers to the limit, he has broken the implicit bargain and can expect, not cooperation from his colleagues, but only retaliation in kind. "A man in the Senate," one senator says, "has just as much power as he has the sense to use. For this very reason he has to be careful to use it properly or else he will incur the wrath of his colleagues."

To play this game properly and effectively requires tolerance and an understanding of the often unique problems and divergent views of the other senators. "No man," one highly placed staff assistant says, "can really be successful in the Senate until he has adopted a *national* point of view. Learning what the other senators' problems are and working within this framework to pass legislation gives him this outlook. If he assumes that everyone thinks and feels the same way he and his constituents do, he will

10 *Ibid.,* June 13, 1956, p. 9153.

be an ineffective legislator." It demands, too, an ability to calculate how much "credit" a senator builds up with a colleague by doing him a favor or "going along." If a senator expects too little in return, he has sold himself and his constituents short. If he expects too much, he will soon find that to ask the impossible is fruitless and that "there are some things a senator just can't do in return for help from you." Finally, this mode of procedure requires that a senator live up to his end of the bargain, no matter how implicit the bargain may have been. "You don't *have* to make these commitments," one senator said, "and if you keep your mouth shut you are often better off, but if you *do* make them, you had better live up to them."

These are subtle skills. Some men do not have them in sufficient quantity to be successful at this sort of bargaining. A few take the view that these practices are immoral and refuse, with some display of righteous indignation, to play the game that way. But these men are the exceptions, the nonconformists to the Senate folkways.

Institutional Patriotism

Most institutions demand an emotional investment from their members. The Senate of the United States is no exception. Senators are expected to believe that they belong to the greatest legislative and deliberative body in the world. They are expected to be a bit suspicious of the President and the bureaucrats and just a little disdainful of the House. They are expected to revere the Senate's personnel, organization, and folkways and to champion them to the outside world.

Most of them do. "The most remarkable group that I have ever met anywhere," "the most able and intelligent body of men that it [has] been my fortune to meet," "the best men in political life today"; thus do senators typically describe their colleagues.[11] The Senate as an institution is usually described in similar superlatives.[12]

A senator whose emotional commitment to Senate ways appears to be less than total is suspect. One who brings the Senate as an institution or senators as a class into public disrepute invites his own destruction as an effective legislator. One who seems to be using the Senate for the purposes of self-advertisement and advancement obviously does not belong. Senators

[11] William Benton, "For Distinguished Service in Congress," *The New York Times Magazine*, July 24, 1955, p. 38; Ralph E. Flanders, "What Ails the Senate?" *The New York Times Magazine*, May 9, 1954, p. 13.

[12] This "institutional patriotism" extends down to the staff level. "I'm an apologist for the Senate and senators," one staff member said in the course of an interview. "When I came here I thought just like the normal liberal that the Senate was bumbling and incompetent, that senators were strictly from Kokomo and that if you wanted something done, you had to go to the Executive Branch. Well, all that is a lot of stuff. It's just not true."

are, as a group, fiercely protective of, and highly patriotic in regard to, the Senate.

This, after all, is not a great deal different from the school spirit of P.S. 34, or the morale of a military outfit, or the "fight" of a football team. But, as we shall see, its political consequences are substantial, for some senators are in a better position than others to develop this emotional attachment.

Influences on Conformity

We have seen that normative rules of conduct—called here folkways—exist in the Senate. Moreover, we have seen that they perform important functions.[13] They provide motivation for the performance of legislative duties that, perhaps, would not otherwise be performed. They discourage long-windedness in a chamber of one hundred highly verbal men who are dependent upon publicity and unrestrained by any formal limitations on debate. They encourage the development of expertism and division of labor and discourage those who would challenge it. They soften the inevitable personal conflict of a legislative body so that adversaries and competitors can meet (at the very least) in an atmosphere of antagonistic cooperation or (at best) in an atmosphere of friendship and mutual respect. They encourage senators to become "compromisers" and "bargainers" and to use their substantial powers with caution and restraint. Without these folkways the Senate could hardly operate in anything like its present form.

Yet the folkways are not universally accepted or adhered to; indeed, there is some covert hostility toward them in certain circles. If most senators do observe them, why not all?

Previous Training and Experience

Senators often express pride in the fact that their chamber is "democratic." "No matter," one senior senator says, "what you were before— a rich man or a poor man, a man with a good reputation or an unknown —you've got to prove yourself in the Senate. It's what you do when you arrive and not what you've done before that determines the amount of respect you get from your colleagues." Or as another has expressed it, everyone "must begin at the foot of the class and spell up."[14] This point of

---

13 That is, the folkways contribute to the survival of the system without change. For a brilliant analysis of the promise and pitfalls of functional analysis see R. K. Merton, *Social Theory and Social Structure* (New York: The Free Press, 1949), Chap. 1.

14 Tom Connally [as told to Alfred Steinberg], *My Name Is Tom Connally* (New York: Thomas Y. Crowell Co., 1954), p. 88.

view overlooks the fact that it is a great deal harder for some men than others to start at the foot of the class.

A former governor who becomes a senator is often accustomed to a higher salary, more power and perquisites, a grander office, a larger staff, and more publicity than the freshman senator enjoys. He is likely to find the pace of legislative life slow and to be frustrated by the necessity of cooperating with ninety-nine equals. To move from the governorship of one of the larger states to the role of apprentice senator is, in the short run, a demotion. The result for the one-time governors is a frequent feeling of disillusionment, depression, and discouragement. "I moved from one world to another," a former governor now in the Senate says. "Back home everything revolved, or seemed to revolve, around the Governor. I had a part in practically everything that happened. There was administration. There was policy making. But down here there was just a seat at the end of the table."[15] At the same time, the other senators complain that the former governors "are the hardest group to handle; they come down here expecting to be big shots" and that they often are unwilling to realize that "they are just one of the boys." Some governors, they feel, never make the adjustment; a larger number make it slowly and painfully.[16] . . .

15 *Providence* (R.I.) *Evening Journal,* February 8, 1956.
16 The same situation seems to occur when a man enters the Senate after long and distinguished service in the House of Representatives. Witness this passage from F. Crissey, *Theodore E. Burton: American Statesman* (New York: World, 1956), pp. 235–36:
"Possibly no man had entered the United States Senate with a feeling of more profound satisfaction and assurance than had Theodore E. Burton. His every personal characteristic marked him as predestined for this high place. 'A born Senator' was a phrase repeatedly on the lips of his friends.
"Yet few Senators have found their service in the 'American House of Lords' more disappointing than Burton did. He met with a disillusionment which irritated and often wounded him. He had become accustomed to being treated with almost unprecedented deference in the House. The entire membership often arose to its feet when he was about to deliver an address and he was listened to with rare attentiveness. Any bill which he opposed was in doubt until the vote was taken.
"He was, in fact, a House institution. . . .
"Accustomed, for years, to this position of power, he was unable, on entering the Senate, to realize that his reputation would not secure for him a consideration not enjoyed by most of the newer members.
"He knew, theoretically, that the seniority rule was applied in the Senate as in no other legislative body; but failed to realize that it was inexorable and undiscriminating; that his many years of service at the other end of the long Capitol corridor could not soften its application. . . . Suddenly, on his promotion to the Senate, he was 'put in his place.' "
It is a rare occurrence indeed when a leader of the House of Representatives runs for the Senate—most of the former congressmen in the Senate served in the lower house for only a few terms. Thus this particular problem of adjustment does not occur with the great regularity that the problem of the former governors does.

Political Ambitions

Higher political ambitions—and for senators this means a desire to become either president or vice-president—can also lead to nonconformity.

First of all, strong and exalted ambitions are likely to lead to restiveness during the period of apprenticeship. A national following is seldom acquired by "being seen and not heard" or through faithful service on the District of Columbia Committee. In order to overcome this initial handicap, the highly ambitious freshman may resort to extreme and unsettling tactics, as, for example, Senator Kefauver is thought by his colleagues to have done in his crime investigation and Senator McCarthy certainly did in his "crusade" against communism. His legislative duties are likely to be neglected in the ceaseless quest for publicity and personal advancement. His ears are likely to be "attuned to noises outside the workaday drone of the Senate chamber."[17] Since the senator with higher ambitions is almost invariably shooting for the presidency, he is likely to be attuned to the voices of somewhat different groups than are most senators. Close presidential elections are won and lost in the doubtful states containing large metropolitan populations. Popularity in these areas is generally a prerequisite for nomination and election to the presidency. Yet these very groups are the ones under-represented in the Senate, the ones most often at odds with its present power structure. To the extent that ambitious senators anticipate the wants of possible future constituents, they find themselves challenging the Senate *status quo....*

There are unwritten rules of behavior, which we have called folkways, in the Senate. These rules are normative, that is, they define how a senator ought to behave. Nonconformity is met with moral condemnation, while senators who conform to the folkways are rewarded with high esteem by their colleagues. Partly because of this fact, they tend to be the most influential and effective members of the Senate.

These folkways, we have suggested, are highly functional to the Senate social system since they provide motivation for the performance of vital duties and essential modes of behavior which, otherwise, would go unrewarded. They discourage frequent and lengthy speech-making in a chamber without any other effective limitation on debate, encourage the development of expertness and a division of labor in a group of overworked laymen facing unbelievably complex problems, soften the inevitable personal conflicts of a problem-solving body, and encourage bargaining and the cautious use of awesome formal powers. Without these folkways, the Senate could hardly operate with its present organization and rules.

[17] Douglass Cater, "Estes Kefauver, Most Willing of the Most Willing," *The Reporter,* November 3, 1955, p. 16.

Nonetheless, the folkways are no more perfectly obeyed than the nation's traffic laws. Men who come to the Senate relatively late in life, toward the close of a distinguished career in or out of politics, have a more difficult time fitting in than the others. So do those elected to the Senate with little prior political experience. The senators who aspire to the presidency find it hard to reconcile the expectations of their Senate colleagues with their desire to build a national following. Finally, all senators belong to, or identify with, many other groups beside the Senate, and the expectations and demands of these groups sometimes conflict with the folkways. This seems to happen most often with the liberals from large, urban two-party states. When confronted with such a conflict situation, a senator must choose between conforming to the folkways, and thus appearing to "sell out," or gaining popularity back home at the expense of good-will, esteem, and effectiveness in the Senate, a course which diminishes his long-run ability to achieve what his followers demand. For this reason, conflicts between the demands of constituents and legislative peers are by no means automatically resolved in favor of constituents.

It would be a mistake to assume that the folkways of the Senate are unchangeable. Their origins are obscure, but sparse evidence scattered throughout senatorial memoirs suggests that they have changed very little since the nineteenth century.[18] Certainly the chamber's small membership and gradual turnover are conducive to the transmission of such rules virtually unchanged from one generation to the next. Yet the trend in American politics seems to be toward more competitive two-party politics; a greater political role for the mass media of communications and those skilled in their political use; larger, more urban constituencies. All these are factors which presently encourage departure from the norms of Senate behavior. In all likelihood, therefore, nonconformity to the folkways will increase in the future if the folkways remain as they are today. Moreover, the major forces which presently push senators toward nonconformity tend to converge upon a relatively small group of senators. Certainly, this is a more unstable situation than the random distribution of such influences—and, hence, of nonconforming behavior—among the entire membership of the Senate.

18 "Should the new legislator wish to be heard, the way to command the attention of the House," George Washington wrote to his favorite nephew, Bushrod, upon Bushrod's election to the Virginia House of Delegates in 1787, "is to speak seldom, but to important subjects, except such as relate to your constituents and, in the former case, make yourself perfectly master of the subject. Never exceed a decent warmth, and submit your sentiments with diffidence. A dictatorial style, though it may carry conviction, is always accompanied with disgust." J. A. Carroll and M. W. Ashworth [continuing D. S. Freeman's biography], *George Washington* (New York: Charles Scribner's Sons, 1957), VII, 591. At least some of the folkways are very old and not restricted to the Senate of the United States!

III

The Committee System

The reasons for the committee system are fairly obvious: without some division of labor the volume of business confronting Congress would be absolutely overwhelming. Congress has responded to this pressure by specializing. While it is not true that committees decide everything and that other aspects of Congress are mere window dressing, there is no doubt that legislative measures receive their most severe consideration in committees and that the outlines of all legislation as well as the details of most proposals are settled in committees or even in subcommittees. It is a fairly safe generalization that the less important or more specific an issue, the greater the probability that the effective decisions about it will be made in committee. As issues become more important, or attract the attention of a larger number of congressmen, the committee still is likely to set the terms of discussion, but the ultimate decisions, both about final passage and about the specific provisions of the bill, will then be made on the floor.

In addition to passing laws, Congress helps shape public opinion and exercises the power of legislative oversight—that is, keeping an eye on what the Executive Branch does. It also appropriates money to run the government. All three of these functions are performed almost exclusively by committees. Once in a great while a speech on the floor will affect public opinion, but generally the important impact in this area comes from committee hearings, which provide far greater opportunities for dramatic newsmaking presentations.

Except for the very few members in each chamber who become party leaders, individual congressmen and senators can leave their mark on public affairs largely by their work on committees. As Chapter 4 showed, most major-ity senators are chairmen of at least one subcommittee, and therefore can exercise a good deal of power in a limited jurisdiction. The same applies to a substantial fraction of all majority representatives.

For all these reasons it is important to recognize the significant differ-ences between the various committees. Some of these are obvious: a few committees, such as Rules, Appropriations, and Ways and Means in the House, or Foreign Relations and Appropriations in the Senate, are par-ticularly desirable assignments. The Foreign Relations Committee, for in-stance, provides unparalleled opportunities for personal publicity, especially since the Senate, unlike the House, permits its committee hearings to be televised. The Appropriations Committees offer their members prime op-portunities for collecting obligations from fellow legislators by doing favors concerning funds for pet projects. On the other hand, the Post Office and Civil Service Committee handles legislation that is not particularly interest-ing to most congressmen or most voters. Since all congressmen want to improve constituent relationships in order to enhance their chances of reelection, and since the committee structure provides them with the best means of doing so, they are necessarily very interested in committee assign-ments which can do them the most good back home. Thus the Interior Committee, while almost worthless to a member from Chicago or New York, is a prized assignment to a congressman from the Rocky Mountains, where much of the land is owned by the federal government and farming is generally possible only with water from federal projects.

The first selection, by Nicholas A. Masters, describes the most important personnel decisions affecting congressmen: their committee assignments. Masters analyzes the procedures, considerations, and participants in this process. His article, like the others in this section, is based on extensive interviewing on Capitol Hill.

Each of the next three selections describes a different House committee. Perhaps because committees are more important in the House, a good deal more scholarly attention has been given to House committees than to Senate committees. The thing to remember in thinking of comparisons with the Senate is that each senator is on several committees, any single one of which is thus less important to him; and that the rules and customs of the Senate enhance the influence of individual senators and thus give a bit more precedence to floor action.

The article by Richard F. Fenno, Jr., on the House Appropriations Committee has become a classic since its publication, and a model for subse-quent research on committees. The focus of this article is the interaction between two committee goals: it *must* process every year a number of complicated and important bills, and it must be able to defend its decisions before a House filled with members hoping to get more money for their individual districts. The committee thus must maintain unity before the House. In the light of these requirements, Fenno describes how the committee leaves a heavy mark on its new members, drastically molding their outlooks so as to make them accept the norms by which the committee does its business.

One important feature of the Appropriations Committee is that its decisions are both numerous and routine, although in their total impact they are, of course, extremely important. On the other hand, the legislation reported by the Ways and Means Committee is neither routine nor voluminous; it is, however, of utmost importance, since this committee has jurisdiction over taxes, social security, and tariffs. These issues traditionally have deep partisan overtones, and therefore the Ways and Means Committee could be a scene of endless wrangling. John F. Manley's article explains how the committee avoids this situation and in fact is remarkably harmonious. His focus on the inner workings of the committee calls attention to many of the same variables stressed by Fenno, including the socialization of new members, the expectations of the House as a whole, and the nature of the subject matter. Manley also describes an important but perhaps temporary factor, the personality and talents of Wilbur Mills, the committee chairman.

The final selection, also by Fenno, describes a committee that, like the Ways and Means Committee, considers important and partisan legislation. But because of the interest groups which are affected by its subject matter, the House Education and Labor Committee has displayed none of the harmony that is found in the Ways and Means Committee. By the same token, unlike the other two committees studied, the Education and Labor Committee is not representative of the House as a whole; its Democratic membership is considerably more liberal and labor-oriented, while its Republican members tend to be more intransigently conservative than the House Republican party. The consequences of this polarization of membership, of the interest groups which lobby the committee, and of the issues which it considers, all tend to make it a bitterly faction-ridden body, with important consequences for the outcome of legislation which it considers.

Needless to say, these three articles do not exhaust the possible subjects of study among congressional committees, but they do suggest the range of variation and point out some important implications for public policy of the particular ways of organizing itself that Congress has adopted. Here, as throughout this book, students should be alert to the interaction of two important themes: in order to get its job done, Congress has adopted, consciously or unconsciously, a variety of procedures, organizations, and priorities. These all help to solve certain "institutional" problems that any independent legislative body with a fairly fixed membership would encounter. But the ways Congress has chosen to solve its problems are not neutral with respect to politics; they have biases in various directions, and the impact of these biases is a major theme in the study of Congress.

7

NICHOLAS A. MASTERS

Committee Assignments in the House of Representatives

Any attempt to understand the legislative process, or to reckon how
well it fullfills its purported functions, calls for a careful consideration of
the relationships among congressmen. The beginning weeks of the
first session of every congress are dominated by the internal
politics of one phase of those relationships, the assignment of
members to committees. Since congressmen devote most of their
energies—constituents' errands apart—to the committees on which
they serve, the political stakes in securing a suitable assignment are
high. Competition for the more coveted posts is intense in both houses;
compromises and adjustments are necessary. Members contest with each
other over particularly desirable assignments; less frequently, one
member challenges the entire body, as when Senator Wayne Morse
fought for his committee assignments in 1953.[1]

The processes and patterns of committee assignments have been only
generally discussed by political scientists and journalists. Perhaps the reason
for this is too ready an acceptance of the supposition that these assignments
are made primarily on the basis of seniority. Continuous service, it is true,

This study was made possible by the support of the Ford Foundation and
Wayne State University. Neither of them, of course, is responsible for any errors
of fact or interpretation.

[1] Ralph K. Huitt, "The Morse Committee Assignment Controversy: A Study
in Senate Norms," *American Political Science Review*, 51 (June 1957), 313–29.

Reprinted from *American Political Science Review*, 55 (June 1961), 345–57,
by permission of the author and publisher. Mr. Masters is Professor of Political
Science at Southern Illinois University at Edwardsville.

insures a member of his place on a committee once he is assigned, but seniority may have very little to do with transfers to other committees, and it has virtually nothing to do with the assignment of freshman members. On what basis, then, are assignments made? Surely, not on the basis of simple random selection.

A recent student sees the committee assignment process as analogous to working out a "giant jig saw puzzle" in which the committees-on-committees observe certain limitations. These committees

> . . . must, of course, be guided by the number of vacancies and by the number of applications for transfer. Care is taken to attain geographical distribution, if not balance. Attention is paid to group desires and to the experience and training of individual legislators. And balance among the various factions of the party is sought. Beyond these more or less objective factors, being in the good graces of the party leader is certainly important in getting on major committees.[2]

This statement leaves significant questions unanswered. What, for example, is meant by geographical distribution or balance? Is every section or region represented in each party on each committee? Or does the committee's subject matter jurisdiction guide the type of geographical representation the committee-on-committees considers? Is the number of assignments allotted to a state party delegation on particular committees restricted? Do state party delegations develop a "vested interest" in certain committees and attempt to maintain continuous representation on them? What groups actively seek representation for their interests on the various committees by campaigning for an individual congressman to fill a vacancy? How influential are they? The study of committee assignments should also throw light on party factionalism, the differences between the parties in performing this organizational task, and the importance attached to the professional and group backgrounds of legislators.

As a step toward answers to these questions this study looks into the formal and informal processes of committee assignments in the House of Representatives.[3]

The special hazards of this study deserve mention. No attempt was made to sample the House. The information derived from each Congressman must be used with caution, for legislators view events from a variety of

[2] George Goodwin, Jr., "The Seniority System in Congress," *American Political Science Review*, 53 (June 1959), 412–36.

[3] Data have been derived from unstructured interviews with members and staffs of the various committees, personal letters and similar papers, official documents of various types, and personal observations. I interviewed members of the committees-on-committees, deans of state delegations, and other members affected by the decisions. The survey covered the 80th through the 86th Congresses, with special attention to the 86th.

perspectives. And finally, in all likelihood, some of the subtleties and nuances of the process have escaped observation. Despite these limitations, relatively crude techniques of analysis can yield significant results. For what sometimes frustrates our understanding of the most unique part of the American legislative process—the committee system—is the lack of organized data and the failure to analyze readily available data.

I. The Committees-on-Committees

In one of the more notable features of the reorganization of Congress in 1911, each party created a committee-on-committees to distribute committee assignments, on the theory, still asserted, that a party committee offers at least an opportunity for all party members to receive suitable assignments. Such a committee would go a long way toward eliminating the arbitrary judgments of the Speaker who, in the past, had used committee assignments as rewards and punishments, to help insure his control of pending legislation.

Though both parties use a committee for this purpose, their methods of selecting its members differ. Each committee therefore needs separate treatment, with comparisons from time to time.

Democrats

By custom the Democratic members of the House Ways and Means Committee, together with the Speaker and Majority Floor Leader (or the Minority Floor Leader when Democrats are in the minority), have constituted the committee-on-committees since 1911. This arrangement is evidently an outgrowth of the former practice of selecting the chairman of Ways and Means as the Majority Floor Leader. Because the Democratic members serve in this dual capacity, and although they are formally designated by the Democratic caucus, they are in fact self-perpetuating. The Speaker and Majority Floor Leader participate extensively in the Committee's deliberations and, of course, have considerable influence on the decisions.

The method of organizing the work of the Committee-on-committees in the 86th Congress was typical. Each member of the Committee was assigned a geographical zone within which his own district lies. (See Table 1.) All zones except two were geographically contiguous. Requests for committee assignments coming from members were handled by their respective zone committeeman. For example, representative Aime Forand from Rhode Island was responsible for the assignment and re-assignment requests of all Democratic representatives from districts within his zone, which includes, in addition to his own state, Connecticut, Maine, Massachusetts and Ver-

Table 1   House Democratic Committee-on-Committees
and Zone Assignments, 86th Congress

Committee Member	Zone	Dems. in State Del.	Fresh-men	Committee Member	Zone	Dems. in State Del.	Fresh-men
Mills (Ark.)	Ark.	6	(1)	Herlong (Fla.)	Fla.	7	(0)
	Del.	1	(1)		Ga.	10	(0)
	Kans.	3	(2)			17	(0)
	Okla.	5	(0)	Ikard (Texas)	Texas	21	(1)
		15	(4)		N. Mex.	2	(1)
Forand (R.I.)	R.I.	2	(0)			23	(2)
	Conn.	6	(6)	Frazier (Tenn.)	Tenn.	7	(0)
	Me.	2	(1)		N.C.	11	(1)
	Mass.	8	(1)			18	(1)
	Vt.	1	(1)	Machrowicz	Mich.	7	(1)
		19	(9)	(Mich.)	Ind.	8	(6)
King (Calif.)	Calif.	16	(4)		Ohio	9	(3)
	Alas.	1	(1)			24	(10)
	Ariz.	1	(0)	Metcalf	Mont.	2	(0)
	Nev.	1	(0)	(Mont.)	Colo.	3	(1)
	Utah	1	(1)		Idaho	1	(0)
		20	(6)		Nebr.	2	(2)
O'Brien (Ill.)	Ill.	14	(4)		N. Dak.	1	(1)
	Wis.	5	(2)		Ore.	3	(0)
		19	(6)		S. Dak.	1	(0)
Boggs (La.)	La.	8	(1)		Wash.	1	(0)
	Ala.	9	(0)			14	(4)
	Miss.	6	(0)	Green (Pa.)	Pa.	16	(4)
		23	(1)		N.J.	5	(2)
Keogh (N.Y.)	N.Y.	19	(2)			21	(6)
		19	(2)	Watts (Ky.)	Ky.	7	(2)
Harrison (Va.)	Va.	8	(1)		Md.	7	(3)
	S.C.	6	(0)		W. Va.	5	(2)
		14	(1)			19	(7)
Karsten (Mo.)	Mo.	10	(0)	Total		283	(63)
	Iowa	4	(3)				
	Minn.	4	(1)				
		18	(4)				

mont. As can be seen from Table 1, each zone representative served an average of approximately 18 members.

Although committee deliberations are closed, the procedure followed is well known among most House members. Each zone representative, speaking in order of seniority, nominates candidates from his zone for the various committee vacancies, usually with supporting arguments. Thereupon the

Committee votes on each of the vacancies, and the nominee receiving the highest number of votes is designated to fill it.

The volume of work before the Committee varies, depending chiefly on the changes resulting from the preceding election. Almost always, however, there are more applications than vacancies; in the 86th Congress 124 applications were made for 75 places to be filled. The major committees were naturally most in demand; applications exceeded vacancies for all committees except District of Columbia, House Administration, Merchant Marine and Fisheries, Post Office and Civil Service, and Science and Astronautics— all regarded as lesser committees. Applicants usually list their order of preference, taking into account not only their personal desires but also advice from other members and their own assessments of where they stand the best chance to land at least an acceptable assignment. Without encouragement from above, an applicant, however much he might prefer to be on the Appropriations Committee, say, would hardly bother (or venture) to ask for what he realizes he has virtually no chance of getting.

Much more than committee structure and manner of procedure is involved in making assignments. Animating and guiding these formal mechanisms are the norms and customs observed when assignments are sought. The pervasive seniority rule, for example, works in a manner not commonly appreciated. Members seeking assignments, and particularly freshmen, channel their requests through the "dean" or senior member of their state party delegation. In negotiations between the Committee-on-committees and the applicants he plays a crucially important role in securing assignments. It is his special responsibility to see that his members receive adequate representation on the various committees. In performing this task, he tries to protect or maintain the delegation's place on a major committee when a vacancy occurs and the seat has previously been held by a member of the delegation; he consults with, and advises, the members of his delegation seeking assignments as to what their chances are, and which committee assignments he will support for them. The dean's decisions must be made in consideration of the needs of his state, the qualifications of his own members, and the necessity for adjusting the requests among his members to prevent duplication on committees. It falls to his lot also to discourage and dissuade members who have unrealistic designs on the major committees—Appropriations, Rules, and Ways and Means.

The importance of the deans of the state delegations may be illustrated negatively. Connecticut, for the first time since 1936, elected six freshman Democrats in 1958. Since the entire delegation was composed of freshmen, no senior member could serve as the dean and apparently there was no time or forethought to form an agreement to become part of an area delegation. So when the committee assignments were made, only two of the six, Chester

Bowles and Frank Kowalski, felt that they had been given as good representation as they were entitled to. Bowles got the assignment of his choice, Foreign Affairs, and Kowalski was assigned to Armed Services because of his extensive military experience. The remaining four were given committee places they did not prefer, namely Science and Astronautics, Education and Labor, Government Operations, and a dual appointment to the District of Columbia and Post Office and Civil Service Committees. The four dissatisfied Connecticut congressmen complained, two of them quite bitterly, that their committee positions would not help them to be reelected—that they had received the "left over" assignments. These assignments had not been made from any desire to penalize them, but apparently because they were orphans with no dean or senior member to fight for their preferences or look after their interests.

If the Democratic Committee-on-committees is judged as a system of collective responsibility among men of equal status, then it is clear that the use of members of a permanent standing committee for this purpose has had almost the opposite effect. Each member does not carry equal weight on the committee. The status and rank of each Democratic member of Ways and Means are carried over to the Committee-on-committees. The ranking Democrat serves as chairman and the status of the other ranking members is unquestionably enhanced by the fact that they also serve as Ways and Means subcommittee chairmen when the Democrats are in the majority. These are the senior members in an institution that respects seniority.

Ways and Means members have had considerable congressional experience prior to their assignment. For the period 1913 to 1958, only five of 86 assignments to this Committee were given to congressmen without any seniority; and each of these five had had previous, but interrupted, congressional service. On the average, members have served at least three consecutive terms prior to being placed on the Committee, and the average is closer to five terms if computations are based simply on prior, rather than continuous, service before selection. The stability of the Committee's membership is also increased by the fact that, although a congressman may sometimes shrink from its responsibilities, only one member has ever left the Committee by his own request. What turnover there is results from death, resignation, or loss of party control, rather than from transfers or election defeat.

For a key functioning unit of the Democratic party's legislative apparatus, so much continuity in the Committee-on-committees makes it ill-designed for flexibility and responsiveness to electoral changes and public opinion trends. Rather, it is more analogous to a firmly entrenched bureaucracy, not completely immune but well insulated, and capable of considerable resistance to any pressures placed upon it.

Republicans

The Republican Committee-on-committees is specially set up for its function and is responsible for no other. It is composed of one member from each state having Republican representation in the House; thereby, a lone Republican from any state is automatically included. Each state delegation determines its member on the Committee. This method might be thought to provide an opportunity to select a new member for each new Congress, but the normal pattern, on the contrary, is for the senior member of the delegation, usually the dean, to assume membership on the Committee and hold it as long as he desires or remains in Congress. Table 2 shows the membership of the Republican Committee-on-committees for the 86th Congress.

The point is sometimes argued that the Republicans make it possible for each state delegation to assume a greater share of the organizational responsibility than the Democratic committee assignment process allows, and consequently that the decentralized Republican method is much more responsive to electoral changes. Actual Republican practice tends to contradict this argument. For the Republicans allow each representative on the Committee-on-committees to cast as many votes as there are Republicans in his delegation. This concentrates the power over committee assignments in the hands of the senior members from the large state delegations. In the 86th Congress, members from seven states—California, Illinois, Michigan, New Jersey, New York, Ohio, and Pennsylvania—controlled 97 of the 153 committee votes.

Not to mask the realities of power, the Republican committee assignments are handled by a Subcommittee which, in the 86th Congress for example, was composed of the senior members from these seven states and two others, with one vote each, evidently added to give a voice to large geographical areas (intermountain and southern) that would otherwise have gone entirely unrepresented. Together the Subcommittee members controlled about two-thirds of the full committee's votes. None of them had served less than four terms in Congress. By custom the Subcommittee is appointed by the Minority Leader (or Speaker, as the case may be) on the authority granted by a resolution of the full Committee. The resolution leaves the membership of the Subcommittee apparently at the discretion of the party leader, but the example just given shows how far he is hemmed in by the practice of appointing the same members from the larger delegations each time a new Congress convenes. The change in the minority leadership in the 86th Congress had no discernible effect on this part of the organizational process.

The Subcommittee receives and considers *all* applications for assignment and transfer, and the full Committee invariably accepts all of its recom-

Table 2   House Republican Committee-on-Committees, 86th Congress

State	Member	Votes	State	Member	Votes
Arizona	John J. Rhodes	1	New Jersey	Frank C. Osmers	9
California	James Utt	14	New York	Mrs. K. St. George	24
Colorado	J. Edgar Chenoweth	1	North Carolina	Chas. R. Jonas	1
Florida	William C. Cramer	1	North Dakota	Don L. Short	1
Idaho	Hamer Budge	1	Ohio	Clarence J. Brown	14
Illinois	Leo E. Allen	11	Oklahoma	Page Belcher	1
Indiana	E. Ross Adair	3	Oregon	Walter Norblad	1
Iowa	Charles B. Hoeven	4	Pennsylvania	Richard Simpson	14
Kansas	Edward H. Rees	3	South Dakota	E. Y. Berry	1
Kentucky	Eugene Siler	1	Tennessee	Howard H. Baker	2
Maine	Clifford G. McIntire	1	Texas	Bruce Alger	1
Massachusetts	William H. Bates	6	Utah	Henry A. Dixon	1
Michigan	Clare E. Hoffman	11	Virginia	Joel T. Broyhill	2
Minnesota	H. Carl Anderson	5	Washington	Jack Westland	6
Missouri	Thomas B. Curtis	1	West Virginia	Arch A. Moore	1
Nebraska	Phil Weaver	2	Wisconsin	John W. Byrnes	5
New Hampshire	Perkins Bass	2	Wyoming	E. Keith Thomson	1

Total—153

Subcommittee Appointed by Minority Leader

State	Member	Votes	Seniority
California	James Utt	14	4 consecutive terms
Idaho	Hamer H. Budge	1	5 consecutive terms
Illinois	Leo E. Allen	11	14 consecutive terms
Michigan	Clare E. Hoffman	11	13 consecutive terms
New Jersey	Frank C. Osmers	9	7 non-consecutive terms
New York	Katharine St. George	24	7 consecutive terms
North Carolina	Charles Raper Jonas	1	4 consecutive terms
Ohio	Clarence J. Brown	14	11 consecutive terms
Pennsylvania	Richard M. Simpson	14	7 consecutive terms

Total—99

mendations. Subcommittee sessions are informal and each member is free to speak for or against any assignment. Information on newly elected members is obtained from the Republican Congressional Campaign Committee and the party leaders pride themselves on having extensive knowledge not only of the professional and personal backgrounds of their colleagues, but also of the constituencies they represent. Members of the full Committee who are not on the Subcommittee are entitled to participate in the determinations if they desire, but they seldom do.

Republicans from small states sometimes object that as a result of the system of proportional voting and large-state domination of the Subcommittee they have no real voice in committee assignments and are often overlooked for assignments to the better committees. Along the same line they complain that the Republican procedure allows no mechanism whereby the small state delegations can combine their voting power in the Committee-on-committees. The critics point to the Democratic practice of letting smaller state delegations select a joint dean in order to be able to negotiate for committee assignments from a position of strength.

Actually, the principal difference between Republican and Democratic practice in formal organization is that the Republicans have built into their system a voting formula that rewards heavy Republican areas; the Democrats offer no comparable leverage to the large delegations. Nor is it likely that Democrats would even consider such a plan as long as the seniority system prevails. For it would only lessen the power of the Southern Democrats by putting more control over committee assignments into the hands of the larger northern, midwestern, and western delegations, with their very different traditions and interests.

There is little to distinguish the manner and procedure followed by an individual Republican or Democratic congressman in securing an assignment. Republican freshman members also work through the deans of the state delegations, but the deans, unlike their Democratic counterparts, are usually members of the Committee-on-committees.

Despite these differences the arrangements in both parties for handling committee assignments have one basic feature in common. Both committees-on-committees are so constituted as to be virtually immune to immediate pressures brought about by electoral changes. This is no accident. Its justification rests on a number of considerations congenial to the norms and customs of the entire body. If junior or freshman members had the responsibility for making committee assignments they would immediately be thrust into difficult and delicate positions, particularly in deciding on transfer requests from senior members. Such decisions might well be controversial enough to damage permanently a junior member's career within the legislature and possibly outside of it. In private as well as public life, organizations seldom allow the newcomer—unfamiliar with the subtleties and the institutional trappings of the process—to make important personnel decisions; and committee assignments are party personnel decisions of the most crucial importance. Senior members simply would not willingly tolerate decisions made in this way. If forced to do so, the pressures, roadblocks and penalties they could evoke might be so severe and difficult to overcome that order in the whole legislative process might be endangered. The system has evolved as it has for these reasons, as well as for more positive benefits, such as the desire to rely on the more knowledgeable judgments of those with greater experience in the legislature.

Finally, the system is intended to give the process a tone of moderation and detachment. Members with seniority are less threatened by an election two years hence, being less subject to the vicissitudes of a competitive district.

After years of experience in a collective body, senior members are readier to recognize the need for compromise and adjustment if work is to be done. Although competitive ambitions among members may be intense, prolonged debate over committee assignments would delay the conduct of legislative business which is already too long delayed by the employment of existing institutional and parliamentary devices.

The Role of the Party Leaders

The role of the party leaders in making committee assignments is difficult to define; no simple definition fits all the realities. Generally speaking, the leadership of each party in the House is formidable and independent to a great degree, though the leaders' power varies with their personal relations with the other members. David Truman explains the dependence of the rank-and-file upon the party leaders as follows:

> The machinery of the House and of its parties is normally available to the ordinary member only, so to speak, on its own terms, because the source of its strength is also the source of its disabilities, namely, numbers. In a House of 435 [now 437] or in a body roughly half that size, as one of the parties, there is a tendency...for the real and formal leadership closely to coincide. A formal, standardized system of communication and control is indispensable to the conduct of affairs in a body of that size.... This standardization of the communication structure implies that initiative tends to be centralized or at least that there are central controls on the flow of business. These the rank-and-file member cannot command or, as sometimes happens in the Senate, supplant. Hence, excepting some aspects of his own voting decisions, the independence of the ordinary member is restricted.[4]

The Democratic and Republican leaders not only play the principal role in the selection of the members of their respective committees-on-committees, but their personal judgments also tend to become the norm for major committee assignments. In practice, the leadership of both parties is directly involved in assignments to all the major committees, though the leaders do not usually concern themselves with applicants to lesser ones.

The party leaders use their power over committee assignments variously, to reward members who have been loyal and cooperative, and to reinforce the strength of their own positions by rewarding members whose loyalty may be suspected but whose strength may no longer be safely disregarded. Party leaders working with the committee-on-committees have in a number of instances offered important committee positions to members with demonstrated followings who were regarded as prospective threats. Such offers are made for the obvious purpose of securing cooperation, and so are frequently labelled as "sell-outs" or "the buying-off process" by some discon-

4 *The Congressional Party: A Case Study* (New York, 1959), p. 195.

tented members. Value judgments on particular cases will vary with individual viewpoints, but it must be recognised that Congress is not the only place where adjustments in the power structure are designed to accommodate or to absorb potentially strong rivals.

A specific example may be offered from the 86th Congress. Prior to the opening of the first session a group of liberal Democrats announced their intention to mobilize forces in the House in order to bring about the passage of legislation they favored. While the movement was underway—letters were being sent to the new Democratic members, as well as to incumbents sympathetic to their cause—Speaker Rayburn intervened, promising to use his influence to prevent the Rules Committee from blocking their bills. The Speaker, working with Chairman Wilbur Mills of the Ways and Means Committee and Majority Leader John McCormack, in order to demonstrate his willingness to cooperate with the group, offered one of their leaders, Lee Metcalf of Montana, an appointment to the Ways and Means Committee. Contrary to expectations, Metcalf said he did not want the assignment; he contended that he preferred to be on Interior and Insular Affairs— important for Montana. The leaders insisted, however, that he had a responsibility to his party to accept the post, and he finally did. Metcalf was the logical choice in a move to head off a possible revolt, because his previous behavior had satisfied the party leaders that he was a "responsible" legislator—a concept that warrants further examination presently.

II. Criteria for Committee Assignments

The committees-on-committees have rules to govern them in assigning members to the twenty permanent standing committees. The Legislative Reorganization Act of 1946 limited members of the House to service on a single committee, but this provision has since been amended as follows: (1) Three committees are *exclusive*—namely, Appropriations, Rules, and Ways and Means. A member who serves on any of these can serve on no other committee. (2) Ten committees are *semi-exclusive;* members may serve on any one of them and any one of the seven non-exclusive committees. The ten are: Agriculture, Armed Services, Banking and Currency, Education and Labor, Foreign Affairs, Interstate and Foreign Commerce, Judiciary, Post Office and Civil Service, Public Works, and Science and Astronautics. (3) Seven committees are *non-exclusive*. A member may serve on any two of these seven, or any one of them and any one of the ten semi-exclusive committees. The seven are: District of Columbia, Government Operations, House Administration, Interior and Insular Affairs, Merchant Marine and Fisheries, Un-American Activities, and Veterans Affairs.

The 1946 Act also fixes the total membership of each committee, although changes can be and are made for the duration of a Congress by means of a House resolution. Party ratios on the Rules and Ways and Means committees are fixed by agreement among the party leaders, while the ratios on other committees ordinarily reflect the House division.[5]

Beyond these ground rules, experience has developed other criteria used in determining committee assignments. In discussing them here, the exclusive committees are treated separately first, because of the special attention given to filling vacancies on them. I will then turn to the variables that affect assignments to all of the committees.

Assignments to Major Committees

The three exclusive committees, Appropriations, Rules, and Ways and Means, are regarded by all in both parties as being of special importance. Other committees—among them Agriculture, Armed Services, and Public Works—deal with issues that affect vital congressional and national interests, but none can lay continuous claim to the power and prestige of the top three. As one Congressman stated, "If you get appointed to one of the top three, you have 'arrived.' "

Although the manner of attaining positions on these committees varies, each nominee must fit a bill of particulars. In practice, as indicated earlier, these lesser leaders are selected by the party leaders in consultation with the members of the committee-on-committees, rather than the other way around. A nominee's name may be first brought up by the party leaders, a committee member, or even by someone not involved in the mechanics, but whatever the technical circumstances surrounding the introduction of his name, if the nominee is assigned, he bears the party leaders' stamp of approval. This is true in both parties.

The principal factors involved in selecting members for a major committee may be grouped under three broad headings: (1) legislative responsibility, (2) type of district represented, and (3) geographical area represented.

(1) *Legislative responsibility.* The most crucial test is whether a candidate is a "responsible" legislator, as the leaders of both parties use that term. What does a member have to be or do—or avoid—in order to be regarded as a responsible legislator?

---

[5] In the 87th Congress a serious conflict arose over the Rules Committee ratio. There was newspaper talk of "purging" the ranking Democratic member, William Colmer from Mississippi, who had supported the Dixiecrat presidential candidacy of Mississippi's Governor Barnett in the 1960 campaign, and who regularly voted with Chairman Howard Smith in the coalition of southern Democrats and conservative Republicans that controlled the Rules Committee. But Speaker Rayburn, in order to break the "stranglehold" the coalition would have over the impending legislation of the Kennedy Administration, advocated instead an increase in the Committee's size. The conflict was resolved in Rayburn's favor by a narrow margin with the entire House participating in the vote. The subsequent appointments, however, were made along the lines suggested in this article.

According to the party leaders and the members of the committees-on-committees, a responsible legislator is one whose ability, attitudes, and relationships with his colleagues serve to enhance the prestige and importance of the House of Representatives. He has a basic and fundamental respect for the legislative process and understands and appreciates its formal and informal rules. He has the respect of his fellow legislators, and particularly the respect of the party leaders. He does not attempt to manipulate every situation for his own personal advantage. In the consideration of issues, he is careful to protect the rights of others; he is careful to clear matters that require clearance; and he is especially careful about details. He understands the pressures on the members with whom he cannot always agree and avoids pushing an issue to the point where his opponents may suffer personal embarrassment. On specific issues, no matter how firm his convictions and no matter how great the pressures upon him, he demonstrates a willingness to compromise. He is moderate, not so much in the sense of his voting record and his personal ideology, but rather in the sense of a moderate approach; he is not to be found on the uncompromising extremes of the political spectrum. Although the notions of those interviewed were somewhat vague on this point, a responsible legislator is apparently one who does not believe that the Congress is the proper place to initiate drastic and rapid changes in the direction of public policy. On the contrary, he is more inclined to be a gradualist, and to see public policy as a sort of "synthesis of opposing viewpoints." In short, a responsible legislator is politically pliant, but not without conviction.

A legislator can demonstrate his responsibility in many ways: how he manages a major bill; what he contributes in committee work; the sort of testimony he presents before other committees; the nature of his remarks on the floor—all these are tests of his responsibility. If he behaves properly in these settings and refrains from criticizing the party leadership—and gets reelected at home—his chances of being selected for a major committee post are very good. In the interviews, both Democrats and Republicans emphasized repeatedly the attention paid to the past performance of major committee applicants. For the major committees are "closed corporations," and their membership is composed only of those who have served their "apprenticeships" on lesser committees for considerable periods of time. Even in an instance in which party leaders feel compelled to appoint a member of a dissident wing of the party in order to gain greater cooperation, they will tend to select the member who most closely conforms to the norms of responsibility.

When the question was raised how southern Democrats, who might be regarded as uncompromising on many questions, yet were appointed to major committees, the interviewees immediately pointed out how the Southerners differ from many of their "uncompromising" northern colleagues:

they never denounce the legislative process as ill suited for public policy formation, they are never frustrated by its intricacies; rather, they master its techniques and use them skillfully and artfully to support their positions. "After all," one Congressman commented,

> the Southerner usually joins this body free from the pressures many of the rest of us face and is usually eager to make his mark. Membership in Congress is the highest political office he is likely to attain and he will devote full time to the legislature. Other members often entertain higher political ambitions or may have to devote the majority of their time to keeping things running smoothly in their districts.

(2) *Type of District Represented.* It would be rare indeed for a member to earn regard as "responsible" in only one or two terms. No freshman has been assigned to the Rules Committee since the Legislative Reorganization Act was passed and only 14 have been assigned to the larger Appropriations Committee and two to the Ways and Means Committee (Table 3). So the concept of responsibility is connected with an element beyond the member's personality, an element that takes into account the nature of his district. The members of the committees-on-committees have something more in mind here than simply a particular member's ability to be reelected. Long tenure by itself is an obvious objective fact, and common sense proof that a district is "safe"; but this is not enough. It is not necessarily to the point either that the member's district may be safe for the incumbent but not for anyone else. The essence of the criterion lies in the terms on which the member is returned rather than in the fact of his return alone. The committee-on-committees wants to feel that his district will not only reelect him but also allow him to operate as a free agent, enabling him to make controversial decisions on major policy questions without constant fear of reprisals at the polls. His district must not be one that forces him to take definite, uncompromising positions, for this would jeopardize his usefulness in committee work. In the terminology of Eulau, Wahlke *et al.,* the district should be one that elects its member as a "trustee" or a "politico" and not as a "delegate."[6] This requirement is of special importance in considering assignments to the Rules Committee; many members would not relish being on this committee despite its power, simply because it is inevitably involved in practically every issue before the Congress.

A related reason for the "safe" district requirement is based on the idea that important committee posts should belong to the professional, the veteran politician who has earned his way up the ladder—the "politico" in preference to the "trustee." A politician from a safe district has fought and

---

[6] "The Role of the Representative: Some Empirical Observations on the Theory of Edmund Burke," *American Political Science Review,* 53 (September 1959), 742–56.

Table 3   Committee Assignments to Freshmen, House of Representatives, 80th–86th Congresses

Committee	Number of Freshman Assignments	
	Repub.	*Dem.*
Exclusive Committees:		
Appropriations	8	6
Rules	0	0
Ways and Means	2	0
Semi-Exclusive Committees:		
Agriculture	13	11
Armed Services	1	11
Banking and Currency	15	20
Education and Labor	17	27
Foreign Affairs	4	10
Interstate and Foreign Commerce	8	10
Judiciary	15	14
Post Office and Civil Service*	22	35
Public Works	20	20
Science and Astronautics†	0	8
Non-Exclusive Committees		
District of Columbia	13	8
Government Operations	24	26
House Administration	11	19
Interior and Insular Affairs	17	28
Merchant Marine and Fisheries	24	26
Un-American Activities	6	1
Veterans' Affairs	33	30
Totals	253	310

Source: Data from *Congressional Directory,* 1st Session of each Congress. Includes only Representatives with *no* previous service at any time. Some Representatives received double assignments, so totals shown are higher than the total of freshmen in each Congress.
* Reams of Ohio, Independent, assigned to Post Office and Civil Service in 82d Congress.
† Created by 86th Congress.

won enough political battles to nail down a district and thus help his party maintain control of the House. In short, he is a sure vote in the battle for control and he should receive the rewards of the system.

Members of the committees-on-committees felt no compulsion to explain away or camouflage this requirement. On the contrary, they argue that a realistic appraisal of the factors operating in our political system reveals that if a member sits on a congressional committee in which compromises must continually be made on matters of major policy, he cannot come from a district that does not allow him flexibility.

(3) *Geographical Area.* A legislator who is responsible and who comes from a district that allows him considerable independence on issues still has no guarantee that he will be selected to fill a major committee vacancy. He simply has a better chance than others. A third factor serves to narrow the range of choice. For both party committees tend to follow the practice of selecting a member from the same state party delegation as the member who vacated the seat, in order not to disturb the existing geographical balance. For example, upon the death or defeat of three members of the Ways and Means Committee, the Kentucky, Michigan, and Pennsylvania Democratic delegations asserted a prescriptive right to have members from their respective delegations chosen to fill the vacancies. Moreover, this practice sometimes extends to other committees. The Ohio Republican delegation, for example, insists that it should have one of its members on the Public Works Committee at all times.

Along this line, each party attempts to have every section of the nation represented on the Appropriations and Ways and Means committees. These are the only two committees, however, on which geographical balance is regarded as especially important. Actually the only geographical rule applied to all committee assignments provides that no state party delegation shall have more than one representative on any committee, except for the largest state delegations where strict application of the rule would be impossible.

General Criteria for All Committee Assignments

The most important single factor in distributing assignments to all other committees is whether a particular place will help to insure the reelection of the member in question. So although it might abstractly seem desirable and logical to place an urban congressman on the Agriculture Committee to protect consumer interests, there is little operative political warrant for such an assignment. Not only do congressmen from urban areas usually refrain from applying for such vacancies when they occur, but the committees-on-committees also insist that members coming from predominantly agricultural areas have first call on them in order that they may use the assignments to protect their tenure in office. Both parties take it for granted that wheat, cotton and tobacco areas should have the majority of representation on the committee. The leaders know that assignment of an urban congressman to the Agriculture Committee would only make him "fair game" for each of the farm lobbies.

The same general reasoning applies to other committees as well. Assignments to Public Works, Interior and Insular Affairs or Merchant Marine and Fisheries are usually based on the ecological make-up of the members' districts, so as to allow them to serve their constituent interests and protect their incumbency. For example, South Dakota Democrat George Mc-Govern's application for transfer to the Agriculture Committee from the Education and Labor Committee was approved primarily on the grounds that his former assignment handicapped his effectiveness in providing service to his constituents and was a disadvantage to him since it had become a major campaign issue in his farm district.

When two or more members stake a claim to the same assignment, on the ground that it is essential to their electoral success, both party committees usually, if not invariably, will give preference to the member with longer service. Members have often maneuvered for a position on a particular committee long before a vacancy existed, and sometimes even long before other applicants were first elected. But open importunity may be self-defeating, for no one likes a pest.

Some Special Cases

The assignment of members to the Education and Labor Committee—with jurisdiction over the explosive issues of school aid, segregation and labor-management relations—has called for the most careful attention to the constituencies of applicants. As the party committees have seen it in recent years, this assignment is no place for a neutral when there are so many belligerents around. Their assignments have produced a standoff between antagonists,[7] and a suggestion during the 86th Congress, dropped in the end, for a partition of the Committee as an alternative to the prospective accession of Adam Clayton Powell of New York to its chairmanship upon the retirement of Graham Barden of North Carolina. Apart from the Southerners and a handful of others from districts safe enough to allow them comfortable independence, Democrats have felt that only members who can afford politically to take an outright pro-labor position—*i.e.,* who get union support for election—should be assigned to this committee.

Members from farm or middle-class suburban districts are discouraged from applying. Service on this committee by a member whose district is relatively free of labor-management or segregation conflicts would only result in raising issues in his district that could prove embarrassing and even politically fatal to the member.

Republicans appear to have concluded, too, that it is impossible to take a moderate position on labor-management issues. They also dissuade members from applying for this committee when it might impair their chances for reelection. Republican assignees, however, are more likely to take a

---

[7] *Cf.* Seymour Scher, "Congressional Committee Members as Independent Agency Overseers: A Case Study," *American Political Science Review,* 54 (December 1960), 911–20.

pro-management or non-labor view for the obvious reason that fewer Republicans receive overt political support from organized labor; more have close ties with management groups.

For the Democratic Committee-on-committees, a special issue affects assignments to what has been commonly described as an unimportant committee, the District of Columbia Committee. Southern legislators attach a great deal of importance to their efforts to maintain representation on that committee and to control it. The objective is to block home rule for the District, with all the implications of extensive Negro participation in District politcal affairs.

More generally, southern congressmen have a more or less collective understanding that in order to maximize their influence on the legislative process they need to spread their strength over all the committees. This involves maneuvering for positions on the "housekeeping" committees. Although *a priori* calculations might seem to argue that dispersing members over twenty committees would weaken rather than strengthen southern control of the House, in actual practice the seniority rule vindicates their strategy. Collectively, congressmen from the South build up more seniority than any other sectional contingent and reap their rewards in committee and subcommittee chairmanships when the Democrats are in the majority.

Organized Interest Group Participation

All members of the committees-on-committees recognized that organized groups outside Congress take a hand in the assignment process from time to time. The influence of such groups is thought to be important, but little evidence is available on its nature and extent. Sometimes, though not often, organized groups formally endorse a nominee for a committee vacancy. For example, Representative Harold B. McSween (Dem., La.), when applying for assignment to the Agriculture Committee, had letters of endorsement from American Farm Bureau representatives placed in his application file. Democrats attempt to placate organized labor by placing pro-labor representatives on the Education and Labor Committee, while Republicans attempt to satisfy the National Association of Manufacturers by appointing pro-business members to the same Committee. The most widely publicized groups connected with assignments to the Ways and Means committee are spokesmen for the oil interests. Democratic members and staff personnel frequently mentioned in interviews that a nominee's acceptability for assignment to this committee often hinged on whether he demonstrated a willingness to oppose any attempts to reduce the oil depletion tax allowance.

Nevertheless, organized groups, with occasional exceptions, appear to refrain from direct intervention in committee assignments; overt intrusion is apt to be resented and so be self-defeating. Rather, they have certain "expectations" about the type of person who should be selected for the vacancies on committees which affect their interests. Each group usually counts several members "friendly" or responsive to their needs. Organized interests do not often concern themselves too much with the selection of a particular member of the "friendly" group so long as one of them is eventually chosen.

Other Considerations

The proposition is sometimes advanced that geographical balance is a deliberate objective in distributing assignments to all committees. If so, it has a low priority. There is no evidence of systematic effort to provide each section with representation on the various committees proportional to its representation in the House. The Appropriations and Ways and Means committees may be considered as exceptions, but even here a much more pressing consideration is representation for the large tax-paying states. An examination of the membership of the Interior and Insular Affairs Committee clearly shows that geographical balance is not necessarily a primary goal for all committees. Of the 19 Democratic members of this committee in the 86th Congress, 17 were from districts west of the Mississippi, and of the twelve Republican members six were from western states. Both committees-on-committees will, indeed, listen sympathetically to an applicant who argues that his section of the nation has no representation on the committee of his choice, but this argument is not a compelling reason for making the assignment. Ordinarily, applications are based on district and state delegation, not regional, considerations. Republican New Englanders, for instance, do not approach committee assignments from the viewpoint that each committee should have a New Englander on it. A notable exception to this generalization sets the southern Democrats apart; as stated earlier, they regularly try to have southern representation on all committees.

Party factionalism is a more serious concern than geographical balance. Republicans and Democrats alike, who were responsible for making committee assignments, vigorously denied the existence of factions within their parties; but readily admitted that their respective groups harbored members with widely divergent viewpoints. Occasional alignments emerge, they acknowledged, but these are regarded as fleeting in character. They asserted that no committee's party representation should be composed exclusively of members who view political issues from the same perspective and claimed to have made a reasonable effort to see that divergent viewpoints within each party find expression on each committee. We have already noted, however, that members on the extremes of the political spectrum are usually passed over for vacancies on the major committees; and a member's location on the spectrum is assessed by the party leadership and the committee-on-committees. It is a matter of opinion, therefore, how well founded is the frequent claim that party representation on each committee is balanced ideologically.

Unfavorable assignments, of little political value to the recipients, are sometimes deliberately given by the powers that be as a mark of disapproval, or for reasons that might be described as "for the good of the order." In one recent instance Dale Alford, Democrat from Arkansas, was said to have been assigned to the Post Office and Civil Service Committee because some members of the Committee-on-committees felt that he had violated the "rules of the game" in his campaign that displaced former Representative Brooks Hays, a widely respected member, in the wake of the Little Rock controversy. Also, there was surprising agreement among those interviewed that the Democratic transfers to the newly created Science and Astronautics Committee—not taken seriously in the House—were made in order to provide the transferees with sinecures, and so to remove some of the less qualified members from the other committees. The transfer offers were made attractive to senior members by promises that they would receive subcommittee chairmanships, which would provide them opportunities to build their niches within the legislative bureaucracy.

The professional background of an individual legislator is seldom in and of itself the controlling factor in his assignment. However, some general rules relating to the professional backgrounds of legislators are followed by both parties. Almost without exception, lawyers only are appointed to the Judiciary Committee. Members with outstanding experience in international relations or with extensive military service are regarded as excellent choices for the Foreign Affairs and Armed Services committees respectively. Other things being equal, former bankers and financiers may be given a slight edge over competing applicants for such committees as Appropriations, Ways and Means, and Banking and Currency. The same holds true for farmers who apply for the Agriculture Committee and for members closely identified with the labor movement who apply for the Education and Labor Committee. But all agreed that holding elective office, particularly a state legislative office, outweighed any other type of professional experience as a qualification for any committee assignment. Holding elective office is regarded as a profession by members of the committees, and they feel that the rewards of the system should go to the professionals. Although the patterns of committee assignments tend to document the importance of professional background, it would be a mistake to assume that the committees-on-committees seek out applicants on this ground. Normally, the reverse is true. Applicants tend to apply for assignments where they think their professional skills can be used to best advantage.

The manner in which a congressman campaigns for a committee is an important factor in the outcome. For example, a member seeking an assignment often solicits the support of members already on the committee. Another technique is to obtain the support of influential political leaders, such as endorsements from the governor, senators, or members of the state legislature. If an individual is comparatively unknown in national politics, he may attempt to familiarize the members of the Committee-on-committees with his background and training as it relates to the type of service he can give on the committee he desires. All these tactics, properly employed, can go a long way toward helping a member get favorable consideration by his party. He must be careful, however, to avoid giving the impression of exerting undue political pressure on the members of the Committee-on-committees. For example, if the committee tells him that a vacancy has already been promised to another, he is *expected* to accept this decision. Attempts to challenge either committee's decisions are generally regarded as serious departures from the norms of conduct in the House.

Religious considerations are not ignored in judging the qualifications of applicants. Most Democratic members interviewed conceded that it was important, when possible, to have at least one Roman Catholic on the major committees, and particularly on the Ways and Means and Education and Labor Committees. Republicans, on the other hand, contended that religious factors had no bearing on their assignments.

Racial and ethnic factors also enter into the calculations occasionally. For example, the Democratic Committee-on-committees thought it made sense to appoint Charles Diggs, Democrat and Negro from the 13th District in Michigan, to the House Foreign Affairs Committee because of his race and because of the emerging prominence of Africa in international affairs. In his letter of application to the Committee, Diggs argued on these grounds. Republicans denied considering racial factors as they denied the relevance of religion.

Finally, a few committee assignments are made virtually at random. Usually a handful of lesser places are left over after the committees-on-committees have argued and settled all the applications. These may be handed out more or less indiscriminately to freshman members. At least two circumstances contribute to this result. One occurs when members fail to make their preferences known or to attract any advance support for their applications. This may stem simply from a freshman member's innocence of the process, or, as in the case of the Connecticut Democratic delegation, from the absence of any senior spokesman in their behalf. A second arises when the committee-on-committees' members, along with the party leadership, have too many prior commitments to give serious consideration to each applicant's stated preference. These commitments may extend to members who are obviously less qualified than those who were passed over.

III. Summary and Conclusion

Committee assignments in the House of Representatives involve all the complexities of an organization whose members "are not automatons but reasoning men and women acting in a setting in which they are subject to a bewildering barrage of conflicting or, at the least, inconsistent, demands— from within their constituencies...."[8] Caution is consequently in order in formulating generalizations to describe the assignment process. In this study I have not tried to go beyond an assessment of the factors taken into account at the time the assignments were made, by those who made them. Whether the behavior, then or later, of those who were assigned is consistent with the reasons given for the assignments, or vindicated expectations expressed, is outside the scope of my endeavor.

From the data, several conclusions can be advanced as hypotheses for future studies:

1. Despite some important differences in the formal structure, both the Democratic and Republican committee assignments are handled by small groups composed of senior members appointed and greatly influenced by the party leaders.

2. Party leaders, working in conjunction with their committees-on-committees, use assignments to major committees to bargain with the leaders of party groups or factions, in order to preserve and fortify their leadership positions and conciliate potential rivals, as well as to reward members who have cooperated.

3. Assignment to the major committees is restricted, with some exceptions, to members who have served two or more terms, who are "responsible" legislators, and who represent districts which do not require them to take inflexible positions on controversial issues.

4. Although a number of factors enter into committee assignments— geography, group support, professional background, etc.—the most important single consideration—unless it can be taken for granted—is to provide each member with an assignment that will help to ensure his reelection. Stated differently, the most impressive argument in any applicant's favor is that the assignment he seeks will give him an opportunity to provide the kind of service to his constituents that will sustain and attract voter interest and support. In distributing assignments the party acts as a mutual benefit and improvement society, and this for the obvious reason that control of the House depends on the reelection of party members.

5. With minor differences, both parties apply the same criteria for making committee assignments. This does not necessarily imply that there are

[8] Truman, *op. cit.*, p. 279.

no differences between Republican and Democratic assignees. It does show that both parties tend to emphasize factors beyond the ideological commitments of the members, and that calculations of party advantage lead them both to substantially the same criteria.

8

RICHARD F. FENNO, JR.

The House Appropriations Committee as a Political System: The Problem of Integration

Studies of Congress by political scientists have produced a time-tested consensus on the very considerable power and autonomy of congressional committees. Because of these two related characteristics, it makes empirical and analytical sense to treat the congressional committee as a discrete unit for analysis. This paper conceives of the committee as a political system (or, more accurately as a political sub-system) faced with a number of basic problems which it must solve in order to achieve its goals and maintain itself. Generally speaking these functional problems pertain to the environmental and the internal relations of the committee. This study is concerned almost exclusively with the internal problems of the committee and particularly with the problem of self-integration.[1] It

The author wishes to acknowledge his indebtedness to the Committee on Political Behavior of the Social Science Research Council for the research grant which made possible this study, and the larger study of legislative behavior in the area of appropriations of which it is a part. This is a revised version of a paper read at the Annual Meeting of the American Political Science Association at St. Louis, September 1961.

[1] On social systems, see George Homans, *The Human Group* (New York: Harcourt, Brace & World, Inc., 1950); Robert K. Merton, *Social Theory and Social Structure* (New York: The Free Press, 1957); Talcott Parsons and Edward Shils, *Toward a General Theory of Action* (Cambridge, Mass.: Harvard University Press, 1951), pp. 190–234. Most helpful with reference to the political system has been David Easton, "An Approach to the Analysis of Political Systems," *World Politics* (April 1957), 383–400.

Reprinted from *American Political Science Review*, 56 (June 1962), 310–24, by permission of the author and publisher. Mr. Fenno is Professor of Political Science at the University of Rochester.

describes how one congressional committee—the Committee on Appropriations of the House of Representatives—has dealt with this problem in the period 1947–1961. Its purpose is to add to our understanding of appropriations politics in Congress and to suggest the usefulness of this type of analysis for studying the activities of any congressional committee.

The necessity for integration in any social system arises from the differentiation among its various elements. Most importantly there is a differentiation among subgroups and among individual positions, together with the roles that flow therefrom.[2] A committee faces the problem, how shall these diverse elements be made to mesh together or function in support of one another? No political system (or sub-system) is perfectly integrated; yet no political system can survive without some minimum degree of integration among its differentiated parts. Committee integration is defined as the degree to which there is a working together or a meshing together or mutual support among its roles and subgroups. Conversely, it is also defined as the degree to which a committee is able to minimize conflict among its roles and its subgroups, by heading off or resolving the conflicts that arise.[3] A concomitant of integration is the existence of a fairly consistent set of norms, widely agreed upon and widely followed by the members. Another concomitant of integration is the existence of control mechanisms (*i.e.*, socialization and sanctioning mechanisms) capable of maintaining reasonable conformity to norms. In other words, the more highly integrated a committee, the smaller will be the gap between expected and actual behavior.

This study is concerned with integration both as a structural characteristic of, and as a functional problem for, the Appropriations Committee. First, certain basic characteristics of the Committee need description, to help explain the integration of its parts. Second comes a partial description of the degree to which and the ways in which the Committee achieves integration. No attempt is made to state this in quantitative terms, but the object is to examine the meshing together or the minimization of conflict among certain subgroups and among certain key roles. Also, important control mechanisms are described. The study concludes with some comments on the consequences of Committee integration for appropriations politics and on the usefulness of further congressional committee analysis in terms of functional problems such as this one.

2 On the idea of subgroups as used here, see Harry M. Johnson, *Sociology* (New York: Harcourt, Brace & World, Inc., 1960), Chap. 3. On role, see specifically Theodore M. Newcomb, *et al.*, *Social Psychology* (New York: Holt, Rinehart & Winston, Inc., 1951), p. 280; see generally N. Gross, W. Mason, and A. McEachern, *Explorations in Role Analysis: Studies of the School Superintendency Role* (New York: John Wiley & Sons, Inc., 1958). On differentiation and its relation to integration, see Scott Greer, *Social Organization* (New York: Random House, Inc., 1955).

3 The usage here follows most closely that of Merton, *op. cit.*, pp. 26–29.

I

Five important characteristics of the Appropriations Committee which help explain Committee integration are (1) the existence of a well-articulated and deeply rooted consensus on Committee goals or tasks; (2) the nature of the Committee's subject matter; (3) the legislative orientation of its members; (4) the attractiveness of the Committee for its members; and (5) the stability of Committee membership.

Consensus

The Appropriations Committee sees its tasks as taking form within the broad guidelines set by its parent body, the House of Representatives. For it is the primary condition of the Committee's existence that it was created by the House for the purpose of assisting the House in the performance of House legislative tasks dealing with appropriations. Committee members agree that their fundamental duty is to serve the House in the manner and with the substantive results that the House prescribes. Given, however, the imprecision of House expectations and the permissiveness of House surveillance, the Committee must elaborate for itself a definition of tasks plus a supporting set of perceptions (of itself and of others) explicit enough to furnish day-to-day guidance.

The Committee's view begins with the preeminence of the House—often mistakenly attributed to the Constitution ("all bills for raising revenue," Art. I, sec. 7) but nevertheless firmly sanctioned by custom—in appropriations affairs.

It moves easily to the conviction that, as the efficient part of the House in this matter, the Constitution has endowed it with special obligations and special prerogatives. It ends in the view that the Committee on Appropriations, far from being merely one among many units in a complicated legislative-executive system, is *the* most important, most responsible unit in the whole appropriations process.[4] Hand in hand with the consensus on their primacy goes a consensus that all of their House-prescribed tasks can be

---

[4] This and all other generalizations about member attitudes and perceptions depend heavily on extensive interviews with Committee members. Semi-structured interviews, averaging 45 minutes in length, were held with 45 of the 50 Committee members during the 86th Congress. Certain key questions, all open-ended, were asked of all respondents. The schedule was kept very flexible, however, in order to permit particular topics to be explored with those individuals best equipped to discuss them. In a few cases, where respondents encouraged it, notes were taken during the interviews. In most cases notes were not taken, but were transcribed immediately after the interview. Where unattributed quotations occur in the text, therefore, they are as nearly verbatim as the author's power of immediate recall could make them. These techniques were all used so as to improve *rapport* between interviewer and respondent.

fulfilled by superimposing upon them one single, paramount task—*to guard the Federal Treasury.* Committee members state their goals in the essentially negative terms of guardianship—screening requests for money, checking against ill-advised expenditures, and protecting the taxpayer's dollar. In the language of the Committee's official history, the job of each member is, "constantly and courageously to protect the Federal Treasury against thousands of appeals and imperative demands for unnecessary, unwise, and excessive expenditures."[5]

To buttress its self-image as guardian of public funds the Committee elaborates a set of perceptions about other participants in the appropriations process to which most members hold most of the time. Each executive official, for example, is seen to be interested in the expansion of his own particular program. Each one asks, therefore, for more money than he really needs, in view of the total picture, to run an adequate program. This and other Committee perceptions—of the Budget Bureau, of the Senate, and of their fellow Representatives—help to shape and support the Committee members in their belief that most budget estimates can, should, and must be reduced and that, since no one else can be relied upon, the House Committee must do the job. To the consensus on the main task of protecting the Treasury is added, therefore, a consensus on the instrumental task of *cutting whatever budget estimates are submitted.*

As an immediate goal, Committee members agree that they must strike a highly critical, aggressive posture toward budget requests, and that they should, on principle, reduce them. In the words of the Committee's veterans: "There has never been a budget submitted to the Congress that couldn't be cut." "There isn't a budget that can't be cut 10 per cent immediately." "I've been on the Committee for 17 years. No subcommittee of which I have been a member has ever reported out a bill without a cut in the budget. I'm proud of that record." The aim of budget-cutting is strongly internalized for the Committee member. "It's a tradition in the Appropriations Committee to cut." "You're grounded in it. . . . It's ingrained in you from the time you get on the Committee." For the purposes of a larger study, the appropriations case histories of 37 executive bureaus have been examined for a 12-year period, 1947–1959.[6] Of 443 separate bureau estimates, the Committee reduced 77.2 per cent (342) of them.

It is a mark of the intensity and self-consciousness of the Committee

5 "History of the Committee on Appropriations," House Doc. 299, 77th Cong., 1st sess., 1941–1942, p. 11.

6 The bureaus being studied are all concerned with domestic policy and are situated in the Agriculture, Interior, Labor, Commerce, Treasury, Justice, and Health, Education and Welfare Departments. For a similar pattern of Committee decisions in foreign affairs, see Holbert Carroll, *The House of Representatives and Foreign Affairs* (Pittsburgh: University of Pittsburgh Press, 1958), Chap. 9.

consensus on budget-cutting that it is couched in a distinctive vocabulary. The workaday lingo of the Committee member is replete with negative verbs, undesirable objects of attention, and effective instruments of action. Agency budgets are said to be filled with "fat," "padding," "grease," "pork," "oleaginous substance," "water," "oil," "cushions," "avoirdupois," "waste tissue," and "soft spots." The action verbs most commonly used are "cut," "carve," "slice," "prune," "whittle," "squeeze," "wring," "trim," "lop off," "chop," "slash," "pare," "shave," "fry," and "whack." The tools of the trade are appropriately referred to as "knife," "blade," "meat axe," "scalpel," "meat cleaver," "hatchet," "shears," "wringer," and "fine-tooth comb." Members are hailed by their fellows as being "pretty sharp with the knife." Agencies may "have the meat axe thrown at them." Executives are urged to put their agencies "on a fat boy's diet." Budgets are praised when they are "cut to the bone." And members agree that, "You can always get a little more fat out of a piece of pork if you fry it a little longer and a little harder."

To the major task of protecting the Treasury and the instrumental task of cutting budget estimates, each Committee member adds, usually by way of exception, a third task—*serving the constituency to which he owes his election.* This creates no problem for him when, as is sometimes the case, he can serve his district best by cutting the budget requests of a federal agency whose program is in conflict with the demands of his constituency.[7] Normally, however, members find that their most common role-conflict is between a Committee-oriented budget-reducing role and a constituency-oriented budget-increasing role. Committee ideology resolves the conflict by assigning top, long-run priority to the budget-cutting task and making of the constituency service a permissible, short-run exception. No member is expected to commit electoral suicide; but no member is expected to allow his district's desire for federal funds to dominate his Committee behavior.

Subject Matter

Appropriations Committee integration is facilitated by the subject matter with which the group deals. The Committee makes decisions on the same controversial issues as do the committees handling substantive legislation. But a money decision—however vitally it affects national policy—is, or at least seems to be, less directly a policy decision. Since they deal immediately with dollars and cents, it is easy for the members to hold to the idea that they are not dealing with programmatic questions, that theirs is a "business" rather than a "policy" committee. The subject matter, furthermore, keeps

[7] See, for example, Philip A. Foss, "The Grazing Fee Dilemma," Inter-University Case Program, No. 57 (University of Alabama, 1960).

Committee members relatively free agents, which promotes intra-Committee maneuvering and, hence, conflict avoidance. Members do not commit themselves to their constituents in terms of precise money amounts, and no dollar sum is sacred—it can always be adjusted without conceding that a principle has been breached. By contrast, members of committees dealing directly with controversial issues are often pressured into taking concrete stands on these issues; consequently, they may come to their committee work with fixed and hardened attitudes. This leads to unavoidable, head-on intra-committee conflict and renders integrative mechanisms relatively ineffective.

The fact of an annual appropriations process means the Committee members repeat the same operations with respect to the same subject matters year after year—and frequently more than once in a given year. Substantive and procedural repetition promotes familiarity with key problems and provides ample opportunity to test and confirm the most satisfactory methods of dealing with them. And the absolute necessity that appropriations bills do ultimately pass gives urgency to the search for such methods. Furthermore, the House rule that no member of the Committee can serve on another standing committee is a deterrent against a fragmentation of Committee member activity which could be a source of difficulty in holding the group together. If a committee has developed (as this one has) a number of norms designed to foster integration, repeated and concentrated exposure to them increases the likelihood that they will be understood, accepted and followed.

Legislative Orientation

The recruitment of members for the Appropriations Committee produces a group of individuals with an orientation especially conducive to Committee integration. Those who make the selection pay special attention to the characteristics which Masters has described as those of the "responsible legislator"—approval of and conformity to the norms of the legislative process and of the House of Representatives.[8]

Key selectors speak of wanting, for the Appropriations Committee, "the kind of man you can deal with" or "a fellow who is well-balanced and won't go off half-cocked on things." A Northern liberal Democrat felt that he had been chosen over eight competitors because, "I had made a lot of friends and was known as a nice guy"—especially, he noted, among Southern Congressmen. Another Democrat explained, "I got the blessing of the Speaker and the leadership. It's personal friendships. I had done a lot of things for them in the past, and when I went to them and asked them, they

---

[8] Nicholas A. Masters, "House Committee Assignments," *American Political Science Review*, 55 (June 1961), 345–57 [Chapter 7 in this volume].

gave it to me." A Republican chosen for the Committee in his first term recalled,

> The Chairman [Rep. Taber] I guess did some checking around in my area. After all, I was new and he didn't know me. People told me that they were called to see if I was—well, unstable or apt to go off on tangents ... to see whether or not I had any preconceived notions about things and would not be flexible—whether I would oppose things even though it was obvious.

A key criterion in each of the cases mentioned was a demonstrable record of, or an assumed predisposition toward, legislative give-and-take.

The 106 Appropriations Committee members serving between 1947 and 1961 spent an average of 3.6 years on other House committees before coming to the Committee. Only 17 of the 106 were selected as first term Congressmen. A House apprenticeship (which Appropriations maintains more successfully than all committees save Ways and Means and Rules[9]) provides the time in which legislative reputations can be established by the member and an assessment of that reputation in terms of Appropriations Committee requirements can be made. Moreover, the mere fact that a member survives for a couple of terms is some indication of an electoral situation conducive to his "responsible" legislative behavior. The optimum bet for the Committee is a member from a sufficiently safe district to permit him freedom of maneuver inside the House without fear of reprisal at the polls.[10] The degree of responsiveness to House norms which the Committee selectors value may be the product of a safe district as well as an individual temperament.

Attractiveness

A fourth factor is the extraordinarily high degree of attractiveness which the Committee holds for its members—as measured by the low rate of departure from it. Committee members do not leave it for service on other committees. To the contrary, they are attracted to it from nearly every other committee.[11] Of the 106 members in the 1947–1961 period, only two men

[9] In the period from 1947 through 1959 (80th to 86th Congress), 79 separate appointments were made to the Appropriations Committee, with 14 going to freshmen. The Committee filled, in other words, 17.7 per cent of its vacancies with freshmen. The Rules Committee had 26 vacancies and selected no freshmen at all. The Ways and Means Committee had 36 vacancies and selected 2 freshmen (5.6 per cent). All other committees had a higher percentage of freshmen appointments. Armed Services ranked fourth, with 45 vacancies and 12 freshmen appointed, for a percentage of 26.7. Foreign Affairs figures were 46 and 14, or 30.4 per cent; Un-American Activities figures were 22 and 7, or 31.8 per cent. Cf. Masters, *op. cit.*

[10] In the 1960 elections, 41 out of the current 50 members received more than 55.1 per cent of the vote in their districts. By a common definition, that is, only 9 of the 50 came from marginal districts.

[11] The 106 members came to Appropriations from every committee except Ways and Means.

left the Committee voluntarily; and neither of them initiated the move.[12] Committee attractiveness is a measure of its capacity to satisfy individual member needs—for power, prestige, recognition, respect, self-esteem, friendship, etc. Such satisfaction in turn increases the likelihood that members will behave in such a way as to hold the group together.

The most frequently mentioned source of Committee attractiveness is its power—based on its control of financial resources. "Where the money is, that's where the power is," sums up the feeling of the members. They prize their ability to reward or punish so many other participants in the political process—executive officials, fellow Congressmen, constituents, and other clientele groups. In the eyes of its own members, the Committee is either the most powerful in the House or it is on a par with Ways and Means or, less frequently, on a par with Ways and Means and Rules. The second important ingredient in member satisfaction is the government-wide scope of Committee activity. The ordinary Congressman may feel that he has too little knowledge of and too little control over his environment. Membership on this Committee compensates for this feeling of helplessness by the wider contacts, the greater amount of information, and the sense of being "in the middle of things" which are consequent, if not to subcommittee activity, at least to the full Committee's overview of the federal government.

Thirdly, Committee attractiveness is heightened by the group's recognizable and distinctive political style—one that is, moreover, highly valued in American political culture. The style is that of *hard work;* and the Committee's self-image is that of "the hardest working Committee in Congress." His willingness to work is the Committee member's badge of identification, and it is proudly worn. It colors his perceptions of others and their perceptions of him.[13] It is a cherished axiom of all members that, "This Committee is no place for a man who doesn't work. They have to

12 One was personally requested by the Speaker to move to Ways and Means. The other was chosen by a caucus of regional Congressmen to be his party's representative on the Rules Committee. Of the 21 members who were forced off the Committee for lack of seniority during a change in party control, or who were defeated for reelection and later returned, 20 sought to regain Committee membership at the earliest opportunity.

13 A sidelight on this attitude is displayed in a current feud between the House and Senate Appropriations Committees over the meeting place for their conference committees. The House Committee is trying to break the century-old custom that conferences to resolve differences on money bills are always held on the Senate side of the Capitol. House Committee members "complain that they often have to trudge back to the House two or three times to answer roll calls during a conference. They say they go over in a body to work, while Senators flit in and out. . . . The House Appropriations Committee feels that it does all the hard work listening to witnesses for months on each bill, only to have the Senate Committee sit as a court of appeals and, with little more than a cursory glance, restore most of the funds cut." *Washington Post,* April 24, 1962, p. 1.

be hard working. It's a way of life. It isn't just a job; it's a way of life."

The mere existence of some identifiable and valued style or "way of life" is a cohesive force for a group. But the particular style of hard work is one which increases group morale and group identification twice over. Hard work means a long, dull, and tedious application to detail, via the technique of "dig, dig, dig, day after day behind closed doors"—in an estimated 460 subcommittee and full Committee meetings a year. And virtually all of these meetings are in executive session. By adopting the style of hard work, the Committee discourages highly individualized forms of legislative behavior, which could be disruptive within the Committee. It rewards its members with power, but it is power based rather on work inside the Committee than on the political glamour of activities carried on in the limelight of the mass media. Prolonged daily work together encourages sentiments of mutual regard, sympathy, and solidarity. This *esprit* is, in turn, functional for integration on the Committee. A Republican leader summed up,

> I think it's more closely knit than any other committee. Yet it's the biggest committee, and you'd think it would be the reverse. I know on my subcommittee, you sit together day after day. You get better acquainted. You have sympathy when other fellows go off to play golf. There's a lot of *esprit de corps* in the Committee.

The strong attraction which members have for the Committee increases the influence which the Committee and its norms exercise on all of them. It increases the susceptibility of the newcomer to Committee socialization and of the veteran to Committee sanctions applicable against deviant behavior.[14]

Membership Stability

Members of the Appropriations Committee are strongly attracted to it; they also have, which bears out their selection as "responsible legislators," a strong attraction for a career in the House of Representatives. The 50 members on the Committee in 1961 had served an average of 13.1 years in the House. These twin attractions produce a noteworthy stability of Committee membership. In the period from the 80th to the 87th Congress, 35.7 per cent of the Committee's membership remained constant. That is to say, 15 of the 42 members on the Committee in March, 1947, were still on

[14] This proposition is spelled out at some length in J. Thibaut and H. Kelley, *The Social Psychology of Groups* (New York: John Wiley & Sons, Inc., 1959), p. 247; and in D. Cartwright and A. Zander, *Group Dynamics: Research and Theory,* 2nd ed. (New York: Harper & Row, Publishers, Inc., 1953), p. 420.

the Committee in March, 1961.[15] The 50 members of the Committee in 1961 averaged 9.3 years of prior service on that Committee. In no single year during the last fourteen has the Committee had to absorb an influx of new members totalling more than one-quarter of its membership. At all times, in other words, at least three-fourths of the members have had previous Committee experience. This extraordinary stability of personnel extends into the staff as well. As of June 1961, its 15 professionals had served an average of 10.7 years with the Committee.[16]

The opportunity exists, therefore, for the development of a stable leadership group, a set of traditional norms for the regulation of internal Committee behavior, and informal techniques of personal accommodation. Time is provided in which new members can learn and internalize Committee norms before they attain high seniority rankings. The Committee does not suffer from the potentially disruptive consequences of rapid changeovers in its leadership group, nor of sudden impositions of new sets of norms governing internal Committee behavior.

II

If one considers the main activity of a political system to be decision making, the acid test of its internal integration is its capacity to make collective decisions without flying apart in the process. Analysis of Committee integration should focus directly, therefore, upon its subgroups and the roles of its members. Two kinds of subgroups are of central importance—subcommittees and majority or minority party groups. The roles which are most relevant derive from: (1) positions which each member holds by virtue of his subgroup attachments, *e.g.*, as subcommittee member, majority (or minority) party member; (2) positions which relate to full Committee membership, *e.g.*, Committee member, and the seniority rankings of veteran, man of moderate experience, and newcomer[17]; (3) positions which relate to both subgroup and full Committee membership, *e.g.*, Chairman of the Committee, ranking minority member of the Committee, subcommittee

15 This figure is 9 per cent greater than the next most stable House Committee during this particular period. The top four, in order, were Appropriations (35.7 per cent), Agriculture (26.7 per cent), Armed Services (25 per cent), Foreign Affairs (20.8 per cent).

16 The Committee's permanent and well integrated professional staff (as distinguished from its temporary investigating staff) might be considered as part of the subsystem though it will not be treated in this paper.

17 "Newcomers" are defined as men who have served no more than two terms on the Committee. "Men of moderate experience" are those with 3–5 terms of service. "Veterans" are those who have 6 or more terms of Committee service.

chairman, ranking subcommittee member. Clusters of norms state the expectations about subgroup and role behavior. The description which follows treats the ways in which these norms and their associated behaviors mesh and clash. It treats, also, the internal control mechanisms by which behavior is brought into reasonable conformity with expectations.

Subgroup Integration

The day-to-day work of the Committee is carried on in its subcommittees, each of which is given jurisdiction over a number of related governmental units. The number of subcommittees is determined by the Committee Chairman and has varied recently from a low of 9 in 1949 to a high of 15 in 1959. The present total of 14 reflects, as always, a set of strategic and personal judgments by the Chairman balanced against the limitations placed on him by Committee tradition and member wishes. The Chairman also determines subcommittee jurisdiction, appoints subcommittee chairmen, and selects the majority party members of each group. The ranking minority member of the Committee exercises similar control over subcommittee assignments on his side of the aisle.

Each subcommittee holds hearings on the budget estimates of the agencies assigned to it, meets in executive session to decide what figures and what language to recommend to the full Committee (to "mark up" the bill), defends its recommendations before the full Committee, writes the Committee's report to the House, dominates the debate on the floor, and bargains for the House in conference committee. Within its jurisdiction, each subcommittee functions independently of the others and guards its autonomy jealously. The Chairman and ranking minority member of the full Committee have, as we shall see, certain opportunities to oversee and dip into the operations of all subcommittees. But their intervention is expected to be minimal. Moreover, they themselves operate importantly within the subcommittee framework by sitting as chairman or ranking minority member of the subcommittee in which they are most interested. Each subcommittee, under the guidance of its chairman, transacts its business in considerable isolation from every other one. One subcommittee chairman exclaimed,

> Why, you'd be branded an impostor if you went into one of those other subcommittee meetings. The only time I go is by appointment, by arrangement with the chairman at a special time. I'm as much a stranger in another subcommittee as I would be in the legislative Committee on Post Office and Civil Service. Each one does its work apart from all others.

All members of all subcommittees are expected to behave in similar fashion in the role of subcommittee member. Three main norms define this role; to the extent that they are observed, they promote harmony and reduce conflict among subcommittees.[18] Subcommittee autonomy gives to the House norm of *specialization* an intensified application on the Appropriations Committee. Each member is expected to play the role of specialist in the activities of one subcommittee. He will sit on from one to four subcommittees, but normally will specialize in the work, or a portion of the work, of only one. Except for the Chairman, ranking minority member and their confidants, a Committee member's time, energy, contacts and experience are devoted to his subcommittees. Specialization is, therefore, among the earliest and most compelling of the Committee norms to which a newcomer is exposed. Within the Committee, respect, deference, and power are earned through subcommittee activity and, hence to a degree, through specialization. Specialization is valued further because it is well suited to the task of guarding the Treasury. Only by specializing, Committee members believe, can they unearth the volume of factual information necessary for the intelligent screening of budget requests. Since "the facts" are acquired only through industry, an effective specialist will, perforce, adopt and promote the Committee's style of hard work.

Committee-wide acceptance of specialization is an integrative force in decision making because it helps support a second norm—*reciprocity*. The stage at which a subcommittee makes its recommendations is a potential point of internal friction. Conflict among subcommittees (or between one subcommittee and the rest of the Committee) is minimized by the deference traditionally accorded to the recommendation of the subcommittee which has specialized in the area, has worked hard, and has "the facts." "It's a matter of 'You respect my work and I'll respect yours.'" "It's frowned upon if you offer an amendment in the full Committee if you aren't on the subcommittee. It's considered presumptuous to pose as an expert if you aren't on the subcommittee." Though records of full Committee decisions are not available, members agree that subcommittee recommendations are "very rarely changed," "almost always approved," "changed one time in fifty," "very seldom changed," etc.

No subcommittee is likely to keep the deference of the full Committee for long unless its recommendations have widespread support among its own members. To this end, a third norm—*subcommittee unity*—is expected to be observed by subcommittee members. Unity means a willingness to support (or not to oppose) the recommendations of one's own subcommit-

18 A statement of expected behavior was taken to be a Committee norm when it was expressed by a substantial number of respondents (a dozen or so) who represented both parties, and varying degrees of experience. In nearly every case, moreover, no refutation of them was encountered, and ample confirmation of their existence can be found in the public record. Their articulation came most frequently from the veterans of the group.

tee. Reciprocity and unity are closely dependent upon one another. Reciprocity is difficult to maintain when subcommittees themselves are badly divided; and unity has little appeal unless reciprocity will subsequently be observed. The norm of reciprocity functions to minimize inter-subcommittee conflict. The norm of unity functions to minimize intra-subcommittee conflict. Both are deemed essential to subcommittee influence.

One payoff for the original selection of "responsible legislators" is their special willingness to compromise in pursuit of subcommittee unity. The impulse to this end is registered most strongly at the time when the subcommittee meets in executive session to mark up the bill. Two ranking minority members explained this aspect of markup procedure in their subcommittees:

If there's agreement, we go right along. If there's a lot of controversy we put the item aside and go on. Then, after a day or two, we may have a list of ten controversial items. We give and take and pound them down till we get agreement.

We have a unanimous agreement on everything. If a fellow enters an objection and we can't talk him out of it—and sometimes we can get him to go along—that's it. We put it in there.

Once the bargain is struck, the subcommittee is expected to "stick together."

It is, of course, easier to achieve unity among the five, seven, or nine members of a subcommittee than among the fifty members of the full Committee. But members are expected wherever possible to observe the norm of unity in the full Committee as well. That is, they should not only defer to the recommendations of the subcommittee involved, but they should support (or not oppose) that recommendation when it reaches the floor in the form of a Committee decision. On the floor, Committee members believe, their power and prestige depend largely on the degree to which the norms of reciprocity and unity continue to be observed. Members warn each other that if they go to the floor in disarray they will be "rolled," "jumped," or "run over" by the membership. It is a cardinal maxim among Committee members that, "You can't turn an appropriations bill loose on the floor." Two senior subcommittee chairmen explain:

We iron out our differences in Committee. We argue it out and usually have a meeting of the minds, a composite view of the Committee.... If we went on the floor in wide disagreement, they would say, "If you can't agree after listening to the testimony and discussing it, how can we understand it? We'll just vote on the basis of who we like the best."

I tell them [the full Committee] we should have a united front. If there are any objections or changes, we ought to hear it now, and not wash our dirty linen out on the floor. If we don't have a bill that we can all agree on and support, we ought not to report it out. To do that is like throwing a piece of meat to a bunch of hungry animals.

One of the most functional Committee practices supporting the norm of unity is the tradition against minority reports in the subcommittee and in the full Committee. It is symptomatic of Committee integration that custom should proscribe the use of the most formal and irrevocable symbol of congressional committee disunity—the minority report. A few have been written—but only 9 out of a possible 141 during the 11 years, 1947–1957. That is to say, 95 per cent of all original appropriations bills in this period were reported out without dissent. The technique of "reserving" is the Committee member's equivalent for the registering of dissent. In subcommittee or Committee, when a member reserves, he goes on record informally by informing his colleagues that he reserves the right to disagree on a specified item later on in the proceedings. He may seek a change or support a change in that particular item in full Committee or on the floor. But he does not publicize his dissent. The subcommittee or the full Committee can then make an unopposed recommendation. The individual retains some freedom of maneuver without firm commitment. Often a member reserves on an appropriations item but takes no further action. A member explained how the procedure operates in subcommittee:

If there's something I feel too strongly about, and just can't go along, I'll say, "Mr. Chairman, we can have a unanimous report, but I reserve the right to bring this up in full Committee. I feel duty bound to make a play for it and see if I can't sell it to the other members." But if I don't say anything, or don't reserve this right, and then I bring it up in full Committee, they'll say. "Who are you trying to embarrass? You're a member of the team, aren't you? That's not the way to get along."

Disagreement cannot, of course, be eliminated from the Committee. But the Committee has accepted a method for ventilating it which produces a minimum of internal disruption. And members believe that the greater their internal unity, the greater the likelihood that their recommendations will pass the House.

The degree to which the role of the subcommittee member can be so played and subcommittee conflict thereby minimized depends upon the minimization of conflict between the majority and minority party subgroups. Nothing would be more disruptive to the Committee's work than bitter and extended partisan controversy. It is, therefore, important to Appropriations Committee integration that a fourth norm—*minimal partisanship*—should be observed by members of both party contingents. Nearly every respondent emphasized, with approval, that "very little" or "not much" partisanship prevailed on the Committee. One subcommittee chairman stated flatly, "My job is to keep down partisanship." A ranking minority member said, "You might think that we Republicans would defend the Administration and the budget, but we don't." Majority and minority party ratios are constant and do not change (*i.e.*, in 1958) to reflect changes in the strength of the controlling party. The Committee operates with a completely nonpartisan professional staff, which does not change in tune with shifts in party control. Requests for studies by the Committee's investigating staff must be made by the Chairman and ranking minority member of the full Committee and by the chairman and ranking minority member of the subcommittee involved. Subcommittees can produce recommendations without dissent and the full Committee can adopt reports without dissent precisely because party conflict is (during the period 1947–1961) the exception rather than the rule.

The Committee is in no sense immune from the temperature of party conflict, but it does have a relatively high specific heat. Intense party strife or a strongly taken presidential position will get reflected in subcommittee and in Committee recommendations. Sharp divisions in party policy were carried, with disruptive impact, into some areas of Commttee activity during the 80th Congress and subsequently, by way of reaction, into the 81st Congress.[19] During the Eisenhower years, extraordinary presidential pleas, especially concerning foreign aid, were given special heed by the Republican members of the Committee.[20] Partisanship is normally generated from the environment and not from within the Committee's party groups. Partisanship is, therefore, likely to be least evident in subcommittee activity, stronger in the full Committee, and most potent at the floor stage. Studies which have focused on roll-call analysis have stressed the influence of party in legislative decision making.[21] In the appropriations process, at any rate, the floor stage probably represents party influence at its maximum. Our examination, by interview, of decision making at the subcommittee and full Committee level would stress the influence of Committee-oriented norms— the strength of which tends to vary inversely with that of party bonds. In the secrecy and intimacy of the subcommittee and full Committee hearing rooms, the member finds it easy to compromise on questions of more or less, to take money from one program and give it to another and, in general,

[19] See, for example, the internal conflict on the subcommittee dealing with the Labor Department. *93 Cong. Rec.*, pp. 2465–2562 *passim; 94 Cong. Rec.*, pp. 7605–7607.

[20] See, for example, the unusual minority report of Committee Republicans on the foreign aid appropriations bill in 1960. Their protest against Committee cuts in the budget estimates was the result of strenuous urging by the Eisenhower Administration. House Report No. 1798, *Mutual Security and Related Agency Appropriation Bill*, 86th Cong., 2d Sess., 1960.

[21] David Truman, *The Congressional Party* (New York: John Wiley & Sons, Inc., 1959); Julius Turner, *Party and Constituency: Pressures on Congress* (Baltimore: Johns Hopkins Press, 1951).

to avoid yes-or-no type party stands. These decisions, taken in response to the integrative norms of the Committee, are the most important ones in the entire appropriations process.

Role Integration

The roles of subcommittee member and party member are common to all. Other more specific decision-making positions are allocated among the members. Different positions produce different roles, and in an integrated system these too must fit together. Integration, in other words, must be achieved through the complementarity or reciprocity of roles as well as through a similarity of roles. This may mean a pattern in which expectations are so different that there is very little contact between individuals; or it may mean a pattern in which contacts require the working out of an involved system of exchange of obligations and rewards.[22] In either case, the desired result is the minimization of conflict among prominent Committee roles. Two crucial instances of role reciprocity on the Committee involve the seniority positions of old-timer and newcomer and the leadership positions of Chairman and ranking minority member, on both the full Committee and on each subcommittee.

The differentiation between senior and junior members is the broadest definition of who shall and who shall not actively participate in Committee decisions. Of a junior member, it will be said, "Oh, he doesn't count— what I mean is, he hasn't been on the Committee long enough." He is not expected to and ordinarily does not have much influence. His role is that of apprentice. He is expected to learn the business and the norms of the Committee by applying himself to its work. He is expected to acquiesce in an arrangement which gives most influence (except in affairs involving him locally) to the veterans of the group. Newcomers will be advised to "follow the chairman until you get your bearings. For the first two years, follow the chairman. He knows." "Work hard, keep quiet, and attend the Committee sessions. We don't want to listen to some new person coming in here." And newcomers perceive their role in identical terms: "You have to sit in the back seat and edge up little by little." "You just go to subcommittee meetings and assimilate the routine. The new members are made to feel welcome, but you have a lot of rope-learning to do before you carry much weight."

---

[22] The ideas of "reciprocity" and "complementarity," which are used interchangeably here, are discussed in Alvin Gouldner, "The Norm of Reciprocity," *American Sociological Review* (April 1960). Most helpful in explaining the idea of a role system has been the work of J. Wahlke, H. Eulau, W. Buchanan, L. Ferguson. See their study, *The Legislative System* (New York: John Wiley & Sons, Inc., 1962), esp. Intro.

At every stage of Committee work, this differentiation prevails. There is 'remarkable agreement on the radically different sets of expectations involved. During the hearings, the view of the elders is that, "Newcomers ...don't know what the score is and they don't have enough information to ask intelligent questions." A newcomer described his behavior in typically similar terms: "I attended all the hearings and studied and collected information that I can use next year. I'm just marking time now." During the crucial subcommittee markup, the newcomer will have little opportunity to speak—save in locally important matters. A subcommittee chairman stated the norm from his viewpoint this way: "When we get a compromise, nobody's going to break that up. If someone tries, we sit on him fast. We don't want young people who throw bricks or slow things down." And a newcomer reciprocated, describing his markup conduct: "I'm not provocative. I'm in there for information. They're the experts in the field. I go along." In full Committee, on the floor, and in conference committee, the Committee's senior members take the lead and the junior members are expected to follow. The apprentice role is common to all new members of the House. But it is wrong to assume that each Committee will give it the same emphasis. Some pay it scant heed.[23] The Appropriations Committee makes it a cornerstone of its internal structure.

Among the Committee's veterans, the key roles are those of Committee Chairman and ranking minority member, and their counterparts in every subcommittee. It is a measure of Committee integration and the low degree of partisanship that considerable reciprocity obtains between these roles. Their partisan status nevertheless sets limits to the degree of possible integration. The Chairman is given certain authority which he and only he can exercise. But save in times of extreme party controversy, the expectation is that consultation and cooperation between the Chairman and ranking minority member shall lubricate the Committee's entire work. For example, by Committee tradition, its Chairman and ranking minority member are both *ex officio* voting members of each subcommittee and of every conference committee. The two of them thus have joint access at every stage of the internal process. A subcommittee chairman, too, is expected to discuss matters of scheduling and agenda with his opposite minority number. He is expected to work with him during the markup session and to give him (and, normally, only him) an opportunity to read and comment on the subcommittee report.[24] A ranking minority member described his subcommittee markup procedure approvingly:

Frequently the chairman has a figure which he states. Sometimes he will have no figure, and he'll turn to me and say, "＿＿＿, what do you think?" Maybe I'll

[23] For example, the Committee on Education and Labor; see footnote 28.
[24] See the exchange in *101 Cong. Rec.,* pp. 3832, 3844, 3874.

have a figure. It's very flexible. Everyone has a chance to say what he thinks, and we'll move it around. Sometimes it takes a long time.... He's a rabid partisan on the floor, but he is a very fair man in the subcommittee.

Where influence is shared, an important exchange of rewards occurs. The chairman gains support for his leadership and the ranking minority member gains intra-Committee power. The Committee as a whole insures against the possibility of drastic change in its internal structure by giving to its key minority members a stake in its operation. Chairman and ranking minority members will, in the course of time, exchange positions; and it is expected that such a switch will produce no form of retribution nor any drastic change in the functioning of the Committee. Reciprocity of roles, in this case, promotes continued integration. A ranking minority member testified to one successful arrangement when he took the floor in the 83d Congress to say:

> The gentleman and I have been seesawing back and forth on this Committee for some time. He was Chairman in the 80th Congress. I had the privilege of serving as Chairman in the 81st and 82nd Congresses. Now he is back in the saddle. I can say that he has never failed to give me his utmost cooperation, and I have tried to give him the same cooperation during his service as Chairman of this Committee. We seldom disagree, but we have found out that we can disagree without being disagreeable. Consequently, we have unusual harmony on this Committee.[25]

Reciprocity between Chairman and ranking minority members on the Appropriations Committee is to some incalculable degree a function of the stability of membership which allows a pair of particular individuals to work out the kind of personal accomodation described above. The close working relationship of Clarence Cannon and John Taber, whose service on the Committee totals 68 years and who have been changing places as Chairman and ranking minority member for 19 years, highlights and sustains a pattern of majority-minority reciprocity throughout the group.

Internal Control Mechanisms

The expectations which apply to subcommittee, to party, to veterans and to newcomers, to chairmen and to ranking minority members prescribe highly integrative behaviors. We have concentrated on these expectations, and have both illustrated and assumed the close correlation between expected and actual behavior. This does not mean that all the norms of the Committee have been canvassed. Nor does it mean that deviation from the integrative norms does not occur. It does. From what can be gathered, however, from piecing together a study of the public record on appropria-

[25] *99 Cong. Rec.,* p. 4933.

tions from 1947 to 1961 with interview materials, the Committee has been markedly successful in maintaining a stable internal structure over time. As might be expected, therefore, changes and threats of change have been generated more from the environment—when outsiders consider the Committee as unresponsive—than from inside the subsystem itself. One source of internal stability, and an added reason for assuming a correlation between expected and actual behavior, is the existence of what appear to be reasonably effective internal control mechanisms. Two of these are the socialization processes applied to newcomers and the sanctioning mechanisms applicable to all Committee members.

Socialization is in part a training in perception. Before members of a group can be expected to behave in accordance with its norms, they must learn to see and interpret the world around them with reasonable similarity. The socialization of the Committee newcomer during his term or two of apprenticeship serves to bring his perceptions and his attitudes sufficiently into line with those of the other members to serve as a basis for Committee integration. The Committee, as we have seen, is chosen from Congressmen whose political flexibility connotes an aptitude for learning new lessons of power. Furthermore, the high degree of satisfaction of its members with the group increases their susceptibility to its processes of learning and training.

For example, one half of the Committee's Democrats are Northerners and Westerners from urban constituencies, whose voting records are just as "liberal" on behalf of domestic social welfare programs as non-Committee Democrats from like constituencies. They come to the Committee favorably disposed toward the high level of federal spending necessary to support such programs, and with no sense of urgency about the Committee's tasks of guarding the Treasury or reducing budget estimates. Given the criteria governing their selection, however, they come without rigid preconceptions and with a built-in responsiveness to the socialization processes of any legislative group of which they are members. It is crucial to Committee integration that they learn to temper their potentially disruptive welfare-state ideology with a conservative's concern for saving money. They must change their perceptions and attitudes sufficiently to view the Committee's tasks in nearly the same terms as their more conservative Southern Democratic and Republican colleagues. What their elders perceive as reality (*i.e.*, the disposition of executives to ask for more money than is necessary) they, too, must see as reality. A subcommittee chairman explained:

> When you have sat on the Committee, you see that these bureaus are always asking for more money—always up, never down. They want to build up their organization. You reach the point—I have—where it sickens you, where you rebel against it. Year after year, they want more money. They say, "Only $50,000 this

year"; but you know the pattern. Next year they'll be back for $100,000, then $200,000. The younger members haven't been on the Committee long enough, haven't had the experience to know this.

The younger men, in this case the younger liberals, do learn from their Committee experience. Within one or two terms, they are differentiating between themselves and the "wild-eyed spenders" or the "free spenders" in the House. "Some of these guys would spend you through the roof," exclaimed one liberal of moderate seniority. Repeated exposure to Committee work and to fellow members has altered their perceptions and their attitudes in money matters. Half a dozen Northern Democrats of low or moderate seniority agreed with one of their number who said: "Yes, it's true. I can see it myself. I suppose I came here a flaming liberal; but as the years go by I get more conservative. You just hate like hell to spend all this money. . . . You come to the point where you say, 'By God, this is enough jobs.' " These men will remain more inclined toward spending than their Committee colleagues, but their perceptions, and hence their attitudes, have been brought close enough to the others to support a consensus on tasks. They are responsive to appeals on budget-cutting grounds that would not have registered earlier and which remain meaningless to liberals outside the Committee. In cases, therefore, where Committee selection does not and cannot initially produce individuals with a predisposition toward protecting the Treasury, the same result is achieved by socialization.

Socialization is a training in behavior as well as in perception. For the newcomer, conformity to norms in specific situations is ensured through the appropriate application, by the Committee veterans, of rewards and punishments. For the Committee member who serves his apprenticeship creditably, the passage of time holds the promise that he will inherit a position of influence. He may, as an incentive, be given some small reward early in his Committee career. One man, in his second year, had been assigned the task of specializing in one particular program. However narrow the scope of his specialization, it had placed him on the road to influence within the Committee. He explained with evident pleasure:

The first year, you let things go by. You can't participate. But you learn by watching the others operate. The next year, you know what you're interested in and when to step in. . . . For instance, I've become an expert on the _____ program. The chairman said to me, "This is something you ought to get interested in." I did; and now I'm the expert on the Committee. Whatever I say on that, the other members listen to me and do what I want.

At some later date, provided he continues to observe Committee norms, he will be granted additional influence, perhaps through a prominent floor

role. A model Committee man of moderate seniority who had just attained
to this stage of acomplishment, and who had suffered through several
political campaigns back home fending off charges that he was a do-nothing
Congressman, spoke about the rewards he was beginning to reap.

> When you perform well on the floor when you bring out a bill, and members
> know that you know the bill, you develop prestige with other members of Congress.
> They come over and ask you what you think, because they know you've studied
> it. You begin to get a reputation beyond your subcommittee. And you get inner
> satisfaction, too. You don't feel that you're down here doing nothing.

The first taste of influence which comes to men on this Committee is compensation for the frustrations of apprenticeship. Committee integration in
general, and the meshing of roles between elders and newcomers in particular, rest on the fact that conformity to role expectations over time does
guarantee to the young positive rewards—the very kind of rewards of power,
prestige, and personal satisfaction which led most of them to seek Committee membership in the first place.

The important function of apprenticeship is that it provides the necessary time during which socialization can go forward. And teaching proceeds
with the aid of punishments as well as rewards. Should a new member
inadvertently or deliberately run afoul of Committee norms during his
apprenticeship, he will find himself confronted with negative sanctions
ranging in subtlety from "jaundiced eyes" to a changed subcommittee assignment. Several members, for example, recalled their earliest encounter
with the norm of unity and the tradition against minority reports. One
remembered his attempt to file a minority report.

> The Chairman was pretty upset about it. It's just a tradition, I guess, not to
> have minority reports. I didn't know it was a tradition. When I said I was going
> to write a minority report, some eyebrows were raised. The Chairman said it just
> wasn't the thing to do. Nothing more was said about it. But it wasn't a very
> popular thing to do, I guess.

He added that he had not filed one since.

Some younger members have congenital difficulty in observing the
norms of the apprentice's role. In the 86th Congress, these types tended
to come from the Republican minority. The minority newcomers (described
by one of the men who selected them as "eight young, energetic, fighting
conservatives") were a group of economy-minded individuals some of
whom chafed against any barrier which kept them from immediate influence on Committee policy. Their reaction was quite different from that
of the young Democrats, whose difficulty was in learning to become economy-minded, but who did not actively resent their lack of influence. One

freshman, who felt that, "The appropriations system is lousy, inadequate, and old fashioned," recalled that he had spoken out in full Committee against the recommendations of a subcommittee of which he was not a member. Having failed, he continued to oppose the recommendation during floor debate. By speaking up, speaking in relation to the work of another subcommittee and by opposing a Committee recommendation, he had violated the particular norms of his apprentice role as well of the generally applicable norms of reciprocity and unity. He explained what he had learned, but remained only partially socialized:

> They want to wash their dirty linen in the Committee and they want no opposition afterward. They let me say my piece in Committee. . . . But I just couldn't keep quiet. I said some things on the floor, and I found out that's about all they would take. . . . If you don't get along with your Committee and have their support, you don't get anything accomplished around here. . . . I'm trying to be a loyal, cooperative member of the Committee. You hate to be a stinker; but I'm still picking at the little things because I can't work on the big things. There's nothing for the new men to do, so they have to find places to needle in order to take some part in it.

Another freshman, who had deliberately violated apprenticeship norms by trying to ask "as many questions as the chairman" during subcommittee hearings, reported a story of unremitting counteraction against his deviation:

> In the hearings, I have to wait sometimes nine or ten hours for a chance; and he hopes I'll get tired and stay home. I've had to wait till some pretty unreasonable hours. Once I've gotten the floor, though, I've been able to make a good case. Sometimes I've been the only person there. . . . He's all powerful. He's got all the power. He wouldn't think of taking me on a trip with him when he goes to hold hearings. Last year, he went to ———. He wouldn't give me a nudge there. And in the hearings, when I'm questioning a witness, he'll keep butting in so that my case won't appear to be too rosy.

Carried on over a period of two years, this behavior resulted in considerable personal friction between a Committee elder and the newcomer. Other members of his subcommittee pointedly gave him a great lack of support for his nonconformity. "They tried to slow him down and tone him down a little," not because he and his subcommittee chairman disagreed, but on the grounds that the Committee has developed accepted ways of disagreeing which minimize, rather than exacerbate, interpersonal friction.

One internal threat to Committee integration comes from new members who from untutored perceptions, from ignorance of norms, or from dissatisfaction with the apprentice role may not act in accordance with Committee expectations. The seriousness of this threat is minimized, however, by the fact that the deviant newcomer does not possess sufficient resources to affect adversely the operation of the system. Even if he does not respond immediately to application of sanctions, he can be held in check and subjected to an extended and (given the frequency of inter-action among members) intensive period of socialization. The success of Committee socialization is indicated by the fact that whereas wholesale criticism of Committee operations was frequently voiced among junior members, it had disappeared among the men of moderate experience. And what these middle seniority members now accept as the facts of Committee life, the veterans vigorously assert and defend as the essentials of a smoothly functioning system. Satisfaction with the Committee's internal structure increases with length of Committee service.

An important reason for changing member attitudes is that those who have attained leadership positions have learned, as newcomers character-istically have not, that their conformity to Committee norms is the ultimate source of their influence inside the group. Freshman members do not as readily perceive the degree to which interpersonal influence is rooted in obedience to group norms. They seem to convert their own sense of power-lessness into the view that the Committee's leaders possess, by virtue of their positions, arbitrary, absolute, and awesome power. Typically, they say: "If you're a subcommittee chairman, it's your Committee." "The Chairman runs the show. He gets what he wants. He decides what he wants and gets it through." Older members of the Committee, however, view the power of the leaders as a highly contingent and revocable grant, tendered by the Committee for so long and only so long as their leaders abide by Committee expectations. In commenting on internal influence, their typical reaction is: "Of course, the Committee wouldn't follow him if it didn't want to. He has a great deal of respect. He's an able man, a hard-working man." "He knows the bill backwards and forwards. He works hard, awfully hard, and the members know it." Committee leaders have an imposing set of formal prerogatives. But they can capitalize on them only if they command the respect, confidence, and deference of their colleagues.

It is basic to Committee integration that members who have the greatest power to change the system evidence the least disposition to do so. Despite their institutional conservatism, however, Committee elders do occasionally violate the norms applicable to them and hence represent a potential threat to successful integration. Excessive deviation from Committee expectations by some leaders will bring counter-measures by other leaders. Thus, for example, the Chairman and his subcommittee chairmen exercise reciprocal controls over one another's behavior. The Chairman has the authority to appoint the chairman and members of each subcommittee and fix its jurisdiction. "He runs the Committee. He has a lot of power," agrees one subcommittee chairman. "But it's all done on the basis of personal friendship. If he tries to get too big, the members can whack him down by majority vote."

In the 84th Congress, Chairman Cannon attempted an unusually broad reorganization of subcommittee jurisdictions. The subcommittee chairman most adversely affected rallied his senior colleagues against the Chairman's action—on the ground that is was an excessive violation of role expectations and threatening to subcommittee autonomy. Faced with the prospect of a negative Committee vote, the Chairman was forced to act in closer conformity to the expectations of the other leaders. As one participant described the episode,

> Mr. Cannon, for reasons of his own, tried to bust up one of the subcommittees. We didn't like that. . . . He was breaking up the whole Committee. A couple of weeks later, a few of the senior members got together and worked out a compromise. By that time, he had seen a few things, so we went to him and talked to him and worked it out.

On the subcommittees, too, it is the veterans of both parties who will levy sanctions against an offending chairman. It is they who speak of "cutting down to size" and "trimming the whiskers" of leaders who become "too cocky," "too stubborn" or who "do things wrong too often." Committee integration is underwritten by the fact that no member high or low is permanently immune from the operation of its sanctioning mechanisms.

III

Data concerning internal committee activity can be organized and presented in various ways. One way is to use key functional problems like integration as the focal points for descriptive analysis. On the basis of our analysis (and without, for the time being, having devised any precise measure of integration), we are led to the summary observation that the House Appropriations Committee appears to be a well-integrated, if not an extremely well-integrated, committee. The question arises as to whether anything can be gained from this study other than a description of one property of one political subsystem. If it is reasonable to assume that the internal life of a congressional committee affects all legislative activity involving that committee, and if it is reasonable to assume that the analysis of a committee's internal relationships will produce useful knowledge about legislative behavior, some broader implications for this study are indicated.

In the first place, the success of the House Appropriations Committee in solving the problem of integration probably does have important consequences for the appropriations process. Some of the possible relationships can be stated as hypotheses and tested; others can be suggested as possible guides to understanding. All of them require further research. Of primary interest is the relationship between integration and the power of the Committee. There is little doubt about the fact of Committee power. Of the 443 separate case histories of bureau appropriations examined, the House accepted Committee recommendations in 387, or 87.4 per cent of them; and in 159, or 33.6 per cent of the cases, the House Committee's original recommendations on money amounts were the exact ones enacted into law. The hypothesis that the greater the degree of Committee unity the greater the probability that its recommendations will be accepted is being tested as part of a larger study.[26] House Committee integration may be a key factor in producing House victories in conference committee. This relationship, too, might be tested. Integration appears to help provide the House conferees with a feeling of confidence and superiority which is one of their important advantages in the mix of psychological factors affecting conference deliberations.

Another suggested consequence of high integration is that party groups have a relatively small influence upon appropriations decisions. It suggests, too, that Committee-oriented behavior should be duly emphasized in any analysis of congressional oversight of administrative activity by this Committee. Successful integration promotes the achievement of the Committee's goals, and doubtless helps account for the fairly consistent production of budget-cutting decisions. Another consequence will be found in the strategies adopted by people seeking favorable Committee decisions. For example, the characteristic lines of contact from executive officials to the Committee will run to the chairman and the ranking minority member (and to the professional staff man) of the single subcommittee handling their agency's appropriations. The ways in which the Committee achieves integration may even affect the success or failure of a bureau in getting its appropriations. Committee members, for instance, will react more favorably toward an administrator who conforms to their self-image of the hard-working master-of-detail than to one who does not—and Committee response to individual administrators bulks large in their determinations.

Finally, the internal integration of this Committee helps to explain the extraordinary stability, since 1920, of appropriations procedures—in the fact of repeated proposals to change them through omnibus appropriations, legislative budgets, new budgetary forms, item veto, Treasury borrowing, etc. Integration is a stabilizing force, and the stability of the House Appropriations Committee has been a force for stabilization throughout the entire process. It was, for example, the disagreement between Cannon and Taber which led to the indecisiveness reflected in the short-lived ex-

[26] *Cf.* Dwaine Marvick, "Congressional Appropriations Politics," unpublished manuscript (Columbia University, 1952).

periment with a single appropriations bill.[27] One need only examine the conditions most likely to decrease Committee integration to ascertain some of the critical factors for producing changes in the appropriations process. A description of integration is also an excellent base-line from which to analyze changes in internal structure.

All of these are speculative propositions which call for further research. But they suggest, as a second implication, that committee integration does have important consequences for legislative activity and, hence, that it is a key variable in the study of legislative politics. It would seem, therefore, to be a fruitful focal point for the study of other congressional committees.[28] Comparative committee analysis could usefully be devoted to (1) the factors which tend to increase or decrease integration; (2) the degree to which integration is achieved; and (3) the consequences of varying degrees of integration for committee behavior and influence. If analyses of committee integration are of any value, they should encourage the analysis and the classification of congressional committees along functional lines. And they should lead to the discussion of interrelated problems of committee survival. Functional classifications of committees (*i.e.*, well or poorly integrated) derived from a large number of descriptive analyses of several functional problems may prove helpful in constructing more general propositions about the legislative process.

[27] See Dalmas Nelson, "The Omnibus Appropriations Act of 1950," *Journal of Politics* (May, 1953).

[28] This view has been confirmed by the results of interviews conducted by the author with members of the House Committee on Education and Labor, together with an examination of that Committee's activity in one policy area. They indicate very significant contrasts between the internal structure of that Committee and the Appropriations Committee—contrasts which center around their comparative success in meeting the problem of integration. The House Committee on Education and Labor appears to be a poorly integrated committee. Its internal structure is characterized by a great deal of subgroup conflict, relatively little role reciprocity, and minimally effective internal control mechanisms. External concerns, like those of party, constituency, and clientele groups, are probably more effective in determining its decisions than is likely to be the case in a well-integrated committee. An analysis of the internal life of the Committee on Education and Labor, drawn partly from interviews with 19 members of that group, appears in *National Politics and Federal Aid to Education* (Syracuse: Syracuse University Press, 1962), by Professor Frank Munger and the author. [The bulk of this analysis appears in Chapter 10 of this reader.] See also Nicholas R. Masters, *op. cit.*, note 8 above, pp. 354–55 [Chapter 7 in this reader]; and Seymour Scher, "Congressional Committee Members as Independent Agency Overseers: A Case Study," *American Political Science Review*, 54 (December 1960), 911–20.

9

JOHN F. MANLEY

The House Committee on Ways and Means:
Conflict Management in a
Congressional Committee

The House Committee on Ways and Means, according to its members, is assigned the responsibility of resolving some of the most partisan issues coming before Congress: questions of taxation, social welfare legislation, foreign trade policy, and management of a national debt which exceeds $300 billion.[1] Yet members of the Committee also contend, at the same time, that they handle most of these problems in a "responsible" way. A Republican member of Ways and Means echoed the views of his fellow Committee members when he said "it's the issues that are partisan,

The author wants to thank several scholars who commented on an early version of this paper: H. Douglas Price, Richard F. Fenno, Jr., Randall B. Ripley, Robert L. Peabody, Nelson W. Polsby, Frederic N. Cleaveland, James D. Barber, Leo Snowiss, Charles O. Jones, and Lewis A. Froman, Jr. I owe a special debt to David W. West, a perceptive friend and adviser who recently left the Committee's staff.

[1] This article is based on interviews conducted during 1964 with twenty of the twenty-five members of the Committee. The average interview ran 80 minutes. Questions were open-ended, no notes were taken during the interview, and all quotations are derived from notes made immediately after each interview. In addition, staff members, lobbyists, and executive department personnel were interviewed, some at great length. As a 1963–1964 Congressional Fellow I worked with Congressmen Thomas B. Curtis (R., Mo.) and Dante B. Fascell (D., Fla.), and was able to observe the Committee directly.

Reprinted from *American Political Science Review*, 59 (December 1965), 927–39, by permission of the author and publisher. Mr. Manley is Assistant Professor of Political Science at the University of Wisconsin.

not the members." A Democratic member went so far as to claim that Ways and Means is "as bipartisan a committee as you have in the House." And a Treasury Department official who has worked closely with Ways and Means for several years believes that it is a

> partisan committee in the sense that you get a lot of partisan voting. But while you get a lot of party votes the members discuss the bills in a nonpartisan way. It's a very *harmonious* committee, the members work very well and harmoniously together. Sure there is partisanship but they discuss the issues in a nonpartisan way.

The purpose of this paper is, first, to describe and analyze some of the factors which affect the Ways and Means Committee's ability to process, in a bipartisan manner, political demands which its members regard as highly partisan issues. Ways and Means is neither racked by partisanship nor dominated by nonpartisanship; conflict and consensus coexist within the Committee and the balance between them varies chiefly with the nature and intensity of the external demands which are made on the Committee. Second, an attempt is made to contribute to the development of an analytical framework, based on Fenno's study of the House Appropriations Committee, which may prove useful for the comparative analysis of congressional committees generally.[2]

For analytical purposes, the Ways and Means Committee is here conceived as a political subsystem of the House of Representatives, charged by the House with a number of tasks, but in the normal course of events

[2]Richard F. Fenno, Jr., "The House Appropriations Committee as a Political System: The Problem of Integration," *American Political Science Review,* 56 (June 1962), 310–24 [Chapter 8 in this reader]. Fenno's approach has been applied to two other committees. See Charles O. Jones, "The Role of the Congressional Subcommittee," *Midwest Journal of Political Science,* 6 (November 1962), 327–44; Harold P. Green and Alan Rosenthal, *Government of the Atom* (New York, 1963), Chap. 2. Other committee studies which may serve as a basis for comparisons include Charles O. Jones, "Representation in Congress: The Case of The House Agriculture Committee," *American Political Science Review,* 55 (June 1961), 358–67; Robert L. Peabody, "The Enlarged Rules Committee," in *New Perspectives on the House of Representatives,* Robert L. Peabody and Nelson W. Polsby, eds. (Chicago, 1963), pp. 129–64; James A. Robinson, *The House Rules Committee* (Indianapolis, 1963); George Goodwin, "Subcommittees: The Miniature Legislatures of Congress," *American Political Science Review,* 56 (September 1962), 596–604; Ralph K. Huitt, "The Congressional Committee: A Case Study," *American Political Science Review,* 48 (June 1954), 340–65. See also Fenno's forthcoming book on the House Appropriations Committee, and his study of the House Education and Labor Committee, in Frank J. Munger and Richard F. Fenno, Jr., *National Politics and Federal Aid to Education* (Syracuse: Syracuse University Press, 1962), Chap. 5 [Chapter 10 in this reader].

enjoying a high degree of operational autonomy.[3] Its primary task *vis-à-vis* the House is the resolution of political demands, many of which involve high stakes in money, power or dogma. To perform this function the Committee must solve certain problems of internal organization and interaction, and these internal problems are inextricably linked to the nature of the environmental demands which the Committee is set up to process. The Ways and Means Committee, in other words, receives from its environment, and it generates internally, demands with which it must cope if it is to maintain itself as a viable subsystem of the House.

These internal and external demands give rise to a set of decision-making norms and roles which govern intra-Committee behavior and regularize its relations with outside actors. Committee norms and roles enable it to manage three distinct but related problems: (1) problems associated with tasks (instrumental interaction); (2) problems of personal gratifications and interpersonal relations (affective interaction); and (3) problems of integration.[4] All three are affected by the type of subject matter and the external demands placed on the Committee; the internal operations of the Committee cannot be fully understood apart from the tasks which the Committee is expected to perform for the House.

The need for internal organization of a heterogeneous group poses integrative problems for the Way and Means Committee. Integration, as defined by Fenno, is

> the degree to which there is a working together or a meshing together or mutual support among roles and subgroups. Conversely, it is also defined as the degree

[3] For the general theory behind this paper see Talcott Parsons and Edward A. Shils, eds., *Toward a General Theory of Action* (New York, 1962), pp. 3–44, 190–233; Talcott Parsons, "Some Highlights of the General Theory of Action," in Roland Young, ed., *Approaches to the Study of Politics*, (Evanston, 1958), pp. 282–301; and Marion J. Levy, Jr., *The Structure of Society*, rev. ed. (New York, 1957), pp. 19–84. For discussions of functionalism see Kingsley Davis, "The Myth of Functional Analysis as a Special Method in Sociology and Anthropology," *American Sociological Review*, 24 (December 1959), 757–72; Irving Louis Horowitz, "Sociology and Politics: The Myth of Functionalism Revisited," *Journal of Politics*, 25 (May 1963), 248–64; Don Martindale, ed., *Functionalism in the Social Sciences* (Philadelphia, 1965).

[4] Parsons and Shils, *op. cit.*, pp. 208–9. These problems are also dealt with in the literature on small groups. See Sidney Verba, *Small Groups and Political Behavior* (Princeton, 1961), pp. 117–43; Josephine Klein, *The Study of Groups* (London, 1956), pp. 115–33; George C. Homans, *The Human Group* (New York, 1950), pp. 319–20; Michael S. Olmstead, *The Small Group* (New York, 1959), Chaps. 4, 5, 6; Barry E. Collins and Harold Guetzkow, *A Social Psychology of Group Processes for Decision-Making* (New York, 1964), Chaps. 3, 10; Dorwin Cartwright and Alvin Zander, eds., *Group Dynamics: Research and Theory* (Evanston, 1953); A. Paul Hare, Edgar F. Borgatta, and Robert F. Bales, eds., *Small Groups: Studies in Social Interaction* (New York, 1955).

to which a committee is able to minimize conflict among its roles and its subgroups, by heading off or resolving the conflicts that arise.[5]

Put in a somewhat different way, as Parsons notes,[6] the integration of roles depends on motivating *individual personalities* in the requisite ways. In order to stimulate the members of a group to contribute to the group's well-being and to the realization of its goals, they must be induced to share certain values and to behave in prescribed ways, either through the distribution of incentives or the application of sanctions, or both.[7] Members must, in a word, be socialized if the group is to be well integrated, and in congressional committees socialization depends on inducements.

Part I, below, deals with three interrelated variables and their relationship to Committee integration: the norm of restrained partisanship, the nature of the subject matter, and the external demands of the House. Part II considers the role of the chairman as an independent variable, describes how Chairman Mills directs the Ways and Means Committee, and offers some reasons why he operates as he does. Part III discusses the socialization process—the Committee's attractiveness, which predisposes the members to respond to socialization, and its ability to satisfy members' personal and political needs. The integration of four key roles, chairman-ranking minority member and newcomer-experienced member, is considered in Part IV. A final section offers some suggestions for comparative committee studies.

I

Minority reports by Republican members of the Ways and Means Committee and motions to recommit on the House floor frequently accompany the major bills reported by the Committee.[8] In addition, the Committee

5 Fenno, *op. cit.,* p. 310 [above, p. 133].

6 Parsons and Shils, eds., *op. cit.,* pp. 24–25.

7 Chester I. Barnard, *The Functions of the Executive* (Cambridge, Mass., 1956), pp. 139–60. Frank J. Sorauf has recently analyzed political parties from an inducement-contribution perspective; see his *Political Parties in the American System* (Boston, 1964), pp. 81–97.

8 *E.g.,* U. S. Congress, House, Committee on Ways and Means, 85th Cong., 2d sess., H. Rept. No. 1761, *Trade Agreements Extension Act of 1958,* pp. 55–87. *Congressional Record,* June 11, 1958, Vol. 104, pp. 10881–82. Committee on Ways and Means, 87th Cong., 2d sess., H. Rept. No. 1818, *Trade Expansion Act of 1962,* pp. 83–104. *Congressional Record,* June 28, 1962, Vol. 108, pp. 12089–90. Committee on Ways and Means, 87th Cong., 2d sess., H. Rept. No. 1447, *Revenue Act of 1962,* pp. B1–B28. *Congressional Record,* March 29, 1962, Vol. 108, pp. 5431–32. Committee on Ways and Means, 88th Cong., 1st sess., H. Rept. No. 749, *Revenue Act of 1963,* pp. C1–C28. *Congressional Record,* September 25, 1963, Vol. 109, pp. 18118–19.

members are clearly split along general ideological lines: the Democrats now overrepresent and the Republicans underrepresent their party's support for a larger federal role.[9] These indices of partisanship do not, however, reflect a critical integrative norm which governs the behavior of members in executive session: *the norm of restrained partisanship.* In the words of one experienced staff member,

> I think you will find that Ways and Means is a partisan committee, there are usually minority views. But partisanship is not that high when they discuss the bill and legislate. About 95 percent of the time the members deliberate the bill in a nonpartisan way, discussing the facts calmly. Then toward the end Byrnes [the ranking Republican] and the Republicans may go partisan. The things the Committee deals with are big Administration issues, so you are bound to get minority views and partisanship. But Byrnes likes to take a nonpartisan attitude toward things and it gets partisan only toward the end. On some votes they go party line but on others they don't. It all depends on the issue.

A couple of Committee members feel that Ways and Means decides most issues on a partisan basis, but the preponderant view is that of a Democrat who declared that "most of the time we go along up to a certain point and then a sharp party vote will come. On the tax bill [Revenue Act of 1964] we went along for a long time without party votes, working very well, then the Republicans lined up at the end against it. There's very little partisanship up to a point, when the political factors come in, and then a partisan vote comes."[10] Or a Republican who said "we try to write the best legislation we can in a nonpartisan way—more so than any other committee. We work in a nonpartisan way. Sure there are philoso-

---

[9] During the 87th Congress the Democratic members of the Committee averaged 81 percent on Congressional Quarterly's index of support for a larger federal role; the Republicans averaged 17 percent. A comparable disparity, 85 percent to 27 percent, shows up during the 88th Congress. Moreover, in both congresses the Democrats and Republicans on Ways and Means now appear to be more "liberal" and less "liberal," respectively, than the rest of their party colleagues. Data compiled from *Congressional Quarterly Weekly Report,* December 28, 1962, pp. 2290–95; October 23, 1964, pp. 2549–53. This may not have been true in earlier years.

[10] This was confirmed by the Committee's ranking Republican member, John Byrnes, in the debate over the 1964 Revenue Act: "We tried to come up with as good a bill as we could. And I say to the Speaker it was not done on a partisan basis —and that has been confirmed by the chairman. It was done on a bipartisan basis, up until the last few days. When they had almost all the drafting completed and perfected, then they said, 'Now we don't need your help any more, boys; we will put the steamroller to work.' But up until then it was on a bipartisan basis." *Congressional Record,* September 25, 1963, Vol. 109, p. 18113. Contrast this with E. E. Schattschneider's account, *Politics, Pressures and the Tariff* (New York, 1935), of the making of the Smoot-Hawley tariff in 1929–30.

phical differences but they never become the partisan legislative fighting that they do on other committees."

The norm of restrained partisanship means that members should not allow partisanship to interfere with a thorough study and complete understanding of the technical complexities of the bills they consider. Members have a bipartisan responsibility to the House and to the nation to write sound legislation. They may disagree over what decisions the Committee ought finally to make but there is a firmly rooted consensus on *how* they ought to go about making them. Several variables affect the norm of restrained partisanship but two of them are of prime importance: (1) the nature of the Committee's subject matter; (2) the relationship between the House and the Committee.

(1) Working in a "responsible" way is valued highly by members of the Ways and Means Committee, and by "responsible" they mean being "conscientious," "thorough," "careful," and "studious." They emphasize the extreme complexity and national significance of the Committee's subject matter and this realization inclines them to constrain partisanship. "We deal with the most complicated, technical subject in the Congress, in the country for that matter, we have to be thorough on Ways and Means," according to a Democrat; a Republican said simply "you just don't mess around with taxes, it can create millionaires or paupers." All the members realize that they have to be responsible, another Democrat contended, and "this means that we don't do things on the basis of partisan or political advantage. We can reach a general consensus. Sometimes what a Republican will offer will be accepted by unanimous consent." A Republican who described the ideal GOP member in terms which made him certain to be in conflict with the Democratic members of the Committee paradoxically added that "partisanship is not too high on Ways and Means—taxes, trade, and social security should not be settled on a partisan basis."

Both partisan and nonpartisan tendencies permeate the Ways and Means Committee and are reflected in the Committee's operating style.

Those members who attend the protracted meetings go through a laborious process of illuminating the implications of arcane tax, tariff, debt, and social security proposals. They are assisted by experts from the executive agencies, the House Legislative Counsel's Office, the staff of the Joint Committee on Internal Revenue Taxation, and at times by employees of the Library of Congress. Legislation is pondered line by line. When the Committee makes a decision it is translated into technical language by the experts ("technicians") and brought back to the Committee for final approval. The decision-making style varies somewhat from issue to issue but in general it is marked by caution, methodical repetition, and, most important, restrained partisanship.[11] "We get together and go through things as twenty-five Americans all trying to do what's for the public good. It's even rare for a bill to be reported out by a 15–10 vote."

But the internal relations of the Ways and Means Committee are not devoid of partisan political or personal disputes. Restrained partisanship is the widely accepted norm governing the Committee's day-to-day operations and it does dampen partisanship and promote integration. It also, on occasion, breaks down. Not all Committee decisions are made in the full Committee meetings. Republican members frequently caucus in order to develop a united front on key pieces of legislation and party line splits are not as rare as some members imply.[12] The norm of restrained partisanship does not stifle all dissension. A Democrat, for example, complained that the "Republicans sit there in Committee, vote for things, let things go by without saying anything, and then come out on the floor with motions to recommit, simply to surprise the Democrats." Personal feuds also erupt from time to time. On the whole, however, the Committee feels that the complex political demands which it must settle are of national importance and should be handled so far as possible on their merits.[13]

(2) Virtually all the major bills reported to the House by the Ways and Means Committee are considered under a closed rule which precludes all floor amendments unless they are first accepted by the Committee. There is no lack of protest against this so-called "gag" rule but many members of the Committee and of the House argue that it saves the members from themselves.[14] Tax and tariff bills are so "sensitive" and "complex" that the

[11] Protests about the Committee's procedure are quite rare, but see the minority views on a 1955 bill extending corporate and excise tax rates in which the Republicans complained about the way a tax credit was "rammed" through the Committee. Committee on Ways and Means, 84th Cong., 1st sess., H. Rept. No. 69, *Revenue Act of 1955*, pp. 36–38.

[12] For a discussion of recent battles fought on the floor over Ways and Means bills see Randall B. Ripley, "The Party Whip Organizations in the United States House of Representatives," *American Political Science Review*, 58 (September 1964), 570–74.

[13] The subject matter of Ways and Means appears to be essentially different from that of the House Education and Labor Committee, at least during recent years. Education and Labor must resolve basic ideological issues whose emotional content has been higher than the issues coming before Ways and Means. For a discussion of the influence of jurisdiction on Education and Labor, see Munger and Fenno, *op. cit.*, pp. 109–12 [pp. 180–83 in this volume].

[14] From 1955–1965, forty-seven bills were debated under closed rules, nine under open or modified open rules, and the rest (over 350 bills) under unanimous consent or suspension of the rules. A typical statement was made by Representative Howard W. Smith in the 1955 fight over a closed rule for the Trade Act: "Mr. Speaker, I recognize the difficulty of many Members of the House on this bill; we all have our own problems in our own districts, but this is a question that affects the whole

House insulates itself from the demands of pressure groups by channeling the pressure into the committee stage of the process. On the few occasions when Ways and Means bills have been considered under open rules, one veteran Democrat claimed, "you had chaos."[15]

Members of the Ways and Means Committee are induced to follow the norm of restrained partisanship when they mark up a bill because of the autonomy which the closed rule gives to the Committee. A Republican, for example, expressed the common view that,

> On our Committee we have a responsibility to the House, we have to do the best job we can. . . . The closed rule prevents amendments and changes so we have to perfect the bill. Other committees can bring a bill to the floor with provisions in it they know will be taken out on the floor. Ways and Means doesn't do this, we can't do this.

One Committee member explained that "there are congressmen who have been here for years and can't understand social security. The average congressman can't understand what we deal with and you just can't open it up on the floor. We try to report well-rounded packages of legislation, the best bills we can. We compromise a lot to get a good bill we can report out. You don't report controversies just for the sake of controversy."

A House vote on whether or not to debate Ways and Means bills under a closed rule is in a sense a vote of confidence in the Committee. The Com-

---

country. . . . It has been recognized ever since I have been on the Rules Committee that bills of this type should be considered, as a practical matter, under a closed rule. The original bill setting up this program, as I recall, and the extensions in 1953 and 1954 were considered under closed rules. Nobody seemed to object at that time; as a matter of fact, both the majority and minority members of the Ways and Means Committee came before the Rules Committee and joined in the usual request that that committee makes of the Rules Committee for a closed rule." *Congressional Record,* February 17, 1955, Vol. 101, p. 1676. On this occasion the closed rule was almost defeated; it was adopted by one vote only after Rayburn took the floor and told his colleagues that "the House on this last vote has done a most unusual and under the circumstances a very dangerous thing. . . . Only once in the history of the House in 42 years in my memory has a bill of this kind and character been considered except under a closed rule. How long it is going to take, how far afield you will go, I do not know. . . . So as an old friend to all of you, as a lover of the House of Representatives and its procedures, I ask you to vote down this amendment offered by the gentleman from Ohio [Mr. Brown]." *Ibid.,* p. 1678.

15 Closed rules do not mean that the House has no influence over the substance of bills reported by Ways and Means. Chairman Mills has a reputation for keeping his ear close to the ground and for gauging House sentiment. House demands, if they are strong enough to attract wide support, are reflected in Ways and Means bills even though no floor amendments are allowed. In order to ease passage of the 1962 Revenue Act, for example, Mills reduced the amount of the controversial investment credit from 8 percent to 7 percent. *Congressional Quarterly Weekly Report,* March 30, 1962, p. 492.

mittee is widely thought to be the master of its esoteric subject matter and almost every member has a stake in maintaining this reputation. The House expects the Committee to polish its bills to near perfection technically and, perhaps more important, to make a satisfactory adjustment of the competing demands which surround Ways and Means bills. This expectation partly explains why Ways and Means is noted for time-consuming diligence, and it also buttresses the Committee's adherence to the norm of restrained partisanship. The distinctiveness of Ways and Means was expressed by one member when he said, "the House is jealous of the Committee. Many members say our bills can't be amended because we know it all, we're the experts. They are jealous." One of his colleagues sounded the same note when he observed that "the House says here are a bunch of smart guys, we won't tamper too much with what they do. The Ways and Means Committee has a reputation of being a well-balanced, level-headed group and the House respects this. . . . You just can't open a tax bill on the floor. The House knows we won't pull any fast ones."

II

If the Ways and Means Committee has been able to manage internal partisan conflict more successfully than the House Education and Labor Committee—and apparently it has—this is due in no small way to the leadership style of the chairman, Wilbur D. Mills (D., Ark.).[16] With the exception of one member who denied that there is a leadership structure within Ways and Means (it is, he claimed, an "amalgamated mess"), members agree that Mills runs the Committee and runs it well.

Mills's fellow Democrats consider him "powerful," "prestigeful," "quite a guy," "clever," "fine," "subtle," "smart," "patient," "expert," "best mind on the Committee," "leader," "key man." Perhaps of greater significance for purposes of integration is that these views are shared by the Republican members. They say Mills is "very effective," "a good synthesizer," "leader," "real student," "master of tax affairs," "fair," "calm," "intelligent," "impartial," "able," "well educated," and "not arbitrary."

Mills promotes integration by treating everyone fairly. He is careful to protect the rights of the Republican members and he gives the Republicans, a former staff member claimed, "pride of authorship" in bills even though the minority members may ultimately oppose them on the floor. Constraints

---

[16] Compare this description of Mills with that of Graham Barden (D., N.C.), former chairman of Education and Labor, whose leadership tended to create rather than resolve internal conflicts. Munger and Fenno, *op. cit.,* pp. 122–24 [pp. 192–94 in this volume].

on participation, both in public hearings and in executive sessions, are very loose.[17] One high ranking Republican said of Mills,

> We deal with things on which Republicans and Democrats are in basic, fundamental disagreement and when you have something like this you are bound to get disagreement and minority reports. I think the major reason things don't disintegrate is Mills. Chairman Mills is very fair and reasonable. I can visualize disintegration and bickering if some of the members now ever become chairman, quite frankly, but all the time I've been on the Committee the chairmen have been reasonable men.

Mills recalls that as a boy he used to hear his father talk about the Ways and Means Committee with William A. Oldfield, an Arkansas congressman who was a member of the Committee during the 64th–70th congresses. When Mills was elected to the House he knew that Ways and Means was a choice assignment and he made an early attempt to get on it. His first try failed largely because he did not lay the proper foundation with the House leadership, but he tried again and with the leadership's support succeeded. Mills's attitude toward the Committee helps explain why he leads it as he does, always sensitive to threats to the Committee's status and prestige; but it is also a source of pride for some of the members. "You hear some criticism of Wilbur," said a Republican, "but he has a high regard for the Committee. *He takes care of it, respects it, and acts to insure its effectiveness on the floor.*" This commitment to the good of the Committee is a subtle factor in Committee integration but its presence is undeniable, even if there is no precise way to measure its importance.

For Mills, the Committee's reputation is dependent upon House acceptance of its bills. He does not like to lose and he usually avoids becoming so committed to an issue that he risks losing a bill on the floor.[18]

---

17 During the hearings on the Trade Expansion Act of 1962, for example, Keogh (D., N. Y.) complained about the amount of time consumed by Curtis (R., Mo.). Mills replied that the Committee would sit until Curtis was through with his interrogation. Committee on Ways and Means, 87th Cong., 2d sess., *Hearings on H.R. 9900, Trade Expansion Act of 1962,* II, 740. On another occasion, Mills moderated an interchange between Representative Bruce Alger (R., Texas) and James B. Carey of the A.F.L.–C.I.O. over whether or not Carey had implied that Ways and Means, by failing to pass the King-Anderson health care bill, was responsible for the death or discomfort of the aged. Mills ruled that Carey did not have to answer Alger's question but he defended Alger's right to propound such a query. Alger took pride in Mills's defense of his rights. Committee on Ways and Means, 88th Cong., 2d sess., *Hearings on H.R. 3920, Medical Care for the Aged,* IV, 1880–83.

18 The most dramatic recent example of how a committee's subject matter can affect its behavior and success in the House was the issue of federal aid to education. See H. Douglas Price, "Schools, Scholarships, and Congressmen: The Kennedy Aid-to-Education Program," *The Centers of Power,* ed. Alan F. Westin (New York, 1964), pp. 53–105.

After waiting sixteen years to become chairman he lost part of the first major bill he brought to the floor; because of his bargaining skill and willingness to compromise, members feel, he has been beaten only once since then on a bill of any consequence.[19]

Part of the reason why Mills tries to accommodate different and sometimes conflicting political demands is the internal composition of the Committee. Two or three of the Democratic members are more conservative than the rest and—before the Committee's party ratio was changed from 15–10 to 17–8—they could determine outcomes by voting with a solid Republican bloc. Conversely, one or two Republicans have been known to "go off the reservation" and vote with the Democrats.[20] Depending on the issue, Mills may have to contain Democratic defections or lure a Republican vote. His base on the Democratic side is large and firm on most issues; even if some Democrats do not attend he can get their proxies. Neither party, however, is completely monolithic on all issues. Levels of commitment vary and in a delicately balanced situation Mills proceeds cautiously to make sure that he has the votes when he needs them. Two staff members commented: "Mills really likes to get a consensus if he can and this is one of the reasons partisanship is relatively low. He lets things settle and tries for agreement. He's just like that." "It's surprising how much Mills gets his own way. He'll sit back very quiet and let the boys thrash it out, let them go at it with their paper swords. Then he'll say we ought to do this and usually that's the way it's done." Committee integration may be positively or negatively affected by the style, ability, and personality of committee chairmen.

The influence of the chairman on integration may also vary with committee structure. For example, the chairman may be a crucial factor in a committee, such as Ways and Means, that does its work in full committee rather than in subcommittees; but he may be less important or have different effects in a committee that operates through relatively autonomous subcommittees (Appropriations).

III

Political socialization is a dynamic and continuous process by which a group perpetuates its norms, values, and roles.[21] It is dynamic in that the content

[19] The first bill Mills lost was a temporary unemployment compensation measure. *Congressional Record,* May 1, 1958, Vol. 104, pp. 7910–11. The second was a conference report to carry out the International Coffee Agreement, *Congressional Record,* August 18, 1964 (daily edition), pp. 19501–7.

[20] See the votes reported in Elizabeth J. Brenner, *The Trade Expansion Act of 1962,* Congressional Quarterly Special Report, pp. 29–30; also the close votes on key sections of the Revenue Act of 1964, *Congressional Quarterly Weekly Report,* August 23, 1963, pp. 1473–83.

[21] Compare this definition with that of Gabriel Almond who says by political

of what is passed on changes with new problems and demands; it is continuous in that it affects both newcomers and experienced members. To the new member socialization involves exposure to and inculcation with the norms of the group. To the experienced member it consists of the maintenance of his conformity to group norms or, if he resists, tension between his values and behavior and those of the group.

Socialization depends upon the attractiveness of the group and upon its ability to regulate behavior through the allocation of positive and negative incentives.[22] Objectively measured, Ways and Means is the most attractive committee assignment in the House. John C. Eberhart compared House committees from 1914 to 1941 and found that Ways and Means had the highest prestige.[23] Similarly, Warren Miller has compared committee assignments between the 80th and 88th Congresses and Ways and Means places first.[24]

Members are attracted to Ways and Means for a variety of reasons. Most frequently mentioned are its power and prestige. Ways and Means is "tops," "the guts of government," a "real blue-ribbon committee," a "choice one." One member, who was neither especially attracted to Ways and Means nor happy with the detailed nature of the Committee's work, said you just don't leave a "blue-ribbon" committee like Ways and Means. "You just go up from Ways and Means," a Democrat said, "you don't go to another committee—Appropriations, Rules, or Interstate. You go to Senator, Governor, that sort of thing. It's a springboard and many members have gone on from it." When asked if he ever tried to shift to a different committee another Democrat replied, "are you kidding! Why leave heaven to go to hell? There's no committee in Congress, including Appropriations, that's as important as Ways and Means. Why step downward once you have reached the top?"

Group identification is high on the Ways and Means Committee and the members usually refrain from behavior that is likely to weaken the Committee's position in the House. The Committee's attractiveness buttresses

---

socialization "we mean that all political systems tend to perpetuate their cultures and structures through time, and that they do this mainly by means of the socializing influences of the primary and secondary structures through which the young of the society pass in the process of maturation. . . . Political socialization is the process of induction into the political culture." Gabriel A. Almond and James S. Coleman, *The Politics of the Developing Areas* (Princeton, 1960), p. 27.

22 Barnard, *op. cit.*

23 Cited in George B. Galloway, *Congress at the Crossroads* (New York, 1946), p. 90. For some critical comments on Eberhart's methodology see James A. Robinson, "Organizational and Constituency Backgrounds of the House Rules Committee," *The American Political Arena*, ed. Joseph R. Fiszman (Boston, 1962), p. 214.

24 Warren E. Miller and Donald Stokes, *Representation in Congress* (Englewood Cliffs, N.J., forthcoming).

the norm that outlaws such behavior. Members may disagree and they may even quarrel among themselves but, as one Democrat said, "we fight our battles in executive session and not in public." A conservative Republican member who almost never agreed with anything supported by the Democrats declared that "we keep personal things to ourselves and we stick together when someone attacks the Committee." The Committee has been criticized by its own members but this happens very rarely.[25] Every member derives satisfaction from the Committee's reputation; they are predisposed by the Committee's attractiveness to follow the ground rules of partisan battle which place rigid constraints on the ways in which disagreement is manifested.

Socialization is also affected by the group's ability to offer the members positive incentives in return for approved modes of behavior. The Ways and Means Committee serves as the source of positive incentives in at least three important ways:[26] (1) affective relations inside the Committee; (2) influence in the House; and (3) relations with constituents.

1. Unlike most other congressional committees (Senate Finance is another example), the Ways and Means Committee functions in executive sessions of the full committee, and not through subcommittees. Members meet in direct face-to-face contact for weeks at a time and this style of deliberation is accompanied by a fairly well defined set of interpersonal norms. Committee meetings are not supposed to be partisan battles; some acrimony does develop but on the whole the members feel that to be effective they must maintain decorum and act in a gentlemanly way. Bitter personal disputes erupt infrequently and even public conflicts which appear to be disruptive of interpersonal relations are often played out in a benign spirit. A Republican who found it difficult to follow these norms was "talked to" by a senior Republican and told that he was losing his effectiveness by being so adamant. If a member starts to berate another member his colleagues will try to restrain him. You "don't attack one man continually" on Ways and Means; "we spar a lot but it never gets serious." "We don't have knock-outs, maybe we are a little more clubby, more closely knit than others." Members believe that they are "responsible" men who

[25] The Committee was reluctantly criticized by a Republican member in 1955 for rushing through H.R. 1, the extension of the Reciprocal Trade Act, without giving the members time to study it or propose amendments. *Congressional Record,* February 18, 1955, Vol. 101, pp. 1743–44.

[26] March and Simon contend that the stronger the individual's identification with a group, the more likely his goals will conform to his perception of group norms. They identify five factors which affect group identification: (1) prestige; (2) perception of shared goals; (3) satisfaction of individual needs; (4) frequency of interaction; and (5) degree of competition between group and individual. In this paper I deal with the first three of these. James G. March and Herbert A. Simon, *Organizations* (New York, 1958), pp. 65–66.

"respect the other fellow" and who "get along pretty well with others."
These attitudes and norms help make the Committee a satisfying group
to belong to. A Republican said,

Relations with the Democrats are usually harmonious. It's like a fraternity where
you have different clubs with different symbols and minor disagreements. There's
a spirit of *camaraderie* that prevails. Oh, we have our differences now and then,
and we jab back and forth, but it never really gets too serious. We are all concerned
with how the Committee looks to outsiders and if there's a lot of bickering the
Committee doesn't look good. Take Banking and Currency for example after
Patman took over. He's arbitrary and the Committee's prestige has sunk way down.
We know that to be an effective committee we must be reasonable.

In the words of a Democrat "everyone's a moderate . . . they screen out those
members who would play for publicity and make a lot of noise. . . ." Two
Democrats attributed their appointments to Ways and Means to personal
characteristics of their rivals as aspirants. One of these "went off half-
cocked," was "controversial" and not "well-liked"; the other was "com-
pulsive" and he would not be right for Ways and Means where members
have to "contain" themselves. Another member said plainly, "we don't want
any screwballs and since I've been a member we haven't had any screwballs.
These men are pretty carefully selected, you know, so you don't get radicals."[27] "Comparing Ways and Means with my former committees, and
with other committees I know of, there is a spirit of cooperation between
Republicans and Democrats. We are members of the 'club' now."

Personal traits are not the only consideration in the recruitment process
to Ways and Means. Seniority, region, and policy orientation are important
and, in many cases, decisive. When these criteria are not of overriding
importance, or when more than one contestant meets them, a popular man
who is "responsible" has an edge over someone who has made enemies, especially on the Democratic side where Ways and Means members are
elected by a vote of all Democratic members of the House; and objective
reasons can usually be found to rationalize affective predilections. These
informal recruitment criteria and norms of behavior combine with the
Committee's attractiveness to produce men who are inclined to follow
group norms, to value harmony, and to promote integration. Members
prefer to disagree amicably if they can; they feel more comfortable in a
low-tension environment and they realize that to protect the Committee's

[27] The same man, a Democrat, explained his election to Ways and Means in
these words: "No one wanted to go much farther north . . . for fear of running into
a radical liberal, and no one wanted to go much further south for fear of running
into an extreme conservative, so they picked me. They wanted a moderate liberal
and a liberal moderate and I fit the bill."

status as the "queen committee" they must manage partisan dissension in a nondestructive way.

As indicated above, partisan considerations and policy orientation are important factors in determining contests over seats on the Ways and Means Committee. In 1963, for example, Phil Landrum of Georgia was denied a seat on Ways and Means largely because he was considered to be too conservative by his Democratic colleagues in the House. Landrum was elected to Ways and Means in 1965 after demonstrating more liberal inclinations by, among other things, guiding the poverty bill through the House.[28] Republicans, on the other hand, want men on Ways and Means who "all fall within pretty much the same general philosophical area" and who will "go down the line" for the party.

2. Membership on the Ways and Means Committee makes one a member of the House elite. Ways and Means members share in the Committee's prestige and, at a more practical level, they are in a good position to accumulate political credits with their colleagues. All congressmen, at one time or another, are concerned with problems that relate to taxes, social security, or trade. On swapping favors one Committee member explained,

> Hell, I'm always being approached by members. It's important, you know. I might go to a member of Public Works once in ten years but they seek my assistance all of the time. Same with all the members of Ways and Means. . . . When I need a favor I can always call on Republicans whom I have helped on Ways and Means bills.

Democrats on Ways and Means have a unique source of influence because of their control over assignments to other committees.[29] Committee assignments in a political system whose life revolves around committees are of major concern to every member of the House. The Ways and Means members normally enjoy—with the exception of assignments to the Rules Committee, which are of special interest to party leaders—a high degree of influence in making appointments. The committee-on-committees function increases their contacts with members from their zone. Newly elected

---

[28] *Congressional Quarterly Weekly Report*, January 18, 1963, p. 46. Landrum's growing liberal tendencies are reflected in his scores on the federal role index: 86th Congress, 33 percent support for a large role; 87th Congress, 61 percent; 88th Congress, 80 percent. *Congressional Quarterly Almanac*, XVI, 1960, p. 136; footnote 9, *supra*.

[29] On the Committee on Committees see Charles L. Clapp, *The Congressman: His Work as He Sees It* (Washington, 1963), pp. 183–212; also Nicholas A. Masters, "Committee Assignments in the House of Representatives," *American Political Science Review*, 55 (June 1961), 345–57. [Chapter 7 in this volume.]

congressmen are indebted to them from the first day they arrive and, as a member moves up the committee hierarchy, he is continually dependent on his representative on Ways and Means.[30] "They call you 'Mr.' and 'Sir' when you are on the committee on committees," one member said. House members "look up to me"; a third member said "*they* come to you and that's very important. Members are always coming to me for things and when I go to them, boy they remember."

In short, the members of Ways and Means stand above many of their peers in the House and they associate this preeminence with the Committee. They are, therefore, induced to follow the norms which insure the continuation of the Committee's stature: restrained partisanship, responsible law making, and reasonable behavior.

3. Most members of the Ways and Means Committee find the Committee a good place from which to satisfy constituent demands. Not every member believes that he can serve his constituents better from Ways and Means than he could from any other House committee, but several do. Moreover, no member's district is so intimately dependent on a committee other than Ways and Means that he risks electoral defeat simply because of his committee assignment.[31] Few members would disagree with a newly appointed member, Dan Rostenkowski (D., Ill.), who told his constituents in a newsletter,

This has been a wonderful year for me. In May I was selected to fill a vacancy on the House Ways and Means Committee. As this is the Committee on Committees, appointment must be made by a vote of the Democratic members of the House, and I am proud to say that I was unanimously chosen by my colleagues. . . . This is the most important committee in the House. . . . It is a most interesting

[30] A "latent function" of the Committee on Committees was evident on the 1963 tax bill, when Mills used the 15 members to help get the bill through the House. Ripley, *op. cit.,* p. 570. Members sometimes take soundings for Mills and act as an informal whip system of their own. As one member remarked, "If I can support it in Committee and on the floor then they [members from his zone] can support it too." When asked what he could do if they did not vote as he did on a Ways and Means bill he added, "Well, suppose if it were [a senior member] I couldn't do very much, but if it were some new member who didn't have a prime committee yet I could do something."

[31] Joel Broyhill, appointed to the Committee in 1964, was thought to be running a grave risk in leaving the District of Columbia Committee and the Post Office and Civil Service Committee because many of his Virginia constituents are government employees who work in the District. Broyhill met the issue head-on by stressing the importance and prestige of Ways and Means and he was reelected, albeit with a somewhat smaller percentage of the vote than he received in 1962. *Washington Post,* October 3, 1964, p. B2. He was reappointed to the District Committee in 1965 without having to yield his seat on Ways and Means, notwithstanding the general rule that membership on the latter is "exclusive."

assignment, but more important, it places me in a position whereby I can be more effective in assisting you with your needs, both personal and legislative.[32]

Intensive bargaining surrounds the myriad parts of a major Ways and Means bill and it is often possible for a member to promote or protect constituent interests by letting it be known that he will support a position unfavorable to the Administration. Executive department representatives may even try to lure Republican support, as evidenced by the late Howard Baker's success in getting one of his favorite proposals included in the Revenue Act of 1964.[33] "You know, you can really do things for your constituents on the Committee. Boy, if you are a horse-trader you can really move. Exports, imports, that sort of thing."

Major legislation is not the only opportunity for serving one's constituents and friends. Ways and Means also processes so-called "members' bills," which are perhaps the best examples of bipartisan cooperation on the Committee. A member's bill is supposed to be a minor piece of legislation that ameliorates the impact of some small feature in the tax laws or makes some "technical" improvement in other laws that come under the Committee's jurisdiction; it is regarded as a "little" thing, of no special interest to anyone other than the Committee member who introduced it.[34]

From time to time during the course of a Congress, Committee members are asked to list in the order of their preference (or chance of passage) those bills which they would like the Committee to consider during "members' bill time." Every member is given the opportunity to call up a bill or bills, depending on how many times they go around the table. If he can get the unanimous consent of his colleagues, his bill will be reported to the House, called up on the House floor by unanimous consent or suspension of the rules, and usually passed without objection.

On April 30, 1964, Chairman Mills stood on the floor of the House and asked unanimous consent for the immediate consideration of twelve mem-

[32] Dan Rostenkowski, "Washington Report," July 20, 1964, p. 2. Congressman George M. Rhodes (D., Pa.), shortly after he was elected to Ways and Means, could take credit for two amendments to a social security bill which were of interest to his constituents. "A Report from Congressman George M. Rhodes," July 16, 1964, p. 1.

[33] For an explanation of this provision see Committee on Ways and Means, 88th Cong., 1st sess., H. Rept. No. 749, *Revenue Act of 1963*, pp. 45–47. It allowed the exclusion from gross income of a limited amount of capital gain received from the sale or exchange of a personal residence by a person 65 years old or over.

[34] Typical members' bills alter the tariff on brooms made of broom corn, provide a credit or refund of self-employment taxes in certain cases, allow the free importation of spectrometers for universities, provide tax-exempt status for nonprofit nurses' professional registries, continue the suspension of duties for metal scrap, etc.

bers' bills.[35] Eleven of these bills were passed by voice vote and one, H.R. 4198 introduced by Representative Shelley (D., Calif.), was defeated when another non-Ways and Means member, Matsunaga (D., Hawaii), objected. H.R. 4198 provided for the free importation of soluble and instant coffee and Matsunaga thought that before it was passed the Hawaiian coffee industry should be consulted. Mills had also intended to call up a bill introduced by Hale Boggs (D., La.), the third ranking Democrat on Ways and Means, but another member of the Committee, Thomas B. Curtis (R., Mo.), prevented it by indicating to Mills that he would object.

Of the eleven bills passed at this time, four were introduced by nonmembers of Ways and Means. The Committee reported these bills as favors to them. Two of the remaining seven were introduced by Republican members of Ways and Means, and five by Democratic members.[36] All twelve were reported unanimously by the Committee and most were supported actively on the floor by the ranking Republican member, John Byrnes (Wis.).

A member's bill may be killed by another member of the Committee, as in the case of the Boggs bill, or it may be killed or postponed by other members of the House, as illustrated by Matsunaga's objection to H.R. 4198. Not every member's bill becomes law. But many do. If influence in the House is defined as the ability to accumulate credits and dispense them with skill, then the members of the Ways and Means Committee, if they stick together, are in a good position to exert influence and satisfy the demands of their constituents and friends.[37] Favors that are "little" in the sum total of things are often large to individual congressmen, and when small favors like these are dispensed over a period of years they amount to a considerable fund of credit on which the Committee (and its Chairman) may draw

[35] *Congressional Record,* April 30, 1964 (daily ed.), pp. 9397–9410. Mills also tried to get S. Con. Res. 19, which expressed the sense of Congress that bourbon whiskey is a distinctive product of the United States and that no imported whiskey should be labeled "bourbon," passed at this time, but John Lindsay (R., N.Y.) objected on behalf of two female constituents whose income came from a small distillery in Mexico. Sober heads prevailed and the resolution passed the House later.

[36] On December 18, 1963, the Committee similarly announced its intention to report 32 members' bills. Seven of them were introduced by nonmembers, 17 by Democratic members, and 8 by Republican members.

[37] For discussions of bargaining see Robert A. Dahl and Charles E. Lindblom, *Politics, Economics, and Welfare* (New York, 1963), Chaps. 12, 13; Lewis A. Froman, Jr., *People and Politics* (Englewood Cliffs, N.J., 1962), pp. 53–58; Robert L. Peabody, "Organization Theory and Legislative Behavior: Bargaining, Hierarchy and Change in the U. S. House of Representatives," a paper read at the annual meeting of the American Political Science Association, New York City, September 4–7, 1963.

if the need arises. Ways and Means reports and passes a relative handful of major bills; it processes dozens of noncontroversial members' bills. When the Committee "cashes in its chips" to pass a major bill the chips are members' bills and other favors which it performs for members of the House.

Members' bills are important benefits which members of both parties enjoy by virtue of their membership on the Committee. They help satisfy the members' need to meet some of the demands of their constituents; and they induce the members to cooperate with one another to this end. The continued success of members' bills depends on the Committee's relations with the House. Members' bills are positive incentives which emanate from the Committee and by helping to promote the members' interests they promote integration.

IV

Committee integration is also affected by the hierarchy of status and role which exists within the group. Members of the Ways and Means Committee play different roles and if the Committee is to be well integrated these roles must be legitimized and ordered.[38] Two sets of roles are of special significance: chairman and ranking minority member, and experienced member-newcomer.

The relationship between the chairman and the ranking minority member is a potential source of conflict in the Committee. Mills, who was elected to the Committee in 1942, has been chairman since 1958. John Byrnes of Wisconsin has 18 years' experience on Ways and Means and has been the ranking Republican member since 1963.[39] Their roles set limits to the degree of cooperation between them and they frequently oppose one another on key policy matters, both within the Committee and on the House floor. There is, however, a good deal of cooperation and mutual respect between them. Both men realize that their positions may be reversed some day and they therefore cooperate on most procedural and some substantive matters.

When the Ways and Means Committee comes to the House floor with a major bill it is often the quintessence of party conflict in the House. But the easy fraternization between Mills and Byrnes even at the height of floor

[38] Parsons and Shils, eds., *op. cit.,* p. 203; John C. Wahlke, Heinz Eulau, William Buchanan, and LeRoy C. Ferguson, *The Legislative System* (New York, 1962), pp. 7–28.
[39] Several people associated with the Committee stated that Mills and Byrnes played prominent leadership roles even before they formally became chairman and ranking minority member.

battles is indicative of the spirit within which the Committee has performed its day-to-day labors.

Mills and Byrnes have jointly sponsored legislation which is referred to Ways and Means and they have collaborated on certain kinds of bills on the floor.[40] One staff member described the two men in these words,

> Mills calls the shots, he runs the show. If a member would like a Committee meeting next Monday, for example, he'd have to get Mills to call it. Every once in a while Mills is questioned about hearings and witnesses but he's very good about it. He discusses these things with Byrnes. The hearings last fall [1963] on beer concentrate were Byrnes's doing. He wanted them, so he and Mills arranged a date. It's quite informal. Mills and Byrnes are good friends. *In many ways they are very similar. Both are dedicated and have no outside life—no hobbies, never take vacations. The Committee is their life. They take work home. They remind me of guys working in a factory who punch in and out, go home and wait for the next work day to begin.*

Members of both parties are "safe" on critical issues and they are, therefore, bound to be opposed on some things. The disintegrative effect of this built-in partisanship is tempered, however, by the tendency of newly elected partisans to accept subordinate roles within the Committee until they become familiar with the subject matter and are accustomed to Committee procedure.

The apprentice role is firmly established on Ways and Means and the new member who wants to be effective does not (even if he could) try to match wits with his more experienced colleagues. This is due in part to the Committee's complex subject matter. One veteran member said that "when I first went on the Committee I used to leave the meetings with a headache, truly a headache! The stuff was just over my head. I just kept plugging along and gradually you catch on. The things we deal with are so complex!" "Detail and technical, oh there's so much detail and it's so technical! You have to take work home and study. Everything is complicated now. Social security has become complicated, tax and tariff too." A junior Democrat added,

> Leadership is pretty constant. The men who sit at the head of the table naturally lead the Committee. They are knowledgeable and have been around a long time. . . . Now that doesn't mean that if I have a question I can't get my oar in.

---

[40] See H.R. 12545 and 12546, 88th Cong., 2d sess., 1964. These bills concern the relative priority of federal tax liens over the interests of other creditors. In addition to their cooperation on members' bills see the debate on H.R. 11865, the 1964 Social Security Amendments, *Congressional Record,* July 29, 1964 (daily ed.), p. 16680.

There's no problem about that. But leadership is as you go up the ladder. Neither ———— nor I will ever be fire-balls on the Committee; we are too old.

Or a junior Republican,

Byrnes and Curtis are real students, are experienced, and know more about it. They *should* lead the Committee. Yesterday, for example, I could have spoken on the Renegotiation Act but I am quite content to let Byrnes and Curtis handle it. They are the experts. I'd tell a new member to get familiar with the four or five major things the Committee deals with. To study hard.

"Jennings is a smart member and Martha Griffiths shows a lot of potential. But we are all learners and beginners, the older members are the ones we listen to." "You have to learn," a Republican said, "and I want to learn. It would be resented if I tried to talk too much or overdid it. . . . So keep your damn big mouth shut a while. If I tried to talk a lot it would be resented, while it wouldn't for an older member."

Newcomers to Ways and Means are expected to "attend religiously, study hard, and pay attention to what the experts are saying." And the "experts" are the experienced members. A new member may participate right away but it is a fundamentally different kind of activity from that of the senior members.[41] Junior members are neither muzzled nor immobilized; they exist in a state of animated quiescence until they have absorbed enough information to make meaningful contributions to the policy discussion.

Friendly and cooperative relations between the chairman and the ranking minority member, plus well established norms of deference governing the degree and kind of participation by senior and junior members, constitute a system of decision-making which is marked by restrained partisanship. During their apprentice period the behavior of new partisans is controlled by the impossibility of rapidly accumulating expertise in the Committee's subject matter. They are exposed to the norms of the group; they soon detect the Committee's leaders; and they learn how to become effective members.

The socialization process is not perfect on Ways and Means but in terms of its ability to negate the influence of divisive partisan factors it compares favorably in recent years[42] with some other committees, most notably the

---

[41] The role of apprentice on the Ways and Means Committee contrasts sharply with the Education and Labor Committee, where newcomers are expected to play a major part immediately. Munger and Fenno, *op. cit.,* p. 119 [p. 189 in this volume].

[42] The importance of time and chairmen becomes clear when one compares the conflict-ridden way the Committee handled the excess profits tax in 1950 with its relatively pacific handling of both the 1962 and 1964 Revenue Acts. For the 1950 bill see Stephen K. Bailey and Howard D. Samuel, *Congress at Work* (New York, 1952), pp. 350–52.

House Education and Labor Committee. It is doubtful if any amount of incentives derived from the Committee, or any number of years experience on the Committee, could result in the total integration of dedicated conservatives like James Utt or committed liberals like George Rhodes, but not even the most ideologically oriented members are immune from the group pressures to restrain partisanship, to articulate dissension in certain ways and not in others, and to contribute to the perpetuation of the Committee as the number one committee in the House.

The major differences in emphasis between Fenno's approach and the one adopted here are that I have stressed the influence of external House demands on the internal operations of the Committee, taken the role of chairman as an independent variable of prime importance to the Ways and Means Committee, considered socialization as a blend of attractiveness and inducements, and attempted a linkage between Parson's focus on integration and Barnard's stress on inducements. Whatever the approach, it is clear that the inner life of congressional committees, a hitherto little explored part of the workings of Congress, deserves the attention of political scientists as a way of increasing our knowledge about legislative behavior and explaining why Congress accepts or rejects the recommendations of its "little legislatures."

10

RICHARD F. FENNO, JR.

The House Committee
on Education and Labor

The special characteristics of the Committee on Education and Labor
as a decision-making institution have had a considerable effect on these
patterns of success and failure. Nearly all of its members agree that
it is probably the most difficult House committee in which to achieve
a consensus and the easiest in which to promote and prolong conflict.
In the words of a leading Democratic proponent of federal aid, "It's a
very discouraging Committee. You can't get a resolution praising God
through that Committee without having a three day battle over it. . . . It's
about the most difficult Committee around. Our executive sessions are
the most exciting things you ever saw."[1] A Republican opponent of federal
aid uses a different perspective but arrives at a similar conclusion.
"We work by trying to split the Democrats on the Committee. And,
actually, we don't have to work very hard. They'll split off by

---

[1] All unattributed quotations in this . . . chapter are taken from interviews
held with 21 members of the House Committee on Education and Labor, one
member of the Senate Committee on Labor and Public Welfare, and with staff
members of both Committees. The interviews were held in Washington in June
1961. They were semi-structured interviews, and the questions were open-ended.
Notes were not taken during the interview, but were transcribed immediately
afterward. The quotations are as near verbatim as the author's power of immediate
recall could make them. In all cases, the respondents were told that their comments
would not be attributed to them.

Reprinted from Frank J. Munger and Richard F. Fenno, Jr., *National Politics
and Federal Aid to Education* (Syracuse: Syracuse University Press, 1962), pp.
109–24, by permission of the publisher.

themselves. . . . Not on the big issues on the final votes, but on amendments and in the Committee. They'll shout at each other, stand up and bang their fists on the table and stomp out."

Unlike its counterpart in the Senate, the House Committee on Education and Labor exhibits an almost classic incapacity as a consensus-building institution. Three basic reasons warrant extended treatment—the nature of the Committee's jurisdiction, the composition of the Committee, and its decision-making procedures.

Jurisdiction

Most of the Committee's internal problems are consequences of the fact that within its jurisdiction fall a high proportion of the most controversial, the most partisan, and the most publicized issues of American domestic politics. The Committee, activated in 1947, cut its legislative teeth on the Taft-Hartley Bill and has been a domestic political battleground ever since. In 1961, two out of President Kennedy's five major domestic programs came before it.[2] All members agreed with two of their colleagues—the first a Republican, the second a Democrat—whose explanations follow:

> This is where the basic philosophies of the two parties really come out strongly. It's a clash of philosophies. You don't get that on Merchant Marine and Fisheries. Oh, what battles! You should see the battles we have in executive session.

> This is probably the most partisan Committee in the House, because this is where the fundamental philosophical battles are fought. . . . The things that identify the administration's domestic program come out of our Committee. You take minimum wage. That's a black and white proposition there. And all of our issues are fundamental, philosophical questions. You don't get that on Space or Foreign Affairs.

If a committee is to function as a consensus-building institution there must be considerable opportunity for compromise and for mutual accommodation of views. Conditions must be maintained in which the legislative techniques of give and take, and of bargaining are possible. It is the chief consequence of nation-wide partisan and philosophical controversies that they seriously limit the development of such internal conditions. A former Republican member reflected on his experience in the 1950's. "Some of us were unalterably opposed to federal aid and some on the other side were just as unalterably in favor of it. . . . There weren't many minds changed by discussion. Everybody had a fixed position when he came there and nobody

---

2 The two were federal aid to education and minimum wage proposals. The other three of Kennedy's big five programs in 1961 were aid to depressed areas, housing, and medical care for the aged.

changed that opinion that I know of." A Democrat, speaking of the situation in 1961, agreed, "The lines are drawn pretty tight on this committee and there isn't much flexibility."

Issues involving the degree and direction of federal participation in such fields as labor-management relations, minimum wage, and education are among those which few legislators can avoid in their election campaigns. Several Republicans recalled debating their opponents on the federal aid issue in 1960; and they recalled, too, having taken a firm stand against all federal aid or a stand, following Vice President Nixon, in support of school construction aid only. Most Committee Democrats, on the other hand, campaigned along with their standard-bearer Senator Kennedy in favor of both a construction and a teachers' salary program. Having assumed more or less unequivocal positions on federal aid before their constituents, members come to their Committee work in an advanced state of commitment and are denied that freedom of maneuver so basic to the production of legislative agreement. They come from their election campaigns trained, positioned, and girded for head-on, showdown Committee conflict.

In another way, too, the jurisdiction of the Committee has hampered consensus building in the field of federal aid. When the Committee was established in 1946, its main focus was considered to be the field of labor—not education. The great majority of Committee members were oriented toward labor problems and professed only minor interest in education. Though there has been a tendency for some members to specialize in educational matters, such members still remain in the minority on the Committee. Since the 1946 decision that the field of education did not warrant a separate committee, many large educational programs of the national government have been placed under the jurisdiction of other House committees.[3] The decision to combine education and labor has thus yielded a weaker and more fragmented effort on behalf of federal aid—by members of Congress and by supporting interest groups—than would surely have resulted from the concentration of educational matters in a committee on education.

Also, educational controversy has been infected with the by-products of labor controversy. Doubtless, internal conflict would be harsh enough in a single education committee, but the tradition of charge and counter-charge accompanying labor-management legislation has certainly not made it any easier for the building of consensus among the same people in another area. There is, of course, an affinity of philosophy between the supporters of organized labor and the supporters of federal aid to education. The record

[3] See Robert M. Rosenzweig, "The Congress—How It Deals With Educational Issues," *Higher Education*, 17 (April 1961), 8–11.

of the AFL-CIO on behalf of federal aid is proof enough. Nonetheless, the Democratic membership of the Committee has been chosen in such a way as to maximize unity on labor matters and with strictly secondary concern for unity on federal aid. The result is that while a Catholic Democrat and a non-Catholic Democrat or a Democrat with many Negro constituents and a Democrat with few Negro constituents can reach agreement on labor matters, they may be pulled in many directions when confronted with the divisive racial and religious issues involved in federal aid.

The passage of time has increased the heat of the federal aid controversy and has done very little, therefore, to reduce Committee conflict. There was a period in the 1940's when information was scarce, when a variety of new approaches were being explored, when there was no legacy of controversy and when, therefore, some attitudes had not crystallized. Between 1943 and 1947, the conversion of Senator Taft to the cause of federal aid took place and helped to settle the issue once and for all in that chamber. But the issue that was settled in the Senate remained a standoff in the House. The opponents win but the proponents keep challenging. And each successive layer of legislative struggle compresses the participants into positions of increasing inflexibility.

The functions of committee hearings, for example, are to add current data to support old positions, and to add current reaffirmations of support or opposition to the store of old political intelligence. They may serve to promote communication between the interest group spokesmen and their own membership, but they have ceased to promote, if they ever did, the communication between proponents and opponents. One member described the federal aid hearings this way. "They don't do any good. And nobody listens to them anyway. The same people say the same things every year. Only the statistics change. But the lines are hard and fast on this issue and nobody changes his mind on or off the Committee. It's a formality.... The teachers groups and these other organizations can prove to their members that they are getting their money's worth for their dues. That's all. They don't change anything." For the newcomer, they may serve an informational function, but they do not convert. One freshman said, "I tried to keep an open mind. I went in there and listened with the attitude, 'let's see if you can convince me I'm wrong.' And the more I heard the more convinced I was that I was right." In the hearing rooms and out, Committee members say, they tend to maintain communications only with one set of interest groups and one set of lobbyists—those with whom they already agree. The only people who may have something new to present, who may represent a potential for change, and who are, therefore, listened to by both sides, are the spokesmen for the president and his administration.

Membership

Conflict inside the Committee on Education and Labor is, ultimately, not a conflict among issues; it is a conflict among individual members. Issues do not battle one another; people do. The selection of Committee members is, therefore, critical in determining the degree, if not the main lines, of internal conflict. The Senate and House committees have dealt, after all, with the same controversial issues, but one has been far more successful at resolving them than the other. To a large degree, this difference is the result of a difference in the personnel of the two groups. The members of the Senate Committee have tended to come from among those of both parties who already are in substantial agreement on the issues of federal aid. The members of the House Committee, on the other hand, have tended to come from among those in their respective parties who already are in the widest disagreement on the issues of federal aid. What this means in the main is that a large minority of Senate Committee Republicans (such as Robert Taft, George Aiken, John S. Cooper, Clifford Case, and Jacob Javits) and Senate Committee southern Democrats (such as Lister Hill, Claude Pepper, Ralph Yarborough) have been far less conservative on the general problem of federal government-educational relations than their counterparts in the House. And it is worth noting that some of the sharpest and most crucial contrasts have been between the respective chairman of the Senate and House committees—namely, Senator Robert Taft (R., Ohio) and Rep. Fred Hartley (R., N.J.), 1947–1949; Senator Lister Hill (D., Ala.) and Rep. Graham Barden (D., N.C.), 1951–1953, 1955–1961.

To concentrate, again, on the House Committee, those who control assignments to it exercise considerable care. On the Republican side, new House members are ordinarily discouraged from applying unless their convictions are firm, their talents for combat considerable, and their districts reasonably safe.[4] Those who cannot be dissuaded and those who must be solicited tend to lean toward the more conservative wing of their party. A rather senior Republican said that he advises anyone who desires a political career to stay off the Committee—unless he is deeply committed. Of himself, he said, "My people didn't vote for me. They voted for what I stood for, my principles. I was elected as a conservative and that's a wonderful thing. . . . It's an awfully unpopular Committee. I take a terrible pounding. But my future is behind me and I don't give a good God damn." "I'm the kind of person," echoed an equally conservative freshman member,

4 See Nicholas A. Masters, "House Committee Assignments," *American Political Science Review*, 55 (June 1961), 354–55 [Chapter 7, pp. 124–27, in this volume.] The four new members in 1961 all won election by less than 55 per cent of the vote; but all were young Republicans who won back normally Republican districts from Democrats who had benefited from the 1958 Democratic sweep.

"who jumps right into these hot spots. So I figured if this was the most controversial committee in the House I'd like to get on it." When the leadership has to fill a slot with some member who has not applied, they may try to ascertain his views beforehand. One member explained, "Halleck called a friend of mine in ——— and said, 'What kind of a guy is this ———? We're thinking of putting him on Education and Labor but we need someone who'll stand up—someone we can count on who won't waver in his views.' My friend replied, 'You don't have to worry about ———.' "

On the Democratic side, too, members are strongly issue-oriented, personally contentious, and deeply committed. They tend to represent the more liberal elements of their party. Party leaders produce this result positively, by encouraging the appointment of labor-oriented congressmen, and negatively, by discouraging the appointment of southerners. To an individual representing a manufacturing or mining constituency a place on the committee dealing with labor matters will have positive electoral advantages. Many Democratic members (15 of the present 19 in either 1958 or 1960) receive financial assistance from the trade unions, and all of these, at least, are dependent upon labor support at the polls.[5] Union lobbyists may actively intercede with the Democratic committee selectors on behalf of congressmen known to be sympathetic to them. On the other hand, no more than four (and usually fewer) southern Democrats have ever been placed on the Committee at one time since its creation—despite the pleas of those southerners who were members of the group. No pretense is made at representativeness on this score; in 1961, 38 per cent of all Democratic congressmen (99 of 263) came from the 11 southern states, but only 11 per cent (2 of 19) of the Committee members did.

Despite the most careful attention to their appointment, the Democratic members of the Committee constitute an extraordinarily heterogeneous group. They are personally much more predisposed to intra-party conflicts than are the Republicans. Moreover, if there is a unifying bond among most of them, it is a bond on the issues involving labor and not education. Whatever other differences there may be among the Republicans on the Committee in 1961, they are all male, non-southern, non-border-state, and Protestant. They are all white, and not one of them represents a constituency with a non-white population of 10 per cent or over. Though 17 per cent of the Roman Catholic House members are Republicans, none is among the Committee Republicans. The 1961 Democratic members, by contrast, include two women, two southerners, two border-state members, seven Roman Catholics, and two Jews. The chairman is a Negro and four

[5] *Congressional Quarterly*, 17 (April 10, 1959), 509–15; *Congressional Quarterly*, 18 (November 11, 1960), 1857.

Democrats represent constituencies with non-white populations of over 10 per cent.[6] These demographic differences are, of course, overlaid with vast differences in personality and political style. Together they make consensus building on the Democratic side especially hazardous—particularly on the issues of school integration and private school assistance.

The combined result of Republican and Democratic appointment practices which is most significant for this study is not only that they guarantee sharp ideological and partisan division on the Committee, but that they intensify internal Committee division. The Congressional Quarterly selected 10 roll call votes in 1961 to distinguish those House members who supported a larger federal role in the nation's economic and social life (e.g., liberals) and those House members who opposed a larger federal role (e.g., conservatives).[7] A majority of Committee Democrats (12 of 19) voted on every occasion to expand government activity; and a majority of Committee Republicans (7 of 12) voted on every occasion in opposition to this expansion. Moreover, if the voting percentages are scaled, every Democratic Committee member voted more often for an expanded federal role than did any of the Republicans.

These ideological and partisan differences inside the Committee are significantly greater than differences on the same issues in the House as a whole. Whereas average percentages among House Democrats were 78 per cent in favor of a larger federal role and 21 per cent against, Committee Democrats averaged 91 per cent in favor and 8 per cent against. House Republicans averaged 12 per cent in favor and 87 per cent opposed, whereas Committee Republicans averaged 7 per cent in favor and 93 per cent opposed. (See Table 1.)

A similar set of 10 roll calls was selected in the Senate. In this case, voting by members of the Committee on Labor and Public Welfare indicates a convergence instead of a divergence of views on the role of the federal government. A majority of Committee Democrats (6 of 10) voted on every occasion to expand the federal role; but only one of the five Republicans voted every time in opposition to such expansion. Three of the five Republicans voted more often for expansion than against it. When Committee voting is compared with Senate voting as a whole it becomes even more obvious that the Committee minimizes rather than magnifies the conflicts inherent in their subject matter. Committee Democrats averaged 90 per cent support for expansion and 10 per cent opposition to it, while the averages for all Senate Democrats were 67 per cent in favor and 33 per cent opposed. Committee Republicans voted 52 per cent in favor and 46

---

[6] Data on the non-white population by congressional districts are taken from U. S. Bureau of the Census, *Congressional District Data Book* (Washington, 1961).

[7] The roll call votes used and the records of each Representative and Senator are listed in *Congressional Quarterly,* 19 (October 20, 1961), 1751–63.

Table 1   Ideological Representativeness of Legislative
           Committees, 1961

	Mean Percentage of Votes in Favor of Expanded Federal Role (10 Roll Calls)	Mean Percentage of Votes in Opposition to Expanded Federal Role (10 Roll Calls)	Index of Liberalism-Conservatism
All House Democrats	78	21	+57
House Education and Labor Committee Democrats	91	8	+83
All House Republicans	12	87	−75
House Education and Labor Committee Republicans	7	93	−86
All Senate Democrats	67	33	+34
Senate Labor and Public Welfare Committee Democrats	90	10	+80
All Senate Republicans	32	64	−32
Senate Labor and Public Welfare Committee Republicans	52	46	+ 6

Source: Congressional Quarterly, 19 (October 20, 1961), 1751–63.

per cent opposed; whereas the averages for all Senate Republicans were 32 per cent in favor and 64 per cent opposed. Both groups on the Committee are substantially more inclined toward increased federal activity than their respective parties in the Senate. This fact is of the utmost significance in facilitating Committee action on federal aid in the Senate.

In the House, given the considerable degree of inflexibility between party groups, the ratio of Democrats to Republicans has assumed considerable importance. During the years of Republican control of the Committee, it was certain that no bill would emerge from the Committee. During the years of Democratic majorities on the Committee only a coalition of Republicans plus southern Democrats could prevent Committee action. Until the 86th Congress in January of 1959, the Republicans plus the southern Democrats constituted a majority of the Committee and, hence, a controlling influence whenever they could agree. In 1959, following the sweeping Democratic congressional victory of the previous November, the liberal Democrats and their interest-group allies succeeded in breaking the long-standing coalition majority. They persuaded Speaker Rayburn to recommend a new party ratio of 20 Democrats to 10 Republicans instead of the previous 17 Democrats to 13 Republicans. Under the previous arrangement 13 Republicans plus Chairman Barden and Georgian Phil Landrum could create a tie vote; and a third, more liberal southerner, Carl Elliott of Alabama, was placed in a strategic position at the ideological center of the Committee and in the eye of most internal storms. Six new Democrats, all supported by organized labor, were given Committee membership in 1959; those southerners who applied were turned down. This membership change constitutes one of the landmarks of the federal aid controversy in Congress.

Procedures

The resolution of internal strife and the formation of legislative consensus are affected greatly by the way in which a committee organizes itself for decision-making. The style of decision-making best suited to these ends would be one which emphasizes mutual accommodation within the group and develops procedures for cooperation and compromise. Frequently, informal and traditional techniques of accommodation will develop on committees—between majority and minority party leaders, between legislatively experienced members and the legislatively inexperienced, between the experts in a particular subject matter and the nonexperts. The Committee on Education and Labor has not devised this style of decision-making to any important degree. It tends to function in a fiercely competitive style in which the techniques are those of naked power and the decision goes to whoever can command a simple majority in a showdown vote. The rules of the game are the formal rules of the House, untempered by private Committee traditions or informal understandings. Committee members have no sense of the Committee as an entity worth worrying about. Sentiments of mutual regard and group solidarity are few. Group morale is not high. The Committee's decision-making procedures do nothing to lower tension or to increase cohesion inside the group.[8]

As described by two leading spokesmen, the atmospheric conditions in which the Committee's federal aid decisions of 1961 were made were typical:

Republican: "The Democrats haven't made a single concession to us on anything. . . . We've dug our heels in. We don't like their tactics and they don't like ours. But what we're doing against the bill isn't any worse than what they are doing to pass the bill. If they aren't going to do some of the things we think are reasonable, we're going to have to oppose the whole thing right down the line."

Democrat: "Boy were they mad. We were slick. But they were trying to be slick, too. They haven't got any interest in aiding parochial schools. They were trying to raise the issue, giggle, sit back and watch the bill die. They play the game right to the hilt."

[8] For a study of a House Committee that contrasts sharply with the Committee on Education and Labor, see Richard F. Fenno, Jr., "The House Appropriations Committee as a Political System: The Problem of Integration," *American Political Science Review*, 56 (June 1962), 310–24. [Chapter 8 in this volume.]

Democrats and Republicans find it difficult to overcome their mutual suspicions sufficiently to establish even minimally harmonious working relationships. Throughout 1961, the Committee chairman and the ranking minority member, whose cooperation should provide the major lubricant of decision-making, conducted a ridiculous public feud over the amount of room space allotted to their respective staffs.[9] A marked lack of communication seems to exist at all other levels of the Committee as well.

Though it is doubtless true that, in the words of one Republican, "Some of our guys hate Democrats more than anything," it often appears that some Democrats hate some other Democrats with a similar passion. Democrats freely admit their natural propensity to fight one another, and a Republican remarked, "There's never that kind of fighting between Democrats and Republicans. They don't expect to convert us. It's like the old situation where they hate the heretic more than they do the infidel." In federal aid decisions, the injection of the segregation issue—splitting northerner from southerner and moderate from liberal—and the parochial school issue—splitting urban Catholic and rural non-Catholic—exacerbates the normal problems of consensus building on the Democratic side. Republicans, less beset by racial and religious differences, and in the minority during all but four years since World War II, have tended to cohere much more frequently—though Eisenhower's support for federal aid split the group in the late 1950's.

One of the most common House traditions that functions as a check on intra-committee conflicts is the informal norm of apprenticeship, which prescribes that committee newcomers should defer to those senior men more experienced in the work of the committee. The freshman should attend meetings, do his homework, say very little, and participate minimally in the making of the group's decisions. The Education and Labor Committee gives virtually no service to this tradition—a tradition which might help countervail against conditions of internecine conflict. The Committee's young men—who happen to be extraordinarily bright, able, and disputatious—are expected to carry a major share of the decision-making burdens. A freshman Republican put this in the strongest language possible. "There isn't any bigger myth than the idea that new people can't do anything. After all this talk about seniority, I was surprised. You know you aren't going to be the Committee Chairman, and you know you aren't going to get to sponsor a major piece of legislation, but other than that you can participate as much as you want. You can even get to take leadership on

---

[9] Their battle was reported in the Capitol Hill newspaper *Roll Call* during March, April, September, and December, 1961. There is, predictably, almost no contact between majority and minority staff members on the Committee.

a bill in Committee. . . . Every time a bill comes out the young members are asked to take five minutes or ten minutes to speak on the floor. They ask us, we don't have to ask. So it's just the opposite from what the myth and fiction of seniority would have you believe." A first-year Democrat spoke for his colleagues when he said: "I was amazed. I was hesitant to do all the things they asked me to do—being a newcomer. I'm the only lawyer on that subcommittee . . . and in drafting the law they relied on me a great deal. A new man has no restrictions at all." The weakness of seniority traditions is evident, also, in the fact that very senior members may be denied the sponsorship of a bill or the chairmanship of a subcommittee to which their rank would otherwise entitle them. Chairman Barden refused to give top Democrat Adam Clayton Powell the chairmanship he wanted, and Powell, when he became chairman, returned the treatment in kind to high-ranking Phil Landrum of Georgia.[10] Without the stabilizing influence of these traditions, decision-making by free-for-all is encouraged. And one can understand the inability of the Committee to exercise any restraining influence whatsoever in regard to proposals such as the Powell Amendment.

Another force which often countervails against an every-man-for-himself technique of legislative decision-making is the presence of subject-matter experts. Committee members will acknowledge the expertise of one or two of their colleagues and will defer to them—not on matters of critical importance to themselves but on technical or factual matters. The expert may not be able to swing ultimate votes, but as the legislation works its way through subcommittee and committee his views will carry substantial weight. The success of federal aid to education bills in the Senate was in large part due to the fact that in committee and out a substantial body of senators were willing to follow an acknowledged expert—Senator Robert A. Taft. Taft's judgment in the Senate in 1947–48 sufficed to settle once and for all a series of questions which have been disputed regularly ever since in the House. It is important to realize, therefore, that there are no acknowledged experts on federal aid to education in the House of Representatives. If there were they would be found on the Committee. Yet every one of the factors thus far discussed militates against the unifying presence of expertise.

Inside the Committee there is no deference accorded even to the work of subcommittees. A subcommittee may have sat many days in hearings and worked long hours over their recommendations, but these are almost always

10 Powell set up a battery of three subcommittees to deal with educational matters, but refrained from assigning them permanent areas of jurisdiction. He offered the chairmanship of the Special Subcommittee on Education to Landrum. Since, however, Powell had no intention of assigning any legislation to the subcommittee if Landrum became its chairman, Landrum declined to serve.

changed by the full Committee. Long-time participants are hard put to remember occasions when substantial alterations have not been made. Regarding federal aid, one senior member remarked: "You can't take a bill before that group unless you know exactly what every section, every paragraph, every line, every word means. There are so many sharpies in there. . . . Someone will try to put another interpretation on it and if you can't refute it, it will stick. . . . Oh! it's a real circus." The Committee has, furthermore, never produced a staff of experts whose independent judgment has carried any weight at all with the members.

Since the Committee does not acknowledge within its own body of supposed specialists any experts on federal aid, it is hardly likely that the Committee will be viewed as conveying expert opinion to the floor. Committee views as such ordinarily carry little persuasion with House colleagues. The normal impression which Committee members manage to create on the floor is one of being wholly unable to agree among themselves—not only between but within parties. Individual Committee members may come to the floor prepared to introduce crippling amendments or, indeed, substitute bills. Members are not usually daunted should a pet amendment, e.g., the Powell Amendment, be defeated in Committee. Said one Democrat in reference to an education amendment, "I tried it in the Committee . . . and I'll try it again on the floor. I haven't told them [his Committee colleagues] I'm going to, but they know that I tried it in Committee and I suppose they know I'll try again. . . . I just believe in it—that's all." Other amendments may come to the floor because the Committee was incapable of dealing with them. "Lots of times . . . if a person has an amendment, he'll hold it back just so we can get the damn bill on the floor. Then he'll propose it on the floor."

To a House membership which already views the Committee as "stacked" via the appointment process, the picture of the Committee in wide disarray on the floor is not conducive to confidence. "Frankly," says one experienced Committee member, "it's not one of the authoritative committees of the Congress—not one of those whose word you take automatically. . . . It lacks stature. In fact most of the bills we report out get completely changed on the floor. . . . It's a power struggle that counts on the floor and not respect for the Committee or the influence of any one individual."

The Committee's modest rank in the prestige hierarchy of House committees operates as both cause and effect of its internal conflicts. Because it is not regarded as having great prestige, House members are only moderately attracted to it. Of the 21 members interviewed, eight had designated it as their first choice for a committee assignment, six had listed it as their second or third choice, and seven members had been requested to go on, or were simply put on, the Committee. Moderate attractiveness means a relatively high rate of turnover among Committee personnel. Of the 30 members of the group in 1961, only three had been members since 1947, seven had been members since 1953, and less than half (14) had been on the Committee for as many as four years (since 1957). Instability of membership is, perhaps, a contributing factor to the Committee's lack of tradition, and lack of group-mindedness. These failures, in their turn, allow internal conflict to flourish, thus further decreasing the prestige of the group among House members.

To write a politically viable federal aid to education bill and to maneuver it successfully through the House Committee requires far more cohesion than the group normally displays. Only exceptional leadership within the Committee or extraordinary pressure without—or both—can produce the requisite internal unity. The many failures of federal aid proponents at the committee stage are due to their inability to combine sufficient Committee leadership, House leadership, administration pressure, and interest-group support to overcome the internal discord of the committee.

Leadership

The Committee has had but one strong chairman since the war—Graham Barden (D., N.C.). Among the members of his Committee, Barden's legislative abilities are already legend. He is invariably described as "a shrewd, smart Chairman," "a very effective Chairman," "absolutely brilliant," "magnificent," and "one of the ablest congressmen in American history." For all of his eight years as chairman, Barden led the Committee in such a way as to create rather than resolve internal conflicts. Most of the time, he worked tirelessly to defeat federal aid legislation; and on the single occasion, in 1949, when he accepted a federal aid bill he did so on such restrictive and uncomprising grounds that he triggered the most acrimonious of all Committee conflicts.

His main tactics were those of delay, divide, and conquer. And his successes were in no small measure due to the fact that these tactics followed the natural grain of a conflict-ridden Committee. "Barden was trying to keep things from being done," said a Democratic member. "He just wanted to filibuster and sow confusion. If it lagged, he would introduce some more." Another Democrat recalled, "He never shut any one up. He'd let you talk yourself around the clock and in circles if you would. One year, he brought in 92 witnesses from the Chamber of Commerce on the school bill and was going to let them all talk. That was his way of doing things." In support of these tactics he relied heavily on the back-stopping votes of the Republicans. A key Republican said, "He ran that committee 100 per cent. I must say that some of us on our side were in substantial sympathy with what he was doing. There was a good deal of support from the Republicans." From his perspective, a Democratic member concurred, "You never had any leadership under Barden—not majority leadership. Under Barden, you had a club. He was a Republican; there's no doubt about that. He was a Democrat in name only. Under him, you had a coalition. And it was very skillful. The coalition ran things until 1959 when Ways and Means decided to enlarge the Committee."

Barden's weapon was a skillful conbination of formal prerogative, informal maneuver, and personal talent. During most of his tenure, for instance, he refused to institute formal Committee rules. Among other things, the Committee had no regular meeting day. "In my first year here," said one member, "we held our first Committee meeting in April and the next one in June." There was, in addition, no time limit placed on the questioning of witnesses during hearings. "I remember once," said a Republican member, "when the very suggestion of a five minute limitation [for each member in questioning each witness] was made, and he hit the roof. He wouldn't hear of any such thing. And he carried the day by sheer bravado or strength of character, call it what you will."

Another prerogative which Barden employed dexterously was his authority to terminate Committee meetings by declaring the absence of a quorum. "Even after 1959 Barden retained a lot of power," exclaimed one Democrat, "we tried holding rump sessions without him but with a quorum. Barden would come in, look around and say, 'I see there's no quorum present,' bang his gavel and it would be all over." A colleague recalled an occasion when the Committee had recessed during a crucial executive session to enable the members to go to the floor to answer a roll call. Barden, however, stayed in the Committee room and sent his clerk to the floor with instructions to call back as soon as the roll call was over and debate had resumed on the floor.

I was one of the first ones back, and Barden was sitting there. He got a phone call, put down the phone, looked around and said "No quorum" and banged the gavel. I jumped up and protested. He said, "No quorum" and left. . . . Technically, he was right. We were supposed to be sitting during debate and should have begun when the floor debate began again. . . . The time table was such that if we didn't complete our work that day we couldn't meet for some time.

In 1956 Barden, who was opposed to the federal aid bill, refused to relinquish his right to control and manage the floor debate on the bill. His allocation of disproportionate time to the opponents plus his dramatic resignation as floor manager near the end of the proceedings added important increments to the unbelievable confusion which accompanied the floor defeat of that year. In the absence of particular Committee rules and in the absence of compensating informal tradition, the rules of the group had to be the same as the rules of the parent House. And in his knowledge of these, Barden far outdistanced the young, aggressive, but legislatively naive liberals on his Committee. "He was a master of parliamentary strategy," said one inexperienced opponent. "He'd lull you to sleep and then hit you with an uppercut. You wouldn't know what the hell had hit you." Another agreed, "We're a young Committee. . . . And it takes a lot of time to learn how the legislative process works. . . . We learned a lot from Barden."

As chairman, Barden could manipulate the various units of the Committee—its subcommittees and its staff. For a considerable period of time, he refused to institute standing subcommittees with specific jurisdiction. The *ad hoc* nature of the Committee structure enabled him to exert close control over the tasks of each subcommittee and over its Democratic membership. In 1957, for example, Barden used his power over subcommittees to head off an incipient liberal revolt in the Committee. He won the support of one senior Democrat to his view on other procedural matters by agreeing to give him a permanent subcommittee of his own. As for the Committee staff, Barden kept it small and inactive as befitted his tactical goals. Democratic Committee members received little research help from the staff and confess to being ignorant of their names. An assistant to one, a veteran Democrat, complained with great feeling, "This committee has the most incompetent, inept staff of any on the Hill. Barden wanted it that way. He could manipulate a dumb staff easier than a smart one. . . . We haven't had a chief clerk or counsel on this Committee for years that knew enough to come in out of the rain." Whether true or not, this is the common perception which pro-federal aid members had of the Committee staff under Barden.

IV

Party Leadership

The party label, essential to electoral victory for representatives and senators, at the same time carries no guarantee at all of loyalty to the party's position in Congress. There are several obstacles to centralized and powerful party discipline. The first of them is the primacy of the individual member's constituency. While he is elected as a Democrat or Republican, no congressman can safely forget that he owes his nomination and election to his contituents, not his national party organization or the president. Thus he cannot easily risk offending significant portions of his electorate, particularly those interests which contributed money or campaign help during elections, or which can command the attention of large numbers of voters. The constituency, therefore, generally comes before party loyalty when there is a conflict. Moreover, the committee system gives a great deal of power to specialists (for knowledge is power in Congress as elsewhere) ; and the seniority system provides a means of choosing committee chairmen that is independent of party loyalty. Indeed, to some extent it runs counter to it. In recent years Democratic committee chairmen in both the House and Senate have given less support to Democratic positions than the average Democratic member of either body.

In the first selection Richard F. Fenno, Jr. provides a bridge between the committee system and the problem of party leadership, describing the place of both institutions in the structure of influence in the House. Fenno considers his problem as being essentially divided into two aspects, the problem of maintenance of institutional patterns, and the problem of decision-making. He places the party leadership in this context, showing its sources of strength and the constraints upon it.

Despite the lack of strong party loyalty, however, it should not be thought that party leaders are without any means of influencing their members. While they do not have control over the ultimate sanction—the ability to withhold renomination—they still set the legislative schedule in both houses; they have a great deal to do with committee assignments; the leadership of the party controlling the White House is the principal channel of communication from the president to his supporters in Congress (and is also the means by which Congress is represented in the White House); and generally, both party leaderships serve as channels of information and foci of attempts to shape legislation on the floor.

Since both parties are far from monolithic, successful party leaders must be able to work with all significant factions in their parties. Congressional leaders tend to be compromisers and accommodators. The impetus for legislation comes primarily from the White House, and is modified chiefly in the relevant committees. With the responsibility for innovation and the development of policy alternatives in other hands, the task of the leaders is not so much to propose legislation as to build majorities for or against it, as the case may be. More than anything, congressional leaders are pre-occupied with the problem of maintaining party unity, with modifying bills so as to make it possible for the maximum number of their supporters to stick together.

The last two selections in Part IV illustrate the generalizations stated above, and in addition provide a series of short case studies of the techniques employed by party leaders. The selection by Rowland Evans and Robert Novak describes the most famous and thoroughgoing example of legislative leadership in contemporary politics—the remarkable skills displayed by Lyndon B. Johnson during his period as majority leader of the Senate. Evans and Novak describe Johnson's enterprising and audacious exploitation of every conceivable resource available to him, including the invention of techniques previously unused by any majority leader. The fact that the aggressive, enterprising Johnson was followed by the low-keyed, retiring Mike Mansfield as leader also illustrates another important thing not only about party leaderships, but also about Congress as an institution: Since so many aspects of the institution are personal, there are tremendous variations possible in the ways that they work, depending upon the personality, skill, and attitudes of individual incumbents in particular roles.

The selection by Randall B. Ripley describes the techniques available to party leaders in the House, and, placed in a context of case studies, categorizes the situations that are likely to confront leaders and the problems that they must overcome. Ripley's selection is based not only on extensive documentary study and interviewing, but also upon a period of direct participant-observation in the office of the House Democratic whip (assistant majority leader). This selection shows to what extent the problem of legislative leaders is to scrape together, by the use of a variety of methods, all of the fragments of power which can be accumulated in order to build majorities for or against legislative measures.

11

RICHARD F. FENNO, JR.

The Internal Distribution of Influence: The House

Every action taken in the House of Representatives is shaped by that body's structure of influence. That structure, in turn, has emerged as a response to two very basic problems of organization. The first is the problem of decision-making. That is, who shall be given influence over what, and how should he (or they) exercise that influence? Influence can be defined simply as a share in the making of House decisions. The House's first problem, then, involves the distribution of these shares among its members and, hence, the creation of a decision-making structure.

The second organizational problem is that of holding the decision-making structure together so that the House can be maintained as an on-going institution. This is the problem of maintenance. How, in other words, should the members be made to work together so as to minimize disruptive internal conflicts? The House must be capable of making decisions, but it must not tear itself apart in the process. It is in response to these twin problems—decision-making and maintenance—that the House's internal structure of influence has developed. And it is by focusing on these two problems that the structure can best be understood.

Decision-Making

Shares in the making of House decisions are not distributed equally among the 435 members. Two sets of formal leadership positions have emerged:

Reprinted from David B. Truman, ed., *The Congress and America's Future* (Englewood Cliffs, N.J.: Prentice-Hall, Inc., 1965), pp. 52–76, by permission of the publisher. Copyright © 1965 by The American Assembly, Columbia University.

the decision-making positions, such as those on the committees, which have been established and maintained by the entire membership of the House, and those positions, such as majority leader and minority leader, which have been established and maintained by the members of the two congressional parties. These two structures of influence, the House structure and the party structure, do overlap—the position of the Speaker, for example, fits into both. But they are distinguishable. Those House members who occupy leadership positions in either structure or both possess the greatest potential for influence in the chamber. Some may not be able to capitalize on that potential; and it is wrong to assume that every man occupying a leadership position is, in fact, a leader. On the other hand, few members of the House become very influential without first occupying a formal leadership position in the House or party structures. Decision-making in the chamber must be described primarily in terms of these two interrelated structures.

House Structure

In 1963, 9,565 bills and 1,731 resolutions were introduced in the House, each calling for a decision. In that same year, one individual member alone reported having received 10,000 letters, kept 900 appointments in his office, and attended 650 meetings, nearly all of which carried requests that he take action of some sort. Individually and collectively, House members are called upon to make decisions, sometimes within the space of a few hours, on matters ranging from national security to constituency service. In short, a body of 435 men must process a work load that is enormous, enormously complicated, and enormously consequential. And they must do so under conditions in which their most precious resources, time and information, are in chronically short supply. The need for internal organization is obvious.

COMMITTEES, DIVISION OF LABOR, AND SPECIALIZATION   To assist them in making their constituency-related decisions, members hire an office staff and distribute them between Washington and "the district." To meet the more general problems the House has developed a division of labor— a system of standing committees. To this they have added a few *ad hoc* select committees and, in conjunction with the Senate, a few joint committees. The 20 standing committees plus the Joint Committee on Atomic Energy provide the backbone of the House's decision-making structure. They screen out most of the bills and resolutions introduced in the House—10,412 out of 11,296 in 1963. On a small fraction, they hold hearings. In fewer cases still the committee will send a modified bill out to the floor of the House for final action. With a few important exceptions, the full House accepts the version of the bill produced by the committee. Decisions of the House for the most part are the decisions of its committees.

The authority of the committees in the chamber rests on the belief that the members of a committee devote more time and possess more information on the subjects within their jurisdiction than do the other congressmen. Specialization is believed to produce expertise. For the non-committee member, reliance on the judgment of the experts on the committee is a useful short-cut in making his decisions. For the committee member, the deference of others is a source of influence. A man of whom it can be said that "he does his homework," "he knows what he's talking about," and "he knows more about that executive bureau than they do themselves" is a prestigeful figure in the House. Members pride themselves on producing, through specialization, a home-grown body of legislative experts to guide them in making their decisions and to serve as a counterweight to the experts of the executive branch. Carl Vinson, George Mahon, and Gerald Ford on military affairs, Wilbur Mills and John Byrnes on taxes, and John Fogarty on medical research are a few such men.

The conditions of committee influence vary. Members are likely to defer to a committee, for example, when the issues are technical and complicated, when large numbers do not feel personally involved, or when all committee members unite in support of the committee's proposal. Some or all of these conditions obtain for committees such as Armed Services and Appropriations, and doubtless help to account for the fact that their recommendations are seldom altered on the floor. Conversely, members are less likely to defer to the judgment of a committee when the issue is of a broad ideological sort, where national controversy has been stirred, or where the committee is not unanimous. These latter conditions frequently mark the work of the Committees on Education and Labor and on Agriculture. Under such circumstances committee influence may be displaced by the influence of party, of constituency, or of a member's social philosophy. Yet even here the committee can determine the framework for later decision-making, and members not on the committee may still be influenced by the factional alignments within the committee.

Committee claims to expertise stem not only from the individual talents of their leaders, but from the abilities of their professional staffs. One of the goals of the Legislative Reorganization Act of 1946 was to strengthen committee staffs. Within the limits of this law, and within budgetary limits voted each year by the House, staff selection is one of the important prerogatives of the committee chairman. Staff size, partisan composition, professional capacity, and duties will reflect his desires. Staff influence varies with the confidence which committee members, and especially the chairman, place in their abilities and their judgment. Where the desire to use a staff and confidence in it exists, staff members constitute a linchpin of internal committee decision-making. When these conditions are not present, it does not make much difference what kind of staff a committee has. Such staff influence as does exist in the House exists here—in the committees. One committee, the Joint Committee on Internal Revenue Taxation, functions primarily as the formal "holding company" for an expert staff which dominates decision-making in that field. In only a few cases does any member of a congressman's personal office staff enter the mainstream of legislative decision-making— in marked contrast to the situation in the Senate. Thus, to advocate larger staff in the House is to argue in favor of the division of labor, of subject-matter specialization, and of an increase in the influence of the twenty standing committees.

COMMITTEE LEADERSHIP AND ITS CONDITIONS   Acceptance of the division of labor as a necessity by House members makes it likely that committee leaders will have major shares in the making of House decisions. Who, then, are the committee leaders and how do their shares vary? In describing the committee-based leaders, it is easy to mistake form for substance. The most common pitfalls are to assume that invariably the most influential committee leaders are the chairmen and to infer that the vital statistics of these twenty individuals characterize committee leadership. Each committee chairman does have a formidable set of prerogatives—over procedure, agenda, hearings, subcommittee creation, subcommittee membership, subcommittee jurisdiction, staff membership, staff functions—which gives him a potential for influence. His actual influence in the House, however, will depend not only upon the prestige of his committee, but also upon his ability to capitalize on his potential and to control his committee. Consequently, many important committee leaders do not hold the position of chairman. They may be subcommittee chairmen, ranking minority members of committees or subcommittees, and occasionally members who hold no formal committee position.

Because House committees differ tremendously in power and prestige, committees like Ways and Means, Rules, and Appropriations necessarily are more influential than committees like Post Office and Civil Service, House Administration, and District of Columbia. These differentials in influence are demonstrated by the House members themselves when, in seeking to change their committee assignments, they regularly trade the possibility of a chairmanship on a low-influence committee for a low-ranking position on a high-influence committee. Circumstance may, of course, alter the relative importance of committees, but at any point in time influential House leaders must be sought among the most influential House committees.

House leaders must be sought, too, among the subcommittee leaders of important House committees. The Committee on Appropriations, for example, divides its tasks among thirteen largely autonomous subcommittees, whose chairmen have as large a share in House decision-making as all but a few full committee chairmen. Thus the chairman of the Appropriations Subcommittee on Foreign Aid exercises more influence over that program than does the chairman of the Foreign Affairs Committee. And the equivalent statement can be made about a half-dozen other Appropriations subcommittee chairmen. When the Reorganization Act of 1946 reduced the number of standing committees from forty-eight to nineteen, it stimulated the growth and the importance of subcommittees. This outcome has obscured the realities of committee-based influence. Analyses of committee leadership which exclude the 123 (as of 1964) subcommittees can be but caricatures of the influence patterns in the House.

The influence of a committee leader in the House depends not only upon the relative power of his committee, but also upon how each committee or subcommittee makes its decisions. To be influential in the House a committee leader must first be influential in his committee. The patterns vary from autocracy to democracy. A chairman who is the acknowledged expert in his field, whose skill in political maneuver is at least as great as that of his colleagues, and who exploits his prerogatives to the fullest can dominate his committee or subcommittee. But his dominance may well proceed with the acquiescence of a majority of the committee. They may, and usually do, expect him to lead. Since a majority of any committee can make its rules, it is impossible for a chairman to dictate committee decisions against the wishes of a cohesive and determined majority of its members—at least in the long run. The aquiescence of his subcommittee chairmen will be especially crucial. On the other hand, since timing is of the essence in legislative maneuver, a short-run autocracy may be decisive in shaping House decisions. A successful chairman, however, must retain the support of his committee, and most chairmen are sensitive to pressures which may arise inside the committee for a wider distribution of internal influence. Long-term resistance to such pressures may bring about a revolt inside the committee which permanently weakens the influence of its chairman. Such revolts occurred, for instance, in the Committee on Government Operations in 1953 and in the Committee on Education and Labor from 1959 to 1961.

It is wrong to assume that most chairmen—even if they could—would monopolize decision-making in their committees. In most cases the creation of subcommittees means a sharing of influence inside the committee. Sharing can be kept to a minimum by designating subcommittees (sometimes simply by numbers) and giving them no permanent jurisdiction of any kind—as has been tried by chairmen of the committees on Armed Services and on the District of Columbia. Or the same result can be produced by withholding jurisdiction over certain bills for the full committee, as is sometimes done by the chairmen of the Armed Services and the Interstate and Foreign Commerce Committees. But where subcommittees are allowed a maximum of autonomy (Government Operations, Public Works, Appropriations, for example) the chairmen may willingly provide leaders of his subcommittees with a base of influence in the House. In the Committee on Government Operations John Moss's Subcommittee on Foreign Operations and Government Information, and in the Committee on Public Works John Blatnik's Subcommittee on Rivers and Harbors come readily to mind. Although the former chairman of the Banking and Currency Committee used the system of numbered subcommittees without permanent jurisdiction as a method of controlling committee activity, he gave to Albert Rains a subcommittee with permanent jurisdiction over housing, thereby enabling Rains to become an influential subject-matter expert. In some cases committee or subcommittee chairmen who work harmoniously with their opposite numbers in the minority party invest the latter with a potential for House influence.

CHARACTERISTICS OF COMMITTEE LEADERS   The chairmen and ranking minority members of the standing committees attain their formal leadership positions through seniority. A variety of rules exist for determining seniority in the case of simultaneous appointments to a committee, but the rules of advancement from that time on are simple to understand and can be applied automatically. A chairman or ranking minority member who retains his party designation and gets re-elected is not removed from his leadership position.

Seniority, however, only partially governs the selection of subcommittee leaders. These positions are filled by the committee chairman (and by the ranking minority member for his side), and he retains sufficient authority over the subcommittee structure to modify the impact of seniority if he so desires. Once a committee member has been appointed to a subcommittee, he usually rises via seniority to become its chairman or ranking minority member. But the original assignment to subcommittees may not be made in accordance with seniority on the parent committee. It may be made on the basis of constituency interests (as is the case with the crop-oriented Agriculture subcommittees), on the basis of prior experience, or on the basis of the chairman's design for influencing subcommittee decisions.

Since the chairman may control subcommittee leadership by his power to determine their jurisdiction and to create or abolish subcommittees, his actions may infuse an important element of flexibility into the rigidities created by strict adherence to seniority. Thus chairmen of the Armed Services and the Post Office and Civil Service Committees have often operated with *ad hoc* subcommittees, hand-picked to consider a particular piece of legislation. The number of Appropriations subcommittees has varied from nine to fifteen since the Reorganization Act, and many of these changes resulted in giving or taking away a subcommittee chairmanship without regard for the claims of seniority.

Normal adherence to the rule of seniority means that by and large committee leaders have had long experience in dealing with their subject matter. Committee-based leadership is founded on subject-matter specialization, and committee-based influence in the House operates within subject-matter areas. Along with information and knowledge, the accumulated experience of committee leaders normally produces practical political wisdom on such matters as how to retain the support of a committee, when to compromise on the contents of a bill, when to take a bill to the floor, how to maneuver in debate, and how to bargain with the Senate in conference —all in a special subject-matter area.

Seniority practices also mean that formal committee leaders represent the traditional areas of party strength—especially the rural South and the rural Midwest and East. In 1964 the twenty Democratic chairmen represented primarily the party strongholds in the South (twelve) and to a smaller degree districts in the urban North (four). The ranking Republicans came in like proportions from rural districts in the Midwest and East (twelve) and from suburban constituencies (four). If one includes the formal sub-committee leaders from the half-dozen most prestigeful committees which have subcommittees (Appropriations, Armed Services, Foreign Affairs, Agriculture, Judiciary, and Interstate and Foreign Commerce), the picture is similar.

What difference does it make to draw committee leaders from safe constituencies? Clearly such interests as can be identified with these areas of the country are advantaged by the makeup of committee leadership. The safest general description of those social interests is that they tend to be conservative, but even this is a gross oversimplification. The important question concerns how the committee chairmen in fact act on those matters which come before their particular committees. By itself the fact that leaders come from safe constituencies tells us only that they will respond to district sentiment that is clear and intense. In all other instances, however, such men remain freer than most other members to use their own judgment in legislative matters without fear of reprisal at the polls. All things being equal, a member who has flexibility of maneuver in the House will be more influential there than one whose constituency obligations leave him without elbow room.

Committee leaders, moreover, defy any easy typology. Representative Howard Smith, Chairman of the Rules Committee, is a prime example of the advantage given to conservative interests by a rural Southern chairman of a key committee. On the other hand, Carl Vinson of Georgia, Chairman of the Armed Services Committee and also a rural Southerner, wielded a critical influence on behalf of President Kennedy's New Frontier proposals. Wilbur Mills, Chairman of the Ways and Means Committee, who represents a rural Arkansas district, followed a pattern of action between these two—steering the Trade Act and the tax cut through his Committee and the House, but blocking Medicare legislation.

The committee structure is a decentralized decision-making system. A fully accurate description of who it is that benefits from the committee structure almost requires, therefore, a committee-by-committee, subcommittee-by-subcommittee, and leader-by-leader analysis.

RULES AND THE DISTRIBUTION OF INFLUENCE   What we have called the House structure of influence (as distinguished from the party structure) results not only from the division of labor by committees but also from the body of formal rules which superintend decision-making. One obvious requirement for the House is a body of rules sufficiently restrictive to prevent unlimited delay and to permit the members to take positive action. Such a set of rules must recognize both a majority's right to govern and a minority's right to criticize. Each is necessary if the rules are to be accepted by both. The accomplishment of this kind of balance is best evidenced by the extraordinary devotion to established rules and to procedural regularity which characterizes every aspect of House action.

Increments of influence accrue to those leaders who understand House rules and can put them to use in their behalf. As they exist in the Constitution, in Jefferson's Manual, in the eleven volumes of Hinds's and Cannon's precedents, and in the forty-two Rules of the House, the procedures of the chamber represent as technical and complex a body of knowledge as any subject-matter area. Influence inside a committee may carry over to the House floor, but success on the floor requires additional skills. Primary among these are the ability to sense the temper of the House and the ability to use the Rules of the House to advantage. A Clarence Cannon, a Howard Smith, or an Albert Rains is a procedural specialist, quite apart from any subject-matter competence he may possess.

The official with the greatest potential for influence in the House, especially in matters of procedure, is the Speaker. Although his importance stems primarily from his position as leader of the majority party, he derives considerable influence from his position as the presiding officer of the House. In this capacity, he exercises a series of procedural controls over House activity. And some of these, in turn, provide opportunities to affect the substance of House decisions. He must recognize any member who wishes to speak on the floor; he rules on the appropriateness of parliamentary procedures; he determines the presence of a quorum; he selects the Chairman of the Committee of the Whole; he votes in case of a tie; he counts and announces votes; he decides in doubtful cases to which standing committee a bill will be assigned; he appoints special or select committees; he appoints the House members to each conference committee; and he maintains decorum in the chamber. The small element of discretion involved in any of these prerogatives occasionally affects legislation. The refusal, for example, of Speaker Sam Rayburn to entertain dilatory tactics before announcing the 203–202 vote extending the draft in 1941 may have prevented a different outcome.

Because the procedural controls of the Speaker extend fairly broadly across the stages through which legislative proposals must pass before they emerge as law, the scope of his procedural influence is probably more important than its weight at any one point. For most House leaders, however, the various decision-making stages represent boundaries which contain their influence. Committee leaders dominate the initial stage of review, reformulation, and recommendation; the Committee on Rules and a few party leaders control the agenda stage; committee leaders, party leaders, and a cluster of other interested members combine to dominate the floor debate and amending stage; a very few committee leaders speak for the House in the conference committee. At each stage a few members normally dominate decision-making. But from stage to stage and from bill to bill, dispersion, not concentration, of influence is the dominant pattern.

THE COMMITTEE ON RULES   No better illustration of these generalizations about influence—its concentration within stages and its dispersion across stages—exists than the Committee on Rules. This Committee owes its great influence in the chamber to the fact that it stands athwart the flow of legislation at one stage—the agenda stage. Since bills flow out of the standing committees and onto the various House calendars in considerable profusion, some mechanism is necessary for sending them to the floor in an orderly fashion. For most important bills these agenda decisions are made by the Rules Committee. By "granting a rule" to a bill the Committee takes it from a calendar, where action is uncertain, and sends it to the floor, where final action is assured. The rule for a bill specifies the length of the debate and the number and kinds of floor amendments to be allowed, and it may remove from challenge provisions which otherwise would violate standing House rules, such as the prohibition against legislation in an appropriation bill.

Commonly referred to as a toll gate or a traffic cop, the Committee obviously functions in the interest of an orderly and efficient flow of business. Just as obviously, however, the Rules Committee functions as a second substantive, policy-making committee for each bill which passes its way. Its fifteen members can exact concessions from the bill's sponsors as their price for granting a rule. Or, as they do on about a dozen bills each year, they can refuse to grant a rule altogether. The Committee thus can wield and threaten to wield a virtual veto over the decision-making process. The veto power is not absolute. Money bills from the Appropriations Committee do not require a rule. A number of bypasses, such as the discharge petition and Calendar Wednesday, are available; but they are clumsy and hence are rarely attempted and hardly ever succeed. The members' devotion to procedural regularity contributes an essential underpinning to Rules Committee influence.

Since House decision is a composite of several formal (and countless informal) decisions, and since at each stage in decision-making a different cluster of House leaders may prevail, supporters of a given bill must build a series of majorities—in the substantive committee, in the Rules Committee, on the floor, and in conference—if they are to be successful. Opponents of a bill, however, need to build but a single majority—at any one stage in the process—to achieve their ends. The Committee on Rules in particular has lent itself to such defensive action. Thus in 1960, when for the first time in history both houses of Congress had passed a federal-aid-to-education bill and the Rules Committee refused to grant a rule so that the bill could go to conference, it was the only place in the entire Congress where opponents of Federal aid could block a majority vote. But it was enough. The consequence, therefore, of the series of stages when accompanied by a corresponding dispersion of influence is to confer a substantial advantage on those interests in society that wish to preserve the *status quo*. House rules make it easier to stop a bill than to pass one.

Party Structure

The complex processes of majority-building involve a party structure of influence which is both different from and yet closely interwoven with the House structure of influence. Considered by itself, the House structure of influence is markedly decentralized—substantively in accordance with committee specialization and procedurally in accordance with a sequence of stages. The party groups organize decision-making across committees and across stages, thereby functioning as a centralizing force in the making of House decisions. Specifically, they organize to elect their own members to the formal leadership positions of the House, to superintend the flow of legislation within and across the various stages, and to determine the substance of policy. Generally, they organize to give some element of central direction to the process of majority building.

THE PARTIES AS CENTRALIZERS   On the record, such centralization as does occur in House decision-making comes about largely as a result of action taken by the party groups. On the other hand, the centralizing capacity of the parties is distinctly limited—so much so that in some ways the net of their activity is to add yet another decentralizing force to that of the House structure. It is a well-established fact that the voting patterns of

House members can be explained better by knowing their party affiliation than by knowing anything else about them. On the other hand, it is an equally well-established fact that on many of the most controversial decisions House majorities must be made up of members of both parties. As organizing, centralizing forces inside the House, the parties have inherent strengths and inherent weaknesses.

Their strength rests in the fact that they are the most comprehensive groups in the House and in the fact that for most members the party is a meaningful source of identification, support, and loyalty. For most of its members, a party label stands for some things which they share in common —an emotional attachment, an interest in getting and keeping power, some perceptions of the political world and, perhaps, certain broad policy orientations. But the unitary party label also masks a pluralism of geographic, social, ideological, and organizational sources of identification, support, and loyalty. The roots of this pluralism lie outside the chamber, in the disparity of conditions under which the members are elected and in the decentralized organization of the parties nationally. As electoral organizations, the two parties are coalitions of diverse social interests and party organizations formed to elect governmental officials—especially the President. No national party hierarchy exists to control the nomination and election of House members or to control their decision-making activity once they are elected. Different House members owe their election to different elements in the party coalition, and they can be expected, in the interests of survival, to respond to their own special local sources of support. Each party label therefore papers over disparate factional blocs and conflicting policy viewpoints. Inside the House as well as outside, the parties remain loose coalitions of social interests and local party organizations.

MAJORITY PARTY LEADERSHIP   Since its members constitute an automatic majority in the House, the larger of the two parties has the greater potential for influence. If the members of the majority party could be brought into perfect agreement, they could produce majorities at every stage of decision-making and transform every party decision into a decision of the House. The fact is, of course, that they cannot. But they do come much closer to the goal than does the minority party. Their successes and failures at maintaining their internal unity and at organizing decision-making provide, therefore, the best insights into the strengths and weaknesses of the party groups in the House.

The majority party achieves its maximum degree of unity and, hence, its greatest success, in filling the leadership positions of the House with its own members. Technically, the whole House elects its Speaker, the chairmen of its standing committees, and the members of each committee. But so long as the majority party prefers to vote its own members into these positions in preference to members of the other party, the decisions are made within the majority party and are only ratified on the House floor. On few, if any, other votes can the majority party achieve unanimity.

The leaders selected inside the majority party—in the Democratic caucus or the Republican conference as the case may be—become leaders in the House. The Speaker, of course, is the prime example and represents the complete interweaving of House and party structure. His dual role gives him a centralizing potential far greater than that of any other member. His effectiveness, however, has varied with the formal authority vested in him by the House and the informal authority he could amass through political skill.

The most successful imposition of party influence upon the House has occurred under strong Speakers—men like Thomas Reed and Joseph Cannon. And the basis of their strength lay in the fact that their formal authority extended into critical areas of personnel and procedure. Speaker Cannon, for example, controlled the Rules Committee by sitting as its chairman. He controlled the substantive committees by selecting their chairmen and members—with or without regard to seniority as he saw fit. Given these and other controls, the majority party leader was able to dominate policy making in the House and become a party leader co-equal with the President. Since 1910, however, the Speaker's formal authority has been modest; and his centralizing influence has been more informal and interstitial than formal and comprehensive. Sam Rayburn's success as Speaker was a triumph of personal skill and only served to obscure the essential modesty of his formal powers.

The majority party elects another leader for the purpose of bringing party influence to bear on the making of House decisions, the majority floor leader. Both he and his counterpart in the minority party remain outside the official House structure. The fact that each of the last eight Speakers served previously as his party's floor leader suggests not only a close working relationship but also some similarity of personal qualifications. In the post-Cannon era, these qualifications have been those of the negotiator. Prime among them has been the recognized ability to command the trust, respect, and confidence of various party factions to the end that the tasks of informal negotiation among them will be facilitated. Successful Speakers and majority leaders are men who appeal personally to their fellow House members and not men whose main appeal is to party elements outside the House. They have been men whose devotion to the House was considered greater than any devotion to ideological causes. These characteristics improve the likelihood that formal party leaders can influence House decision-making. The Speaker and the majority floor leader constitute the nucleus of that somewhat amorphous group in the majority party known as "the leadership."

Such centralization as the majority party is able to bring to House decision-making springs from them.

In barest organizational terms, the job of the majority floor leader is to manage the legislative schedule of the House by programming the day-to-day business on the floor. In so doing, he avails himself of the full range of the Speaker's procedural controls. He also avails himself of the party whip and his assistants who inform members of the schedule, take polls to assess party sentiment, round up members when a vote is to be taken, and generally channel communications between leaders and followers. In their execution, obviously, these scheduling and communications functions shade into the most crucial kinds of procedural concerns—setting legislative priorities, determining strategies of timing, planning parliamentary maneuver. And these functions, in turn, bring opportunities to affect the substance of decisions. The success of many a bill depends more upon when it is called up than on anything else. The effectiveness of the majority party in centralizing House decision-making depends upon its ability to control the procedural flow of legislation. Such success depends in turn upon the ability of the speaker, the majority leader, and the whips to pool their resources to this end.

PARTY LEADERSHIP AND COMMITTEE PERSONNEL   Whether viewed as a control over personnel, procedure, or policy, one fundamental limitation on majority party influence in the House is the inability of its leaders to select committee chairmen. All committee chairmen do, of course, come from the majority party; but the only action which that party takes is to ratify the workings of seniority. More than anything else, this practice perpetuates the separation of House and party structures of influence. The subject-matter committees dominate policy making in their areas of specialization. The Rules Committee exercises a crucial influence over the flow of legislation. But to the degree that the majority party leaders cannot select the chairmen of these committees, their control over procedure and policy is restricted. When the leaders of the party and the committee leaders are in basic disagreement, centralized control is impossible. If in such circumstances unity between members of the same party is to be achieved at all, it must be brought about by the subtle processes of negotiation, bargaining, and compromise.

Lacking influence over the selection of committee chairmen, the most important control over committee personnel which remains within the purview of elective party leaders is that of filling committee vacancies. On the Democratic side, committee assignments are made by action of the Democratic members of the Ways and Means Committee. The selection of Democrats for that Committee, by the entire caucus, is among the most important decisions made in that party. Accordingly, Speaker Rayburn kept tight control over that process, screened the candidates carefully, and maintained his influence in all their subsequent deliberations. Committee assignments on the Republican side are made by a committee comprised of one member from each state which has a Republican congressman—with each member having as many votes as there are Republicans in his state's delegation. The party leader is the chairman of the group; he also chooses and then chairs the subcommittee which actually does the work. Thus Joseph Martin and Charles Halleck have exercised a direct influence on committee assignments.

These personnel decisions can have important consequences for House decision-making. If there are enough vacancies on a given committee, the impact of committee assignments on committee policy may be immediate—as happened in the filling of six vacancies on the Education and Labor Committee in 1959. In this case, a new majority was created which pushed a new set of rules through the committee, overrode the chairman, and got the first general aid-to-education bill in history through the House. If the policy balance is close, a single appointment may be decisive. Those Democrats who in 1962 defeated Representative Landrum's bid for a seat on the Ways and Means Committee, in caucus and against the wishes of Speaker McCormack, believed that the fate of President Kennedy's trade program, of his tax program, and of the Medicare bill might be at stake in that single assignment. But even if no short-run effect can be foreseen, changes in committee leadership and policy may be effected. So reasoned the Democrats with their five "liberal" appointments to the Appropriations Committee and the Republicans with their five "conservative" appointments to the Foreign Affairs Committee in 1963. It is important to understand that seniority is but one among a large number of criteria that custom prescribes for filling vacancies. Party leaders are not at all bound by it, and the process, therefore, has great potential as a means for impressing party influence on the House.

Typically, a formal party leader does not dictate to his "Committee on Committees." Rather he negotiates with them in making committee assignments. The reason for this is simply that the members of these important committees represent the various elements in the party coalition and, as such, may be important party leaders in their own right. Among the Democrats on the Ways and Means Committee are customarily found representatives of the big-city delegations (New York, Philadelphia, Chicago, Detroit), of key state delegations (California, Texas), and of regional groupings (New England, Southeastern, and Border states). The membership of the key Republican subcommittee will include representatives from all the large state delegations—New York, Pennsylvania, Ohio, California, and Illinois. The most influential members of these committees—men like the late Thomas O'Brien, dean of the Illinois Democratic delegation, and Clarence

Brown, veteran leader of the Ohio Republican delegation—are the leaders of party factions. These factions represent important sources of electoral strength and they are the building blocks of the party inside the House as well. In making party decisions, the Speaker and majority leader must always negotiate with the leaders of such coalition elements—thus, in effect, broadening "the leadership" itself into a kind of coalition.

PARTY LEADERSHIP AND POLICY MAKING   Further evidence of the fragmentation of party groups can be found in the attempts by each to organize for the making of policy. Formally the Democratic caucus can make such decisions and bind all House Democrats to vote as directed. But the exceptions are kept sufficiently broad so that no one is, in effect, under any constraint. Furthermore, so deep has been the cleavage between the northern and the southern factions of the party in recent years that the caucus never meets to discuss policy. To do so, say the leaders, would only heat up factional division and make their task of negotiation among the elements of the coalition more difficult. The Democrats also have a steering committee, a smaller group containing representatives of all factions—also designed to discuss and recommend policy positions. But for fear that it, too, might exacerbate disunities, it has not met in recent years.

The Republicans have a representative Policy Committee which has been active and whose chairman, at least, is recognized as a member of the Republican "leadership." Typically, however, its main function is one of facilitating communication among various Republican factions—East and Midwest, suburban and rural, young and old, liberal and conservative. Where a policy consensus already exists, the Policy Committee will state the party position. Where disagreement exists, the Policy Committee is powerless to make a statement of party policy—much less enforce one on its members. If dissident party members refuse to be bound by policy pronouncements worked out within the chamber, they are of course far less willing to listen to the counsels of party groups outside Congress, whether the national committees or such *ad hoc* groups as the Democratic Advisory Council and the All-Republican Conference.

Nothing makes clearer the decentralized nature of policy making by the congressional parties than an examination of certain other policy-oriented groups which exist within (and between) the parties. The most elaborate of these is the Democratic Study Group. These 125 northern and western liberals have concerted their efforts by settling policy positions, by organizing their own whip system to deliver the vote, and by looking even to the financing of House campaigns for like-minded individuals. Conservative southern Democrats also meet (now under the leadership of Omar Burleson of Texas) to discuss issues and strategy on matters of regional concern. Across the two parties, linked by the informal communications of their leaders, a coalition of Democrats and Republicans has operated off and on since 1938 as an informal policy alliance. Similarly the party delegations from each state meet to discuss and seek unity on policies of interest to them. In the Republican party especially, each "class" of first-term party members forms a group in whose meeting party policy is discussed. Smaller discussion groups —the Marching and Chowder Society, the Acorns—persist as forums in which sympathetic party members can talk shop. And, even more informally, members talk policy at regular coffee hours, during workouts in the gym, at poker games, in visits along the same corridor in the office buildings or between nearby Washington residences. The communication networks of congressmen are infinitely complex and, in the absence of two party hier-archies capable of making policy, all of these less formal sources of consulta-tion become consequential for policy making.

Such policy leadership as comes to the party group comes most impor-tantly from the President. To the members of his party in the House, his program provides a unifying, centralizing influence. It reduces the necessity for any active policy-making organ for his party. To the members of the other party, presidential initiatives furnish targets to shoot at. Activity is stirred among the minority party's policy-making organs in an attempt to put together some coherent opposition. But, on the evidence, factionalism in the party which cannot claim the President remains more pronounced than in the party which can. The optimum conditions for policy leadership by the majority party in Congress occur when the President is of the same party. Under other conditions fragmentation is harder to check. Even under the best of circumstances, however, the limitations on the President, not in proposing but in disposing of his program, must be recognized. Since he does not control the electoral fortunes or the House careers of most of his own party members, he may not be able to give them what they most want or discipline them if they fail to follow him. He too, therefore, is normally cast in the role of a negotiator with the elements of his party coalition and, when necessary, with elements of the other party coalition.

MAJORITY BUILDING BY THE MAJORITY PARTY   The decisions with which the party groups are concerned thus are made by processes of negotia-tion and bargaining. Through these processes party leaders try to build and maintain the majorities they need to control House personnel, House proce-dure, and House policy. In the era since Speaker Cannon, the success of the majority party leaders has depended more on a mixed bag of resources than on any massive concentration of formal authority. Typically, in any effort at any stage, "the leadership" of either party can depend on a hard core of support within the party, based on a sympathy of views and overlaid with a sense of party loyalty. Members have, as well, an ingrained respect for the constituted authority of their party leader. All things being equal, party members feel more comfortable when they find it possible to be "with" the party leadership rather than against it. The negotiations of "the leadership" center on making this support possible for a majority of members.

A successful leader of the majority party will put his experience and his political intuition to work in assessing what is possible for key individuals on the committees and in factional blocs. At any point in time, he must make a judgment as to the "temper of the House," what its dominant sentiments are, and what things it can or cannot accept. And the same is true for committees, for blocs, or for individuals. In making these assessments and then negotiating for support the effective Speaker avails himself of his own good personal relations with members, his reputation for fairness, for integrity, for trustworthiness, and for political judgment. He extends his own capacities by using the talents of those friends and protegés whom he locates in every House group. Through them he maintains a line into every committee, every bloc, and every informal group. With them, "the Speaker's boys," he shares his party leadership and, in return, secures a broader base of support than he might otherwise get. Through personal friendship—such as that which existed between Sam Rayburn and Joseph Martin—he maintains a line into the opposition party. Through these networks he identifies the views of others and calculates what concessions he can make before the costs exceed the benefits. He learns whether he can build a majority with his own party or must rely upon negotiations with the other party as well. He decides how partisan a tone he wishes to give to the contest. By adding up support in terms of large blocs, he can determine whether the policy he supports has a fighting chance. If it does not, he is likely to wait, for he will not willingly commit his prestige in a losing cause.

If the large bases of support have been secured and the task of majority building boils down to persuading a few waverers, the knowledge which the party leaders possess of individual idiosyncrasies plus the availability of rewards and punishments may then come into play. The leaders do, after all, influence committee assignments. Through the Congressional Campaign Committee they influence the distribution of campaign money, often in small amounts, but badly needed nonetheless. Through the Congressional Patronage Committee they influence the distribution of a few jobs. Through their procedural controls they may influence the disposition of bills on the Private Bill Calendar, the Consent Calendar, and bills passed by a suspension of the rules. Through their contact with the President they may be able to influence the disposition of a "pet project" of a given member—a dam, a post office, a research laboratory, a federal building. By manipulating rewards and punishments like these, the leaders can bargain for increments of support— in the committees or on the floor.

Majority party leaders negotiate in order to overcome the decentralizing tendencies of party factionalism and the committee system. It follows, then, that the sternest challenge to the centralizing capacities of "the leadership" arises when they confront a dissident party faction in control of an important committee. And, since "the leadership" is normally trying to construct a majority on behalf of some positive action, the greatest test of all occurs when an entrenched party faction uses the advantages of the rules to defend the *status quo*. In recent years the classic contests of this sort have occurred between the leadership of the majority Democratic party and the bipartisan coalition of Southern Democrats and Republicans operating from the bastion of the Committee on Rules.

Since the mid-1930s the party leadership has had to fight for its view that the Rules Committee is an arm of the majority party leadership. The Committee has alternately acceded to this view and fought to retain an autonomous role in the making of House decisions.

Over the past twenty years factional splits in the Democratic party have made the Democratic leadership's relation to the Rules Committee an unstable one. In 1949 the leadership sought and gained by House vote a twenty-one day rule, which provided a procedure by which the chairman of a committee might gain recognition by the Speaker and bring a bill to the floor if the Rules Committee refused to act favorably upon it within twenty-one days of its referral. While it was in force, eight rather important bills were moved to the floor via this route. After a two-year trial and aided by gains in the 1950 elections, however, the Southern Democrats and Republicans in the House repealed the twenty-one day rule and restored the coalition to its position of dominance inside the Committee.

In some respects the twenty-one day rule increased the influence of the Speaker; but it also increased the influence of committee chairmen. Speaker Rayburn regarded it as a very mixed blessing. In any case, during most of the 1940s and 1950s, when it was not in effect, Rayburn frequently had to rely on Republican leader Joseph Martin to provide him with the margin of victory on the Committee.

In 1961, in the wake of a number of defeats in the Rules Committee, in the presence of a new and less cooperative Republican leader, and faced with the prospect of implementing the new Democratic President's program, Speaker Rayburn decided to challenge Chairman Howard Smith for control of the Rules Committee. It was a contest that neither man wanted; and it could only have come about, at did the revolt against Speaker Cannon in 1910, under conditions of serious and irreconcilable differences over policy. The Speaker employed the full range of his authority and skills in this contest and pushed his influence to its outermost limits. He succeeded in enlarging the membership of the Committee from twelve to fifteen—from eight to ten for the majority-party Democrats and from four to five for the minority. Then he added two personal choices to the Democratic side.

With eight dependable Democratic votes, the task of majority-building has subsequently been much easier. Still, it should be noted that the Speaker could not have won his 217-to-212 victory without the votes of twenty-two Republicans, most of whom were sympathetic to his policy goals. And it should also be noted that a single defection among the "dependable" eight can still thwart majority-building by the majority party—as it did on federal aid to education and on the urban affairs bill in 1961.

Clashes between the majority-party leadership and the Rules Committee go to the heart of the structural separation between House and party. Proposed changes in that larger relationship thus almost inescapably must center on Rules Committee activity.

The relations between the Democratic party leadership and the Rules Committee illustrate something about the social interests served by the majority party leadership. When the same party "controls" both the Presidency and Congress, the majority party leadership is more likely than the committee chairmen to be a vehicle through which interests in society opposed to the *status quo* can assert themselves. Given the fact that presidential programs are likely to be pointed more toward change than many committee chairmen desire, the majority party leadership will most often operate against the influence of the committees. From the perspective of conservatively and liberally oriented groups outside Congress, the twenty-one day rule and the Rayburn-Smith contests involved the distribution of real advantages and disadvantages.

This identification of the majority party leadership and liberal interests is only approximate, however. Majority leaders are by no means obedient to every presidential desire. Since majority party leaders are chosen for their ability to communicate across party factions, they may work hand in glove with a conservatively oriented committee to preserve the *status quo*. By blocking legislation the Rules Committee, for example, can and often does serve the interests of the leadership. (In some cases it keeps off the floor legislation on which members do not want to have to vote and then provides a whipping boy for them to blame for the resultant inaction.) Neither conservative nor liberal social interests bear a one-to-one relationship to particular elements of the House structure.

Maintenance

Decentralized and yet distributing influence unequally among the 435 members, the decision-making structure of the House is essentially a semi-oligarchy. This semi-oligarchical structure has been in existence since shortly after the revolution of 1910. In order fully to understand that structure it is necessary finally to understand those internal processes by which it has maintained itself. Structural stability is the result, in brief, of internal processes which have served to keep the institution from tearing itself apart while engaged in the business of decision-making.

The disruption of the influence structure of the House is prevented through the existence of certain general norms of conduct which are widely held and widely observed by House members and which function to minimize internal conflicts. Foremost among these is the norm that members be devoted to the House as an institution, that they do not pursue internal conflicts to the point where the effectiveness of the House is impaired. Immediately after he is elected and sworn in, the Speaker customarily voices this norm and his total allegiance to it. Similarly, the minority party leader graciously accepts the results of the election, thereby symbolizing the minority commitment to the House as an institution. From this over-arching rule of conduct follows the norm that all formal rules and informal traditions of the House should be observed.

Two distinguishable clusters of such rules and traditions are of special importance to the preservation of the existing structure. One cluster functions to maintain harmony between those who hold leadership positions in the House and those who do not. It is the seniority-protégé-apprentice system of norms. A second cluster functions to maintain harmony among those members who hold leadership positions. This is the negotiation and bargaining system of norms. Together the two systems maintain the degree of centralization-decentralization which gives to the House its semi-oligarchical characteristics.

These clusters of norms represent what most members regard as proper behavior. By word and by example they are taught to the newcomers of the House in the earliest years of their tenure. Members who learn them well and whose behavior demonstrates an attachment to them are rewarded with increased influence. Conversely, members who seriously and persistently deviate from them are punished by diminution of their influence. Members may be denied or given the potential for leadership that goes with such formal positions as subcommittee leader or party leader. Or, if they are committee chairmen, rewards and punishments may affect their capacity to maximize the potential for influence. But for these socializing and sanctioning mechanisms, the structure of influence would be quite different from the one just described.

The Seniority-Protégé-Apprentice System

The seniority rules which govern the selection of committee chairmen draw a great deal of attention in commentaries on Congress. What does not draw attention is the fact that these rules are only the most visible ones out of a large and complex body of norms which superintend the House career of every member. Seniority governs ultimate leadership selection; but for all those who do not hold leadership positions, the rules which count represent the other side of the coin. Seniority rules rest on the basic assumption that a man must first spend time learning to be a representative, just as he learns any other occupation. Seniority signifies experience, and experience brings that combination of subject-matter knowledge and political wisdom which alone is held to qualify a man for leadership in the House. Before a member can be certified as an experienced senior member, he must first be an apprentice and a protégé.

Every new member of the House is expected to observe an apprenticeship —to work hard, tend to his constituency, learn his committee work, specialize in an area of public policy, appear often but speak very seldom on the floor, and cooperate with the leaders of his committee and of his party. Naturally, this is the time in their careers when House members are most critical of the system which denies them influence. The proportion of newcomers to non-newcomers is, therefore, a key index of potential conflict in the House influence structure. It was, for example, the extraordinarily large number of new Republicans that made possible the overthrow of Charles Hoeven, the Chairman of the Republican Conference, in 1963. Normally, however, the number of newcomers is sufficiently small so that they have difficulty in organizing to combat the existing leadership structure.

House members believe there is no better judge of a man's worth than the institutional judgment of the House. The assessment and reassessment of one's colleagues—the calculation of each member's "Dow Jones average" —goes on without end. Indeed, this searching scrutiny of one another is an occupational necessity for men whose business is majority-building. After a term or two or three of apprenticeship, men on whom the judgment of the formal leaders is favorable will be rewarded—with an assignment to a more prestigeful committee or with an assignment to one of the committees of his party. The more promising among the newcomers will become the protégés of committee and party leaders. Protégés of a committee chairman may turn up as a special confidants, as subcommittee chairmen, or as floor managers of minor bills. Protégés of the Speaker turn up as Chairmen of the Committee of the Whole, as participants in strategy meetings, or as "a leadership man" on various committees. No mark of preferment, however slight, escapes the notice of the membership. These protégés, with three or four terms of service, have reached an intermediate stage in their House careers. They will have demonstrated their ability, their devotion to the House, and their willingness to cooperate with its leaders. They will be expected to assume the grinding responsibilities of House decision-making and to exercise an independent influence in the chamber. As other members see them, they have gained in stature and are marked as the future leaders in the chamber.

As the protégés see it, they have been rewarded for their apprenticeship with a gratifying measure of influence. They have been given, too, time in which to ponder and prepare for the eventualities of formal leadership.

The seniority-protégé-apprentice system emphasizes a gradual and well-modulated ascent to positions of formal leadership. In its early stages this process of leadership selection is affected by the behavior of the individual member and by the reaction of the leaders to him. The idea of a ladder is basic; but members are sorted out and placed on different career ladders. By their third term most members will be embarked on a House and party career that will follow a fairly predictable path. And in its climactic stage, the process is totally predictable, automatic, and quick. Custom has made this nearly as true for the succession from majority leader to Speaker as is has for the succession to committee chairmanships. The seniority-protégé-apprentice system is basically a system for minimizing conflict among members over who shall exercise influence and who shall not. Its apprentice norms damp down a potential conflict over leadership between newcomers and the more experienced members. Its rules for rewarding the newcomer with a predictable degree of influence keep most of those in mid-career reasonably satisfied with their prospects. Finally, at the point where conflict would be greatest, namely, where formal leadership positions are at stake, the system proscribes conflict entirely.

The seniority-protégé-apprenticeship system is a regulator of many relationships in the chamber—not merely a way of picking committee chairmen. The system must be considered in its entirely as it functions to stabilize the internal structure of influence. It must be considered, too, as a system which touches almost every activity of the House. Consequently, proposed changes in the seniority-protégé-apprentice system cannot be considered as minor. They would produce a new distribution of influence in the House.

The Negotiation and Bargaining System

An organization like the House, in which influence is distributed among forty or fifty different leaders, risks the danger of irreconcilable conflict among them. And it is to prevent such internecine struggle from destroying the institution that a system of norms has developed to govern the business of majority-building.

The negotiation and bargaining system of norms defines for the members how majority-building should proceed. The over-arching norm of this system is that compromise through negotiation be accepted as the proper way of making decisions in the chamber. No individual or group ought to expect to get exactly what it wants from the process. Each must "give a little and take a little" if majorities are to be built and the institution is to survive. A corollary of this norm is that all conflicts should be as de-personalized as possible and that policy disagreement should not produce personal animosities. Members should "disagree without being disagreeable." Only thus will it be possible to negotiate and bargain with one's colleagues on a continuing basis and construct new alliances with former opponents. From these basic norms of conduct flow other rules to govern those interactions between specific leaders or specific groups where conflict might be expected to arise.

Working back through the structure as we have described it, one obvious point of conflict is that between committees or between a committee and the rest of the House. One source of such conflict was reduced considerably by the elaboration of committee jurisdictions in the Reorganization Act of 1946. Committees which authorize programs still conflict, however, with the Appropriations Committee, which must act on the money for those programs. Between the two, however, there normally exists a mutual recognition that the Appropriations Committee should not define programs, i.e., legislate, in an appropriation bill and that the authorizing committee must accept the dollar figure set by the appropriating committee. To keep this conflict to a minimum, informal consultation between the two committees frequently occurs so as to exchange information and to negotiate outstanding differences of opinion. In general, it is the acceptance of the norm of specialization that minimizes inter-committee conflict. On this basis, committees negotiate treaties of reciprocity ranging from "I will stay out of your specialty if you will stay out of mine" to "I'll support your bill if you will support mine." Committee leaders share the desire to preserve their autonomy within the House and will come to each other's aid when they perceive a threat to the committee system in general. The survival of them all demands, and produces, a norm of mutual respect one for another.

Inside the various committees, conflict is frequently held down by similar norms of negotiation. Where influential subcommittees exist, as on the Appropriations Committee, the rules of specialization and reciprocity underpin a system of mutual subcommittee support. To the degree that the committee leaders share their influence and bargain with other members of the committee in working over a piece of legislation, internal committee conflict may be minimized. Also inside the committee, conflict may be averted by obedience to norms which stress a minimum of partisanship—as they do on the Armed Services Committee—and which produce a close working relationship between chairman and ranking minority member and their respective party groups.

One especially delicate relationship involves that between the majority party leadership and the committee chairmen—the sore point of House and party structure. The disruptive potentialities of this kind of conflict are well illustrated by the struggle between Speaker Rayburn and Chairman Smith of the Rules Committee, causing damage that took Speaker McCormack much of his first year to repair. But this case is an extraordinary one precisely because actions taken in accordance with the usual norms of negotiation and bargaining failed. Most of the time the two kinds of leaders cooperate —sometimes on the basis of a policy agreement, but always on the basis of a mutual need. The party leaders need the support of the committee leaders if they want any bill at all to get to the floor; the committee leaders need the support of the party leaders if they want procedural assistance and sufficient supporting votes on the floor. So committee leaders remain amenable to the wishes of the party leaders; but the party leaders by and large defer to and support the specialized committees. Sanctions and the threat of sanctions are, of course, available on both sides and may be used. But knock-down, drag-out battles within the majority party are events to be avoided at nearly any cost. The committee leaders risk a loss of influence inside and outside their committees; and the party leaders risk the permanent loss of sources of support which they may need on later issues.

Given the fact that partisanship runs deep in the structure of influence, the norms which keep inter-party conflict at a minimum are perhaps the most important of all. Without them the House could not survive as we know it. The existence and the observance of such rules were symbolized in the trust, the friendship, the consultation, the exchange of information, and the mutual assistance between Sam Rayburn and Joseph Martin and, similarly, between Nicholas Longworth and John Garner before them.

Most basic to inter-party relations are the continuous consultations between the respective leaders on the legislative program. The rule that the majority should schedule the business of the House is accompanied by the rule that the minority should be apprised of that schedule in advance and that minority objections or suggestions should be entertained where possible. Here again, there is mutual need. For the majority, speed and order may be of the essence. The minority cannot obstruct indefinitely, but it can surely disrupt the smooth flow of House business. On the other hand, for the minority, predictability is critically important. They do not want to live under constant threat of parliamentary tricks, snap roll call votes, or unscheduled sessions. Informal working agreements and trust between majority and minority lubricate House decision-making. Similar agreements as to the size and party ratio of each committee, together with the agreement not to interfere in each other's committee assignment processes, undergird the committee system.

The fact that all-out conflict between the parties is subject to certain limiting norms at every stage in decision-making means that when a majority is built, its decision is more likely to be accepted as legitimate and supported as such by the minority. This is doubly essential in a system where much of today's majority may be found in tomorrow's minority.

Since the divisions within each party make intra-party conflict likely, some note should be made of those norms which help to keep such conflict from disrupting the party altogether. Foremost, perhaps, is the rule that no man is required to show complete party loyalty. A great many reasons are acceptable as excuses for going "off the reservation" and against "the leadership." Constituency and conscience are recognized as taking precedence over party, and a vote cast on these grounds will not be held against a member. On the other hand, in return for this degree of freedom, party leaders do expect that when a man is importuned specifically and directly on a vote, he will do everything he can to "go along." Party members who seek immunity even from this degree of give and take will receive no rewards at the hands of the leadership. But, as we have seen, the leaders must take the party coalition as they find it. Thus they preside over negotiations which take place among the elements of the coalition and preserve its loose unity. Such negotiations dominate internal party organs. Committee assignments are negotiated among party blocs in accordance with formulas that give proportionate representation to party factions. Similarly, all factions will be represented on party policy organs. And party leaders, as we have noted, will be chosen from those most able to communicate on a basis of trust and respect with all factions.

Conflict is the very life blood of a decision-making body in a free society. Yet it is amazing how much of the time and energy of House members is devoted to the business of avoiding conflict. The reason for this is simple. Excessive conflict will disrupt and disable the entire internal structure. In the interests of stability, therefore, a cluster of norms calling for negotiation and bargaining is operative at every point where conflict might destroy the institution. In view of the criticisms frequently pointed at bargaining techniques—"back scratching," "log rolling," "pork barrelling," "vote trading" —it should be noted that these techniques are designed to make majority-building possible. Negotiations in which exchanges of trust or exchanges of tangible benefits minimize conflict pervade every attempt to exercise influence in the chamber. If they were replaced with new rules of conduct, a wholly new structure for decision-making would have to be inaugurated in the House.

Conclusion

This essay has attempted to describe the existing structure of influence inside the House of Representatives. And it has used the problems of decision-making and maintenance as the vehicles for that description. The reader has been invited to view influence relationships in the House as they function to solve these two basic organizational problems. Present relations within and between committees and party units have been treated as one solution to the problem of decision-making. Seniority and bargaining norms have been considered in terms of their contribution to maintenance. Obviously, many other structural arrangements can be devised to deal with these same problems. The pre-1910 Speaker-centered structure comes most readily to mind. This essay, however, offers neither blueprints nor prescriptions. To those who may be concerned with alternative arrangements, the suggestion here is simply that they focus their attention on the twin problems of decision-making and maintenance.

In choosing to highlight decision-making and maintenance as crucial *internal* problems, the essay declares a bias in favor of an influential House of Representatives. If one believes that the House should be dominated either by a powerful President or by a national party organization, then neither decision-making nor maintenance are significant internal problems. They will have to be solved—but the solution will come from outside the chamber. And the internal structure of influence will be a mere shadow of the external structure of influence. To those, therefore, who would prefer a weaker House of Representatives, this essay will miss the mark and, hence, have little to offer. To those who wish to preserve or strengthen the influence of the House of Representatives within the American political system, this analysis of one kind of internal structure may help in assessing the likely consequences of another.

12

ROWLAND EVANS / ROBERT NOVAK

The Johnson System

... Through most of its history, the Senate had been a cockpit of debaters
—Websters and Calhouns, La Follettes and Tafts. Only twice before
Johnson's rule had a Majority Leader achieved real power and control.
The first occasion was a two-year reign by the imperious Republican
aristocrat, Nelson W. Aldrich of Rhode Island, in 1908 and 1909.
Under Aldrich, the majority leadership reached its peak of institutional
authority. Aldrich had sole power to name all members of standing
committees—a power destined for short life in a feudal-like institution whose
members possessed baronial equality. Not until the long tenure of Democrat
Joseph Robinson of Arkansas—Minority Leader from 1923 to 1928 and
Majority Leader from 1928 to 1937—was the Senate again brought
under tight control. Robinson utilized his personal authority, born of
fourteen years as party floor leader, to compensate for his lack of
institutionalized power.

Lacking both Aldrich's institutional power and Robinson's long tenure,
Johnson had to concoct his own System. Highly personalized and
instinctive as it was, the Johnson System stemmed from no grand
master-plan or tightly organized chart. Simply stated, the System can be
broken down into two interlocking components: the Johnson Network

Reprinted from *Lyndon B. Johnson: The Exercise of Power* (Cleveland:
The World Publishing Company, 1966), pp. 95–97, 99–107, 111–17, by permission
of The World Publishing Company and George Allen & Unwin, Ltd.
An NAL book. Copyright © 1966 by Rowland Evans and Robert Novak.
Messrs. Evans and Novak are nationally syndicated political columnists.

and the Johnson Procedure. The Network was the source of Johnson's power, the tool essential to put into effect the Procedure that enabled one man to tame the Senate and bring it under control for the first time in eighteen years.

J. Allen Frear, a Delaware farmboy who became a successful small-town, pint-sized banker in Dover, Delaware, was elected to the United States Senate in 1948 and served two terms there before his defeat in 1960. Obscured by his luminous fellow Democrats in the Class of '48, Frear's trademark was his piercing, high-pitched response to Senate roll calls (much to the amusement of the galleries). Otherwise, he was invisible. Nevertheless, this pleasant little nobody became an important link in the Johnson Network.

At heart a conservative Democrat, Frear generally voted the conservative position—unless Lyndon Johnson wanted him to vote otherwise. Almost without exception, Frear's vote—or non-vote—was Johnson's for the asking, a fact abundantly clear to the astonished gallery in 1959 during the debate on a tax bill. Johnson was supporting an amendment to repeal special tax advantages for dividend income put into law by the Republican-controlled Congress of 1954. In a rare miscalculation, Johnson had miscounted the vote and when the roll call was completed, he found himself beaten by a single vote, 41 to 40. Frear had shrieked "no" on the amendment. Unsolicited by Johnson, he voted as a Delaware conservative. But now Johnson shouted across the Senate floor to Frear: "Change your vote!" Surprised, almost stunned by the command, Frear hesitated. Johnson shouted again, "Change your vote!" Frear did, and the amendment carried.

Indispensable to the Johnson System were generous rewards for consistent good conduct. While distinguished economist Paul Douglas spent years angrily and anxiously waiting for a seat on the tax-writing Finance Committee, Frear went on it quickly (as well as onto the Banking and Currency Committee). Moreover, Johnson did all in his power for Frear's pet bill: a tax-relief measure for Delaware's dominating industry, E. I. Du Pont de Nemours & Company. Du Pont's request was opposed even by the conservative Treasury Department of the Eisenhower Administration.[1]

Most members of the Johnson Network were not so faithful as Allen Frear. He was the ideal, not a typical, member of the Network—a collection of Republicans and Democrats, Northerners and Southerners, liberals and conservatives, great figures and mediocrities. In varying degree, Johnson could count on them all for help.

At the core of the Johnson Network were his peers—Senate grandees to whom he turned more for advice than for votes. Richard Russell, of course;

---

[1] The fact that a combination of liberal Democrats and Eisenhower Administration officials prevented passage of the Du Pont bill contributed to Frear's defeat in 1960. Ironically, the bill passed in 1961, with support from the Kennedy Administration.

Clinton Anderson; Styles Bridges, the Senate's senior Republican; and—one to whom he turned far more often than most realized—his old seat-mate from the Class of '48, Robert S. Kerr. Sometimes unsure of himself on the fine points of complex bills, Johnson often picked Kerr's retentive brain. Once when White House officials traveled secretly to Capitol Hill to give Johnson a confidential advance peek at a new Eisenhower farm bill, they were taken aback to find Kerr waiting for them with Johnson.

Essential to the Johnson Network was the informal, uncoordinated system of lieutenants that he established soon after becoming Majority Leader. Senator Earle Clements of Kentucky—now the Majority Whip—was general handyman and assistant to Johnson and was still able to move moderately well among all factions of Senate Democrats (though he had become increasingly distrusted by the liberals). Taking up that slack with the liberals was Senator Hubert Humphrey of Minnesota. By 1955, though the general public and even much of the Senate failed to realize it, the one-time stereotype of ADA-style liberalism had become a full-fledged lieutenant of Lyndon Johnson. They still disagreed about many matters, just as Russell and Johnson often disagreed. But as much as Russell, though less openly, Humphrey was a Johnson man.

The most important of Johnson's lieutenants in 1955 was no Senator at all. Bobby G. Baker, now twenty-six, had been promoted to Secretary of the Senate Majority when the Democrats regained control in 1955, approved routinely by the Senate Democratic caucus on the Majority Leader's recommendation. Baker promptly remade that job to fit his own specifications, just as Johnson was remaking the majority leadership to fit his. Thus, a routine housekeeping sinecure became in Baker's hands—and with Johnson's blessing —a position of great authority. Mistakenly shrugged off for years by many Senators as a cloak-room chatterbox, Baker now began to eclipse Senator Clements himself as Johnson's top assistant. When Johnson was running the Senate from the Bethesda hospital bed after his heart attack, he relayed his instructions through Bobby Baker. The bouncy, ingratiating—and immensely able—young man from Pickens, South Carolina, came to be called "the ninety-seventh Senator" and "Lyndon, Jr.". . .

But the Johnson Network was not so much a system of lieutenants as of personal alliances that transcended partisan, ideological, and geographic lines. Johnson slowly built up a cadre of supporters who would vote for LBJ —even, on occasion, against their ideology, their conscience, and their political self-interest, depending on the issue and the Senator. The cadre included: Dennis Chavez, an aging New Mexico Democrat; George (Molly) Malone, an eccentric McCarthyite Republican from Nevada; Democrat Stuart Symington of Missouri, vigorous air power man (whose long relationship with Johnson cooled for personal reasons in the late 1950s) ; liberal Republican Margaret Chase Smith of Maine; Harry Flood Byrd, conservative Democrat and national high priest of fiscal responsibility; Richard Neuberger, liberal Democrat of Oregon. East, West; rich, poor; left wing, right wing—all in greater or lesser degree were part of the Johnson Network. With other, less conspicuous members of the Network, they made up perhaps one-quarter of the Senate—more than enough to provide the balance of power on most issues.

To build his Network, Johnson stretched the meager power resources of the Majority Leader to the outer limit. The mightiest of these was his influence over committee assignments. Still, it was not comparable to the absolute power enjoyed by Nelson Aldrich a half century before. As chairman of the Democratic Steering Committee, Johnson steadily widened the breach in rigid seniority rules, working delicately with a surgical scalpel, not a stick of dynamite.

In January, 1955, his ally and adviser, Clinton Anderson, pressed his claim for an overdue assignment on either Foreign Relations or Finance. Each committee had one vacancy. But former Vice-President Alben Barkley, who had just returned to the Senate as a "freshman" from Kentucky in the 1954 elections, asked for the Finance Committee—a request that could scarcely be denied. A further complication was the still unresolved problem of Wayne Morse, the Oregon maverick who had bolted the Republican party in the 1952 campaign and, after two years in the political wilderness as an "Independent," now joined the Democratic caucus in 1955. Morse's decision was vital to Johnson. It provided him with the narrow one-vote margin he needed to cross the bridge, incalculably important in terms of power, from Minority Leader to Majority Leader. Thus, it was incumbent upon Johnson to give Morse a good committee assignment, and Morse wanted Foreign Relations.

Johnson duly explained these facts of life to Anderson, who agreed not to insist (as he well could have) on either Finance or Foreign Relations. But Johnson remembered his old friend's personal loyalty and, on a 1956 speaking engagement in New Mexico, he publicly—and unexpectedly— promised that Clint Anderson would become the next chairman of the Joint Atomic Energy Committee. That post, because of New Mexico's Los Alamos atomic installation, would solidly enhance Anderson's prestige. To make good his promise, Johnson was required to jump Anderson over none other than Richard Russell, who outranked Anderson on the joint committee. . . .

And as chairman of the Joint Atomic Energy Committee, Anderson was even more pleased than he would have been on Foreign Relations. The only grumbling over Johnson's ingenious shuffling came from Russell, who had not agreed in advance to step aside for Anderson. But the grumbling was private and soft, not public and bitter. Lyndon Johnson could count on Dick Russell not to make a public fuss about such matters.

Two years later, Anderson was the center of far more devious committee maneuvers by Johnson. After the presidential election of 1956, Estes Kefauver of Tennessee and John F. Kennedy of Massachusetts, who had competed on the National Convention floor at Chicago for the vice-presidential nomination the previous summer, were competing again—this time for a single vacancy on Foreign Relations. Johnson, who had backed Kennedy against Kefauver at Chicago, was now trying to bring Kennedy closer to his orbit. He was determined to have the vacancy go to Kennedy over Johnson's old foe, Kefauver. But how to get around Kefauver's four-year seniority bulge over Kennedy? In December, 1956, long before Congress convened, Johnson telephoned Anderson with a most curious question: "How are you getting along with your campaign for the Foreign Relations Committee?"

Anderson was puzzled. Could Johnson have forgotten that his "campaign" had ended two years earlier? But Johnson persisted.

"This may be your chance," he said.

Before Anderson could reply that he had his hands full as chairman of Atomic Energy, Johnson rushed on.

"You have seniority now over Jack Kennedy," Johnson explained. "But if you don't claim it, Estes Kefauver may get there first."

Johnson's ploy suddenly came through to Anderson. Both Anderson and Kefauver were members of the Class of '48, and therefore had equal seniority. If they both applied for the one vacancy on the Foreign Relations Committee, Johnson could throw up his hands in the Steering Committee, declare a standoff—and give the vacancy to Kennedy. Anderson went along with this neat strategy, and Kennedy was given the seat, just as Johnson wanted.

Johnson's use of power to influence committee assignments cut both ways. "Good" liberals, such as Humphrey, could be prematurely boosted into the Foreign Relations Committee, and a "bad" liberal, such as Kefauver, could be made to cool his heels for years. A "bad" liberal such as Paul Douglas could be barred from the Finance Committee for eight long years, while five fellow members of the Class of '48 (Kerr, Long, Frear, Anderson, and Johnson himself) and one from the Class of '50 (Smathers) were finding places there.[2] Senators who dared to function too far outside the Johnson Network waited long to get inside the prestige committees.

In these clandestine committee maneuvers, Johnson seldom exposed his

[2] This extraordinary treatment of Douglas also reflected Johnson's desire to keep the Finance Committee free of Northern liberals opposing special tax advantages for the oil and gas industry. But if Douglas had been a "good" liberal in the Humphrey mold, Johnson could have shaved a point, since the Finance Committee was already so stacked in favor of the oil and gas industry.

hand. But in the routine committee shifts, he enjoyed wringing out the last drop of credit. One evening in early January, 1955, shortly after the committee assignments for the 84th Congress had been settled and announced, Johnson invited a couple of friends into his Majority Leader's office in the corner of the Capitol for a political bull session over Scotch and sodas. Nothing relaxed him more than these feet-up, hair-down chats. They invariably lasted well into the night and they invariably ended in long, often hilarious LBJ monologues, full of ribald yarns and racy mimicry.

Suddenly, he interrupted himself. "My God," he said, "I forgot to call Senator Stennis and congratulate him." Stennis had been valuable to Johnson a month earlier in the McCarthy censure fight, and now had just landed a coveted seat on the Appropriations Committee—thanks to Lyndon Johnson. Johnson reached over, cradled the phone between his shoulder and chin, and dialed.

Mrs. Stennis answered the phone, and the conversation commenced. "Ma'm, this is Lyndon Johnson, is your husband there?...He isn't?...Well, I must tell you, Ma'm, how proud I am of your husband and how proud the Senate is, and you tell him that when he gets home. The Senate paid him a great honor today. The Senate elected your husband to the Appropriations Committee. That's one of the most powerful committees in the whole Senate and a great honor for your husband. I'm so proud of John. He's a great American. And I know you're proud of him, too. He's one my finest Senators...." Accompanying this monologue were nods and winks in the direction of Johnson's fascinated audience.

Johnson went on to tell Mrs. Stennis how the Steering Committee had selected her husband unanimously for the Appropriations spot and how the full Senate had unanimously concurred, but implicitly he was belaboring the obvious—that it wasn't the Steering Committee or the full Senate that really was responsible. It was LBJ.

Johnson quietly commandeered other bits and pieces of Senate patronage that previous Majority Leaders ignored. To cement his budding alliance with Senator Margaret Chase Smith, for instance, he arranged for a special staff member of the Senate Armed Services Committee to be appointed by her and to be responsible to her alone, even though she was a Republican on the Democratic-controlled committee, and only fourth-ranking Republican at that.

Although in the past, office space for Senators, a source of sometimes intense competition, had been distributed by strict seniority as a routine housekeeping chore of the Senate's Sergeant-at-Arms, Johnson quickly perceived its value as a weapon of influence and fitted it into his growing system of rewards and punishments. When Paul Douglas lost that top-floor capitol office to Johnson in 1955, the Senate took notice. It was a dramatic sign of the consequences of a lack of rapport with the Majority Leader. Johnson skillfully exploited the gleaming New Senate Office Building in 1958, with its spanking new suites, as an inducement for help on the floor. Senator Mike Monroney of Oklahoma, sometimes troublesome for Johnson, was brought into line on one bill with the award of a handsome corner suite that Johnson knew Monroney coveted.

Johnson also kept his ears open to discover which Senator—or Senator's wife—was really anxious to go on which senatorial junket abroad. At a cocktail party early in 1957, Johnson was chatting with the wife of Frank Church, the young, newly elected liberal Democrat from Idaho. Mrs. Church innocently revealed that she had always wanted to see South America. Knowing that Frank Church might become a valuable addition to the Johnson Network, the Majority Leader saw to it that he was named to the very next delegation of Senators to visit South America.

Even before that, however, Frank Church had reason to be grateful to Lyndon Johnson. Bitterly opposed by the Idaho Power Company and other private-power interests because of his public-power stand, Church was hard-pressed for funds in his 1956 campaign for the Senate. He sent an S.O.S. to the Senate Democratic Campaign Committee in Washington. Senator Smathers, chairman of the Campaign Committee, was dubious about pouring money into what seemed a hopeless cause in a small Mountain State. But Johnson and Bobby Baker argued Church's cause, and their wishes prevailed.

De facto control of the Campaign Committee's funds was one of Johnson's least obvious but most effective tools in building his Network. He controlled the distribution of committee funds through both its chairman—first Earle Clements and later George Smathers—and through its secretary, Bobby Baker. More often than not, the requests for campaign funds were routinely made to Baker, and the money was physically distributed by him. Johnson further tightened his control when Clements was named the committee's executive director after his Senate defeat in 1956. Johnson got the most out of the committee's limited funds (at that time a mere four hundred thousand dollars) by shrewdly distributing them where they would do the most work. In the small Mountain States like Idaho, a ten-thousand-dollar contribution could change the course of an election. But in New York or Pennsylvania, ten thousand dollars was the merest drop in the bucket. Johnson and Baker tried to reduce contributions to Democrats in the industrial Northeast to the minimum. Since Senators seldom bite the hand that finances them, these Westerners were naturally drawn into the Johnson Network, while the Eastern liberals tended to remain outside.

But this ingenious stretching of the Majority Leader's limited stock of patronage could not by itself explain the brilliant success of the Johnson

Network. The extra, indeed the dominant, ingredient was Johnson's over-whelming personality, reflected in what came to be known as "The Treat-ment."

The Treatment could last ten minutes or four hours. It came, enveloping its target, at the LBJ Ranch swimming pool, in one of LBJ's offices, in the Senate cloakroom, on the floor of the Senate itself—wherever Johnson might find a fellow Senator within his reach. Its tone could be supplication, accusa-tion, cajolery, exuberance, scorn, tears, complaint, the hint of threat. It was all of these together. It ran the gamut of human emotions. Its velocity was breathtaking, and it was all in one direction. Interjections from the target were rare. Johnson anticipated them before they could be spoken. He moved in close, his face a scant millimeter from his target, his eyes widening and narrowing, his eyebrows rising and falling. From his pockets poured clip-pings, memos, statistics. Mimicry, humor, and the genius of analogy made The Treatment an almost hypnotic experience and rendered the target stunned and helpless.

In 1957, when Johnson was courting the non-Senate Eastern liberal establishment, he summoned historian and liberal theoretician Arthur Schlesinger, Jr., down from his classroom at Harvard. Wary at the prospect of his first prolonged meeting with Johnson (whom he suspected of disdain-ing the liberal cause), Schlesinger had in his mind a long list of questions to ask Johnson. Never known for shyness, Schlesinger was nevertheless on his guard when he entered Johnson's Capitol office and sat in front of the great man's desk.

The Treatment began immediately: a brilliant, capsule characterization of every Democratic Senator: his strengths and failings, where he fit into the political spectrum; how far he could be pushed, how far pulled; his hates, his loves. And who (he asked Schlesinger) must oversee all these prima donnas, put them to work, knit them together, know when to tickle this one's vanity, inquire of that one's health, remember this one's five o'clock nip of Scotch, that one's nagging wife? Who must find the hidden legislative path between the South and the North, the public power men and the private power men, the farmers' men and the unions' men, the bomber-boys and the peace-lovers, the eggheads and the fatheads? Nobody but Lyndon Johnson.

Imagine a football team (Johnson hurried on) and I'm the coach, and I'm also the quarterback. I have to call the signals, and I have to center the ball, run the ball, pass the ball. I'm the blocker (he rose out of his chair and threw an imaginary block). I'm the tackler (he crouched and tackled). I'm the passer (he heaved a mighty pass). I have to catch the pass (he reached and caught the pass).

Schelesinger was sitting on the edge of his chair, both fascinated and amused. Here was a view of the Senate he had never seen before.

Johnson next ticked off all the bills he had passed that year, how he'd gotten Dick Russell on this one, Bob Kerr on that one, Hubert Humphrey on another. He reached into his desk drawer and out came the voting record of New Jersey's Clifford Case, a liberal Republican. You liberals, he told Schlesinger, are always talking about my record. You wouldn't question Cliff Case's record, would you? And he ran down the list and compared it to his voting record. Whatever Johnson had on those two lists, he came out with a record more liberal than Case's.

Johnson had anticipated and answered all of Schlesinger's questions. The leader rolled on, reiterating a theme common to The Treatment of that time. He'd had his heart attack, he said, and he knew he'd never be President. He wasn't made for the presidency. If only the Good Lord would just give him enough time to do a few more things in the Senate. Then he'd go back to Texas. That's where he belonged.

Breathless now, ninety minutes later, Schlesinger said good-by and groped his way out of Johnson's office. Eight years later, he was to record his impressions. Johnson had been "a good deal more attractive, more subtle, and more formidable than I expected." And, he might have added, vastly more entertaining.

The Treatment was designed for a single target or, at most, an audience of three or four. In large groups, what was witty sounded crude, what was expansive became arrogant. It was inevitable, then, that when Johnson allowed The Treatment to dominate his "press conferences" a sour note entered his relations with the press. Reporters en masse didn't like being on the receiving end of The Treatment. Johnson's failure to understand that annoyed the press, which in turn made Johnson increasingly wary and suspicious. Unable to tame the press as he tamed so many Senators, he foolishly took offense at routine questions, and was quick to find a double meaning in the most innocent point raised by a reporter. Although Senate reporters and Washington's top columnists were captivated in their *private* sessions with Johnson in his office or at LBJ Ranch, his press conferences were fiascoes. They simply could not be harnessed to The Treatment.

One additional bit of Johnson glue held his Network together. Whenever a seventy-five-cent cigar came his way, Johnson would not forget to stick it in his pocket and save it for Senator Carl Hayden of Arizona, a notorious cigar-chomper and chairman of the Senate Appropriations Committee. When William Knowland became a grandfather for the fourth time, Johnson took the floor of the Senate to make the event a historical footnote in the *Congressional Record*. When the wife of Felton (Skeeter) Johnston, a veteran Senate employee who became Secretary of the Senate in 1955, went to the hospital for major surgery, Lyndon Johnson offered to help pay the bill. These small favors and courtesies were elaborately planned by Johnson and graciously carried out. They built Johnson a bottomless reservoir of good will.

Johnson's meticulous attention to such details predated his Senate leadership. In 1952, Westwood, the only daughter of Virginia's Senator Harry Byrd, met a tragic death. Johnson drove from Washington to Winchester, Virgina, for the funeral. As Johnson told the story in 1955, he was amazed to discover that he was the only Senator present. The courtly old Virginan was deeply touched. When Johnson sought Byrd's vote on a labor issue years later, it was Byrd who recalled the funeral and gave Johnson his vote.

While constructing his elaborate Network, the Majority Leader was also building the largest staff ever assembled by a single Senator. Each of the many hats worn by Johnson—Senator from Texas, Senate Majority Leader, chairman of the Democratic Policy Committee, chairman of the Democratic Conference, chairman of the Democratic Steering Committee, chairman of the Defense Preparedness Subcommittee, chairman of the Appropriations Subcommittee on the State, Commerce, and Justice Departments, and (after 1958) chairman of the new Space Committee—each of these hats entitled him to government-paid employees.

Despite the size of this little bureaucracy, the weakest element in the Johnson System was his staff. Throughout his Senate career, he maintained a stable, highly successful relationship with only two staff aides: Walter Jenkins and Bobby Baker.

Jenkins joined Johnson in 1939 fresh from the University of Texas, and except for an unsuccessful race for Congress in a special Texas election in September, 1951, stayed for twenty-five years. He became Johnson's invaluable first assistant, the steadiest rock on the staff. Jenkins ruled the "Texas office" (Johnson's suite in the Senate Office Building, devoted to Texas affairs, which Johnson seldom visited), but was given highly confidential duties that ranged far afield. He was general office manager, personnel chief, private secretary, shorthand stenographer, and errand boy. Johnson rattled off daily chores, from trivial to top secret, and the uncomplaining, unsmiling Jenkins would jot them down in shorthand and get them accomplished. Privy to every scheme in Johnson's brain, Walter Jenkins never complained about his sixteen-hour days, the abuse the Senator would sometimes fling out to relieve his own tension, or the assignment of the most menial chores. The single clue to the suppressed emotional turbulence inside this devoted poker-faced servant were periodic attacks of a skin rash.

235 ROWLAND EVANS / ROBERT NOVAK

Johnson's other staff intimate was Jenkins' antithesis. Bobby Baker was a natural-born politician who wore his moods on his face; he was gregarious, glad-handing, gossipy, and smart as a fox. If Jenkins would have lost his right arm before revealing a secret Johnson scheme, Baker gloried in passing juicy tidbits to his friends in the Senate and among the press, not to damage but to advance the Majority Leader's objective.

Moreover, the Johnson-Baker relationship was altered subtly by the fact that Baker was technically an employee not of Johnson himself but of all the Democratic Senators. This partially explained why there was about Baker none of the hangdog look of the discreet servant that distinguished Walter Jenkins and most of Johnson's own staff. Baker talked out on his own and on occasion even talked back to Johnson, as one day when Johnson halted a reporter in the reception room just off the Senate floor and upbraided him about a story published that morning. Baker listened for a moment, then interrupted. "Now, Senator, that's silly," he said. "You shouldn't say that. That was a damn good story and you ought to appreciate it." To most members of Johnson's regular staff, talk like that was beyond imagining. . . .

At the opening of the 1951 Senate session, when Richard Russell named Lyndon Johnson as floor manager of the universal military training bill (his first major floor assignment), the Senate could justly claim itself to be "the world's greatest deliberative body." The Korean War was raging, and President Truman badly needed passage of the bill to bring the armed forces to full strength. But the Senate took its time, as it had since its earliest days. Debate on the bill—stretching from February 27 to March 9—had the urgency of a chess game at an exclusive men's club. There was an unhurried discursive tone as the learned Senators—Richard Russell, Wayne Morse, Robert Taft, Henry Cabot Lodge, Herbert Lehman—probed every corner of the bill. The sessions seldom ran beyond six o'clock in the evening, and the chamber was closed over the weekends. Senator Ernest McFarland, the Majority Leader, tried to hurry the Senate along, but he wasn't overly concerned by the languorous pace or the frequency and uncertainty of roll calls on amendments. As floor manager of the bill, Johnson naturally joined in debate, delivering long, rambling speeches. But Johnson did not enter the game with the zest of a Taft or Russell. He seemed impatient with this kind of Senate.

The Senate had always been that way, even in the days of Nelson Aldrich and Joe Robinson. In 1883 the young Woodrow Wilson wrote of the Senate in *Congressional Government:*

It must be regarded as no inconsiderable addition to the usefulness of the Senate that it enjoys a much greater freedom of discussion than the House can allow itself. It permits itself a good deal of talk in public about what it is doing, and it commonly talks a great deal of sense.

But it would not be hurried, and, without a rule of germaneness, it could not stick to the point, as Senator Lester Hunt of Wyoming perceived in 1952, on the eve of the Johnson System. Hunt complained: "Any state legislature in the United States would make the Senate of the United States look very bad in connection with procedure." Indeed, the "procedure" of the Senate was geared to slow talk, not vital action.

Johnson was quite aware that he could never establish an efficient procedure by modernizing the encrusted Senate rules. His only recourse, then, as the new Majority Leader, was by trial and error, to evolve slowly the Johnson Procedure—along with the Network, the second major component of the Johnson System.

The principal ingredient of the Procedure was flexibility. On any major piece of legislation, never make a commitment as to what will pass; determine in advance what is *possible* under the best of circumstances for the Senate to accept; after making this near-mathematical determination, don't reveal it; keep the leader's intentions carefully masked; then, exploiting the Johnson Network, start rounding up all detachable votes; when all is in readiness, strike quickly and pass the bill with a minimum of debate.

Essential to making the Johnson Procedure work in this fashion was divided government: a Democratic Majority Leader and a Republican President. Freed of obligation to shepherd a White House program through a Democratic Senate (because the White House was in Republican hands), Johnson could hold his own cards and play his own game. Although divided government had come to Washington before, as recently as the Republican 80th Congress of 1947–48 under President Truman, no previous leader in a divided government had had Johnson's political wit. Besides, Johnson genuinely wanted to *pass* bills, not just block everything sent up by the Republican President.

Johnson had another advantage: the Johnson Intelligence System. Unlike his predecessors, Johnson was constantly probing beneath the Senate's bland exterior to discover what the Senate was really thinking. The Intelligence System was a marvel of efficiency. It was also rather frightening. One evening in the late 1950s, Senator Thruston Morton of Kentucky (the Republican who defeated Earle Clements in 1956) dined with seven political reporters at the Metropolitan Club. The meeting was off-the-record. The reporters had been working as a team for several years. All were sworn to secrecy, and there had never been a leak. Morton laid bare some fascinating behind-the-scenes divisions in the Republican party. A few days later, one of the reporters called on Johnson in his Capitol office. Johnson bitterly chided him and the Washington press corps for writing column after column about the divisions in the Democratic party while ignoring internal tensions in the

Republican party. To prove his point, Johnson dipped into one of the deep wire baskets on his desk and fished out a memorandum on the "confidential" Morton session—complete in every detail.

The thoroughness of Johnson's Intelligence System worried his fellow Senators, some of whom began to half doubt the security of their own telephone conversations. But Johnson needed no help from electronic eavesdropping. His intelligence had a dazzling multiplicity of sources tucked away in surprising places all over Washington. Bobby Baker and his team of cloakroom attendants were in constant touch and conversation with Senators. Johnson's staff was alert to report what they heard on the floor from other Senators and their staffs. The Johnson Network of friendly Senators kept him informed. Johnson himself was constantly probing and questioning other Senators in the cloakrooms, over late-afternoon drinks, during hamburger lunches, in his office. Occasionally aides of other Senators were invited to lunch with the Majority Leader. Immensely flattered, they eagerly volunteered what they—and more important, what their bosses—were thinking.

Speaker Rayburn and the Texas congressional delegation kept Johnson fully informed about what was going on inside the House. Beyond this, moreover, Johnson had loyal friends scattered throughout the government agencies who regularly tipped him on developments.

Johnson took special precautions to maintain a flow of intelligence about the activities of liberal Democrats, his greatest source of trouble in the Senate. Gerry Siegel and later Harry McPherson, his two most liberal staff members, kept lines open to staff members of liberal Senators and sometimes liberal Senators themselves. Robert Oliver, the United Auto Workers staff member from Texas who had maneuvered the CIO behind Johnson in his 1948 campaign and who was now Walter Reuther's chief lobbyist in Washington, was in constant touch with both Johnson and the liberals. But the most important conduit to the liberals was Hubert Humphrey. Johnson had such intimate knowledge of liberal battle plans to reform Rule XXII (the filibuster rule) in January, 1957, that liberals suspected a leak in their own camp. Specifically, they suspected that Humphrey, Bob Oliver, or possibly both, were passing word of their secret meetings to the Majority Leader.

The distillation of intelligence was the head count—the report on how each Senator would vote on a given issue. This delicate judgment of each Senator's intentions was entrusted to Bobby Baker, who compiled the famous head counts in their final form. Baker's head counts were an invaluable asset for Johnson not available to labor, to business, to the Republicans, or even to the White House. Baker's invariably precise count not only gave Johnson the odds on a bill, but what votes he had to switch. This enabled Johnson to energize the Network and get a sufficient number of Senators to change their votes, or at least arrange for Network Senators who opposed the Johnson position to linger in the cloakroom while the roll was called.

Johnson controlled the speed of the actual roll call by signaling the reading clerk—slowing it down until the Senator with the deciding vote (on Johnson's side, of course) entered the chamber, then speeding it up (by a quick rotary movement of his forefinger) when the votes he needed were in hand.

Very infrequently the Johnson-Baker count would be off by a single tally. Perhaps an anti-Johnson Senator would return unexpectedly from out of town to vote. If that happened, Johnson would flash an S.O.S. to the cloakroom and a Network Senator would emerge, then signal the reading clerk that he wanted to cast his vote and tip the balance to Johnson.

That was the dramatic culmination of the Johnson Procedure. Never had a Majority Leader maintained so precise a check on the preferences and the possibilities of every colleague. But inherent in the Johnson Procedure were basic changes in the daily operation of the Senate, changes emanating from the personality of the Majority Leader and evolving so slowly that they were ignored by the public and scarcely recognized in the Senate itself. Yet they were insensibly transforming the Senate. No longer was it the deliberative body described by Woodrow Wilson in 1883 and found relatively intact when Lyndon Johnson arrived in 1949.

These were the mechanical devices of the Johnson Procedure that transformed the Senate:

Unanimous Consent

This was merely a matter of getting all Senators to agree in advance to debate a bill for a fixed time and then to vote. It had always been used in the Senate, but used sparingly and mostly for minor bills.

Johnson transmogrified this occasional procedural device into a way of life. He applied it to every major bill. And so, gradually, attention and interest deserted the once stately public debate and centered on the cloakroom where Johnson, in nose-to-nose negotiations, hammered out his unanimous consent agreements to limit debate. Sometimes these were extremely complex, containing an intricate maze of provisos and codicils.

Occasionally Johnson forged a unanimous consent agreement adhered to by all interested parties (or so he thought), only to hear one maverick Senator (perhaps emboldened by too many nips from the bottle) shout "no" when the agreement was formally offered, thereby depriving Johnson of his unanimous consent. Angry at being crossed, Johnson would storm into the cloakroom and when the glass door had swung shut, would let himself go with an angry soliloquy against the nonconformist who was well beyond hearing on the Senate floor. Then, composing himself, the glass door would swing open and Johnson would return to the floor, drape his arm around the offender, find the cause for objection (perhaps nothing more than a desire to make an extra two-hour speech), satisfy him—and then propound another unanimous consent request to the Senate. He seldom was turned down twice on one bill.

Thus did Lyndon Johnson revolutionize the Senate, severely modifying its proud heritage of unlimited debate without changing a single rule. Of course, the filibuster was still available as an ultimate weapon. And of course any Senator could block unanimous consent and keep the debate going. In fact, however, few did. Debates grew shorter—and ever less important.

Aborted Quorum Calls

When Johnson first arrived at the Senate, the Majority Leader still followed the ancient practice of demanding that a quorum of Senators (forty-nine out of ninety-six) be on the floor for an important debate. As Majority Leader, Johnson demanded more and more quorum calls—but with a new purpose: to fill gaps in the Johnson schedule. Instead of recessing the Senate for an hour or two as in the past, Johnson would ask for a quorum call and wait, sometimes for close to an hour, while the reading clerk droned slowly through the names. Then, when Johnson was ready for the Senate to resume, he would suspend the calling of the roll. These aborted quorum calls held the Senate in suspended animation while Johnson worked out his deals in the cloakroom. Soon, nobody answered the quorum calls. The ever-increasing proportion of the Senate's day spent in meaningless recital of names of Senators who did not bother to answer was a symbol of the decay of Senate debate under the Johnson Procedure.

Night Sessions

In the 1920s, the Senate recessed for luncheon and then returned in the afternoon for more debate. That leisurely practice ended long before Johnson's arrival. But before the Johnson Procedure was instituted, the Senate session was a civilized twelve noon to five o'clock, except under extraordinary conditions.

Johnson changed that. When a debate neared completion, he drove the Senate into night session—beyond nine o'clock, to eleven, to midnight. Late hours, he shrewdly calculated, dulled the desire for debate. With senatorial brains addled by fatigue and generous libations poured in anterooms, combativeness diminished. The Senator who was ready to fight Johnson at three o'clock on this line until the snows came was only too ready by midnight to accept a unanimous consent agreement—*any* unanimous consent agreement—if only he could go home to bed. By driving the Senate into night sessions, the Johnson Procedure further reduced and deadened debate.

Stop-and-Go

Born of necessity after his heart attack, this technique became a positive asset to Johnson. Because doctor's orders called for Johnson to make frequent rest trips back to the LBJ Ranch, he compressed packets of complex legislation into a single week or so, then let the Senate limp along with little or no business (under the loose guidance of the Majority Whip). As the years passed, Johnson out of choice began to legislate in bursts of activity followed by spells of torpor—even when he was not home in Texas.

In 1959, Johnson brought this technique to perfection. He drove the Senate into passing important bills on January 5 and 6 during two long sessions. Next followed a lull to March 11 in which the Senate was virtually inoperative. Johnson then harassed the Senate to overtime work and passed four bills between March 11 and 23. Two bills were passed in April, two in late May and then quiet, until a frenetic burst of activity between June 25 and July 9 brought the Senate to the point of exhaustion with the passage of four major bills. Again a long pause, then the frenzied session-end burst of activity with five bills passed between September 5 and 14.

Stop-and-go was the twin sister of the night session. Exhausted by the numbing consideration of one bill after another in a short time span, the Senate was infinitely more pliable and at the mercy of Johnson's debate-limiting, unanimous-consent agreements. It was another nail in the coffin of debate.

The techniques employed by Johnson weakened, very nearly destroyed, the Senate as a debating society. But in place of a debating society, Johnson did not substitute a parliamentary body that functioned with a comprehensive set of rules, such as the House of Representatives or the British House of Commons. For the Senate functioned under Johnson only because of the Johnson System—the Network and the Procedure, both so attuned to one man's genius they had no chance to survive him.

Johnson's Senate procedure was a natural extension of Johnson's personality. Because he was no orator, his genius was not to sway men's minds in forensic debate. Besides, he thought it a waste of time. He knew that Senators seldom revealed their inner nature in public talk, and discovering that inner nature was at the core of the Johnson System. With rare exceptions, the Senate's important work was done in bilateral negotiations, with a premium on secrecy.

But when it came to those rare exceptions when Johnson wanted a single major speech to administer the coup de grace to his opposition, he was a master at setting the stage on the floor of the Senate and at squeezing out the last drop of drama.

Thus, as the annual debate on foreign aid droned to a conclusion and Eisenhower dispatched urgent messages to Johnson and Knowland to hold the line, Johnson carefully staged a debate-closing speech for the bill by the chairman of the Foreign Relations Committee, elder statesman Walter George, whose resonant voice gave off the vibrant timbre of a cathedral organ.

Lesser Senators prepared the way for the chairman's final appeal. As the last of the second-stringers rose to his feet, Johnson sent another Senator into the cloakroom to alert George. Johnson's agent led the old man across the hall to the comfortable quarters of the Secretary of the Senate and poured him a glass of a particular fine old wine that George fancied. Allowing time for George to sip his wine, Johnson finally crossed into the office of the Secretary himself and led George back into the chamber. The Senate quickly filled up—because Johnson had passed the word he wanted a full attendance. Relaxed and lubricated, George spoke for the better part of an hour, excoriating the small minds who opposed the foreign aid bill— his arms pumping the air, his magnificent voice filling the farthest reaches of the chamber. The moment the old man stopped, Johnson signaled to the reading clerk and the roll was called on the foreign aid bill, the conclusion foregone.

The George performance was out of the old pre-Johnson Senate, now becoming extinct, smothered by the Johnson System. Johnson himself seldom attempted a major speech. Instead, he read brief statements from a type-written sheet of paper, often mumbling inaudibly into his chest.

Just as Thomas Jefferson was a strong President who weakened the presidency as an institution, so did Lyndon Johnson tame the Senate and make it work for him but leave it a weaker institution than he found it.[3]. . .

3 Jefferson wielded his power through his leadership of the Republican majority in the House. When Jefferson left the presidency, real power remained in Congress. His successors were unable to continue Jefferson's control of the party in Congress. Presidential power faded for nearly a generation until Andrew Jackson restored the health of the presidency as an institution. This was prophesied two months before Jefferson's inauguration by Chief Justice John Marshall, who wrote in a letter to a friend: "Mr. Jefferson appears to me to be a man who will embody himself with the House of Representatives. By weakening the office of President, he will increase his personal power." Just as Johnson was followed by a weak Majority Leader in Senator Mike Mansfield, so was Jefferson followed by a weak President in James Madison.

13

RANDALL B. RIPLEY

Techniques of Contemporary Leaders

Most of the thousands of bills introduced into the House each year are
ignored by the party leaders, who assume that the standing committees will
do whatever is necessary. Sometimes, however, they must use all of their
resources to achieve a favorable decision on a significant bill. This chapter
examines the techniques available to the leaders as they struggle for
legislative success.

Floor business is the principal preserve of the leaders. This is where they
direct most of their attention and have their greatest impact. This is
especially true of majority leadership, which is responsible for scheduling
the business on the floor and developing efforts to enact it.

Leaders do not often attempt to influence committee business. Partisan
influences on committees from the leaders, the administration, and some
senior committee members are apparent in numerous case studies, but
such studies emphasize that the parties are much more important
on the floor than in committees.[1] A study of the Landrum-Griffin Act

---

[1] Studies of the Taft-Hartley Act, the Rent Control Act of 1949, and the Excess
Profits Tax of 1950 all seem to point in this direction. See Stephen K. Bailey and
Howard D. Samuel, *Congress at Work* (New York, Holt, Rinehart & Winston, Inc.,
1952), pp. 284–86, 346–51, and 429–30. Also, Bailey's study of the Employment

Reprinted from *Party Leaders in the House of Representatives* (Washington:
The Brookings Institution, 1967), pp. 114–23, 125–30, 132–38, by permission
of the publisher. Copyright © 1967 by The Brookings Institution. Mr. Ripley is
Professor of Political Science at Ohio State University.

242

of 1959, for example, indicates that the floor activity was almost all concerned with problems that tended to divide the two parties, although the Republicans desisted wherever they could in order to retain the Democratic allies essential to their success.[2] A study of the failure of the proposal for an Urban Affairs Department in 1961–62 shows how a clash between the House Republican Policy Committee and the Democratic President helped create a partisan tone in all of the ensuing debate.[3]

Clem Miller, in his remarkable series of letters to his constituents about the House, indicated the paramount importance of the floor, both for developing a feeling of party unity and as the place where the party leaders exercise the greatest influence.

> The House Floor is a great meeting place. . . . One gets a line on upcoming legislation or party strategy, and so on. . . .
>
> In recent weeks we have been talking about the locus of congressional power. Let us now relate it to the Floor of the House. Previously, we have seen that as an issue mounts in importance, ability to influence on the Floor of the House lessens.
>
> We have also seen that debate changes few votes. Now let us consider how votes *are* changed. Members do change the votes of other Members and Members do switch from vote to vote. This is done on a personal basis. . . .
>
> Voting lines are set by the committee chairmen (and by each committee's senior minority member) and hence by the Leadership; that generally is sufficient to carry the day; and finally . . . individuals may shift back and forth within this framework in response to personal appeals and deeply ingrained prejudices.[4]

To understand the contemporary leaders' techniques for influencing outcomes on the floor, they will be investigated in two ways. First, a catalog of eight techniques will be discussed, using specific examples. Second, the majority party leaders will be shown using a variety of techniques as they sought support for five different bills in the Eighty-eighth Congress (1963–65).

Act of 1946, despite its conclusions that deny the presence of party influence and responsibility, makes clear that during the floor fight in the House, party leadership was an important factor. Ultimately, of course, the southern Democratic-conservative Republican alliance carried the day, but the maneuvering was largely partisan. See Stephen K. Bailey, *Congress Makes a Law* (New York: Vintage Books, 1964), pp. 237–38, 173–78.

[2] Alan K. McAdams, *Power and Politics in Labor Legislation* (New York: Columbia University Press, 1964), pp. 214, 226–27, 277–78.

[3] Judith Ann Heimlich, "The Urban Department Mr. Kennedy Did Not Get" (unpublished manuscript prepared for a Brookings Institution project).

[4] Clem Miller, *Member of the House* (New York: Charles Scribner's Sons, 1962), pp. 4, 107, 109.

A Catalog of Current Techniques

Developing Committee Unanimity

Leaders of both parties can develop unanimous support for a particular position among their members on the standing committee handling the bill. With no defections among committee members in debate or in voting, the rest of the party members are more likely to follow.

Party members on a standing committee can take the lead in developing an alternative to the proposals of the other party or the administration. Under Presidents Kennedy and Johnson, some Republicans have made efforts to develop alternative positions by working through the party members on committees as well as the party leaders. In the Eighty-seventh and Eighty-eighth Congresses (1961–65), this usually involved a caucus and agreement on the part of committee Republicans before approaching Minority Leader Charles Halleck to ask for a meeting of the Policy Committee or the full conference. Only a few Republican committee delegations made such efforts; others felt that the opposition should merely oppose majority proposals.

In 1963, Republicans on the Ways and Means Committee met and worked out an alternative to the Democratic plan for a tax cut. They took their proposal to the Policy Committee, which in turn recommended a conference. The conference ratified the plan, and when it was embodied in the recommittal motion on the floor only one Republican voted with the majority against the motion and 173 Republicans voted for it, although the Democrats kept their own losses low enough to win.

Republicans on the Judiciary Committee met throughout 1963 to develop a united position on civil rights legislation. As a result, leading party members on the committee received much of the credit for passage of the bill with a high degree of Republican support.

In the Eighty-ninth Congress (1965–67), the Republican pattern of committee-leadership consultation changed. The new Minority Leader, Gerald Ford, encouraged all committee delegations to develop alternatives to almost all major Democratic proposals, including the Appalachia program (Public Works Committee), education (Education and Labor Committee), and Medicare (Ways and Means Committee). The Minority Leader and others in the leadership met with all Republicans on a standing committee to discuss various alternatives. After a unanimous position was reached, the Minority Leader sent a letter to all Republicans announcing the party position. Republican support for these proposals on the floor was high—although, given the small number of Republicans in the House, few victories were won.

Scheduling

The majority party alone has the power to manipulate the scheduling of floor business to suit its own ends. Generally, the majority leadership does not try to spring "surprises" in scheduling major bills: the usual tactic is to delay until the time is right for passage. This can mean delay of a day or two until attendance is more favorable, or it can mean a delay of many months to obtain needed support for a proposal.

The chronology of the bill providing subsidies for both growers and manufacturers of cotton, which the House passed on December 4, 1963, suggests the uses the majority party leaders can make of scheduling delays. A subcommittee of the House Agriculture Committee held hearings on the bill February 5, and the full committee reported it June 6. On June 11, the Secretary of Agriculture wrote the chairman of the committee, Harold Cooley of North Carolina, that the administration strongly supported the bill. On the next day, however, the House killed a proposed extension and expansion of the area redevelopment program, with Cooley and many other southerners voting against the administration. One Democratic leader remarked immediately after this defeat, "Harold Cooley can forget the cotton bill."

Feeling against the southerners continued so high throughout the summer that the leaders and administration would not risk bringing the bill to the floor. In mid-August Cooley and other high-ranking southerners on the committee met with Majority Leader Carl Albert, Majority Whip Hale Boggs, and Albert Rains of the Banking and Currency Committee to determine whether a trade could be arranged whereby southerners would support a new version of the area redevelopment bill in return for northern and liberal support for the cotton bill. No agreement could be reached.

By the week of October 21, Cooley had decided to schedule the cotton bill for the week after Veterans Day (November 11). The Speaker announced this decision, and on October 25, Albert and Boggs signed a letter to all Democrats outlining the objectives of the bill. On October 28 the whip organization began polling all Democrats on the question: "Will you vote for the 1963 cotton bill?" At a meeting on October 31, the Speaker reported that Democratic defections would require forty Republican votes to pass the bill. He rescheduled it for the week of November 18, giving the supporters an extra week to find the votes.

By November 8, on the basis of the whip poll results, the Speaker again decided to postpone the bill until the first week in December.

By chance, the cotton bill was the first major legislation before the House that was of primary importance to the new President, Lyndon Johnson. Just thirteen days after the assassination of President Kennedy, the House acted. During the week before the vote, the leaders used extensively (and almost exclusively) the argument that no Democrat should vote against the bill and help defeat the new President in his first test. With the Democratic leaders keeping all assistant whips on the floor to prevent members from straying, the House passed the bill on December 4. Even then forty-eight Democrats voted against it, but thirty-four Republican votes pulled the leadership and the new President through to success. The whip poll begun in October left at least seventy Democratic votes in doubt. Before the Speaker let the bill come to the floor, the poll was showing only twenty-five defectors, with another eight unsure. (Some of the forty-eight votes cast in opposition would probably have been changed if it were certain they were needed for a leadership and presidential victory.)

Two bills increasing the pay of federal employees, including congressmen, came to the House floor in 1964. The first version lost early in the session by a roll call vote of 222 to 184. After several months of work on recalcitrant Democrats, the leaders again brought it to the floor in June. This time it passed, 243 to 157. Before the Speaker had scheduled it the second time, he personally checked with enough members to know that it would win. Only then did he authorize the Majority Leader to announce that the bill would come to the floor in less than forty-eight hours.[5]

In dealing with the Appalachia bill in 1964, the Democratic leaders had a long fight—first with the Public Works Committee and then with the Rules Committee—before being able to schedule it for floor action. Continuing absences during September forced postponement, until finally Congress adjourned without action.[6] Early in the more heavily Democratic Eighty-ninth Congress, the administration won an easy victory despite the loss of fifty-six Democrats, a number that in 1964 would probably have defeated the bill.

Taking Official Party Positions

A technique available to the leaders of both parties is to state and disseminate official party positions on proposed legislation. Both information and some pressure accompany the dissemination.

Since 1962, the Democratic leaders customarily write all their members

---

5 *Washington Post,* June 14, 1964.

6 The *Wall Street Journal,* September 3, 1964, indicates that the Appalachia bill was scheduled for floor action on Wednesday, September 2, but the number of Democratic absences on the preceding day forced the Speaker to postpone the bill. Had it come up, it is likely that the leadership and the President would have suffered a stinging defeat at the start of a national election campaign.

explaining the bill in question and asking for a certain kind of vote. For example, on the 1963 tax reduction bill, the Speaker, Majority Leader, Whip, and chairman of the Ways and Means Committee sent a short letter and digest of the bill to all Democrats twelve days before floor action was scheduled. They said simply, "The passage of this bill is essential to our national well-being. A motion to recommit, which would be highly destructive of the bill, will be made. We urge that you be present for the debate, and that you vote to defeat the motion to recommit and for final passage of the bill."

The minority pattern in the Eighty-eighth Congress was for the Policy Committee to take a position and then communicate it to various regional and class groupings of Republicans through their representatives on the committee. Sometimes John Byrnes, chairman of the Policy Committee, would himself write all Republicans. In the Eighty-ninth Congress, party positions were taken either in the conference or simply in a letter from the Minority Leader after consultation with members on a standing committee.

Phone Calls and Personal Contacts

The leaders of both parties rely heavily on telephone and personal contacts (often on the floor) in trying to persuade members to act in a certain way. Since 1962, for example, the Democratic leaders meet a week or two before an important vote to decide which members should be contacted and by whom. On the basis of these discussions, the Speaker, Majority Leader, Whip, and committee chairman involved each take a list of members to contact.

Arranging Speakers for the Floor

It is often important who speaks for or against a bill, not so much for what he says as for who he is. The leaders of both parties are eager to get their most respected members to speak for their position. This is particularly true of members who often disagree with the leaders. Thus, Democratic leaders often seek speeches from southern conservatives, while Republican leaders seek speeches from northeastern liberals.

In the fight to defeat the Republican recommittal motion on the 1963 tax bill, the Democratic leaders were able to persuade George Mahon, then second-ranking on the Appropriations Committee and a highly respected Texan with a moderately conservative voting record, to speak against the Republican motion. They also persuaded Omar Burleson, another conservative Texan of great seniority and reputation, to speak against the motion and for the bill. That Mahon and Burleson spoke and made effective arguments seems to have convinced a sufficient number of wavering Democrats to defeat the recommittal motion.

Persuading disliked members not to speak on their side is also something that the leadership must do. During the debate on the cotton bill in December 1963, the Speaker told two ranking southern Democrats on the Agriculture Committee not to speak for the bill because they would both lose votes. When another unpopular southerner did speak for it, the observation of one liberal westerner was, "There's another nail in the coffin."

Managing the Voting Pattern[7]

There are three major aspects to leadership management of the voting pattern on the House floor. First, the leaders of both parties can try to make sure that key men vote the right way. This is obviously important on roll calls, where certain respected figures provide voting cues for a number of other members. It can also be true on teller votes, during which members on each side line up in the center aisle of the House and are counted by tellers appointed by the chairman of the Committee of the Whole. For example, during the House debate on the student loan provisions of the health professions assistance bill in 1963, a Republican offered an amendment that would have made segregated programs ineligible for funds. Had it passed, enough southerners would probably have voted against the bill on final passage (a roll call visible to their constituents) to defeat it. Yet it was difficult for northern supporters of the bill who came from pro-civil rights districts to vote against the anti-segregation amendment. Thus when the teller vote on the amendment was held, the Democratic leaders persuaded four of their five Negro members to vote against it, graphic proof to liberal Democrats that the amendment could be attacked as a sham.

Second, the leaders of both parties can ask probable opponents to be

[7] The analysis in this section is based in part on material found in Lewis A. Froman, Jr., and Randall B. Ripley, "Conditions for Party Leadership: The Case of the House Democrats," *American Political Science Review,* 59 (March 1965), 59–61.

There are four types of voting in the House: (1) roll calls, in which each member votes individually and publicly when his name is called by the clerk; (2) teller votes, in which those voting aye first pass up the center aisle of the House, followed by those voting nay, and are counted by members appointed as tellers by the chair; (3) divisions, in which those voting aye, followed by those voting nay, stand and are counted by the chair; and (4) voice votes.

Pairs are used to record the position of absent members on a roll call. A regular legislative pair is an agreement to neutralize the votes of one absent member on each side of a question. A live pair results in a net gain of one vote for one side or the other because a member actually present is paired with an absent member. There are also "general pairs," which have no legislative value in that no position is announced for either of the absent members.

absent when a vote is cast. Rarely will more than two or three members of either party be persuaded to miss a final roll call deliberately. More were persuaded, however, on the second bill raising federal pay in 1964. An entire committee, made up largely of opponents, was convinced by the Democratic leaders to take a field trip the day of the vote. It is normal for five or more members of both parties to be missing by request on roll calls on recommittal motions and for ten or more to absent themselves during teller votes.

Third, the leaders have some leeway in manipulating the type of vote that is used on a particular matter. The minority is limited largely to supplying the people necessary to force a roll call vote (one-fifth of those present must concur in such a demand), or a teller vote (44 in the House and 20 in the Committee of the Whole must concur), instead of a voice vote. In addition to this, because of their control of the schedule, the majority leaders can adjourn the House if a series of teller votes looks as if it will result in too many unwanted amendments, postpone a roll call from one day to another, or force the House to stay in session and hold a roll call on a particular day rather than waiting until the next day.

The leaders of both parties generally have greater control over the behavior of their members on votes that have relatively low visibility to the voting public, the press, the political leaders at home, and other members of the House. Roll call voting on final passage of measures is the most visible. Roll calls on recommittal motions, which send a bill back to a standing committee, often with instructions to make specific changes and report the bill back to the floor, are somewhat less visible, especially if the motions do not include specific instructions, because the implications of such votes are more obscure to the electorate. Roll calls on specific amendments and procedural questions are even less visible.

Division and voice voting are often simply party votes because they happen so quickly, and because few members know the nature of the choice being made. As the members scurry from the cloak-rooms, many Democrats only want to know the position taken by the floor manager (usually the committee or subcommittee chairman) ; Republicans ask for the position of their contingent on the committee.

Teller voting, because it takes longer (and it is therefore easier to identify members as they line up to vote), and because members are notified by bells located in their offices and throughout the Capitol and House Office Buildings, is subject to more strenuous efforts by the leaders to keep members in tow. More members are likely to vote on teller votes than on divisions or voice votes, and a large number of voice and division votes are reversed because the leaders have time to call members to the floor. These exertions are rewarded by a substantial amount of party unity on most teller votes even by members who, if forced to a roll call, would vote against the leaders. . . .

Meeting Demands from Within the Party

Sometimes the members of a party will make demands the leaders feel they must accept. The skill in using this technique comes when accession can be transformed, at least partially, into manipulation. Early in 1964, for example, after the House had defeated the first bill raising federal employees' pay (including the pay of members of Congress), there was much disagreement about what the second bill should contain. California Democrats caucused three times and each time decided that they would demand that the full $10,000 increase for members be retained as the price for their support of the bill. The leaders knew that if the $10,000 provision were left unchanged, the bill would almost surely be defeated again. About a week before floor action, the leaders let it be known that floor consideration would be postponed unless the California Democrats (and some other liberals) would support a $7,500 raise for members. The President and the leaders asked Democratic members of the Senate Post Office and Civil Service Committee to promise to restore the $10,000 and stand by that position in conference. Thus the lure of possible success in conference was held out to liberal Democrats in exchange for their support, and the House passed the bill.[8]

In 1965 the administration farm bill called for an additional subsidy for wheat that would be financed by a tax on millers and bakers. The latter immediately made clear that they would pass the cost of the tax on to the consumer by raising the price of bread. This led numerous urban and suburban Democrats, usually staunchly loyal to the leaders, to protest forcefully to the Speaker. The Speaker in turn informed the White House and Department of Agriculture that the provision would have to be dropped or Democratic votes would defeat the bill; the administration capitulated.[9]

The overthrow of Minority Leader Halleck in 1965 came in part because the members felt that he had not acceded to enough of their legislative requests. Republicans on standing committee delegations striving to develop alternatives to Democratic proposals felt that he had not been willing to listen to them. For example, when Widnall sought to have the Republican Policy Committee resist its natural urge to oppose the mass transit bill because a number of Republicans favored it, the committee refused and asked for Republican unity in opposing the bill. When Republicans on the Education and Labor Committee sought to develop alternative education

---

[8] See the *Washington Post,* June 14, 1964, for the best story covering some of these events.

[9] See the *Washington Post,* August 17 and 18, 1965.

bills, they found Halleck unsympathetic. Younger members who had experienced this kind of reaction were among the leaders of the anti-Halleck group.

Majority Leaders in Action:
Four Cases in the Eighty-eighth Congress[10]

The House Raises the Debt Limit, May 1963

In 1963, the House raised or extended the limit on the national debt three different times. The hardest and closest fight occurred in May, over a bill raising the limit in two stages—from $305 billion to $307 billion for about a month, and then to $309 billion for two more months. The Ways and Means Committee took over eight weeks to act on the Secretary of the Treasury's request. A straight party vote in the committee on May 2 favored the bill; the report was made to the House on Monday, May 6.

The leaders knew from the outset that this would be a close fight. Thus they immediately asked the Whip to take a poll to find whether Democratic members would favor the bill. An attendance check was also started to ascertain who would be in Washington and able to vote on Wednesday, May 15, and Thursday, May 16. The Speaker waited for the results of this before deciding definitely that the bill should be brought to the floor May 15.

Results of the poll on the question of the bill itself were given to the Speaker as they were recorded. On Tuesday, May 7, the Speaker telephoned seven Democrats reported as opposed or doubtful about the bill, persuading them to give commitments that they would vote for it. On the same Tuesday, the whip organization distributed to all Democrats a single sheet statement about the importance of raising the debt limit and the consequences of not raising it. This statement had been prepared by the Treasury but carried no identifying label.

The two principal lobbyists for the Treasury believed—as did Chairman Wilbur Mills of Ways and Means—that Minority Leader Halleck did not really want to defeat the bill, but only wanted to give the Democrats a scare. The rest of the leadership, however, felt that Halleck was intent on victory and proceeded on that assumption. The Treasury representatives also worked hard on Democratic members, starting with a list of forty-seven suggested by the Whip's office on May 6.

10 For an excellent description of the passage of a bill in the Eighty-seventh Congress that also illustrates the leaders of both parties using a number of techniques, see Don F. Hadwiger and Ross B. Talbot, *Pressures and Protests* (San Francisco: Chandler Publishing Co., 1965), pp. 193–209, 233.

Chairman Mills played an active role as part of the leadership. On Wednesday, May 8, he sent all Democrats a letter from Secretary of the Treasury Douglas Dillon explaining the difficulties that might be posed if the bill failed. Mills also asked the Democratic members of Ways and Means to talk to all members they represented on the Committee on Committees and make a personal appeal for support of the bill. Dillon was successful in getting Robert Anderson, the last Secretary of the Treasury in the Eisenhower administration, to call Halleck and ask him not to create difficulties for Dillon by trying to defeat the bill. Anderson also called John Byrnes, ranking Republican on Ways and Means and chairman of the Policy Committee. These appeals made no apparent difference to Halleck or Byrnes, however.

On Friday, May 10, McCormack, Albert, John Moss (the deputy whip), and Mills met with Lawrence O'Brien, chief of White House congressional liaison, three O'Brien assistants, the administrative assistant to the Whip, and the Assistant Secretary of the Treasury for congressional liaison. Mills reviewed a list of all Democrats and announced their reported position on the bill. When a member was announced as doubtful or against the bill, the Speaker or Majority Leader called him immediately and urged him to support it. Likewise, when a member favoring the bill was reported as planning to be absent, the Speaker called him and asked him to stay. One member who was asked to cancel a trip abroad (which he did) used the occasion to arrange an appointment with O'Brien for himself and another Democrat to talk about a proposed veterans hospital consolidation in their districts.

Mills repeated his belief that Halleck really would not defeat the bill if the Republican recommittal motion failed. He said he would try to get the Parliamentarian to arrange a meeting between himself and Halleck to see if an agreement could be reached whereby enough Republicans would vote for final passage to guarantee success if the Republican motion was defeated. Mills also said he had discussed the bill with some Republicans who favored a tax cut and had made it clear to them that if the debt limit bill was defeated, there would be no tax cut bill.

The meeting ended with the general feeling that the vote on recommittal would be no particular problem. Conservative southern Democrats could vote against that motion because it also included a debt limit increase, although smaller than the administration measure. The consensus was that the vote on final passage would be extremely close, with the Democrats probably having enough votes to win by two or three even if no Republicans voted for the bill. Mills said that he needed an accurate head count the afternoon before the bill came to the floor so that it could be delayed if necessary.

On Monday, May 13, after the first quorum call, the whip organization called the offices of favorable members not answering the call to make sure they would be back by Wednesday. The House leaders, Mills, the Treasury, and the White House continued to contact the few remaining Democrats whose votes were in doubt. The final whip poll (completed by the morning of Tuesday, May 14) showed 203 Democrats present and voting aye, thirty-five Democrats present and voting nay, ten who would be absent, and eight whose position still could not be clearly ascertained. These results made the chances of success look shaky and so the leaders (principally the Speaker) proceeded to obtain commitments from thirteen Democrats opposed to the bill that they would vote for it if their votes were needed for victory. Thus the leaders felt that they could count on about 215 Democrats if they absolutely needed them, which would be enough to win without Republican help. Copies of a list of the thirteen pocket votes were distributed to McCormack, Albert, Boggs, Moss, and Mills, so that they could quickly spot these men on the floor. Last minute efforts on Wednesday were made to get the maximum attendance on the floor. Two members attended in wheel chairs.

All the preparations paid off. After the Republican recommittal motion had been defeated 222 to 195, the House passed the administration bill 213 to 204, with a lone Republican joining 212 Democrats. Only thirty-two Democrats defected. Three of the pocket votes were used, probably at the initiative of the member himself, rather than because of a specific request of the leaders.

In this single fight, then, the leaders used most of the techniques available to them. Mills was successful in producing Democratic unity in the committee; the schedule was timed to the benefit of the party position; letters and explanatory material were sent to all Democrats; there were numerous phone and personal contacts; and an effort (although abortive) was made to obtain some Republican votes. . . .

Trading in the House:
Food Stamps for Wheat-Cotton, April 1964[11]

In June 1963, the Agriculture Committee held hearings on a bill to establish a food stamp program to guarantee the needy an adequate diet. Democratic Congresswoman Leonor Sullivan of Missouri had been sponsoring similar bills for almost a decade. The committee could not agree on a number of specific points and reached no agreement until early the fol-

[11] For a fuller version of this story see Randall B. Ripley, "Bargaining in the House: The Food Stamp Act of 1964" (unpublished manuscript prepared for a Brookings Institution project).

lowing February when it tabled the bill eighteen to seventeen, with the aid of five defecting southern Democrats. The food stamp bill appeared to be dead.

Two developments occurred, however, that helped save the bill. First, liberals on the Rules Committee held up a tobacco bill that was supported by the anti-food stamp southerners on the Agriculture Committee. The liberals demanded a favorable report on the food stamp bill as the price for releasing the tobacco bill. The Agriculture Committee agreed to this demand on March 4.

Second, on March 6, the Senate added a wheat program to a cotton measure passed by the House the previous December, and the amended bill was returned to the House, where it almost immediately became linked to the food stamp bill. Both the administration and the Democratic members of the Agriculture Committee had a large stake in favorable House action on the wheat-cotton bill, but it was evident that there was a sizable number of potential nay votes among urban Democrats. These votes, with a solid Republican front against the bill, could defeat it.

Kenneth Birkhead, head of congressional liaison in the Agriculture Department, and the House Democratic leaders conceived the necessity of tying the wheat-cotton bill to some bill that would appeal to urban Democrats. They wanted to arrange a trade.

Until the House on March 12 defeated a pay raise for government employees, there had been talk that the pay raise and wheat-cotton might be linked, but after farm votes helped kill the pay raise, the urban Democratic anger grew. Gradually, during March, it became clear that the trade would involve the food stamp bill and the wheat-cotton bill. No formal announcement was made, nor was any formal meeting held to reach agreement between leaders of urban and rural blocs. Instead—typical of the operations of the House—the psychological climate had become favorable. The more individual members and the press discussed a possible trade of rural votes on food stamps for urban votes on wheat-cotton, the more firmly the idea took hold in the minds of the members. The trade was based on shared perceptions of a legislative situation, bolstered by individual lobbying efforts relying on the trade as a persuasive point.

During the weeks before Easter vacation, it became evident that the wheat-cotton bill was in much more danger of losing than was the food stamp bill. Thus most of the lobbying activity on the part of the executive and Democratic House leaders was aimed at passing wheat-cotton. The Speaker obtained pocket votes from nine northeastern Democrats as insurance.

The floor debate on April 7 and 8 was heated. All knew that the wheat-cotton bill was scheduled to follow the final action on food stamps, and there

were many references to the upcoming—and more costly and controversial
—legislation. The leaders asked for whip polls on both bills. They showed
that 212 Democrats would vote for the food stamp bill, enough to win even
without Republican help if there was the usual number of absentees. On
the other hand, only 197 Democrats were likely to vote aye on the wheat-
cotton bill—not enough if Republican lines held.

The House finished general debate on the food stamp bill and read the
first section for amendment on Tuesday, April 7. On Wednesday, April 8,
the House met an hour earlier than usual and resumed the amending process.
During this process, the Republicans raised a civil rights question in an
attempt to woo southern Democrats away from the program. They stressed
that the pilot programs had, with a few exceptions, not been located in the
South, and that Title VI of the pending civil rights bill would prevent much
of the region from benefitting from the program.

Nevertheless, the Democratic ranks held during teller votes, and five
Republican amendments objectionable to the leaders were defeated, includ-
ing an amendment requiring matching state funds that the Agriculture
Committee had adopted over the protests of its chairman.

In the midst of the amending process, the House recessed for two hours
to pay respects to the late General Douglas MacArthur, whose body lay in
state in the rotunda.

Chairman Cooley of the Agriculture Committee moved to cut off debate
at six o'clock P.M. and the House passed this motion. The Committee of the
Whole rose; the Speaker resumed the chair and prepared to order a final
roll call. A Republican demanded an engrossed copy of the bill. The
Democrats were prepared for this possibility, and the printer was ready to
accomplish the task within a few hours. The Speaker then let debate open
on the rule for the wheat-cotton bill. Within a few minutes, liberal
Democrats, including Mrs. Sullivan, realized that this might mean that the
final vote on wheat-cotton would come before the final vote on food stamps.
She quickly let the Speaker know that this would be unacceptable because
the southerners, after voting aye on wheat-cotton, might either leave the
chamber or vote nay on food stamps. Thus the Speaker interrupted the
debate and declared a recess, acting under the agreement that had allowed
the earlier recess to honor MacArthur.

The House reconvened at 9:05 P.M. and the Republicans protested
vigorously that the recess agreement had been used to give the Speaker an
unforeseen power. They offered a motion to adjourn and demanded a roll
call, on which the motion was defeated. The minority then exercised its right
of offering a recommittal motion, which provided that the amendment on
state matching be restored to the bill. This was defeated 195 to 223. The
House then passed the food stamp bill by a vote of 229 to 189.

To complete the day, an hour-long debate on the wheat-cotton bill was held, and the House passed it 211 to 203 before adjourning at 12:44 A.M.

An analysis of the last three roll calls indicates the degree of success of the trade of food stamps for wheat-cotton among Democrats. Twelve Democrats were absent for all three votes. Six more were absent for one or more of the three roll calls, but supported the administration when they voted. One hundred eighty Democrats supported the administration on all three roll calls and might best be labeled as "reliable traders." Twenty-six members were "hard-line liberals," voting with the administration twice on the food stamp bill and against the wheat-cotton bill. Twelve members were "hard-line conservatives," voting against the food stamp bill twice and for the wheat-cotton bill. Eight members were "half-hearted traders," voting with the administration on one food stamp roll call and against it on the other and for the wheat-cotton bill. Eight Democrats were against both programs on all three roll calls.

The trade was 82 percent successful in that only the hard-line liberals, hard-line conservatives, and half-hearted traders explicitly violated the terms of the bargain. Even if only the reliable traders are counted, the trade was 71 percent successful.

In this case the House leaders were successful partly because of the techniques they used: they managed the voting sequence and schedule so as to make the trade most effective; they made numerous phone and personal contacts; they helped channel demands from both the urban and rural segments of the party in such a way that all demands could be met and the administration could be satisfied at the same time.

The House Supports the Poverty Bill,
August 1964

During the spring of 1964, a subcommittee of the Committee on Education and Labor held hearings on the proposed antipoverty program. From the outset, the Democrats made clear that they wanted the entire credit for this program in an election year. The Republicans did not know exactly how to react. Not until late April did they put forth their own alternative, which generated unanimous Democratic opposition and only partial Republican support. But at least they were sure they wanted to do nothing to help President Johnson and the Democratic leadership in the House. The Democrats sought unity by having a southerner, Phil Landrum of Georgia, steer the bill through the committee and on the floor.[12]

At the end of the subcommittee hearings, Democrats on the full Education

[12] See the *Baltimore Sun,* April 20, 1964, for a good account of how some parts of this political fight developed.

and Labor Committee caucused for several weeks to discuss a number of changes and reach a unified position. By mid-May the committee was ready to begin executive sessions on the bill. After resolving a number of controversial issues—including race and church-state relations—the committee on May 26 voted to report the bill by a straight party-line vote.

The bill went to the Rules Committee and the leadership expected swift action. On June 2, Carl Albert and Hale Boggs sent a letter to all Democrats urging them to support the bill. The Rules Committee, however, did not take up the bill until mid-June, and then Chairman Howard Smith, an opponent, indicated that he thought Republicans should have many witnesses testify at hearings. Finally, on July 28, by an eight to seven vote, Rules cleared the measure.

Floor debate began on Wednesday, August 5. A whip poll early in the summer showed that the vote would be very close, with a number of southern Democratic defections. Only minimal help could be expected from the Republicans.

On the morning of August 6, Sargent Shriver, the man who would head the poverty program if it came into being, had breakfast with three representatives from North Carolina to persuade them of its merits and solicit their votes. The North Carolinians asked him if Adam Yarmolinsky, a well-known liberal Democrat and official in the Defense Department, would be in the program and Shriver, in a moment of candor, said that Yarmolinsky would, indeed, be appointed to an important post. The North Carolinians reacted adversely. They thought Yarmolinsky radical and alerted the other members of their delegation. That afternoon, at a large meeting in the Speaker's office, the dean of the North Carolina delegation attacked Yarmolinsky vigorously and demanded a promise that he would not be in the program as the price for their support of the bill. Chairman Adam Clayton Powell of the committee and floor manager Landrum agreed. The speaker and Shriver called the White House and got the needed guarantee from the President, and the North Carolinians then filed in to hear Shriver repeat the promise.[13]

After this affair, the whip poll on the morning before the day of the vote showed 200 Democrats in favor, five absent, and four doubtful. The 200, when increased by expected help from Republicans representing poverty-stricken areas, would be enough to pass the bill. To help insure Republican support, the administration encouraged a former Eisenhower Secretary of Health, Education and Welfare, Marion Folsom, to endorse the bill in telegrams to nine Republicans, including Halleck.

[13] On the sacrifice of Yarmolinsky see Rowland Evans and Robert Novak, "The Yarmolinsky Affair," *Esquire,* February 1965; and the story by Mary McGrory in the *Evening Star* (Washington), August 12, 1964.

The final vote came on Saturday, August 8, and the House passed the bill 226 to 185. Seven of the nine North Carolina Democrats voted for it. Twenty-two Republicans joined 204 Democrats in supporting the bill.

In this case the key technique had been the development of committee unanimity among Democrats. The leaders miscalculated by assuming that capitulation to the North Carolina demand was essential to victory, but their use of other techniques was more skillful and helped produce the favorable outcome.

V

Power in Congress

All of this book, of course, concerns the exercise of power in Congress, which is affected by elections, the committee system, lobbyists, and so on. But this section draws together analyses of aspects of power in Congress unexplored elsewhere in this book—in particular, minority rule and reforms designed to make Congress more responsive to majorities.

The first selection, by Howard E. Shuman, deals with the intricate procedural rules of the Senate. The rules are a crucial aspect of policy-making, yet are so complicated and detailed that describing them fully would exhaust the patience of anyone but the most dedicated specialist. Shuman illustrates their importance by examining a few Senate procedures and a few instances of their consequences. In so doing, he shows how these rules affected the outcome of political struggles; in this case, how, fifteen years ago, champions of civil rights legislation were handicapped not only by the rules, but by their opponents' superior parliamentary skill.

Shuman wrote a gloomy chronicle of futility and defeat for civil rights bills. In the dozen years after his article Congress passed civil rights legislation far beyond the fondest dreams of the liberals who struggled so ineffectually in the mid-1950s. But along with the passage of these measures, these same years have seen an equally impressive series of frustrations for attempts to reform the procedural issue most important to Shuman—the filibuster. My article on this topic brings the history of unlimited debate up to the end of the 1960s and uses the filibuster as a vehicle to examine several important themes in congressional politics.

This article demonstrates that a majority of senators have consistently preferred to maintain the principle of minority rule embodied in the filibuster. The recent history of attempts to reform the filibuster rule also illustrates how remarkably indifferent presidents have been to this presumed impediment to their influence over Congress. Finally, the unhappy experiences of reformers in this area show that often the Senate folkways described in Chapter 6 by Donald R. Matthews are not always applied equally to all senators.

An important theme running through many discussions of congressional shortcomings is the presumably unfair power to frustrate the majority wielded by a determined minority or a single individual, be they party leaders or (more recently) a single committee chairman. In the third selection Charles O. Jones examines two of the most interesting and significant examples of such arbitrary individual power, the legendary Speaker Joseph Cannon, whose heyday was the first decade of the century, and the equally celebrated "Judge" Smith, whose power was based both on his chairmanship of the Rules Committee and his position as the leader of the southern Democratic bloc in the House of Representatives. Both of these men earned the denunciations of liberals and of reformers for the way they conducted themselves—in particular, for the way they balked the aspirations and proposals of liberal congressmen. Both Speaker Cannon and Judge Smith eventually found their power severely limited, however, and this is the point of Jones' article: while the House of Representatives, through a combination of necessity, habit, and rules, has given its leaders great power, there are limits within which those powers can be exercised. Thus both Smith and Cannon found, to their grief, that while they could get away with a good deal, they could not get away with anything.

Smith and Cannon are by no means exceptions, although they are perhaps the most conspicuous and spectacular examples of mighty congressional leaders brought to grief by their own excesses. The history of Congress records a number of committee chairmen, for instance, who have been too enthusiastic, or too imprudent, in the ways they used their undenied power. The point of such cases is important: congressmen are willing to tolerate a certain amount of arbitrary exercise of influence, but they do not, for the reasons spelled out by Jones, find it possible to tolerate repeated excesses. Here, as in so many other instances throughout this book, the importance of a good tactical sense and of an ability to develop and maintain informal alliances is seen to be an important aspect of congressional influence.

14

HOWARD E. SHUMAN

Senate Rules and the Civil Rights Bill: A Case Study

The rules of the Senate of the United States are only 40 in number and comprise only 49 of the 832 pages of the *Senate Manual*. Yet, when literally invoked they can bring Senate business to a standstill. They are most often ignored or circumvented by unanimous consent in order that the Senate may operate conveniently as a deliberative and parliamentary body. To pass legislation when they are invoked is a formidable enterprise.

Just as the law is said to be no better than the procedures by which it is carried out, so the substance of legislation is shaped and modified by the procedures that may be required under the Senate rules, or by the mere threat to invoke those procedures, for they are compelling. The procedures preceding and surrounding the passage of the first civil rights bill in over 80 years illumine and illustrate the effect of the rules on the substance of legislation as have few other legislative controversies in recent years.

The Senate rules are the product of sectionalism. They were designed to prevent action unacceptable to a sectional minority. Among the more important specific rules with this design are: sections 2 and 3 of Rule XXII—the filibuster rule; section 1 of Rule XXII, which makes a tabling motion not debatable and which, therefore, acts as a "negative" form of majority cloture for, if successful, it can stop talk and kill a bill

Reprinted from *American Political Science Review*, 51 (December 1957), 955–75, by permission of the author and publisher. Mr. Shuman is administrative assistant to Senator William Proxmire and during the events described in this article was legislative assistant to Senator Paul H. Douglas.

or amendment without a vote on the merits;[1] Rule XXVI, which requires that all reports and motions to discharge a committee of a bill must lie over one legislative day—in practice this can mean several weeks if the Senate recesses from day to day rather than adjourns; Rule XL which requires one (legislative) day's notice to suspend the rules; Rule VII, which requires that a petition to discharge a committee be filed in the so-called morning hour, except by unanimous consent; and the same Rule VII which when literally followed requires the reading of the Journal in full, the presentation of messages from the President and reports and communications from executive departments, and numerous other time-consuming procedures in the morning hour, and so may preclude the opportunity for discharge petitions to be reached, for at the close of that hour the Senate must proceed to the unfinished or pending business; and two unwritten rules, first, of seniority, and second, the rule of recognition under which the chair recognizes either the Majority or Minority Leader as against other Senators who are seeking recognition. This can prevent a Senator from making a timely motion or point of order to which the leadership is opposed and so helps give the leadership command of the parliamentary situation.

How these rules affected the course of the civil rights debate and the strategy of both sides in the 1956 and 1957 sessions is now to be shown.

I. The Abortive Civil Rights Bill of 1956

With only a few days of the 84th Congress remaining in July, 1956, the House of Representatives, by a margin of 279 to 126, passed H.R. 627, a bill substantially the same as H.R. 6127 of the 85th Congress, part of which is now the law of the land. A small band composed of Senators Hennings, Douglas, and Lehman and finally supported by Senators Langer, Ives, and Bender, attempted to gain Senate action on the bill when it came from the House. This move was made notwithstanding the determined opposition of both Majority and Minority Leaders which, in the end, proved crushing.

Senator Douglas was guarding the Senate floor as the House passed the bill, and left his seat to go to the House chamber to escort H.R. 627 through the long corridor from the Speaker's to the Vice President's desk. As he was walking to the House he was passed, unknowing, by a messenger carrying the bill to the Senate. With Senator Douglas outside the Senate chamber and with Senator Hill of Alabama in the chair, the bill, with jet-age speed, was read a first and second time and referred to the Senate Judiciary Committee where its Senate counterparts had languished for two years.

[1] The Senate has no similar form of "majority" cloture which could end debate and bring a vote on the substance of a bill or an amendment.

This action took place by unanimous consent and so by-passed the specific provisions of Rule XIV, which require three readings of a bill prior to passage, "Which [readings] shall be on three different days," but state that bills from the House of Representatives "...shall be read once, and may be read twice, on the same day, if not objected to, for reference...."

An attempt was then made under Rule XXVI, section 2, to file a petition to discharge the Judiciary Committee from the further consideration of H.R. 627. Except by unanimous consent the petition must be introduced in the morning hour.

On the same calendar day the bill came from the House a unanimous consent request to file the petition was blocked by a motion of the Majority Leader to recess overnight. At the beginning of the next day's session, in what would ordinarily have been the morning hour, the Senator from Georgia, Mr. George, ruled that the petition could not be filed, except by unanimous consent, for the Senate had recessed the previous evening and, in fact, had not adjourned since the evening of July 13, *i.e.,* 10 days previously. Although the date was then July 24, the legislative day was July 16, and thus technically there was no morning hour for the routine business of filing bills, reports, petitions, etc. Individual Senators then objected to further unanimous consent requests to file the petition. The Senate recessed that day and did not adjourn overnight until July 26, the evening before adjournment *sine die.* In the meantime a motion by Senator Douglas to adjourn for five minutes, in order to bring a new legislative day and a morning hour, was defeated by the crushing vote of 76 to 6.

In the morning hour on the last day of the session, the discharge petition was finally filed. But a discharge petition, under section 2 of Rule XXVI, must lie over one further "legislative" day. If consideration of the petition is not reached or is not concluded in the morning hour or before 2 o'clock on the next "legislative" day, it goes to the calendar. Then the motion to proceed to its consideration and the motion on passage of the petition are both subject to unlimited debate, unless cloture is applied to each. Such action, even if successful, would only result in placing the bill itself on the calendar, where it in turn must lie for another "legislative" day. The motion to proceed to its consideration and the motion on final passage are also both subject to unlimited debate, unless cloture is applied. Thus the filing of the petition came too late to bring action in the 84th Congress. Even if commenced at the beginning of a session, and even if 64 votes were obtainable for cloture on each of the four occasions when they are potentially necessary, the process of discharging a committee can be drawn out over several weeks, and even months, if the rules of the Senate are literally invoked.

Although this attempt was abortive the experience was useful to the civil rights proponents in 1957. It brought a familiarity with the rules of the

Senate which can only be gained from step-by-step proceedings under them; from it they concluded that action must begin very early in the session if it were to be successful; they saw that the route of discharging a committee meant meeting countless roadblocks, which could only be stormed and surmounted by determined efforts and with overwhelming bi-partisan support; and they concluded that a fight to change Rule XXII was essential because the inadequacy of cloture had either killed previous civil rights bills or brought their death by the mere threat of a filibuster.[2]

II. The Fight to Change Rule XXII

The effort to change Rule XXII was made at the opening of the 85th Congress in January 1957. In the past Rule XXII has been the gravedigger in the Senate graveyard for civil rights bills. Section 2 of Rule XXII requires 64 affirmative votes to limit debate and section 3 provides that on a motion to proceed to the consideration of a change in the rules there can be no limit on debate of any kind. The rules of the Senate have carried over from Congress to Congress and changes in them have been made only after a unanimous consent agreement has been reached narrowly limiting the language and amendments which could come before the Senate.

Because of section 3, the only chance of success seemed to lie in a move at the beginning of a Congress that the Senate proceed to adopt new rules, relying on Article I, Section 5 of the Constitution, which provides that "...each House may determine the rules of its proceedings." Such a motion was made in 1953 and was defeated by a vote of 70 to 21. Its opponents argued then that a civil rights bill would be passed, and that the rules should be changed only by ordinary processes of piecemeal amendment.

In 1957 the vote to table the motion to proceed to the consideration of new rules was carried, 55 to 38. Three absentees, Senators Neely and Wiley, and Javits, who had not yet taken his seat, opposed tabling and so brought to 41 the total who favored adopting new rules. Thus a shift of seven votes, plus a Vice President's favorable vote or ruling, was all that was now required to change Rule XXII. This was a major gain over 1953, for these 41 votes were obtained over the concerted objections of the leadership of both parties.

The size of the vote and its near success caught Southern Senators on the horns of a dilemma. They knew that any actual and organized use of the filibuster would ultimately bring an end to Rule XXII, and they also knew

---

[2] Since 1917, or for 40 years, cloture has been successful on only four of twenty-two attempts and never on a civil rights bill. Sixty-four votes have been forthcoming only three times, all in the period 1917 to 1927. Thus, no cloture motion has successfully prevailed in the last 30 years.

that if they did not use the filibuster Congress would most likely pass a civil rights bill. The fight to change Rule XXII thereby produced a climate in which not only a meaningful bill could pass but, it can be persuasively argued, a bill much stronger than that which was actually passed. The arguments and the parliamentary strategy involved in the Rule XXII fight were therefore crucial.

The opponents of the change relied basically on a single argument, namely, that the Senate was a continuing body, and as two-thirds of its members carry over from Congress to Congress, its rules should therefore also carry over from Congress to Congress as they have in the past.

The proponents argued that whatever the Senate had done in the past it had explicit constitutional power to adopt its rules at the beginning of a new Congress. Unlike their course in 1953, when the attempt to adopt new rules was hastily devised, the proponents did not meet the continuing body argument head on, but argued instead that it was immaterial whether the Senate was a continuing body or not. Acceptance of the continuing body argument did not deny to a majority of the Senate the right to adopt its own rules. Proponents also argued that proceedings on all bills and resolutions, as well as on treaties, begin again in a new Congress; that the Senate is newly organized and new committees are appointed; and that the newly elected one-third, even though only one-third, could alter the party alignment and thus provide a new majority and a new mandate which it had the right to carry out.

A second argument by the opponents, less used but probably more telling than the first, was that until the adoption of new rules the Senate would be in a parliamentary "jungle." Senator Russell combined with this argument a threat to proceed to rewrite each of the 40 rules of the Senate.

In rejoinder the proponents argued that the House of Representatives entered and left the parliamentary "jungle" in a very few minutes at each new Congress. They proposed that until the rules were adopted the Senate should proceed under general parliamentary rules including the motion for the previous question under which debate could be shut off by a simple majority. The proponents also relied on the precedents of the Senate to support the contention that majority cloture could be applied, for it was shown that the previous question rule was a part of the Senate rules from 1789 to 1806 and was used to bring debate to a close on several occasions.

The potential parliamentary moves were extremely involved, but basically the proponents sought to gain a ruling from the Vice President that their motion to proceed to the immediate consideration of the adoption of new rules was in order. This was their strongest position but, in the end, it was not gained.

It was their strongest position for a variety of reasons. To succeed, strong bi-partisan support was needed. The Democratic Party, by its nature, was split on the issue and could not provide a majority of votes. This was true even though the Democrats have traditionally supplied more votes on procedural issues in support of civil rights, and occasionally more on substantive civil rights issues, than the Republicans. In 1953, of the 21 votes for the adoption of new rules, 15 were Democratic. Only 5 Republicans and Wayne Morse, then an independent, voted for the change. That year Vice President Barkley let it be known that he would rule such a motion in order. But he had no opportunity to do so for Senator Taft gained the floor and gave immediate and prearranged notice that he would move to table the motion and thus shut off argument after a short debate. In 1957 with a Republican Vice President and with Republican votes needed to win, it was obvious that the strongest position would follow from a favorable ruling by the Vice President, and on the vote to uphold or overturn his ruling. The Democrats could provide no more than half of their numbers in support of such a favorable ruling. But the Republicans could provide, potentially, almost all of their votes if the issue were one of supporting their own Vice President.

In 1953 it mattered little whether the motion to proceed to the adoption of new rules were tabled, or whether a point of order were made and a ruling sought, for there would still have been a limit to the number of potential Democratic votes on this issue in support of a Democratic Vice President. The Republicans were obviously under no political pressure to support the ruling of a Democratic Vice President who was to leave office in a very few days.

In 1957 it was a different matter. Whether the vote came on a motion to table or on an appeal from the ruling of the Chair was critically important. If a Republican Vice President now ruled favorably, he would no doubt be supported by more than a majority of his own party which, combined with the Democratic support, could provide the winning margin. The proponent group knew that they would make gains over 1953 however the Vice President ruled, but if he ruled for them there was an opportunity for spectacular gains and perhaps a victory.

The strategy was therefore devised that the mover of the motion to proceed to the consideration of new rules for the Senate should also couple with his motion a parliamentary request for a ruling from the Chair that the motion was in order. If this were not done a motion to table would no doubt be made, thereby cutting off debate and bringing an immediate vote. The proponents of a change in Rule XXII not only had more to gain from a ruling from the Chair but also felt that time for debate, which could educate and arouse public opinion, was necessary to the success of the effort. A steering committee representing those who favored adoption of the new rules therefore met with the Vice President to advise him of their proposed course of action. They did not seek nor did they receive the Vice President's opinion as to the merits of their proposal.

They were advised, however, that the Majority Leader had informed the Vice President that immediately following the motion to proceed to the consideration of new rules he would seek recognition for the purpose of tabling that motion. The Vice President then gave his opinion that under the precedents of the Senate a point of order could not be coupled with the substantive motion, and that under the unwritten rule of recognition he must recognize the Majority Leader as against some other Senator seeking the floor. This meant, of course, that once the motion was made the Majority Leader would be recognized to move to table that motion and thereby shut off debate before any other Senator, including the mover of the motion, could raise a point of order.

The unwritten rule of recognition thus brought the vote on the issue of Rule XXII on the least advantageous grounds for the proponents of new rules and an end to the filibuster. It was, however, very ironic that the proponents of unlimited debate should immediately move to shut off debate on the question of changing Senate Rule XXII which, in effect, provides for unlimited debate. Recognition of this anomaly led to a unanimous consent agreement which fixed a limited time for debate on the tabling motion. When the motion to proceed to the consideration of new rules was made, consequently, and was sent to the desk and read by the clerk, the Majority Leader sought and gained recognition. He proposed to table the motion which, but for the unanimous consent agreement, would have cut off debate immediately; as it was, debate was limited and the issue came to a vote as had been planned.

In the course of these events the Vice President gave it as his informal opinion, though not as a formal ruling, (1) that a majority of the Senate could adopt new rules at the beginning of a new Congress if it wished; (2) that Section 3 of Rule XXII was unconstitutional for it allowed a previous Senate to bind a majority of a future Senate;[3] and (3) that until such time as the Senate either adopted new rules or by some action, such as the tabling motion, acquiesced in the old rules, the Senate would proceed under its previous rules except for those which could deny a majority of the Senate the right or opportunity to adopt new ones, or, in short, sections 2 and 3 of Rule XXII.

Thus, the unwritten rule of recognition and the use of the tabling motion

---

[3] It has been asked why, if the Vice President believed section 3 was unconstitutional, Senators did not press the issue later in the session. The answer is that the Vice President's position was that it was unconstitutional to the extent that it bound one Senate by the actions of a previous Senate. However, if the new Senate agreed to be bound, *i.e.*, acquiesced in the old rules as it did when the tabling motion was successful, section 3 would remain in effect throughout the 85th Congress.

as a negative form of majority cloture, not available to the proponents of a motion, bill, or amendment, were decisive parliamentary weapons in the fight over Rule XXII and the filibuster.

Although the fight was lost it nevertheless brought several clear gains to the proponents of the civil rights bill and of majority rule, apart from the dilemma of the Southern Senators over their future use of the filibuster. First, rhetorically, it foreshadowed the end of the effectiveness of the argument that the Senate is a continuing body with necessarily continuing rules. The debate showed it to be irrelevant as well as circuitous to argue that the rules carry over because the Senate is a continuing body, and that the Senate is a continuing body because the rules carry over. Second, substantively, the episode brought clear bi-partisan gains over 1953; the Democratic vote increased from 15 to 21, and the Republican from 5 to 17. While the press was predicting an overwhelming defeat for the 1957 effort those close to the scene estimated quite accurately that approximately 40 would support the motion to proceed to the adoption of new rules. Third, tactically, this fight gave a political urgency to civil rights legislation which it might not otherwise have had, and improved immeasurably the chances for a meaningful bill.

III. Filibuster by Committee

H.R. 6127 passed the House on June 18, 1957. In the Senate its companion bill, as well as some 15 other civil rights bills, still had not been acted on by the Judiciary Committee.

This inaction followed precedent. In the 83d Congress four civil rights bills were reported from the Subcommittee on Constitutional Rights to the full Judiciary Committee, where they died. In the 84th Congress, the Constitutional Rights Subcommittee reported three bills on February 28, 1956 and a fourth bill on March 4, 1956, to the full Judiciary Committee; but they too died following 10 days of hearings by the full committee spread over the 11-week period from April 24 to July 13. In the 85th Congress, after every legitimate attempt by Senator Hennings and his colleagues to gain action on the bills, not one was reported to the Senate during the entire session. A chronology of the efforts to report a bill to the Senate will show how filibuster by committee takes place.

A number of civil rights bills were introduced during the first days of the session. On January 22, Senator Hennings moved in committee that February 18 be set as the deadline for ending hearings on them and that a vote on the legislation and the reporting of a bill to the Senate should not be delayed beyond one further week. This motion was not acted on.

Four days later, on January 26, the 14 bills by then in committee were referred to the Constitutional Rights Subcommittee.

On January 30 Senator Hennings, the chairman, presented an omnibus bill to the subcommittee and moved that it be reported to the full committee. The motion was defeated.

The subcommittee then agreed to hold hearings and Senator Hennings moved that these should begin on February 12 and be limited to two weeks, after which the subcommittee should act on the bills immediately. This motion was defeated.

Hearings by the subcommittee did begin on February 14 and ended after three weeks on March 5. On March 19, the subcommittee approved S. 83 and reported it, along with majority and minority views, to the full committee.

On March 21, Senator Hennings introduced S. 1658; its language was identical with that of H.R. 6127.

On April 1, in the full committee, Senator Hennings moved that the Judiciary Committee dispose of civil rights legislation by April 15. He was unable to obtain a vote on this motion.

On April 8, Senator Hennings intended to renew his motion, but there was no meeting of the committee owing to the absence of a quorum.

On April 15, Senator Hennings moved that S. 83 be voted on by May 6. The committee took no action.

On May 13, at the next meeting, Senator Hennings desired to move that the committee meet every morning and all day, when the rules of the Senate permitted, and in the evenings if necessary, so that a vote on the bill could be taken by May 16. He was unable to obtain recognition to make this motion.

On June 3, the committee added the sweeping "jury trial" amendment to the bill.

On June 10 and June 17, Senator Hennings was unable to gain recognition during committee meetings.

On June 18 the House passed H.R. 6127 and it was sent to the Senate.

How was it possible for the Judiciary Committee, which contained only a minority of Southern Senators, to delay action on civil rights for such a lengthy period of time? Under Section 134 (c) of the Legislative Reorganization Act, "No standing committee of the Senate...shall sit, without special leave, while the Senate...is in session." Under Section 133 (a) of the same Act, each standing committee is required to fix a regular day on which to meet. The regular meeting day of the Senate Judiciary Committee is Monday. While the Senate is often in recess on other days of the week, it is invariably in session on Monday, because that day is set for the call of the calendar of unobjected-to bills, and because the Constitution provides that neither House may adjourn for more than three days without the consent of the other. Consequently, when the hour of 12 noon arrives or when, as in the latter stages of the session the Senate meets at an earlier hour, any member of the Judiciary Committee may make a point of order that the Committee may no longer sit. This was done, and was one means of postponing action.

In addition, by the chairman's power to recognize an opponent first, and by his power to hold off a vote on a motion until such a member has concluded his remarks on it, it was easy for the chairman either to prevent a motion from being offered or to prevent action on a specific bill during the Committee's normal two-hour meeting. Further, the unwritten rule of seniority has generally placed a Southern Senator in the chair when the Democratic Party controls Congress. While Rule XXIV reads that "...the Senate, unless otherwise ordered, shall proceed by ballot to appoint severally the chairman of each committee...," this rule was not enforced either when Senator Eastland was first appointed chairman, on the death of Senator Kilgore, or at the beginning of the 85th Congress when he was reappointed. There was neither a ballot nor a motion to "order otherwise." Finally, on several Mondays it was impossible to muster a quorum.

IV. Placing H.R. 6127 on the Senate Calendar

Faced with this situation, a small group of pro-civil-rights Democratic Senators met a few days prior to the passage of H.R. 6127 by the House of Representatives, to determine on a course of action when that bill arrived in the Senate.

Several possibilities were canvassed. These included: (1) moving to send H.R. 6127 to the Judiciary Committee with instructions to report it to the Senate on a specific date; (2) allowing H.R. 6127 to go to Committee but moving to discharge the Judiciary Committee from further consideration either of that bill or of one of several of the Senate bills; (3) moving to suspend the rules under Rule XL in order to place H.R. 6127 on the calendar; and (4) moving to place the bill on the calendar under Rule XIV.

After consultation with the Senate Parliamentarian the group ruled out the first possibility, of sending the bill to committee with instructions to report it to the Senate on a day certain. Such instructions may be added to a motion to refer or to commit only when the bill itself has been motioned up and is actually before the Senate. Before the bill could come before the Senate it had first to be placed on the calendar, and then to be motioned up. Such a motion is subject to unlimited debate unless cloture is applied. This procedure was therefore evidently impossible, notwithstanding later statements by Senator Morse who, in justifying his opposition to placing the bill directly on the calendar, asserted that instructions to report the bill on a day certain could have been added after the second reading.

Similarly, as we have already seen, the method of discharging a committee is lengthy, and was probably impossible for legislation as controversial as a civil rights bill. More specifically, the steps involved in this procedure include:

1. Filing a discharge petition during the morning hour.
2. A successful motion to adjourn so that a new legislative day may arrive.
3. Reaching the petition during the morning hour, in which case it would go to the foot of the calendar if debate were not concluded in two hours; or, if it was not reached in the morning hour, motioning it up at a later stage.
4. Moving to proceed to consideration of the petition, after it has reached the calendar, and after one legislative day has elapsed (which requires an intervening adjournment), when such a motion becomes in order.
5. Securing a vote on this motion, which is debatable and requires either unanimous consent or cloture and 64 affirmative votes to bring the debate to an end. Passage of this procedural motion requires only a simple majority.
6. Securing a vote on the next motion, to agree to the petition to discharge the committee. This motion too is debatable and requires cloture.
7. Placing the bill, now discharged from committee, at the foot of the Rule VIII calendar, which follows automatically if the previous steps are successful. It must remain there for another legislative day, which requires another successful motion to adjourn in order to reach a new legislative day.
8. Moving to proceed to consideration of the bill and securing a vote on this motion, which is by now in order, is debatable, requires cloture to end debate, and a simple majority for passage.
9. Moving to agree to the bill and securing a vote on it, after all amendments have been dealt with; this again is debatable and requires cloture.

In the face of determined opposition, and without the help of the party leadership, the procedures outlined here would take a minimum of five to eight weeks even if there were 64 votes in support of action at every stage, which was by no means certain. The group therefore determined that the route of discharging the Judiciary Committee was impractical; indeed, that the votes and physical endurance necessary to break four successive potential filibusters made it impossible.

Suspending the rules of the Senate in order to place the House-passed bill on the calendar was also considered. This procedure is no near cousin of the method of moving to suspend the rules and pass the bill, which is a short-cut frequently used in the House of Representatives and common in state legislatures, where with the backing of the party leadership and a disciplined two-thirds vote at hand an opposition minority can be steam-rollered. In the Senate version it has the advantage merely of reducing from four to three the number of potential filibusters and cloture motions to be met.[4] On the other hand, in comparison with the discharge procedure, it has two immediate drawbacks. First, because the tradition that all matters, unless by unanimous consent, should go to a committee before floor action is rightly very strong, suspension of the rules is open to the charge of by-passing the committee; the discharge procedure at least makes a gesture of giving the committee a chance to act. Second, because the suspension procedure has been so rarely used, it is open also to the charge of novelty in procedure—an unorthodox means of gaining an unorthodox end. The steering group of civil rights senators therefore discarded this alternative, and in fact concluded that if a choice had to be made between the two, the discharge route was preferable.

Finally, the possibility of placing the House-passed bill on the calendar under Rule XIV was canvassed. The relevant parts of Rule XIV read as follows:

> No bill or joint resolution shall be committed or amended until it shall have been twice read, after which it *may* be referred to a committee; bills and joint resolutions introduced on leave, and bills and joint resolutions from the House of Representatives, shall be read once, and may be read twice, on the same day, if not objected to, for reference, but shall not be considered on that day nor debated, except for reference, unless by unanimous consent. [Section 3, emphasis added.]

> Every bill and joint resolution reported from a committee, not having previously been read, shall be read once, and twice, if not objected to, on the same day, and

---

[4] The steps involved in suspending the rules in order, to place the bill on the calendar run as follows: (1) When the bill arrives from the House, either a motion that it be laid before the Senate, or a wait until the presiding officer laid it before the Senate in order to object to the second reading of the bill on the same day. (2) Simultaneously giving notice of an intention to move to suspend the rules, and reading or placing in the *Record* the terms of the motion. (3) Gaining an adjournment to bring a new legislative day. (4) On the new legislative day and after the reading of the Journal, either calling up the motion to suspend the rules, or waiting until the presiding officer laid the bill before the Senate for a second reading. At this time, and prior to the customary referral to committee, gaining recognition to prevent such a reference by calling up the motion to suspend the rules. Since no motion to proceed to the consideration of that motion would be necessary, one potential filibuster is avoided at this point. (5) Securing a vote on the motion to suspend the rules, which is debatable and would require cloture to stop a filibuster. An affirmative two-thirds vote of those present and voting on this motion would send the bill to the calendar. (6) From this stage on the procedure is the same as with the discharge method—an adjournment to bring a new legislative day, when a motion to proceed to the consideration of the bill would be in order; a vote on this motion, which is debatable and would require cloture; disposition of amendments and a vote on final passage, which again is debatable and would require cloture.

placed on the Calendar in the order in which same may be reported; and every bill and joint resolution introduced on leave, *and every bill and joint resolution of the House of Representatives which shall have received a first and second reading without being referred to a committee, shall, if objection be made to further proceeding thereon, be placed on the Calendar.* [Section 4, emphasis added.]

Although infrequently used, this seemed to be a relatively simple and direct method of placing the House-passed bill on the calendar. If it could be attacked for by-passing the committee, it was nevertheless a well settled part of the rules of the Senate; and, compared with many rules, its meaning appeared to be crystal clear. On that count it was therefore preferable to suspending the rules. And although perhaps less orthodox than discharging the committee, it reduced the potential number of filibusters in finally passing the bill from four to two. It was decided, therefore, that this method had the best, and perhaps the only, chance of success.

On June 14, following press reports that a group of Republican senators, including their leadership, were also considering using Rule XIV to place the bill on the calendar, a group of 15 Democratic liberals issued a statement in which they (1) urged the Judiciary Committee to report out a bill promptly, (2) stated that, while they preferred to act on a Senate bill, if a Senate bill were not reported they would join and cooperate with any other senator or groups of senators on either side of the aisle who wished to place the House bill on the calendar under Rule XIV, (3) gave formal notice of their intention to do so to the leadership and whips on both sides of the aisle, to the Parliamentarian, and to all other Senators, and (4) gave notice that they would not give unanimous consent to any motion to refer the House-passed bill to committee and formally requested that they be notified before the bill was laid before the Senate or referred, so that they might be in their places to ask certain parliamentary questions or to make certain motions. This last request grew out of the experience in 1956, when the House-passed bill was referred to committee while interested Senators were not on the floor. A further important reason for giving notice was that bills from the House as well as bills introduced in the Senate are ordinarily, for the convenience of all, read perfunctorily, not actually laid down by the presiding officer, and automatically referred to committee. Even when a bill is actually laid before the Senate, this can be done at any time and while the floor is unguarded, for under section 7 of Rule VII,

The Presiding Officer may at any time lay, and it shall be in order at any time for a Senator to move to lay, before the Senate, any bill or other matter sent to the Senate by the President or the House of Representatives, and any question pending at that time shall be suspended for this purpose. Any motion so made shall be determined without debate.

Thus with a senator who opposed civil rights in the chair, another senator could move to, or the chair without a motion could, lay the House bill before the Senate and have it referred before another senator could gain recognition to object.

Certain precautionary steps were therefore taken. The first was to try to make certain that a senator in sympathy with the move to place the bill on the calendar, or the Vice President, would be in the chair when the bill arrived at the desk. Teams of senators were organized to guard the floor at all times. Arrangements were made with House members to notify key senators of the step-by-step actions on the bill in the House. Further, it was publicly pointed out that when the bill arrived the Senate would be in executive session considering the Atomic Energy Treaty, and hence that the bill would remain in limbo at the desk until the Senate moved back into legislative session. As the Senate can move back and forth from legislative to executive session by a simple unanimous consent request, attention was called to this fact so that senators would not lower their guard and stay off the floor during executive sessions under the mistaken impression that no action on the bill could be taken. Sheets of instructions were issued to the Democratic senators in sympathy with the move, in which parliamentary details were outlined; these instructed them to object to any attempt to read the bill a second time or to refer it, and to call for a quorum when in doubt. As a result, the rights of individual senators were protected as they had not been in 1956. Agreements were entered into at almost every stage for a specific time when action would take place and motions would be made, so that the rights of each senator could be asserted.

H.R. 6127 was laid before the Senate on June 19. It was read a first time, after which Senator Russell asked unanimous consent that it be read a second time on that day. Objections were heard from Senators Knowland and Douglas.

At this time Senator Russell argued that Rule XXV took precedence over Rule XIV. He claimed that following the procedures under Rule XIV would "...throw out the window the laws, the rules, and the Constitution in order to get at 'these infernal southerners' in a hurry." His major argument rested on the premise that the changes made in the rules by the Legislative Reorganization Act of 1946 superseded other rules with which they were inconsistent. In his view the language of Rule XXV, which enumerates the subject matter over which specific committees have jurisdiction, was in conflict with Rule XIV and therefore took precedence over that rule. He quoted Section 101 (a) of the Reorganization Act which reads, in part, "...such rules shall supersede other rules only to the extent that they are inconsistent therewith," and Section (k) of Rule XXV which reads:

Committee on the Judiciary, to consist of fifteen Senators, to which *shall be referred* all proposed legislation, messages, petitions, memorials, and other matters relating to the following subjects. [Emphasis added.]

A list of subjects then follows, including "civil liberties." Senator Russell urged specifically that the phrase "shall be referred" is mandatory and superseded sections 3 and 4 of Rule XIV.

The proponents of the move argued that nothing could be clearer than the language of Rule XIV; that Rule XXV was not mandatory concerning referral but merely a specification of the subject matter over which each committee had jurisdiction; that the history of the Legislative Reorganization Act showed this to be true; that there were numerous examples of House bills going directly to the calendar both by precedent and under Rule XIV; and that the phrase "shall be referred," should not now be construed as mandatory when it had not been so on hundreds of other occasions.[5]

Development of the argument brought out examples of House-passed bills which were automatically placed on the Senate calendar when a Senate companion bill was already on the Senate calendar, and examples of a House-passed bill placed on the calendar prior to the Senate bill being placed there, when it was known that a Senate bill would soon be reported. Further, although this point was not made on the floor, it is well known that, especially on the last day of a session, numerous House-passed bills are motioned up on the floor of the Senate when there are no Senate companion bills. There have even been examples of the bill clerk officially referring a bill to a committee and entering that referral in the Journal, only to find that the House bill is motioned up and passed in the last few hours before adjournment. In such cases the Journal has been corrected after the fact

5 There were only a few examples of a bill going to the calendar under Rule XIV prior to 1946. Since then procedures under this rule were followed once on May 3, 1948 when Senator Downey of California objected after second reading to further proceedings on the Tidelands Oil bill, which then went directly to the calendar. Immediately following that action and on the same day Senator Fulbright attempted to do the same thing to the oleomargarine tax repeal bill. However, the chair (then the President pro-tempore, Mr. Vandenberg) had first recognized Senator Wherry, who raised the issue of committee jurisdiction before Senator Fulbright made his objection. In a series of parliamentary questions and votes the bill eventually went to committee, but it is quite clear from a thorough reading of that incident that it did not conflict with Senator Downey's action. Senator Vandenberg stated not only that it did not conflict but that the issue turned finally "...upon the pure question as to who is first recognized by the Chair to assert his rights under these conflicting rules." He said specifically: "There is no collision whatever between the precedent of yesterday and the precedent of today.... It is the view of the Chair that the question of precedence in a case of this character depends entirely on who raises the point first. Since the question of jurisdiction has been raised first it is the view of the Chair that the question of jurisdiction takes priority."

to show that the bill was sent to the calendar, in order to be there legitimately when motioned up. These examples added considerable weight to the argument that the phrase "shall be referred" in Rule XXV was by no means mandatory. Since these bills were sent to the calendar by a private decision of the Vice President or his agent, it was argued that what one man could do *in camera* under the precedents a majority of the Senate could do openly under the provisions of a specific rule.

On June 20, Senator Knowland objected to the "further proceeding thereon" immediately after H.R. 6127 was read a second time. Senator Russell raised the point of order that Rule XXV took precedence; and debate on this point, which is not debatable except at the pleasure of the Chair, took place for several hours. One problem concerning the use of Rule XIV bothered some Senators, namely, that a "single" Senator, by objection, could prevent a bill going to committee. The proponents of the move argued that while such a case might theoretically arise, there would no doubt, on an issue of such importance as a civil rights bill, be a point of order, such as Senator Russell raised; and that a majority of the Senate would, in fact, decide whether the bill should go to the calendar or to the committee.

Senator Case of New Jersey was particularly concerned about a single Senator's objection sending the bill to the calendar, and felt that greater support for the move could be obtained if some method were found to decide the issue more directly by majority vote. He proposed that, after the second reading, a motion rather than an objection should be made, to send the bill to the calendar. He had numerous discussions with the Vice President on this point and prepared a detailed memorandum outlining his views. The Vice President's opinion on the Russell point of order reflects, to a considerable extent, these original views of Senator Case.

The leaders of the liberal Democratic group, while sympathizing with Senator Case's position, believed that if a specific motion were made to place the bill on the calendar following the second reading, rather than an objection by a single Senator under Rule XIV, such a motion would be debatable and hence would require 64 affirmative votes and cloture to end debate. If this were true then the attempt to place the bill on the calendar could not succeed.

This point was overcome by the opinion of the Vice President, who stated (1) that Rule XXV did not require a mandatory referral to committee; (2) that if objection were made under Rule XIV and no point of order were raised the bill would go directly to the calendar; but (3) that if a point of order were raised the effect of it would be to put the substantive question, "Shall the bill be referred," in which case the issue would be decided by a majority vote. A filibuster at this stage was precluded when the Vice President went on to state that a motion to table could lie against the point of order. A simple majority, therefore, could end debate by moving to table the point of order. No such tabling motion was made, but the fact that it could be made allowed the Senate to vote on the substantive issue, "Shall the bill be referred?" The vote was 35 to sustain Senator Russell's point of order and 45 who opposed; and the bill went to the calendar.

Major Results of the Maneuver

There were at least three major, and perhaps historic, results of this action. In the first place it was probably the only method by which a civil rights bill could have been placed in a position to come before the Senate. Without it the civil rights bill would no doubt have languished again in the Senate Judiciary Committee until the end of the Congress. This procedural move was a major and essential step towards the final passage of the bill.

Secondly, for the first important occasion since 1938, the coalition of Southern Democrats and conservative Republicans was shattered. The *quid pro quo* of that coalition has long been that Southern Democrats would provide enough votes to defeat liberal social and economic legislation while the conservative Republicans provided the votes to defeat civil rights moves. Now, for the first time, a coalition of Northern Republicans and liberal Northern Democrats had acted together on a procedural issue to further the progress of a civil rights bill. This was all the more significant for, in the past, the conservative Republicans had furnished their votes in support of the South mainly on procedural rather than substantive issues, such as the 1949 appeal from the decision of the chair and amendment to Rule XXII which made it even more difficult than before to shut off debate. They provided just enough votes or absentees so that cloture could not be applied to previous civil rights bills. They opposed and defeated the 1953 and 1957 attempts to adopt new rules of the Senate at the beginning of a new Congress. In that way the Republicans hoped to avoid the charge of opposing civil rights, for they professed their willingness to support, at least in part, the bills themselves on which, in almost every case, they prevented action. This was playing both sides of an issue and, because procedural niceties are little understood by the public and even more difficult to explain, they avoided condemnation for opposing civil rights which was the real effect of their actions.

In place of this coalition two new coalitions emerged. One was the Knowland-Douglas Axis, as Senator Russell referred to it, on the civil rights issue. This coalition is probably limited to civil rights and was more the result of public opinion, of the Republican gains in the Negro districts in 1956, possibly of the personal Presidential ambitions of individual Senators, and of the effective filibuster by committee, than the basis for any agreement or tacit arrangement for mutual support on other issues.

The other coalition was a revival of cooperation between the Southern and Western Democrats together with the remaining hard core of the Republican right wing. In many respects this coalition was not new for it has operated for years on such economic issues common to both areas as legislation on sugar cane and sugar beets, rivers and harbors and reclamation projects, the wool tariff, the silver subsidy, aid to the Western mining industry, and similar matters. As the course of the civil rights debate continued, this combination became dominant and civil rights, apparently, was added as a part of the bargain.

A third and most important effect of the vote was that for the first time in many years the Senate asserted a disciplinary jurisdiction over one of its committees. In theory, at least, committees of the Senate should be the servants of the Senate as a whole. Notoriously, in practice this has not been so. Examples include the unwillingness of the Senate to deal with the excesses of investigating committees; the tacit arrangement whereby the leadership, committee chairmen, and those Senators who are within or who are seeking admittance to the "inner circle" join to provide 52 to 55 votes to defeat motions and amendments on the floor when offered by individual Senators who are not members of the committee; and the unwritten rule of the Senate leadership that it supports the substance of committee action without regard to opposition by what may be even a majority of the party. In this respect, placing the civil rights bill on the calendar was unique and precedent setting. Although committees will no doubt continue to operate substantially as they have in the past, the possibility or threat of similar action may well serve to allow action by the full Senate on controversial bills of great importance for which there is overwhelming support and which otherwise would die in a committee stacked against them.

V. The Debate on H.R. 6127

Although the vote to take up the bill was 71 to 18, the new Southern-Western coalition proved powerful enough to effect major changes in the bill itself. They forced the deletion of Section III of the bill and they added a jury trial amendment to the voting section which, as it passed the Senate, would have made the bill least effective in those areas of the Deep South where it was most needed.

Apart from the coalition, two other major factors operated towards weakening the bill. The first was the press conference statement of the President on Section III, saying that it was not his intention that the Attorney General should have the power to initiate civil rights suits under that Section and the 14th Amendment. The second was the fact that the press centered its coverage almost wholly on the contest—the strategy and maneuverings in connection with the bill—and avoided, almost completely, the moral and substantive grounds for supporting it in the first place. For example, Senator Douglas placed in the Record a detailed legal brief on the jury trial amendment and contempt proceedings, showing that no "right" to trial by jury was being denied by the provisions of the bill. This was ignored by the press. County-by-county figures on Negro registration in the South were also detailed, as were the various subtle methods by which Negroes are denied the franchise; and these too were largely, although not entirely, ignored. Further, Senator Javits and others made lengthy and even brilliant rebuttals of the attack on Section III of the bill which were little reported and went almost unnoticed even by such papers as the *Washington Post* and the *New York Times*.

On three further occasions after the bill was taken up the rules of the Senate, together with other internal and external factors, affected the substance of the bill materially. These include the abortive attempt on the part of the Knowland-Douglas forces to modify Section III when it was clear, following the President's press conference, that it would otherwise be stricken; the various revisions of the jury-trial amendment; and the successful use of the unanimous consent device to bring a third reading and deny the possibility of further amendments at the late stages in the debate.

Striking Out Section III

Once the bill was before the Senate, Senators Anderson and Aiken moved to strike out Section III. This section would have permitted the Attorney General to seek injunctive remedies under the equal rights provisions of the 14th Amendment in cases affecting the use of schools, busses, public parks, etc., either on his own initiative, or at the request of an aggrieved party, or at the request of local public authorities which, in practice, would generally have meant school boards. Despite repeated claims to the contrary during the course of debate, the bill gave him no power to issue court orders or to decide how fast school integration must proceed. The remedies sought were milder in form, though easier, it was hoped, to obtain, than the criminal penalties now available against those who deny rights guaranteed under the Constitution; they were to supplement, not supplant, these penalties. The Little Rock, Arkansas case has since shown something of the potential effectiveness of the injunctive remedies. But the Attorney General was able to act in that case only because the original court order was sought by the Little Rock School Board, and because the court then invited him to intervene. Section III would have given the Attorney General the right to take the initiative.

When it was clear, after the President's press conference, that Section III would be deleted, the Knowland-Douglas forces sought to reach agreement on some substitute which could gain majority support. The Knowland position was that such an amendment should allow the Attorney General to intervene only when he was requested to do so by the local school boards or officials. The Douglas group's position was that the amendment should enable the Attorney General to intervene in these cases and also when an aggrieved party sought his intervention. Both versions abandoned the provision for the Attorney General to initiate action on his own and without specific request.

The parliamentary situation was that the amendment to strike out Section III could only be decided after perfecting amendments to the section in its original form had been offered and voted on. Under the rules even though the motion to strike out was offered first, its priority for purposes of voting was last. The Knowland forces were unable to agree to the Douglas amendment, largely because they felt they could not push beyond the President's position; but the two groups tried to work out a strategy whereby they would fall back step by step, attempting to pick up strength as they did so. They decided that Senator Knowland should first offer his amendment, and that Senator Douglas would then move to substitute his own amendment for it. In this way they hoped that the liberal Democrats and other supporters of the stronger position could vote for the Douglas motion and when defeated, as they no doubt would have been, they could join the Knowland position as the next defensive move.

Because of the rules and precedents of the Senate this strategy had eventually to be abandoned. The supporters of the Douglas position were willing to fall back a step at a time, but could not agree to support a weaker provision when it was presented against a stronger position. They could vote for the Douglas motion as against the Knowland motion. They could vote for the Douglas or the Knowland motion as against the Anderson-Aiken motion to strike out Section III. They could not vote for the Douglas or the Knowland motion if either were to lie against Section III.

The parliamentary situation made it impossible to carry out their strategy. Once the Douglas motion was defeated there was no way in which the Knowland motion could be made to lie against the Anderson motion to strike Section III. The issue would have been between the Knowland motion and Section III, in which case the liberal Democrats and some Republicans would have felt compelled to vote against the Knowland motion. This was true because of the precedent that a motion to strike is only voted on after the perfecting amendments to the basic provisions of a section have been disposed of. Efforts to substitute a weaker provision for the existing Section III were therefore abandoned at this stage. It was decided to let the vote come on the Anderson motion to strike, and to offer a revised Section III at a later stage, preferably following a victory on some substantive issue.

The Moving Target

Yet another example of the effect of the rules of the Senate on the substance of legislation may be seen in the successive revisions of the jury trial amendment. It is a cardinal principle of most parliamentary procedures that once a motion is offered it belongs to the full body and not to the mover. The parliamentary body determines what action should be taken, *i.e.,* to amend, commit, refer, etc. This is not true of the Senate of the United States. An amendment, even after it is offered, belongs to the mover of the amendment and until such time as the yeas and nays have been ordered, he may amend it, revise it, or change it as he sees fit. In this fashion the jury trial amendment was changed almost from day to day, not by any vote of the Senate but by the offering or acceptance of revisions on the part of its mover, Senator O'Mahoney. As Senator Douglas said on the floor, the opponents of the jury trial amendment were "shooting at a moving target." The initial point at issue was the definition of the criminal contempts to which a jury trial would be made applicable—an exceedingly intricate technical question.

The first version met strenuous objection. The distinction it drew between civil and criminal contempt was whether or not questions of fact were at issue. As any good defense lawyer could raise a question of fact, the effect of this version was to allow a jury trial in all contempt cases.

The second version attempted to distinguish between civil and criminal contempt on the basis of whether or not the act committed was a crime. The traditional distinction between the two types of contempt, often hard to draw in practice, turns on whether the action of the court is for the purpose of compelling compliance with a previous court order, or for the purpose of punishment for failure to carry out the order. Thus in a voting case, a local registrar could be held in contempt for failing to carry out the court's order, but so long as he could remove that contempt by compliance with the order it would be civil contempt. Once the day for election had arrived and passed, and the defendant was no longer able to remove his contempt by compliance, then the contempt would be criminal, for the court could send him to a jail or impose a fine only for the purpose of punishment. Since almost all obstructive actions connected with voting in federal elections are criminal, the effect of the second version was to grant a jury trial in contempt cases arising from interferences with voting.

In the third version of the O'Mahoney amendment the orthodox distinction was finally drawn between civil and criminal contempt. In an attempt to gain more widespread support for it, however, the amendment was broadened to apply not only to voting cases but to all contempt actions under federal law. At least 40 other statutes were affected, but primarily this revision was aimed at gaining labor support, particularly from the Railroad Brotherhoods and the United Mine Workers, who were sensitive about past abuses of labor injunctions and who, in turn, influenced a number of key votes in the Senate. This provision was a most radical departure from existing procedures. Like the second version, it was merely accepted on the floor by Senator O'Mahoney, and no vote was taken on the question of substituting it for the previous version.

At this stage the question of passage of a jury trial amendment was touch and go. Those opposed to it still appeared to be in the majority. Finally, a fourth version was offered to meet the complaints over the absence of Negroes from Southern juries, and so to pick up a few more votes. Federal law sets certain standards for service on Federal juries, but also provides that no one may serve on a federal jury who is incompetent to serve on the grand or petit jury under the laws of his state. As one must be a voter or qualified elector in Texas, Arkansas, Mississippi, South Carolina, and the Parish of New Orleans in order to be eligible to serve on a local grand or petit jury, and as Negroes are largely excluded from voting in these states, this means that by law Negroes are also excluded from federal jury service there. The fourth version, offered by Senator Church, repealed the provisions of the United States Code which excluded those from federal jury service who could not meet state qualifications. The effect of this final version was to provide the margin of strength to pass the jury trial amendment. However, as Negroes are excluded from jury service in other Southern states, in practice and by other means, it is doubtful that this change will have much practical effect.

The right to revise and modify an amendment at the will of its sponsor played a large part in attaching a jury trial amendment to the bill, for had the vote come on the first, second, or possibly the third version, it appears fairly certain that the amendment would have been defeated; and that, once defeated, the forces favoring it could not have recovered enough strength to pass even a greatly modified new amendment.

Unanimous Consent

The final instance in which parliamentary practice affected the substance of the bill occurred following the jury trial amendment vote and prior to the vote on the remaining amendments. Senator Russell referred to it in a speech on August 30, after the bill had passed, in which he justified and explained the failure of Southern Senators to filibuster the bill and took great credit for watering it down. He had this to say on the floor:

When we had arrived at this particular stage of the proceedings in the Senate I happened to learn that a determined effort would be made to revive some of the provisions of Part III that had been stricken from the bill. The new amendment appeared harmless on its face, but if it had been adopted it would have placed the stamp of congressional approval on the erroneous, if not infamous, decision of the Supreme Court requiring the mixing of the children in the public schools without regard to the wishes of the parents of either race. We, therefore, quickly closed the bill to amendments in order to assure that none of the victories that we had gained would be snatched from us.[6]

What happened was that a bi-partisan group determined to try to revive a part of the Section III previously stricken. Before they could offer their amendment a unanimous consent agreement was reached, at a time when there was general commotion on the floor, limiting further proceedings to those amendments which had already been offered and printed and confining the time for debate to 30 minutes on each amendment. Senator Douglas was within minutes of offering the revised Section III amendment and was prevented from doing so by Senator Johnson's unanimous consent request which was made and agreed to at a time of confusion when his request could not be heard in the chamber. Apparently a gentlemen's agreement had also been reached that all further amendments would be voted down by voice vote and without a roll call.

VI. The Filibuster: A Paper Tiger?

One final point should be made concerning the effect of the rules of the Senate on the substance of the civil rights bill. A number of highly competent journalists who were not close to the debate, or who have since been misled by the interpretations placed on it by some, have asserted that the absence of a filibuster at any stage in the proceedings on the floor represented a willingness on the part of the Southern opponents to accommodate themselves at least to the voting rights provisions of the bill. A closer view leads to the opposite conclusion, that the passage of the bill represents no compromise or accommodation on the part of the Deep South Senators at all. Rather, the failure to filibuster may be regarded as a carefully calculated decision to avoid consequences which would have been worse, from the Southern point of view, than those of the bill as it passed the Senate.

6 *Congressional Record,* August 30, 1957, p. 15171 (daily ed.).

Throughout the debate, and preceding the votes on Section III and the jury trial amendment, the threat of a filibuster was used to gain support for both these amendments. Senator Russell has since frankly admitted what many on the inside felt sure of at the time, namely, that the South would not filibuster and that the threat of doing so was more effective than the reality would have been. Notwithstanding the arguments made earlier in the year, that no meaningful civil rights bill could be passed unless Rule XXII was changed, the filibuster, after the Rule XXII fight and after the bill was placed on the calendar, became a paper tiger. In retrospect it seems clear that the Southerners did not dare to use it because they feared the results would be the loss of Rule XXII and the passage of a much stronger bill than was passed. They were sufficiently convinced that a filibuster would so outrage the country and the Senate that they had more to lose than to gain by its use. This accounts for the severe condemnation of Senator Thurmond by his Southern colleagues following his 24-hour "talkathon."

The Southern group decided, instead, to attempt to filibuster the bill to death in committee. In this they were successful; they could have kept it throttled there indefinitely. However, as a result of the great increase in votes for a change in Rule XXII and the vote to place the bill on the calendar, they knew they could not successfully transfer that filibuster to the floor. In Senator Russell's words:

In years gone by, it has been a great source of pride to me that our group was able to defeat bills of this nature when they were forced to the consideration of the Senate. In the case of H.R. 6127 we were from the outset faced with greater odds than ever before...[7]

There was not a man among us who was not willing to speak against this iniquitous bill until he dropped in his tracks. We would have done so, but for the conviction, growing out of our knowledge of the Senate and the experience of many years in this body, that a filibuster was certain to make a bad bill infinitely worse...[8]

Our group held numerous meetings and the wisdom of launching a filibuster was often discussed. All members of the group were living with the problem from day to day, defending the things dearest to our heart while under heavy fire. At no time did any member of our group declare in any of our meetings that it was his belief that a filibuster was advisable, much less that one could be successfully waged. The contrary view was expressed on innumerable occasions...[9]

They therefore decided to avoid a filibuster while using the threat of it to gain their points. They decided also to keep debate relevant, and with

[7] *Ibid.*, p. 15172.
[8] *Ibid.*, p. 15171.
[9] *Ibid.*, pp. 15171–72.

one or two very glaring exceptions this was done. With the wholehearted support of Senator Johnson, the Democratic leader, they then pressed for the two basic amendments which, from their point of view, would gain the least offensive result. In this, too, they were successful. They took this course not from any desire for accommodation or willingness to compromise but because a different course would, from the Southern position, "make a bad bill infinitely worse."

Although the filibuster was not used, the existence of Rule XXII made it still possible for Senator Russell to claim that:

> ...the fact that we were able to confine the Federal activities to the field of voting and keep the withering hand of the Federal Government out of our schools and social order is to me, as I look back over the years, the sweetest victory of my 25 years as a Senator from the State of Georgia.[10]

Because of the filibuster rule, the unwillingness of some professed supporters of civil rights to see that the South dared not filibuster at this time, the consequent surrender to the mere threat of its use, and the skillful tactics of Senators Russell and Johnson, the bill as passed by the Senate was largely a victory for the forces of segregation. As civil rights proponents saw it, all their sweat and struggle to overcome the parliamentary obstacles had led to a bill which, except for a few minor gains, was almost form without substance. They took what consolation they could in watching the House revise it enough to make it a modest forward step.

[10] *Ibid.*, p. 15172.

15

RAYMOND E. WOLFINGER

Filibusters: Majority Rule, Presidential Leadership, and Senate Norms

Unlimited floor debate is a rarity among national legislatures and the glory of the United States Senate. The influence of filibusters on the fate of proposed civil rights legislation and the attempts made by some senators to change the rules so as to weaken that influence have been a persistent subject in contemporary political history and have provided a basis for several generalizations about both the Senate and the American political system. In some important respects these generalizations are based on a misreading of the evidence, as I hope to show in this article.

Filibusters touch on several important and familiar themes: (1) they are a major weapon used by a parochial Congress to block presidential programs; (2) for a generation they were the means used to veto civil rights bills supported by legislative majorities; (3) they illustrate the importance of apolitical congressional norms, in this instance senatorial commitment to unlimited debate. As the following narrative demonstrates, all three of these generalizations are in need of revision.

I

Most Senate motions, including any to consider ("take up") a bill, as well as to pass it, are subject to unlimited debate unless cloture is imposed, and

I am grateful to J. Vincent Buck, Nelson W. Polsby, and Leroy N. Rieselbach for comments on earlier drafts of this paper, which is a product of participation in the Study of Congress sponsored by the American Political Science Foundation with the aid of a grant from the Carnegie Corporation.

the Senate's Rule 22 requires a two-thirds vote for cloture. Weak as it is, Rule 22 has been on the books for only half a century. There were no limits at all on debate before 1917, and thus a handful of determined senators could frustrate a majority's desire to pass a bill.[1] From 1865, when the use of unlimited debate for this purpose became firmly established, until 1950, thirty-six proposed legislative measures were delayed or defeated by filibusters, most of which lasted only a few days.[2] All but eleven of these measures eventually were passed in some form. The exceptions—those bills totally defeated by unlimited debate—were almost all civil rights measures.[3] Numerous appropriations bill were also casualties of filibusters.[4] There is no way of knowing for sure how many other measures were shelved or modified by the threat of unlimited debate, but threatening to talk a provision to death is a commonplace Senate tactic, particularly in the closing days of a session when members are anxious to adjourn.[5]

Beginning with Henry Clay in 1841, many senators tried one means or another of limiting debate, but it was not until the emotional period just before our entry into the First World War that the Senate adopted any such restriction. Early in 1917 a dozen western progressives succeeded, by means of a very unpopular filibuster, in defeating President Wilson's bill to arm merchant ships. The infuriated Wilson uttered his famous denunciation of the filibusterers: "A little group of willful men, representing no opinion but their own, have rendered the great Government of the United States helpless and contemptible." He also called the Senate into extraordinary session. Three days later it adopted, by a vote of 76 to 3, an amendment to Rule 22 providing that debate could be limited by a vote of two-thirds of those senators present and voting; after cloture had been imposed, each senator could speak for one hour. This change in the rules was introduced by Senator Thomas S. Martin of Virginia. That a Southerner sponsored the cloture rule can be viewed either as an historical irony or as an illustration of the hollowness of pure principle as a motivation in any behavior concerning filibusters.

From the adoption of the Martin Resolution until 1964 there were twenty-eight cloture votes, five of which passed. Four of these successful

---

1 During the Senate's first years its rules provided for ending debate by moving the previous question, but this provision was eliminated at the beginning of the nineteenth century. See William J. Keefe and Morris S. Ogul, *The American Legislative Process,* second ed. (Englewood Cliffs, N.J.: Prentice-Hall, Inc., 1968), p. 256.

2 George B. Galloway, *Limitation of Debate in the U. S. Senate* (Washington: Library of Congress, Legislative Reference Service, 1958), p. 29.

3 *Ibid.,* p. 30.

4 Galloway reports that there were eighty-two of these between 1876 and 1916 alone; *ibid.,* p. 3.

5 For a modern example of this tactic see Ralph K. Huitt, "The Outsider in the Senate: An Alternative Role," in Ralph K. Huitt and Robert L. Peabody, *Congress: Two Decades of Analysis* (New York: Harper & Row, Publishers, 1969), pp. 166–68.

attempts occurred before 1928; the fifth, on the Communications Satellite (Comsat) Bill of 1962, is of special interest and will be discussed shortly. Cloture was not attempted on a civil rights bill until 1938; from then through 1962 there were eleven cloture votes on this issue, all unsuccessful.[6]

Over the years since 1917 various parliamentary rulings gradually established the precedent of barring cloture on procedural motions. Since motions to take up a bill are procedural motions, the 1917 change lost all meaning. This development was fully apparent in 1948 when, relying on precedents, Senator Arthur Vandenberg, the presiding officer, sustained a point of order against a cloture petition, observing that "in the final analysis, the Senate has no effective cloture rule at all...a small but determined minority can always prevent cloture...the existing Senate rules regarding cloture do not provide conclusive cloture."[7] The Senate did not vote on appeal of this ruling, which came during the post-convention special session.[8]

Soon after the new Congress convened in 1949 several liberal senators, cheered on by President Truman, moved for new rules to reimpose some control over unlimited debate. After weeks of argument on the floor they gained a provision applying cloture to procedural motions, but at a price dictated by the Republican-Dixiecrat coalition: motions to change the rules were exempted from cloture and the necessary majority was changed from two-thirds of those present and voting to two-thirds of the total membership. (Both of these restrictions were removed ten years later.)

Four years later the opening of the Eighty-third Congress ushered in an era in which liberal attempts to strengthen Rule 22 became almost a biennial ritual. Down through the years there have been two proposals; the more moderate would change the required cloture majority from two-thirds to three-fifths; the other would provide for cloture fifteen days after a vote won by a simple majority. None of the liberal campaigns against Rule 22 has been successful. But because the Senate's resolution of this question over the years reveals a good deal about its members' attitudes toward majority rule, a brief and selective chronicle of the fights over Rule 22 is useful.[9]

[6] *Congress and the Nation* (Washington: Congressional Quarterly Service, 1965), p. 1415.
[7] Galloway, *op. cit.*, p. 18.
[8] A vote early in 1949 had the effect of affirming Vandenberg's ruling. See John G. Stewart, "Independence and Control: The Challenge of Senatorial Party Leadership" (Chicago: unpublished doctoral dissertation, University of Chicago, 1968), p. 92.
[9] The principal sources are Galloway, *op. cit.*; *Congress and the Nation, op. cit.*; Howard E. Shuman, "Senate Rules and the Civil Rights Bill," *American Political Science Review*, 51 (December 1957), pp. 955–75 [Chapter 14 in this reader]; Alan Rosenthal, *Toward Majority Rule in the United States Senate* (New York: McGraw-Hill Book Company; 1962); and various issues of *Congressional Quarterly Weekly Report.*

II

These controversies always occur at the beginning of a Congress because otherwise motions to amend the rules unquestionably would be subject to unlimited debate unless restricted by a two-thirds vote. The liberals' goal has been to bring a motion to revise Rule 22 to a vote under circumstances where a simple majority would suffice to change the rules. In introducing such motions at the opening of a Congress they argued that the Senate could not be bound forever by rules adopted by past Congresses; thus at the very beginning of a Congress the old rules would not be in effect unless they went unchallenged, and in this state of nature general parliamentary rules would apply. In contrast to the Senate's rules, the latter regulations provide that a member can bring a pending motion to a vote by moving the previous question; this motion is not debatable and carries by a simple majority. The basis of the liberal case is Article I, Section 5 of the Constitution, which states that "each House may determine the rules of its proceedings." The defenders of Rule 22 point to Rule 32, which reads in part, "The rules of the Senate shall continue from one Congress to the next Congress unless they are changed as provided in these rules." The merits of the case, on which a great deal of talmudic argumentation has been displayed by both sides, are irrelevant to the concerns of this article.

In 1953, during the first of these fights, the liberals quickly learned that the champions of unlimited debate did not intend to apply the principle to proposals to change Rule 22. The Eighty-third Congress opened on January 3, 1953. On January 7 the Majority Leader, Robert A. Taft (R-Ohio) announced that the Republican Policy Committee had voted against a change in Rule 22, and moved to table a motion by Senator Clinton P. Anderson (D-N.M.) to consider new rules. The nondebatable tabling motion (dubbed "negative cloture" by some liberals) carried by a vote of 70 to 21. It was opposed by fifteen Democrats, five Republicans, and Wayne Morse of Oregon, then an Independent in transition from the Republican to the Democratic party.

Much the same thing happened in 1957. Anderson again offered his motion on opening day and the Majority Leader—by now Lyndon B. Johnson—immediately moved to table it. Vice President Nixon issued various "advisory opinions" to the effect that Article I, Section 5 empowered each Congress to make its own rules and that, given the opportunity, he would so rule. This was no more than an informal expression of opinion, however, and in any event was beside the point, for Johnson's tabling motion carried, 55 to 38. All but six northern Democrats voted "no," but the Republicans were for it by a three-to-two ratio.

Two years later, following a landslide that produced fifteen freshman

Democrats, the liberals again prepared an assault on Rule 22. But Johnson took the initiative on opening day by offering proposals to extend cloture to attempts to change the rules and to relax the majority required for cloture to two-thirds of senators present and voting. The next day Johnson yielded the floor so Anderson could offer his familiar motion, then moved to table it and won by 60 to 36. After the liberals lost two more lopsided votes Johnson's palliatives passed handily and forestalled further action in 1959.

The 1960 election brought a new spirit of hope to liberals. Both party platforms in 1960 promised changes in Rule 22 and Kennedy's election suggested that the White House, which had eschewed any involvement during the Eisenhower years, might join the fight, thus making it more of a party issue and reinforcing the liberals with the prestige and pressure available to a newly elected president. Kennedy, who had opposed Rule 22 while in the Senate, promised an ambitious legislative program to "get this country moving again" and surely would want to remove one notorious obstruction to progressive legislation. With these hopes liberal senators— notably Paul H. Douglas (D-Ill.) and Joseph S. Clark (D-Penn.)—pressed Kennedy for a commitment to help. Clark met with the President-elect in December and professed to be satisfied with the outcome. A week later, however, Kennedy issued an Eisenhower-like statement to the effect that it was up to the members of both houses of Congress to work out their own rules. The reformers' campaign was further weakened when Kennedy's staff passed the word that he did not intend to ask Congress for civil rights legislation. Other developments were even more discouraging. Various liberal senators, including Anderson, Hubert H. Humphrey (the new majority whip and previously an opponent of Rule 22), and Mike Mansfield (the new majority leader and also an opponent of Rule 22 in the past), all said or were reported to have said that the time was not ripe for an attack on the rule. Eventually, however, Anderson agreed to repeat his old role of proposing three-fifths cloture, Mansfield appeared to be neutral, and Humphrey, after vaccillating almost until the opening prayer of the new Congress, finally joined the reformers.

Despite these and other disquieting signs and a general air of pessimism in the press, the liberals approached the beginning of the Eighty-seventh Congress with outward optimism. The incoming administration seemed above the battle; Nixon, with two weeks to go as presiding officer, still maintained that each Congress could make its own rules by majority vote; and a head count showed that a probable majority was in favor of at least three-fifths cloture. The liberals planned to allow more than a week of debate and then to move the previous question. Nixon was expected to rule that this motion was in order, the inevitable southern appeal of the ruling could be tabled without debate, the Senate could vote on the moving of the previous question and then on the proposed changes, beginning with the more extreme majority cloture and falling back to the Anderson proposal if the first one was rejected.

After a few days of debate Mansfield and the Republican leader, Everett M. Dirksen, said they would move to refer both proposals to the Rules and Administration Committee for "further study." Mansfield promised that the reform proposals would be reported to the floor "at a later date" and that "the minority leader join[s] with me in assuring the Senate that we shall do everything in our power to bring such a measure to a vote in this body."[10] Word soon spread that Kennedy favored the referral in order to dispose of an issue that otherwise would jeopardize his legislative program by antagonizing southern committee chairmen. The liberals argued desperately that postponement would cost them their procedural advantage; when the issue came before the Senate later in the session, debate on it could not be limited except by a two-thirds vote. Furthermore, they would lose the help of a presumably sympathetic presiding officer, for Johnson, the new Vice President, had made no secret of his hostility to changing Rule 22. (Johnson was thought to have played an important part in the maneuvering on this issue in 1961.) Mansfield's motion carried by a vote of 50 to 46, with Democrats and Republicans evenly divided.

The "later date" for consideration of rules changes turned out to be very late indeed. Mansfield waited almost until the end of the session and then announced that the Anderson proposal, S. Res. 4, would be called up on Saturday, September 16, and that he would immediately file a cloture petition to avoid wasting time. The liberals, additionally handicapped by having to find a two-thirds majority for cutting off debate before there had been any debate, and doing so at the end of a session when everyone wanted to go home, pleaded for a delay until the next session began in January. Both party leaderships, supported by the ordinarily leisurely Southerners, insisted on handling the matter with dispatch. Cloture was rejected on the 19th by a vote of 37 to 43, again with both parties split evenly. Mansfield then moved successfully to table his motion to consider S. Res. 4, and the issue was dead until 1963.

In 1963 Johnson refused to rule whether a majority could cut off debate at the beginning of a Congress. Instead, he put the question to the Senate itself, saying that since 1803 such constitutional issues invariably had been decided by the members, not by the presiding officer. The question Johnson referred to the Senate was debatable and his action thus had the effect of requiring a two-thirds vote to end debate. Three days later the Senate approved a motion to table this question devised by Mansfield and Dirksen.

[10] Rosenthal, *op. cit.*, p. 23.

The motion passed, 53 to 42, with all the Southerners, two-thirds of the Republicans, and more than a third of the northern Democrats voting in favor. Five days later Mansfield filed a cloture petition. Although the 54–42 vote was ten votes short of the two-thirds needed, the liberals at least had a majority, the first time since 1950 that this had happened on a cloture vote related to civil rights. The civil rights groups turned furiously on Johnson. One of their spokesmen claimed that the Vice President's ruling revealed that his first loyalty was to southern racists.

The successful cloture vote on the Civil Rights Bill of 1964 took some of the edge off the attempt to amend Rule 22 at the beginning of the Eighty-ninth Congress. The customary two reform proposals were referred by unanimous consent to the Committee on Rules and Administration. Two months later they were reported back to the Senate, along with a five-to-four committee vote recommending against their adoption. No further action was taken. It seems likely that President Johnson's ambitious legislative program, none of which appeared threatened by a filibuster, led to a gentle-man's agreement to forget about the issue.

In 1967 the liberals finally brought to a vote the question of whether a majority of senators could change the rules at the beginning of a session—and lost by more than twenty votes. George McGovern (D-S.D.) moved that the Senate vote immediately to end debate on a motion to take up a rules change proposal and then, if the motion carried by majority vote, proceed to further decisions on rules reform. Dirksen raised a point of order against McGovern's motion, calling it a violation of Rule 22. Vice President Humphrey said he would follow precedent and refer the question to the Senate for decision. But unlike Johnson in 1963, who referred the liberal motion to the Senate, Humphrey submitted this question: "Shall the point of order made by the Senator from Illinois be sustained?"[11] He also said that Dirksen's point of order was subject to a tabling motion and that if it were tabled, McGovern's motion would be in order and the way cleared to adopting a three-fifths cloture rule by a series of simple majority votes. Since a tabling motion is nondebatable and carries by a simple majority, Humphrey's action created a parliamentary situation diametrically opposed to the one produced by Johnson's seemingly similar ruling four years earlier, for as a result of his ruling the rules could be changed by a simple majority.[12] At last the liberals stood at the threshold they had been seeking since 1949, and at last they learned the naked truth: confronted by a clear

[11] Quoted in *Congressional Quarterly Weekly Report,* January 20, 1967, p. 88.
[12] Humphrey's ruling was carefully designed to allow the issue to be decided by majority vote and yet not violate the unbroken precedent that the presiding officer should refer constitutional questions to the Senate for its decision. This strategy had been planned in concert with the reformers. See Stewart, *op. cit.,* pp. 125–28. (Stewart was Humphrey's legislative assistant at the time.)

chance to amend Rule 22 uncomplicated by procedural distractions, a solid majority of senators went on record against majority rule. McGovern's motion to table Dirksen's point of order was defeated, 37 to 61; and the point of order then sustained, 59 to 37. On both roll calls only eight Republicans joined with just under two-thirds of the northern Democrats on the losing side. Mansfield, who supported Dirksen's point of order, then brought the issue to a close by filing a cloture petition which, as expected, was rejected by 53 to 46, thirteen votes short of the necessary two-thirds. Nine Republicans and four northern Democrats who voted for cloture voted against tabling Dirksen's point of order, the key vote on this issue in 1967.

After the brutal reality of the 1967 votes the 1969 revival of the issue produced little more than an anticlimax. Humphrey's decision in 1967 had been widely interpreted as an example of his general betrayal of liberalism.[13] In 1969, having endured two more years of vilification on this theme, the lame duck Vice President made the ruling his radical critics had demanded, with results no different from the earlier outcome. Humphrey announced that if a simple majority voted for cloture on a motion to take up a rules change resolution, he would rule that the majority had prevailed; and that if this ruling were appealed, the vote on the appeal would give the Senate a chance to decide the constitutional question of whether a simple majority could amend the rules at the beginning of a new Congress. The vote on the cloture motion was 51 to 47, Humphrey ruled that cloture had been imposed, this ruling was appealed, and reversed by a 45 to 53 vote.

This chronicle of unrelieved liberal defeats over Rule 22 contains important clues for understanding the role of unlimited debate in the Senate and in the national political system. The clearest conclusion to be drawn from these recurring episodes is that most senators consistently have opposed carrying the principle of majority rule so far as to weaken or abolish a minority's power to prevent the Senate from voting on a bill. Prior to 1967 it had been easier for many observers to believe that most senators disliked Rule 22 and would be willing to reform it if only a motion to do so could be brought to a vote. The outcome in 1967 exposed what the previous motions to table and refer to committee had obscured: most senators like Rule 22.

III

A second lesson from this history is that three presidents, who might be considered the natural enemies of the obstructive, sectional, anti-

<hr>

[13] See, e.g., Robert Sherrill and Harry W. Ernst, *The Drugstore Liberal* (New York: Grossman Publishers, 1968), p. 142.

majoritarian filibuster, have been remarkably unconcerned by the threat it poses to their goals. They have, in fact, appeared much more disturbed by attempts to weaken the filibuster. It seems that neither Eisenhower nor Kennedy nor Johnson ever did anything to help amend Rule 22. Indeed, while firm evidence is elusive, it appears that at least Kennedy and Johnson covertly encouraged dropping the issue. (Harry S. Truman, on the other hand, was a vociferous advocate of reform in 1949, although there is no indication that his efforts went beyond advocacy. His public statements on this issue were quite maladroit, devoid of the necessary bipartisan spirit, and usually at odds with the efforts of the Democratic leadership, often to the point of being a hindrance rather than a help.[14])

One school of political scientists, of whom James M. Burns has come to be the symbol, argues that this kind of behavior is unnatural, that by the very nature of things presidents should try to centralize power, and that when they do not, they are not only failing to play their role correctly but are also making a serious strategic error.[15] Since most presidents have made the same mistake, it might be useful to consider why they persist in behaving in such an apparently wrongheaded manner. The answer, I think, will also explain why most senators submit to minority rule.

One common explanation for the Senate's tolerance is that many senators anticipate a day when they may need to filibuster to protect some cherished interest of their own. It is said, for example, that the senators from Nevada oppose restricting debate because the gambling interests in their state, foreseeing future proposals for greater federal taxation or regulation, count on the filibuster for protection. This may be true, but it is also true that there are few Negroes and many ex-Southerners and Mormons in Nevada, and that the balance of constituent attitudes there is not favorable to civil rights. Moreover, it has been a long time since a liberal represented Nevada in the Senate.

I think it closer to the truth that filibusters essentially are for bills involving salient and emotional issues, of which the prime contemporary example is civil rights. Despite conservative filibusters to prevent elimination of Section 14(b) of the Taft-Hartley Act in 1965 and 1966 and liberal ones on Comsat and to preserve the Supreme Court's reapportionment decisions in

---

14 Stewart, *op. cit.,* pp. 87–91. For Truman's failings in congressional liaison see Rowland Evans and Robert Novak, *Lyndon B. Johnson: The Exercise of Power* (New York: New American Library, Inc., 1966), Chap. 3.

15 For Burns' criticisms of Franklin D. Roosevelt on this score see his *Roosevelt: The Lion and the Fox* (New York: Harcourt, Brace & World, Inc., 1956), pp. 375–80. The closest nonacademic parallel to Burns is *The New Republic,* which habitually urges presidents to act more presidential.

1964 and 1965,[16] Rule 22 reform is almost wholly a civil rights issue. The familiar bloc of lobbyists institutionalized in the Leadership Conference on Civil Rights—including labor, liberal, and Negro organizations—takes the field on Rule 22 disputes just as it does on substantive bills. The hard core of senatorial votes in defense of Rule 22 is from the South, and the onslaught is led by the most liberal senators. The principal difference between voting on civil rights bills and on Rule 22 is that moderate Democrats and most Republicans other than the small liberal bloc tend to oppose rule reform, as do the leaderships of both parties.

The extent to which filibusters are reserved for civil rights legislation can be illustrated by examining the issues on which conservatives used this weapon against liberal bills in the Eisenhower, Kennedy, and Johnson Administrations. All such cases in which the threat of obstruction was sufficiently serious to lead to a cloture petition are summarized in Table 1. All concern civil rights except the unsuccessful attempt to repeal Section 14(b), which permits states to adopt right-to-work laws. (President Johnson supported this measure, but without discernible enthusiasm, and the White House let it be known that the President would not push very hard for its passage.[17] It was generally felt that the bill's progress represented the Democratic party's debt to the labor movement rather than political calculations or ideological conviction.) The other seven cases all concern civil rights, a fact which strongly suggests that filibusters are a realistic threat only to a narrow element of a president's program and often are directed at bills about which the president is not very enthusiastic. The table also shows quite a strong relationship between presidential involvement and failure of filibusters. The only deviant case, the Civil Rights Act of 1966, was passed two years later after a hairsbreadth cloture vote.

During the 1950s and early 1960s political observers often classified civil rights measures as part of a general liberal legislative agenda. In fact, however, the issue was something of a special category in the minds of many Democratic politicians, particularly those who prided themselves on their pragmatism. They calculated that significant civil rights legislation could not be passed, that attempts to do so would damage Democratic unity, and moreover that such efforts were politically unnecessary for national Democratic electoral success. Civil rights was thought to be something of an obsession of impractical liberals, and political leaders often expressed

16 Two other successful conservative filibusters, against home rule for the District of Columbia in 1966 and against confirmation of Abe Fortas as Chief Justice in 1968, were motivated in part by racial considerations.

17 Eric F. Goldman, *The Tragedy of Lyndon Johnson* (New York: Dell Publishing Company, 1968), p. 334.

Table 1   Conservative Filibusters against
Liberal Legislation, 1953–1968*

Year	Bill	Cloture Vote	Votes Needed	Presidential Pressure	Cloture Imposed
1960	Civil Rights	42–53	64	low	no
1962	Restrict Literacy Tests	43–53†	64	low	no
1964	Civil Rights	71–29	67	high	yes
1965	Voting Rights	70–30	67	high	yes
1965	Repeal Section 14(b)	45–47	62	low	no
1966	Repeal Section 14(b)	51–48‡	66	low	no
1966	Civil Rights	54–42§	64	high	no
1966	D.C. Home Rule	41–37	52	low	no
1968	Open Housing	65–32‖	65	high	yes

Source (except for last two columns): *Congressional Quarterly Weekly Report,* January 17, 1969, p. 140.
* Includes only filibusters on which a cloture petition was filed and excludes non-legislative issues such as rules reform and the Fortas confirmation.
† On a second roll call a few days later the vote was 42–52.
‡ Two days later the vote was 50–49.
§ A few days later the vote was 52–41.
‖ This successful vote was preceded by three unsuccessful ones.

annoyance at the intrusion of the issue on their expectations. Thus during his period as majority leader Johnson complained: "I want to run the Senate. I want to pass the bills that need to be passed. I want my party to do right. But all I ever hear from the liberals is Nigra, Nigra, Nigra."[18]

In 1961 and 1963 President Kennedy helped defend Rule 22 not because he liked it, but because involvement in rule reform was not worth the price he would pay in party unity, since he had no intention of pressing Congress for action on the only issue likely to bring forth a filibuster. Much as his decision may have shocked liberal Democrats, they were unlikely to vote against his proposals, in contrast to the southern Democrats, who held the keys to his legislative success. The Kennedy Administration eventually did introduce and fight for significant civil rights legislation, but only after the Birmingham demonstrations in the spring of 1963 altered the political climate and forced a major policy shift in the White House.[19] Much the same pattern was followed in 1965. At the opening of the Eighty-ninth Congress in January 1965 President Johnson had no plans to introduce civil rights legislation. The dramatic brutality marking suppression of demonstrations in Selma, Alabama, led Johnson to much the same re-arrangement of his legislative program that his predecessor had made two

[18] Quoted in Evans and Novak, *op. cit.*, p. 119.
[19] David B. Filvaroff and Raymond E. Wolfinger, *The Civil Rights Act of 1964* (forthcoming).

years before, and again, with the Voting Rights Bill of 1965, civil rights legislation became an urgent White House goal.[20]

The narrow range of issues on which filibusters occur explains the durability of Rule 22, for if filibusters were more widely used, Rule 22 would not be so difficult to change. The senate could not tolerate promiscuous filibusters in which any minority resorted to unlimited debate to avoid defeat. Filibusters do more than prevent just one bill from passing; they keep the whole Senate from functioning, committees cannot meet (except by unanimous consent), and the need to remain available for quorum calls keeps senators from tending to many other kinds of business. The filibusterers themselves must be organized and disciplined. For these reasons filibusters— as opposed to the use of unlimited debate for on-the-spot tactical purposes —generally are reserved for issues on which a minority of senators represent very intense and salient opinion. If they were used more often, or more capriciously, the Senate would amend Rule 22 so as to exert more control over its proceedings, with the president cheering it on.

This point—as it pertains both to the Senate and the president—can be illustrated by comparing the filibuster to another classic obstructive device, the House Rules Committee, and by contrasting the new Kennedy Administration's behavior on the two procedural struggles that ushered in the opening of Congress in 1961, the Rule 22 fight in the Senate and the enlargement of the Rules Committee in the House. At the time of Kennedy's election the Rules Committee consisted, as it had for some years, of eight Democrats and four Republicans. Two of the Democrats, Chairman Howard W. Smith (Va.) and William M. Colmer (Miss.), were ultra-conservatives who frequently sided with the four Republicans to make a six-to-six deadlock and thus block liberal legislation on a *variety of issues*. This obstruction, however, did not interfere with committee meetings, floor business, or House activity other than the blocked measure. Since the Rules Committee's obstructive potential was focused and thus less disruptive of the good order of the House than was the filibuster of the Senate's, it could be more widely used —and was. It was responsible for the death of several important liberal bills in the late 1950s. This is not to say that Smith could have stopped any legislation he disliked; if this were the case, the country's laws would be very different from what they are.[21] But the Rules Committee's potential for blocking Kennedy's legislative program was far more dangerous than the continuation of an unamended Rule 22. Since Kennedy had no plans for

20 Goldman, *op. cit.*, pp. 337, 376–77.

21 Nor does it mean that Smith did not eventually lose a good measure of his power as a consequence of exercising it too eagerly. In this connection see Charles O. Jones' important article, "Joseph G. Cannon and Howard W. Smith: An Essay on the Limits of Leadership in the House of Representatives," *Journal of Politics,* 30 (August 1968), 617–46 [Chapter 16 in this reader].

civil rights legislation he had no cause to fear the filibuster and no incentive to inflame southern Democrats by trying to weaken it. But he did want to pass other social welfare legislation, some of which the Rules Committee had blocked in past years.[22] Therefore he leaped eagerly into the fight when liberal Democratic congressmen proposed enlarging the Rules Committee from twelve to fifteen so it would be composed of ten Democrats and five Republicans, replacing the old six-to-six deadlock with an eight-to-seven Administration majority. Rallying Speaker Sam Rayburn, he exerted every resource of his new administration in a tremendous campaign to enlarge the committee, succeeding by a margin of five votes.[23] The conclusion, I think, is clear: the filibuster is not used often enough on issues important to either presidents or a majority of the Senate to motivate them to weaken its power.

By itself this conclusion is not startling, but its implications run counter to the widespread interpretation of American politics that sees the president (especially if he is a Democrat) and his legislative allies—representing modern, urban, majoritarian America—opposing a more conservative grouping based on traditional, rural, consensual ideas. This view is held by such diverse interpreters of the political scene as Burns and the late Willmoore Kendall.[24] Yet there are times when the President is not so much the advocate of liberal measures as their would-be undertaker, at odds with his presumed allies in Congress. In recent years the most important of these issues often has concerned civil rights, and therefore in this respect the President has not been part of the coalition trying to make the policy-formation process more responsive to majority rule. In Burns' terminology, the president in these circumstances has been allied with the "congressional Democratic party," opposed to the goals supposedly pursued by the "presidential Democratic party."[25]

[22] *Ibid.*; James A. Robinson, *The House Rules Committee* (Indianapolis: Bobbs-Merrill Company, Inc., 1963); Frank J. Munger and Richard F. Fenno, Jr., *National Politics and Federal Aid to Education* (Syracuse: Syracuse University Press, 1962), pp. 132–36; Richard Bolling, *House Out of Order* (New York: E. P. Dutton & Co., Inc., 1965), Chap. 10; and Hugh D. Price, "Race, Religion, and the Rules Committee," in Alan F. Westin, ed., *The Uses of Power* (New York: Harcourt, Brace & World, Inc., 1962), pp. 1–71.

[23] There are many descriptions of the enlargement of the Rules Committee. See, e.g., Bolling, *op. cit.*; and Milton C. Cummings, Jr., and Robert L. Peabody, "The Decision to Enlarge the Committee on Rules: An Analysis of the 1961 Vote," in Robert L. Peabody and Nelson W. Polsby, eds., *New Perspectives on the House of Representatives*, second ed. (Chicago: Rand McNally & Co., 1969), pp. 253–81.

[24] See James M. Burns, *The Deadlock of Democracy: Four-Party Politics in America* (Englewood Cliffs, N.J.: Prentice-Hall, Inc., 1963), Part III; and Willmoore Kendall, "The Two Majorities," *Midwest Journal of Political Science*, 4 (November 1960), 317–45. I should add that neither of these authors explicitly states that presidents are deadly enemies of Rule 22.

[25] *Ibid.*

IV

Readers familiar with some of the leisurely filibusters of the period before 1964 might think that my characterization of their disruptive impact on the Senate is exaggerated. This is a fair judgment, but it is important to note that these languid affairs were not "true filibusters" in which a determined minority balked a majority. Two conditions must be met before a particular filibuster could validly be judged a minority veto: (1) House passage of the bill being filibustered; (2) a majority vote for cloture.[26] In other words, there must be evidence that the bill would have passed but for the filibuster. On closer examination of the historical record, it appears that these conditions were met only once between the end of World War II and 1964. The filibuster, then, does not deserve its fearsome reputation for defeating civil rights bills, but was instead a convenient scapegoat.

Of the eleven cloture votes on civil rights in this period, none came close to success. A simple majority was attained on only four of the eleven. The first of these four was a 48–36 vote in 1946 on a bill to establish a federal Fair Employment Practices Commission (FEPC). It is not at all clear that this was the true cause of the bill's death, however, for in the House an FEPC bill was bottled up in the Rules Committee.

In the same year a House-passed bill to prohibit poll taxes was stopped by filibuster, but won a simple majority in the cloture vote, 39 to 33. This is the only one of the four bills with simple majorities on cloture that also passed the House—that is, the only one that seemingly would have become law but for the filibuster. It is worth noting, however, that earlier in 1946 the Senate had tabled an attempt by Senator Wayne Morse to add this measure as a rider to another bill. This suggests that some of the votes for cloture were cast by senators fairly secure that they would not win.[27]

In 1950 two cloture votes on FEPC failed, 52–32 and 55–33. The latter was the closest approach to success on a civil rights cloture vote prior to

---

[26] It might be argued in rebuttal that votes on a cloture motion may reflect senators' views on the procedural issue of unlimited debate rather than their opinion of the bill being filibustered, and that therefore a significant number of senators voting against cloture on a bill might nevertheless vote for the bill itself if given the opportunity, and vice versa. The most that can be said for this argument is that it should be reformulated to state that, in given circumstances, senators' procedural preferences are more important to them than their substantive views, when the two are in conflict. Even this proposition is not very necessary to the argument, however. As my discussion of the Comsat filibuster shows, procedural issues of this kind seldom keep senators from voting so as to further their policy preferences.

[27] Although fifteen Republican senators voted for cloture and seven opposed it, sixteen others did not vote, which indicates either that the issue was not very salient to some Republicans or that they were staying away from the crucial vote as a means of ensuring the bill's defeat.

1964, falling nine votes short. In the same year an **FEPC** bill finally reached the floor of the House, but once there it was amended to remove all enforcement powers. Thus while a majority of the Senate favored an FEPC with power to enforce prohibitions against discrimination, a majority of the House was against it. Once again, the filibuster may have borne more than its proper share of guilt for the failure of FEPC.

Ten years passed before another cloture vote on civil rights legislation.[28] The cloture petition on the Civil Rights Bill of 1960 seems to have been more of a liberal grandstand play than a constructive attempt to strengthen the bill. The petition was filed even before a bill had reached the House floor, at least in part because of fears by the liberals in each party that the other party would appear the more dedicated to civil rights.[29] Cloture failed by 42 to 53, with Democrats split evenly and twelve Republicans in favor to twenty against. Neither party leadership nor the President supported cloture, and the bill eventually passed by the House was subsequently accepted by the Senate without major damage.

As with other aspects of the 1962 bill restricting the use of literacy tests in voter registration, the filibuster against it was largely ceremonial. No action was taken by the House on this measure, nor did a simple majority of the Senate favor it. Although ostensibly it was an Administration bill, the White House and Justice Department barely went through the motions of supporting it. No serious attempt was made to exhaust the desultory southern filibuster before resorting to cloture which, as in 1961, was timed by the leadership to dispose of the issue as quickly as possible and thus minimize the Democratic party split.

During the civil rights filibusters of the early 1960s the liberals were haunted by failure from start to finish. Their characteristic disorganization was less consequential than it might have been if the issue had ever been in doubt. Much of their behavior seemed to be for the sake of ceremony and Negro voters rather than constructive legislative purposes, as in 1960.

In short, from the war until 1964 only one civil rights bill was killed chiefly by unlimited debate, the anti-poll tax bill of 1946. During the Eisenhower and Kennedy Administrations no civil rights filibuster was strongly opposed by the leadership of either party or by the Executive

[28] The threat of unlimited debate may have been responsible for the 52 to 38 vote to delete "Part III" (empowering the Attorney General to initiate suits to prevent denial of equal protection of the laws) from the 1957 Civil Rights Bill, but it is by no means certain that this was the decisive factor, in view of President Eisenhower's distaste for this provision. See Evans and Novak, *op. cit.,* pp. 124–40; and Shuman, *op. cit.,* pp. 970–75 [pp. 279–85 in this reader].

[29] Statements about events in 1960 are based on my observations while a Congressional Fellow that year. Statements about civil rights politics in subsequent years are based on interviews with most of the politicans and lobbyists involved and my observations while a member of Senator Humphrey's staff in 1964.

Branch, and no cloture vote won even a simple majority. Thus while the filibuster is, as Dahl says, one of several governmental features that "provide a minority veto,"[30] it is a veto that is seldom exercised by a minority against a majority.

V

None of these judgments can be made of one other recent filibuster, against the Communications Satellite Bill of 1962, on which the Senate voted cloture for the first time since 1927. At issue was an Administration bill, already passed by the House, to authorize a private corporation to own and operate a commercial communications satellite system based on federally financed research. Some liberal Democratic senators denounced the bill as a giveaway of public resources and announced that they would filibuster it. The bill was debated for five days in June and again from July 26 to 31. On August 10 it came before the Senate for the third time and the next day the leadership filed a cloture petition. Cloture was invoked on August 14 by a vote of 63 to 27, three votes more than were needed.

The voting patterns made it quite clear that the principle of devotion to unlimited debate had its limits.[31] Every one of the thirty-four Republicans voted, and only the two most conservative, Barry Goldwater of Arizona and John Tower of Texas, voted against cloture. Seventeen Republican senators who had never before voted for cloture on a civil rights or rules change measure in the 1960s voted for it on Comsat.

The behavior of the Southerners and their conservative northern Democratic allies is even more interesting. All of the eighteen inveterate southern filibusterers (those from all former Confederate states less Texas and Tennessee) supported the Comsat bill. Eleven of them voted against cloture, including their leader, Richard B. Russell of Georgia, who said, "I'll vote to gag the Senate when the shrimps start to whistling 'Dixie.' "[32] These eleven could afford their procedural principles, however, for the other seven filibusterers made cloture possible, two by voting for it and the other five by not voting.[33] Two other conservative Democrats who had never voted for cloture, Alan Bible of Nevada and Robert Byrd of West Virginia, also

---

30 Robert A. Dahl, *A Preface to Democratic Theory* (Chicago: University of Chicago Press, 1956), p. 55.

31 For a similar interpretation see Keefe and Ogul, *op. cit.*, pp. 259–60.

32 Quoted in the *1962 Congressional Quarterly Almanac*, p. 378.

33 The only known "principled" vote for cloture by an opponent of the bill was by Clark, who stuck to his belief that a majority of senators should be able to vote on an issue when they wanted to. Frank Moss of Utah voted against the bill and paired for cloture. The other nine senators who voted against the bill all voted against cloture.

abstained. If any five of these seven anti-cloture senators had voted, 65 votes would have been required to stop debate, two more than the Administration mustered. Undoubtedly two more conservatives could have been induced to vote for cloture at the cost of compromising their principles. All in all, ten Democrats failed to vote, eight of whom announced their opposition to cloture and voted for the bill on final passage.

Less conspicuous events after cloture shed light on the relative durability of one Senate norm—that every member should have his say—and the extent to which this courtesy is extended equally to different senators. According to the rules, each senator may speak for a total of one hour after cloture has been imposed. Together with quorum calls and a minimum of twenty minutes to complete a roll call on an amendment, this gives diehard filibusterers further chances to obstruct proceedings. The liberals intended to exploit these rules, but quickly discovered that there were limits on the fabled Senate norms of respect for fellow members and opportunities for full discussion. As soon as a liberal offered an amendment, the leadership moved to table it, thus cutting off debate and forcing an immediate vote. The liberals lost every tabling motion and never mustered more than twenty votes. Most tabling motions carried by voice vote, which speeded up the proceedings even more. All in all, the liberals offered 122 amendments, some of which would have restored provisions in the bill the President originally had sent to Congress. Since many of these provisions had been amended in the House, restoring them in the Senate would have necessitated either House acceptance of the Senate amendments or referral of the bill to a conference committee to compromise the differences in the two versions of the bill. If the bill went to conference, however, the motion that the Senate accept the conference committee report could be filibustered. Nevertheless, the leadership could have permitted debate on these amendments and then let the Senate "vote them up or down," since it clearly had the votes to defeat all amendments. Instead the leadership chose speed over comity and ruthlessly pressed on to final passage by moving to table every amendment offered after cloture.

Two years later, when cloture was imposed on the Civil Rights Bill of 1964, the leadership faced a similar problem: how to respond to the more than five hundred amendments which the Southerners had filed and could call up one by one in order to delay the vote on final passage. At the meeting where this was discussed Senator Mansfield expressed his fears that the long controversy over the bill would end with the defeated Southerners deeply embittered and inclined to vent their feelings on other aspects of the Administration's program. Insisting "We've got to keep our party together," Mansfield was so solicitous of the filibusterers that he suggested trying to give each of them more than the allotted hour for speaking.

Senator Clark objected and urged that amendments be tabled as they were offered and that no time be lost in bringing the bill to a final vote. But other senators shared Mansfield's concern for party unity, which prompted Clark to ask bitterly, "Who worried about the liberals' feelings in the Comsat debate?" A conciliatory attitude prevailed, however, and the Southerners prolonged Senate proceedings for nine days after cloture by calling up and speaking for 104 unsuccessful amendments, all of which were the subject of roll call votes. Moreover, the leadership (in concert with Senator Dirksen) accepted several amendments offered by Southerners after private negotiations and, usually, redrafting.

The contrast between the leadership's behavior in 1962 and its behavior in 1964 can be explained principally by the identity of the filibusterers in the two cases, and in part by the solidity of the pro-cloture coalitions. The Comsat filibusterers were mostly rather junior senators and none was a committee chairman at the time, while the 1964 filibusterers included ten of the Senate's sixteen standing committee chairmen, as well as the chairmen of seven of the twelve subcommittees of the Committee on Appropriations. The Southerners were bitter at losing the cloture vote and Mansfield, characteristically preoccupied with maintaining party unity in the long run, wanted to avoid any further possible annoyances. He disliked the divisiveness of civil rights bills and felt that Southern chairmen took their revenge on this issue by delaying Administration legislation, particularly appropriations bills. The Comsat rebels, on the other hand, had neither the committee power of the Southerners nor their freedom to embarrass the Administration.

The leadership's willingness to accept amendments that were trifling or could be rendered harmless was motivated by a desire to be helpful to certain Southerners, for whom successful amendments were trophies to display at home. (One of them confided, "Down home, being against the bill isn't good enough; you've got to put in amendments, too.") Russell Long of Louisiana was most successful at this bargaining, principally because he was expected to succeed to the chairmanship of the Finance Committee fairly soon, and thus was a good man to propitiate.

Finally, there were fears that too arbitrary a stance might inflame enough touchy senators to risk losing their support on important amendments, for some Republicans were dubious about various provisions in the bill. Indeed, the Southerners gathered enough Republican support on one damaging amendment to come within four votes of winning. Fears of provoking a reaction from their shaky coalition led the leadership to give the Southerners all the leeway they wanted and also to accept several trifling amendments from Republicans. (Three of these were from Jack Miller of Iowa, who kept banging out new amendments on a cloakroom typewriter while the debate was in progress.[34] Dirksen eventually tired of this and, when approached by Miller with yet another trivial amendment, thundered, "Enough of this cheese-paring, Jack.") There were no such problems on Comsat, where the filibusterers clearly had no chance to win any votes on amendments, and so could be treated less tenderly.

These events do not seem consistent with the picture of the Senate suggested by those writers—notably William S. White—who stress that body's weighty respect for prerogatives, courtesy, and deliberation.[35] These norms are by no means limited to Rule 22, of course, but provide that every senator should have his say, in contrast to the large and impersonal House, where bills are briskly debated and voted up or down. Now there is no doubt that the Senate displays far more respect for individual members' sensibilities than the House.[36] My point here is that this solicitude—an important and constant factor in the leadership's strategy throughout the 1964 filibuster—varies significantly with the exigencies of the legislative situation (which is not so surprising) and the characteristics of those senators whose prerogatives are subject to violation. The contrasting post-cloture events in 1962 and 1964 suggest the existence of a Senate folkway that may take precedence over the norm of comity: some senators are more equal than others.[37]

White, the prototypical interpreter of senatorial norms, also offers, in his concept of the "Inner Club," a characterization of the Senate that seemingly accomodates my proposition.[38] But his argument about the "Club" differs from what I am arguing in two respects: (1) The advantages of being in White's Club are not that one then benefits from the norms of equality, courtesy, and so on. These, he implies, are universal save for the rare outcast. (2) Senators are in the Club by virtue of their conformity to

[34] The leadership was extraordinarily accomodating about granting unanimous consent to present amendments which had not been introduced before cloture.
[35] The standard work is White's *Citadel* (New York: Harper & Row, Publishers, 1956).
[36] For a useful discussion and demonstration of this point and its implications see Lewis A. Froman, Jr., *The Congressional Process* (Boston: Little, Brown, 1967), pp. 6–15 [Chapter 4 in this reader].
[37] A more explicit discussion of Senate folkways is in Donald R. Matthews, *U. S. Senators and Their World* (Chapel Hill: University of North Carolina Press, 1960), Chap. 5 [Chapter 6 in this reader] ; and Huitt, *op. cit.* For both these writers folkways or norms are individual role expectations, while I have broadened the terms to apply to leadership behavior, or collective senatorial decisions. This somewhat different usage is one of the reasons why my discussion of "unequal norms" is not directly at variance with Matthews, although it is not in consonance with his picture of the Senate.
[38] White, *op. cit.*, Chaps. 7–10. For a strong critique of the Inner Club theme see Nelson W. Polsby, *Congress and the Presidency* (Englewood Cliffs, N.J.: Prentice-Hall, Inc., 1965), pp. 32–43.

role expectations, while the Southerners in 1964 were the beneficiaries of their formal institutional positions (their chairmanships), not their level of group acceptance.

VI

To sum up the foregoing: (1) Filibusters have been so unthreatening to various presidents' legislative programs that the actual postwar occupants of the White House either have remained aloof from attempts to curb this presumed impediment to their power or have even covertly helped defeat and distract such efforts. (2) With one possible exception, in no case between the war and 1966 was the filibuster responsible for the death of a civil rights bill supported by majorities in Congress. (3) Far from being the most devoted advocates of full and free discussion as a general principle, irrespective of politics, supporters of filibusters often have displayed uncommon zeal to deny their opponents unlimited debate, most notably when changes in the rules were proposed, when the votes to support such arbitrary treatment were assured, and/or when the squelched senators were relatively junior.

16

CHARLES O. JONES

Joseph G. Cannon and Howard W. Smith: An Essay on the Limits of Leadership in the House of Representatives

That the House of Representatives is characterized by bargaining has been well established by many scholars of that institution[1] and suggests that leaders of that body must be skilled negotiators. Ultimately each representative, even the freshman, has some bargaining power (at minimum—his vote). It is on this basis of bargaining that the "middle-man" thesis of congressional leadership has been developed.[2] Rightly or wrongly House leaders must attend to their majorities.

Financial support for this study was provided by the American Political Science Association's Study of Congress, Professor Ralph K. Huitt, Director, and the Institute of Government Research, University of Arizona. The author wishes to acknowledge the comments of Richard Cortner, Conrad Joyner, John Crow, Phillip Chapman, and Clifford Lytle.

[1] For a sample of this literature see: David B. Truman, *The Governmental Process* (New York: Alfred A. Knopf, Inc., 1951); Bertram M. Gross, *The Legislative Struggle* (New York: McGraw-Hill Book Company, 1953); Robert L. Peabody and Nelson W. Polsby, eds., *New Perspectives on the House of Representatives* (Chicago: Rand McNally & Co., 1963); and particularly Robert L. Peabody, "Organization Theory and Legislative Behavior: Bargaining, Hierarchy and Change in the U. S. House of Representatives," unpublished paper delivered at the Annual Meeting of the American Political Science Association, New York, 1963.

[2] The "middle-man" thesis of congressional leadership is discussed in David B. Truman, *The Congressional Party: A Case Study* (New York: John Wiley & Sons, Inc., 1959). See also Samuel C. Patterson, "Legislative Leadership and Political Ideology," *Public Opinion Quarterly,* 27 (Fall, 1963), 399–410 (condensed).

Reprinted from *The Journal of Politics,* 30 (August 1968), 617–46, by permission of the author and publisher. Mr. Jones is Professor of Political Science at the University of Pittsburgh.

Two types of majorities in the House are of interest here—procedural and substantive. Procedural majorities are those necessary to organize the House for business and maintain that organization.[3] They are formed at the beginning of the session. Leaders are selected and provided with a number of bargaining advantages so that the House may perform its functions in the political system. Normally, membership of procedural majorities and minorities coincides with that of the two political parties.[4]

Substantive majorities are those necessary to pass legislation in the House. Whereas procedural majorities are relatively stable in membership, the make-up of substantive majorities may well differ issue to issue, since many substantive measures cut across party lines. Leaders are expected to build substantive majorities—employing the many bargaining advantages provided by their procedural majorities. They are not expected, nor do they normally have the power, to force members into substantive majorities.

House leaders must take care not to lose touch with any sizeable segment of their procedural majorities. On most issues they will find the basis for substantive majorities in their own party. Obviously, party members have views on the substantive matters before the House. If he wishes to remain in office, a leader must hold himself accountable to his procedural majority when building substantive majorities and accommodate important substantive changes among segments of his procedural majority. House leaders have latitude in their behavior, to be sure, and the process of defeat and/or reform is often painfully slow, but the leader who maintains himself in a responsible position of authority over a long period of time must be adaptive, communicative, accommodating, and accountable.

What if a House leader fails to behave in this way? In the short run, it probably will not make much difference. In the long run, however, aberrant behavior is bound to cause trouble for the leader with segments of his procedural majority. If it is a case of a leader exceeding the authority given to him, or failing to meet the expectations of his followers, he may simply be removed. But what if he has developed sources of power which make him independent of his procedural majority? That is, he is exercising authority which is real—it is incorporated into the position he holds—but is contextually inappropriate because it violates the bargaining condition in the House. Under these circumstances removing the leader is not the

3 Richard F. Fenno, Jr., has eloquently discussed the organizational problems of the House in his essay in David B. Truman, ed., *The Congress and America's Future* (Englewood Cliffs, N.J.: Prentice-Hall, Inc., 1965) [Chapter 11 in this reader].

4 Lewis A. Froman, Jr., and Randall B. Ripley note that the two parties maintain the highest level of cohesion on procedural questions. See "Conditions for Party Leadership: The Case of the House Democrats," *American Political Science Review*, 59 (March 1965), 52–63. Much of this essay tends to support their general argument.

whole solution. One may expect some House members to be concerned enough about the potential of divorce between the procedural majority and its leader to press for reform. One may further expect that in these situations the House will define the limits of leadership in that body as it debates reform.

There are two spectacular cases of "excessive leadership" in the House in this century. Joseph G. Cannon, as Speaker, had become an exceptionally powerful figure in American politics. He had a wide variety of sanctions available and he used them all. Nearly 50 years later, Howard W. Smith, as Chairman of the Committee on Rules, also had an impressive array of prerogatives—all of which he used to his advantage. The purposes of this essay are to examine the authority of these two men, how they exercised this authority in relationship to their procedural majorities, and the reaction and ultimate loss of their majorities. The findings not only tend to support the "middle-man" hypothesis but provide a clearer indication of its meaning as defined by the members themselves.

The Case of Uncle Joe Cannon

The House leadership situation in 1910 should have satisfied many of the responsible party scholars. There was no question that the Speaker was responsible for leading the House. Since his election in 1903, Speaker Joseph G. Cannon had enjoyed rather substantial procedural majorities and due to the growth of the speakership and Cannon's interpretation and use of his powers, a procedural majority carried with it awesome authority. He could appoint committees—including the chairmen—determine the schedule of business, recognize members on the floor, appoint members to conference committees, dispense favors of various kinds.

Cannon's Exercise of Power

Particularly significant was Speaker Cannon's power as chairman of the Committee on Rules. The Committee was small—never over five members prior to 1910. The three-to-two edge of the Republicans was potent, however, since the Speaker appointed the members carefully—insuring that they agreed with his views.[5] Champ Clark's view of the Committee was widely shared: "I violate no secret when I tell you the committee is made up of

[5] Cannon allowed the Democrats to select their members, though he did not have to make this concession. He did so because he thought that by giving the minority leader this power, the Democrats would fight over committee assignments. See William R. Gwinn, *Uncle Joe Cannon: Archfoe of Insurgency* (New York: Bookman Associates, 1957), p. 97.

three very distinguished Republicans and two ornamental Democrats. [Laughter]...there never would be a rule reported out of that committee that the Speaker and his two Republican colleagues do not want reported."[6]. . . .

A second center of power which the Speaker dominated was the Committee on Ways and Means. It was the custom to have the Chairman of Ways and Means serve as the majority floor leader. Sereno Payne, New York, served Cannon in these two important posts during his speakership. There was considerable overlapping membership between Rules and Ways and Means. Between 1903 and 1907, Dalzell and Grosvenor were second- and third-ranking Republicans on Ways and Means. Dalzell remained in both positions throughout Cannon's speakership.[7]

The list of grievances against Cannon and his lieutenants on Rules and Ways and Means lengthened with each year of his speakership. A frequent complaint was that Speaker Cannon abused House Rule X, which gave him the power to appoint the standing committees. He had made some spectacular appointments and adjustments prior to 1909—selecting Tawney, Minnesota, as Chairman of Appropriations in 1905, even though Tawney had never served on that committee; Overstreet, Indiana, as Chairman of Post Office and Post Roads in 1903, even though Overstreet had never served on that committee; and Scott, Kansas, as Chairman of Agriculture in 1907 over Henry, Connecticut (whom Cannon removed completely from the Committee) and Haugen, Iowa. In 1909, however, Speaker Cannon appeared to shift assignments about at will. Though seniority was not an inviolable rule at this time, it was relied on as a significant factor in committee assignments.[8] Twelve Republicans had not voted for Cannon for Speaker in 1909 and seniority was certainly no protection for them. . . .

Speaker Cannon was not above delaying the appointment of committees until his wishes on legislation had been met. In the famous 61st Congress, he appointed the important Rules and Ways and Means Committees on March 16, the second day of the session. Most of the remaining appointments had to wait until the Payne-Aldrich tariff bill was in the conference committee—nearly five months after the session began.[9]

---

6 *Congressional Record,* 61st Cong., 2d sess., March 17, 1910, p. 3294.

7 Cannon also preferred to have his whip on Ways and Means. James Tawney (Minnesota), James Watson (Indiana), and John Dwight (New York) all were on that Committee while serving as Whip under Cannon.

8 For discussions of seniority and its development, see George Goodwin, "The Seniority Sytem in Congress," *American Political Science Review,* 53 (June 1959), 596–604; George B. Galloway, *History of the House of Representatives* (New York: Thomas Y. Crowell Company, 1961); and particularly Nelson W. Polsby, "The Institutionalization of the U.S. House of Representatives," *American Political Science Review,* 62 (March 1968), 144–68.

9 See Paul D. Hasbrouck, *Party Government in the House of Representatives* (New York: The Macmillan Book Company, 1927), p. 37.

Joe Cannon did not limit himself to managing committee appointments. He also managed the output of the House. George Norris describes one of his early experiences on the House Committee on Public Buildings and Grounds. The Committee discussed drafting a public building bill and Norris soon learned that the Speaker would ultimately decide whether the Committee should proceed or not. "The senior Democratic member of the committee, Representative Bankhead of Alabama...actually made a motion that the chairman of the committee should seek a conference with the Speaker and ascertain whether or not we should be allowed to have a public building bill at that session."[10]

There were many examples of the frustrations of the insurgents in dealing with Speaker Cannon's Committee on Rules during the debate in 1910 to remove the Speaker from that Committee. One involved a first-term congressman from New York, Hamilton Fish. He had unsuccessfully sought to get a hearing before the Committee on a resolution which called on the Committee on Post Office and Post Roads to inquire into the feasibility and the desirability of establishing a parcel-post system. The colloquy between Fish and Walter I. Smith, Iowa, a member of the Committee on Rules, is worth recording here as an example of how various senior members would treat a freshman.

MR. SMITH. I deny that a hearing has ever been refused.

MR. FISH. Mr. Speaker, I have the evidence in writing that I asked a hearing and none has been granted me.

MR. SMITH. Well—

MR. FISH. I will ask the gentleman, in the six weeks that the resolution has been before the Committee on Rules why he has not answered my request and given me the privilege of a hearing?

MR. SMITH. Does the gentleman ask that question?

MR. FISH. Yes; why have you not given me a hearing?

MR. SMITH. I wrote the gentleman in person that while I did not approve of a parcel post myself I was opposed to suppressing any measure, and that I was willing to give him a hearing and report the bill adversely.

MR. FISH. I would ask the gentleman, then, why he did not give me a hearing?

MR. SMITH The gentleman never appeared and asked for a hearing.

MR. FISH. But I have written time and time again asking for it.

MR. SMITH. Oh, written—[11]

Fish's subsequent question to John Dalzell, also a member of the Rules Committee, regarding how a member extracted a bill from a committee which did not wish to report it, went unanswered.

---

[10] George Norris, *Fighting Liberal* (New York: The Macmillan Company, 1945), p. 109.

[11] *Congressional Record,* 61st Cong., 2d sess., March 17, 1910, p. 3300.

Managing the work assignments of congressmen, managing their work, and managing the rules by which their work would be done—such were the powers of the Speaker. Yet still other sanctions were available to him. Speakers have always had a number of temporary and honorary appointments which they can make. In some cases these are much sought after—for publicity, prestige, or for some other special purpose. Norris reports one such appointment which he sought. William C. Lovering, Massachusetts, a close friend of Norris and an early insurgent congressman, died February 4, 1910. Norris wished to be appointed to the committee representing the House at the funeral.

I hoped the Speaker, recognizing my close ties with Mr. Lovering, would accord me the privilege of paying my respects to a very dear friend, as a member of the House committee. Without seeing the Speaker about it personally, I had one or two friends approach him; and they reported he refused absolutely to approve my selection. It was a long time before the deep resentment which this aroused in me disappeared.[12]

This awesome list of powers exceeded that exercised by any previous Speaker. It was exceedingly difficult for the insurgent members to "force" the Speaker to accommodate their views because (1) he had so many sanctions available and could discipline not only them but any members who might otherwise be enticed to join them, and (2) the insurgent Republicans did not want to defeat Cannon so as to elect a Democratic Speaker, who would likely be no more accommodating to their views. Thus, Cannon had a considerable advantage and could ignore the changes occurring within his own procedural majority—he had developed a certain amount of independence from that majority.

The Warning Signals

Speaker Cannon and the regular Republicans had ample warning of the unrest among their more progressive brethren during the 60th and 61st Congresses. In fact, members made no effort to hide their dissatisfaction in speeches on the House floor. Twelve insurgents refused to vote for Cannon for Speaker at the opening of the special session in 1909, called by President Taft to consider the tariff. And a combination of insurgents and Democrats defeated the motion to adopt the rules of the preceding Congress. Minority Leader Champ Clark followed this victory with a resolution which would have increased the size of the Committee on Rules, removed the Speaker from the Committee, and taken from the Speaker his power of appointing all committees except Ways and Means. With insurgent support, the stage

12 Norris, *op. cit.*, p. 144.

was set for revolution at that moment, but John J. Fitzgerald (D-New York) and 22 bolting Democrats voted with the majority of Republicans to defeat Clark's move and Cannon was saved. Fitzgerald then offered a compromise motion of his own which established a unanimous consent calendar, a motion of recommital (for use by the minority), and increased the majority necessary to set aside Calendar Wednesday.[13]

Calendar Wednesday itself had been adopted at the close of the 60th Congress and though it did not meet the reform standards of the insurgents, there were strong hopes that it would limit Cannon's power. These hopes were dashed rather soon and rather decisively. A call of standing committees every Wednesday allowed committee chairmen to take bills which had been reported off the calendar for House consideration. With the changes as a result of the Fitzgerald compromise, the procedure could be dispensed with only by a two-thirds majority. A variety of devices was used to neutralize the procedure—adjournment required only a simple majority and was used to avoid Calendar Wednesday; bills of great length and complexity were called up and debated on successive Calendar Wednesdays (all nine Calendar Wednesdays were devoted to one bill in the third session of the 61st Congress).[14]

The Consent Calendar was more of a victory for the rank-and-file. There was a unanimous consent procedure in existence wherein any member could move consideration of a bill. The Speaker, theoretically, had no greater power of objection than any other member. In practice, however, the Speaker required advance notice of a unanimous consent request before he would recognize it. Thus, members had to clear such requests with Cannon before they could even be recognized on the floor.[15] The rules change created a Calendar for Unanimous Consent. The Speaker's consent was no longer required for a unanimous consent motion.

It was unlikely that these reforms would satisfy those members who were increasingly alienated from their own party. The 1908 elections resulted in a further reduction of the size of the House Republican majority. Cannon had a slim 29-vote majority in his first term as Speaker. Roosevelt's election in 1904 brought with it a 114-vote majority for Republicans in the House. This was reduced to 58 in 1906 and to 47 in 1908. Many of the new Republicans elected in 1906 and 1908 were from states in the Middle West

---

[13] Hasbrouck, *op. cit.*, pp. 4–6.

[14] The principal student of these changes is Joseph Cooper. See "Congress and its Committees," unpublished Ph.D. dissertation, Harvard University, 1961. See also Chang-wei Chiu, *The Speaker of the House of Representatives Since 1896* (New York: Columbia University Press, 1928), Chap. VI. Actually, for rather complicated reasons, the insurgents hadn't voted for Calendar Wednesday; see Cooper, *op cit.*, Chap. II.

[15] Hasbrouck, *op. cit.*, p. 126.

CHARLES O. JONES

and were soon to join veteran insurgents like Henry Cooper, Wisconsin; Gilbert Haugen, Iowa; and George Norris, Nebraska. Thus, not only was Cannon's majority being reduced but regular Republicans were being replaced by members who were potential threats to Cannon's leadership. The result was that if enough members absented themselves on crucial votes, the insurgents would hold the balance of power. For the insurgents the time had come. Speaker Cannon would be taught some fundamental lessons about leadership in the House of Representatives. Though he had developed impressive power as Speaker and found that he didn't have to make accommodations to a changing procedural majority in the short run, there were other alternatives available to the insurgents. They could always take their one bargaining advantage—the vote—and join the Democrats to curb the powers of the Speaker.

The Revolt

The full-scale revolt against Cannon began on March 16, 1910. . . .
Following the debate on House Joint Resolution 172, Norris pulled from his pocket a resolution to change the rules of the House. In his autobiography, Norris observes:

. . . I had carried it for a long time, certain that in the flush of its power the Cannon machine would overreach itself. The paper upon which I had written my resolution had become so tattered it scarcely hung together.[16]

Norris announced: "Mr. Speaker, I present a resolution made privileged by the Constitution.". . . Norris found a way to circumvent the House Committee on Rules for effecting a rules change. His "privileged" resolution would reorganize the Rules Committee by increasing its size, having members selected by groups of state delegations, and removing the Speaker from the Committee. Norris argued that his resolution was privileged under the Constitution because in Article I, Section 5, paragraph 2, it stated "Each House may determine the rules of its proceedings." The Speaker ordered the clerk to read the resolution. "The moment the reading clerk saw it he smiled, for he recognized the fact that the great fight on the rules of the House was on."[17]
. . .Speaker Cannon then ruled that "the [Norris] resolution is not in order." Norris appealed the decision of the chair and the Speaker was overruled (162 Republicans supporting Cannon and 34 Republicans voting with 148 Democrats against him). An amended version of the Norris resolu-

[16] Norris, op. cit., p. 126.
[17] New York Times, March 18, 1910, p. 1.

tion then passed the House 193 to 153. A total of 43 insurgent Republicans crossed over on this key vote to defeat the Speaker. . . .

Defining the Limits of Leadership

In debate the Cannon forces set forth the following argument—basically a party responsibility position with important modifications. The people had elected a majority of Republicans to the House of Representatives. That majority had selected a leadership group which acted for the party and therefore for the country. There is a necessary coincidence between electoral majorities, procedural majorities, and substantive majorities which must not break down. That is, no member may leave the majority without severe penalty. Those members who reject the party leadership are rejecting the Republican party and its mandate from the people to manage the House and its work. The leadership would provide mechanisms whereby individual members could make their opinions known. Mr. Fassett of New York spoke for the Cannon forces:

> We are robust partisans, every one of us. . . . I take it that no Democrat was elected to cooperate with our party nor was any Republican elected to hand over the Republican control of this House to our political opponents. . . . A man ought to have opinions and convictions. He ought not to be a political chocolate eclair. . . . In my judgment, the place to adjust differences of opinion on unimportant questions, and on important questions of public policy and party policy is not in public, where one minority uniting with another minority may make a temporary majority; but in the family caucus . . .[18]

Mr. Gardner of Michigan noted the importance of two parties which put the issues before the people in debate and the threat caused by actions of the sort contemplated by Norris.[19] Mr. Nye of Minnesota observed that "Parties are a necessity, and the great power and effectiveness of the Republican party has been largely its cohesiveness. Its followers have stood shoulder to shoulder and fought the battle against a political foe."[20]

But it was left to Speaker Cannon, following his defeat, to summarize the position most eloquently.

> THE SPEAKER. Gentlemen of the House of Representatives: Actions, not words, determine the conduct and the sincerity of men in the affairs of life. This is a government by the people acting through the representatives of a majority of the people. Results cannot be had except by a majority, and in the House of Representatives a majority, being responsible, should have full power and should exercise

18 *Congressional Record,* 61st Cong., 2d sess., March 17, 1910, p. 3302.
19 *Ibid.,* p. 3305.
20 *Congressional Record,* 61st Cong., 2d sess., March 19, 1910, p. 3430.

that power; otherwise the majority is inefficient and does not perform its function. The office of the minority is to put the majority on its good behavior, advocating, in good faith, the policies which it professes, ever ready to take advantage of the mistakes of the majority party, and appeal to the country for its vindication.[21]

After his defeat, Cannon surprised both his friends and his enemies by entertaining a motion to declare the office of Speaker vacant so that the new majority could proceeed to elect a new Speaker. It was a perfectly consistent maneuver on his part—consistent with his notion of party leadership in the House of Representatives. If a new majority had formed, and the recent vote indicated to him that such was the case, then that new majority "ought to have the courage of its convictions, and logically meet the situation that confronts it." Though Cannon's action was consistent with his notions of party leadership, it is likely that this move was less honest consistency than it was impressive strategy. If he felt strongly about the logic of his theory of party leadership, he could have easily resigned. He did not resign, however, because, in his words, he declined "to precipitate a contest upon the House...a contest that might greatly endanger the final passage of all legislation necessary to redeem Republican pledges..." and because resignation would be "a confession of weakness or mistake or an apology for past actions."[22] Neither reason is convincing. A lengthy and divisive contest could as easily ensue as a result of declaring the office vacant. Cannon himself noted that he was entertaining the motion so that the new majority could proceed to elect another Speaker. There was no reason to think that Cannon would be the only nominee. Further, if Cannon was consistent with the party responsibility theory, he would have resigned, not because of his analysis of his personal weakness or strength or because of his view of whether he had made mistakes or not, but due to the simple fact that on a paramount issue, *he had been defeated.* Other considerations were irrelevant.

In short, Cannon, and probably his cohorts, believed more in strong, personal party leadership with limited accountability to party membership, let alone the nation as whole, than they did in the classic party responsibility position. There is abundant evidence for this interpretation in their behavior before 1910, in the actions of the cabal before the debate in 1910, and in the Cannon maneuver following his defeat. He chose the strategy of entertaining the motion to declare the office vacant so that he might regain control of the situation. At the time, it looked very much as though he might succeed. As he proudly notes in his autobiography: "I was given more votes than at the beginning of Congress and when I went back to resume

21 *Ibid.,* p. 3436.
22 *Ibid.,* p. 3437.

the Chair I received a demonstration from both sides such as the House has seldom witnessed."[23]

It was precisely this "limited accountability" interpretation of party leadership in the House which defeated Cannon. It was not, and is not, consistent either with the structure of the House as noted above or the "middle-man" concept of leadership which is fostered by this structure. The insurgents articulated an interpretation much more consistent with the structure of the House. Whether theirs was a good or bad theory; whether it was well articulated or not; these are not relevant to the present argument. Though their position was much less tidy, and required considerable painful unraveling in the 1910 debate, it was more in the mainstream of the traditions of party leadership in Congress.

The insurgents argued that Cannon and his supporters had simply gone too far. Each congressman is an individual who is potentially part of a majority—procedural or substantive. On substantive issues, the insurgents argued, the Republican leadership was not attuned to new attitudes among Republicans. Leaders were using sanctions provided by procedural majorities to force—rather than build—substantive majorities. Leaders who do not attend to new opinions, and recognize their force, must face the consequences of losing their procedural majorities. Mr. Lindbergh of Minnesota argued the case for the insurgents as follows:

> ...when I look back over the proceedings of this House, and when I know, and the entire country knows, that by indirection the will of this House has been thwarted time and time again, then I say, when we have a resolution before us, which proposes to do by direction the will of the House, it is time now and here on this occasion to manifest our power, to enforce the rule of the majority, in the language that has frequently been expressed by the able Speaker of this House. I say now and here, in the light of what has occurred over and over again, in defeating, in holding back, in preventing bills that have been introduced in this House, which were in accord with the wish of the entire country at large—I say, when those bills have time and time again been pigeonholed by select committees, that now ... the House can by a direct vote do directly the will of the House ...[24]

John Nelson of Wisconsin also stated the insurgents' case vigorously. He observed that their duty was unpleasant—but that theirs had been an unpleasant experience in the House for some time. They had foregone the many privileges of the "regulars"—e.g., patronage and power—for the sake of principle. Their punishment was severe for failing to "cringe or crawl before the arbitrary power of the Speaker and his House machine." Nelson

---

[23] L. White Busbey, *Uncle Joe Cannon: The Story of a Pioneer American* (New York: Henry Holt, 1927), p. 266.

[24] *Congressional Record,* 61st Cong., 2d sess., March 17, 1910, p. 3300.

then discussed the problems of majorities, rules, leadership, and representation.

> The eloquent gentleman from New York [Mr. Fassett] says the majority must control, but what is the majority? Speaker Reed emphatically said: "There is no greater fallacy than this idea that majority and minority are predicated on political parties only." Why should the subject of the rules be a party matter? At what convention did the Republican party adopt the present rules of the House? The Speaker says he represents the majority. But how? He and his chief lieutenants—favorites or personal friends, a small minority within the majority—call themselves the party and then pass the word on to the rank and file of the Republican membership to line up or be punished. What is the controlling force? Party principles? No. The Speaker's power under the rules. . . . We are no less Republicans because we would be free Members of Congress. We do not need to be kept on leading strings. We are free representatives of the people, and we want freedom here for every Member of every party.[25]

It seems quite clear that Nelson's remarks may be interpreted in line with the analysis suggested here. Cannon's exercise of power was inconsistent with the bargaining condition in the House and therefore "free representatives" would form a new majority which would change the sanctions available to the Speaker.

The argument of the Democrats was very much like that of the insurgents. Oscar W. Underwood was led to conclude that leadership in the House should not be centered in the speakership—at least as it was exercised by Cannon. The Cannon "system" had to be overthrown.

> We are fighting a system, and that system is the system that enables the Speaker, by the power vested in him, to thwart and overthrow the will of the majority membership of this House. We recognize to-day that there has to be leadership; that some man must be the leader of the majority and some man must be the leader of the minority, but we say the place for that leadership *is not in the Chair*.[26] [Emphasis added.]

In summary, the insurgent Republican members were led to take the drastic action of leaving their party to join the Democrats on a major

---

[25] *Ibid.*, p. 3304.

[26] *Congressional Record,* 61st Cong., 2d sess., March 19, 1910, p. 3433. Interestingly, Underwood later became the principal leader of the House during the 62nd Congress as majority leader. The Democrats were in a ticklish spot. They wanted to emphasize the internal divisions in the Republican Party so as to win the 1910 elections, but did not want the Republicans either to get credit for reform or to reunite after reform. One news story suggested that the Democrats wanted Cannon to win, so as not to lose an issue in 1910 (*New York Times,* March 19, 1910). The Democrats also had to consider the problems for themselves of a drastic change in the Speaker's power, should they gain control of the House in 1910.

procedural change because they were convinced that the Speaker's authority had allowed him to ignore segments of his procedural majority. They were unable to reach him directly in pressing for representation of their views. As their numbers grew, they merely waited for the right moment—primed to take action sometime to make the Speaker more accountable. Mr. Norris' resolution served as the catalyst for action.

The Case of Judge Smith

In 1961, the House voted 217 to 212 to enlarge the Committee on Rules from 12 to 15 members. By this action, the House took the first of a series of steps to curb the power of the Committee and its chairman, Howard W. Smith of Virginia. The Committee had, since 1937, developed an anti-administration nature. Southern Democrats and Republicans joined to defeat presidential proposals. There was considerable evidence to suggest that these actions more often than not had the tacit support of a bipartisan majority in the House. As Lewis J. Lapham concluded:

> ...it is perfectly true that a very good case can be developed for supporting the proposition that the Rules Committee, though out of sympathy with the majority party program as defined by the President and his supporters, did in fact faithfully represent majority sentiment in the House.[27]

Adolph Sabath (D-Illinois) chaired the Committee every Congress, except the 80th, between 1939 and 1952. Though he personally supported Democratic presidents and their programs, he was extremely weak and ineffective as Chairman. Lapham observed that "the *Congressional Record,* since 1939, is replete with candid admissions by Mr. Sabath that he was 'helpless' in the face of an obstinate majority on the Committee which he could not control."[28]

In 1953, conservative Republican Leo Allen (Illinois) again chaired the Committee, as he had in the 80th Congress. And in 1955, after the Democrats recaptured control of Congress in the 1954 elections, Howard W. Smith became chairman. Smith had been influential on the Committee before his accession to the chairmanship. He and Eugene E. Cox of Georgia were the principal leaders of the Southern Democratic-Republican coalition during Sabath's long tenure as chairman. Smith was first appointed to the Committee in 1933—over the objections of the then-Speaker, Henry T. Rainey of Illinois. As chairman, Smith was free to exercise his considerable powers

[27] Lewis J. Lapham, "Party Leadership and the House Committee on Rules," unpublished Ph.D. dissertation, Harvard University, 1954, p. 137.
[28] *Ibid.,* p. 123.

to stifle legislation which he and his southern Democratic and Republican colleagues opposed. In some cases the legislation was part of President Eisenhower's program—in other cases attempts by the Democratic majority in the House to enact their own legislation.

Smith's procedural majority was of a different sort than that provided Speaker Cannon. Whereas Cannon was elected to office, Smith achieved his position of leadership through seniority. Thus, in accepting seniority as a procedure for committee chairmanships, the Democrats had to accept Howard W. Smith as chairman of the Committee on Rules. To "defeat" Smith, the Democrats would have to strike a blow against the whole seniority system. Thus, Smith, like Cannon, had a considerable advantage. He had a certain amount of independence from his procedural majority. Up to a point, he could afford to ignore it in exercising the considerable reservoir of power in the Committee on Rules. He proceeded to do just that.

Chairman Smith's Exercise of Power

How did Smith develop and use his powers? Two careful students of the House Committee on Rules, James A. Robinson and Walter Kravitz, have examined the influence of the Committee on legislation during this period.[29] Both indicated the wide variety of powers available to the Committee at the height of its influence. The more overt actions were to refuse to grant a hearing for a rule and to refuse to grant the rule. During the 84th Congress, Robinson found that only four requests for hearings were refused and 11 rules were denied. During the 85th Congress, 20 requests for hearings were refused and nine requests for rules were denied. In addition to these more obvious exercises of power, the Committee could force changes in the legislation as a condition for granting a rule, they could delay granting a rule until the mood of the House changed for some reason, they could grant a rule with conditions for debate which the authors did not want, they could threaten to refuse a rule. All of these tactics were relied on during the 84th and 85th Congresses. And, as is indicated by both Robinson and Kravitz, the legislation which was affected was often important legislation—the doctors' draft, housing, statehood for Alaska and Hawaii, aid to education, civil rights, depressed areas aid, presidential disability, absentee voting, appropriations measures, federal judgeships.

---

[29] See James A. Robinson, *The House Rules Committee* (Indianapolis: Bobbs-Merrill, Company, Inc., 1963); and the several useful unpublished research papers on the House Committee on Rules produced by Walter Kravitz of the Legislative Reference Service, Library of Congress. See also, Christopher Van Hollen, "The House Committee on Rules (1933–1951): Agent of Party and Agent of Opposition," unpublished Ph.D. dissertation, Johns Hopkins University, 1951.

Warning Signals Again

In 1958, the Democrats won a sweeping victory throughout the nation. They increased their margin in the House by 49 seats and their margin in the Senate by 17 seats. A number of Democratic liberals in the House went to the Speaker and proposed that the party ratio on the Committee on Rules be changed from eight Democrats and four Republicans to nine and three. They further pressed for the return of the 21-day rule. Speaker Rayburn convinced them that they should not press for the changes. He assured them that legislation would be brought out of the Committee.[30]

The 1958 elections were of considerable importance to Chairman Smith and his power base. It was at this time that his procedural majority began to change drastically. There were 48 congressional districts in which Democrats replaced Republicans. What was the significance of this trade for Chairman Smith? The *Congressional Quarterly* provides economy support and opposition scores for the 85th Congress and for the first session of the 86th Congress.[31] The 48 House Republicans who were replaced by Democrats in 1958 had an average economy score of 42.9 and an average economy opposition score of 42.0 in the 85th Congress. Their Democratic replacements in the 86th Congress, 1st session, had an average economy score of 9.3 and an average economy opposition score of 86.3. Obviously this new group of congressmen was considerably more liberal than the Republicans who left Congress in 1958, and markedly less dependable for Chairman Smith.

If Chairman Smith wished to retain his position of power in the long run, several developments made it evident that he would have to make some accommodations during the 86th Congress. Speaker Rayburn had given the reformers his assurance that important legislation would not be delayed and thus had put his prestige on the line. The new Democrats were anxious to develop a legislative record for the 1960 presidential elections. Criticism of the Chairman and his committee had continued to mount during the 85th Congress. And, the new Democrats had served notice of their intentions with their reform suggestions during the early days of the 86th Congress (much as the progressive Republicans had placed Speaker Cannon on notice 50 years earlier).

The record shows, however, that Chairman Smith continued to block legislation. He relied on the same techniques as before, despite the fact that a new, restive majority was emerging in the House—a majority which ulti-

---

[30] See Congressional Quarterly, Inc., *Congress and the Nation*, p. 1425. See also William MacKaye, *A New Coalition Takes Control: The House Rules Committee Fight 1961* (New York: McGraw-Hill Book Company, 1963).
[31] *Congressional Quarterly Almanacs*, Vols. 14 and 15.

mately could deprive Chairman Smith of much of his influence through procedural changes. During the 86th Congress, the Committee on Rules denied 31 requests for hearings and 11 requests for rules. As before, the Committee was a major factor in practically all significant legislation to come before the House—either by preventing its consideration on the floor or by influencing the substance of the legislation. But the most controversial action of the Committee was that taken in 1960 to defeat the first broad scale federal aid to education bill since the Morrill Act of 1862. Following the passage of the bill in both houses, the Committee on Rules invoked its power to deny the request for a rule allowing the House of Representatives to agree to a conference so as to resolve the differences between the House and Senate versions of the bill. The result, of course, was to kill the bill. By this action, the Committee on Rules seemed to place itself above majority action by *both* the House and the Senate. It became obvious to the liberal and moderate Democrats that Chairman Smith was not going to make accommodations. They concluded that their only alternative was to curb the power of Chairman Smith and his Committee on Rules.

The Limits of Leadership Reemphasized

The 1960 elections brought to the White House an energetic young President of the twentieth century. He had campaigned on a platform of "action." Though his majority in the House was 20 less than the Democratic majority of the 86th Congress, it was still sizeable and it was made up of many members who were extremely critical of the Committee on Rules. If the President's program was to receive favorable consideration in Congress, it would have to receive favorable consideration in the Committee on Rules. Unless changes were made, it was unlikely that the Committee would be so cooperative.

The results of the power struggle between the young President, his Speaker, and Chairman Smith have been well chronicled and thus only the sequence of events needs repeating here.[32] Our interest is not in the details of what happened but rather in the arguments which were made, since these arguments should provide clues in defining the limits of power for leaders in the House. A brief sequence of events is provided in Table 1.

As might be expected there are parallels between the debate in 1910 and the debates during the 1961–1965 period (of which the 1961 debate was the most crucial). As in 1910, those who pressed for change in 1961 argued in

---

[32] Note in particular, in addition to Robinson and MacKaye, the two articles in Peabody and Polsby—one by Peabody and one by Peabody and Milton C. Cummings, Jr.; and Neil MacNeil, *Forge of Democracy: The House of Representatives* (New York: David MacKay Co., Inc., 1963), Chap. 15.

Table 1   Sequence of Events in Decline of Power
of House Committee on Rules, 1961–1965

Event	Date	Vote
Enlargement of Committee from 12 to 15 for 87th Congress	January 31, 1961	217–212 GOP-22–148 Dem-195–64
Permanent Enlargement of Committee from 12 to 15	January 9, 1963	235–196 GOP-28–148 Dem-207–48
Reinstitution of the 21-day rule and tranfer of power regarding sending bills to conference.*	January 4, 1965	224–201† GOP-16–123 Dem-208–78

* The second change permitted the Speaker to recognize a member to offer a motion to send a bill to conference.
† On a motion to close debate. Rules changes actually passed by voice vote.

favor of leadership accountability to the majority. The Committee on Rules was a roadblock to the majority. It was not allowing the House to vote on measures which a majority in the House wished to vote on. Despite the fact that the majority party had a 2 to 1 majority on the Committee, Chairman Smith and second-ranking Democrat, William Colmer (Mississippi), would frequently vote with the four Republicans on important legislation to prevent it from coming to the floor. John A. Blatnik (D-Minnesota), head of the Democratic Study Group, and therefore a principal leader in adopting the rules changes, stated the case as follows:

> My constituents did not cast a free ballot for the office of U. S. Representative to Congress to have the functions of that Office limited by one or two or even six other Members. They understand that in a body as large as this the majority shall be established in caucus and put forward in the form of legislation by the leadership chosen by the majority. It is difficult to explain to them how 2 members of the majority [Smith and Colmer] can desert the majority's program, join with 4 members of the minority and among them determine the course of action of 431 other Members of this House. . . . Does their judgment supersede the cumulative judgment of the legislative committees? Do they have some inherent right . . . to determine the course of legislation. . . ? It would appear that they at least think so.[33]

Thus, though Blatnik, and others who pressed for change, agreed that any leader or any leadership committee had latitude in exercising power, they also agreed that there should be limits beyond which leaders are not permitted to go. To the reformers, the Committee on Rules ultimately should be a part of the majority leadership. That meant something very specific. For example, to Paul J. Kilday (D-Texas), it meant that:

[33] *Congressional Record,* 87th Cong., 1st sess., January 31, 1961, pp. 1582–1583.

...the Committee on Rules is an arm of the leadership of the majority party....
one who assumes membership on the Committee on Rules must be prepared to
exercise a function of leadership. His personal objection to the proposal is not always
sufficient reason for him to vote to deny the membership of the whole House the
opportunity to express its approval or, equally important, the opportunity to
express its disapproval.[34]

Speaker Rayburn expressed much the same sentiment:

I think that the Committee on Rules should grant that rule whether its membership is for the bill or not. I think this House should be allowed on great measures
to work its will, and it cannot work its will if the Committee on Rules is so
constituted as not to allow the House to pass on those things.[35]

Frequent references to 1910 were made. At the time "too much control
was centered in the Speaker...." "Today... we fight a system which has
deposited too much power in the Committee on Rules..."[36] according to
Sidney R. Yates (D-Illinois). What is the definition of "too much power?"
It is that situation when leaders have been permitted to exercise greater
authority than was intended by the procedural majority in the House.

The Limited Accountability Theory Restated

The arguments of Smith and his supporters also bore the characteristics
of the 1910 debate. Speaker Cannon believed in limited accountability and
so did Smith. Though their positions of leadership were different, and therefore one would not expect exact parallels between the two situations, the
two had similar views of leadership and accountability. To Chairman Smith,
the whole effort to enlarge the Committee was both unnecessary and prema-
ture. In a series of circumlocutions (some of which were contradictory),
Smith and his cohorts argued as follows:

1. The Committee has been wrongly charged—it does not block important legislation which requires "emergency action." As Clarence Brown (R-Ohio), ranking
Republican on the Committee on Rules, and close colleague of Chairman
Smith, noted: "In my nearly a quarter of a century of service here, I have
never known of a single instance, when the House leadership desired a bill to
be brought to a House vote, that such measure was not voted upon."[37]
2. The Committee will delay on measures which are not "emergency" measures
but "nothing is lost and much is gained by delay.... 'haste makes waste'...John
Nance Garner...once was reported to have said, 'The country never suffers
from the things that Congress fails to do.' "[38]

[34] *Ibid.*, p. 1574.
[35] *Ibid.*, p. 1579.
[36] *Ibid.*, p. 1581.
[37] *Ibid.*, p. 1575.
[38] *Ibid.*, p. 1577.

3. The majority can always work its will—it can go around the Committee on Rules by relying on Calendar Wednesday, discharge petition, and suspension of the rules.
4. Much more legislation is killed in other standing committees than in the Committee on Rules.
5. How can the president know that his program will not be enacted? He has just arrived on the scene. It would be better to leave the "packing" resolution on the calendar for two years and then assess the situation when the evidence is in.
6. The Chairman is willing now to insure that "no obstacles" would be interposed "to the five major bills that the President has publicly announced as his program for this session."

This example of a Smith accommodation is very revealing and brings us to an analysis of his broader view of his position of leadership. He did not consider it necessary generally to work with his party leaders and membership in passing legislation but he was willing to allow five major bills to reach the floor. This offer was considered "audacious" by the reformers. Blatnik expressed their views:

Who else would have the audacity and arrogance to even suggest that in exchange for our agreeing to the status quo they would permit us to consider five pieces of legislation said to be the cornerstone of the new administration's domestic program? This offer was an insult to the House and its Members. The fact that it was a bona fide and sincere attempt only heightens the frightening picture of two men telling a nation that they will permit five bills to pass if they can reserve their right to kill off any others that do not meet with their approval.[39]

How could this type of proposal be offered by Smith? Clearly, he saw it as a definite concession. "All of the five bills which the President has announced as his program for this session...are five bills that I am very much opposed to...."[40] Smith did not consider that he had an obligation to support his party's legislation just because he chaired the committee which scheduled that legislation.

When I made this pledge to the Speaker and to the Members of this House, it is a pledge I made when I first became chairman of the Rules Committee. That is, *I will cooperate with the Democratic leadership of the House of Representatives just as long and just as far as my conscience will permit me to go.*[41] [Emphasis added.]

The convenience of holding oneself accountable to "conscience" is that only the individual himself is involved in defining accountability. This self-interpretation was the very thing that was objected to by the reformers. It

---

39 *Ibid.*, p. 1583.
40 *Ibid.*, p. 1576.
41 *Loc. cit.*

meant that the majority could not be assured of cooperation from one of their leaders. Speaker Rayburn, among others, expressed his concern.

> The gentleman from Virginia says that he is not going to report anything that violates his conscience and then winds up his talk on the floor by saying you have nothing to fear from the action of the Committee on Rules.[42]

In 1963 the Committee on Rules was permanently expanded to 15 members. Many of the same arguments were invoked but the political situation had changed. The reformers could now defend their experiment— pointing out that the dire predictions of those opposed in 1961 had not come true. Even the Republicans seemed to accept the 15-member committee, though they tried to have the party division changed from 10 Democrats and 5 Republicans to 9 Democrats and 6 Republicans. The best the opponents of a 15-member committee could do was to reiterate their earlier arguments and note that the committee's performance in the 87th Congress was little different than before—it, too, blocked legislation.[43] For Judge Smith's part, he focused his attention on southern Democrats, warning that:

> ...this matter of packing the Rules Committee affects more closely our area of the country than anywhere else.... I hope that none of my southern friends are going to be complaining around here when certain measures come up, and come up quite promptly, if the Committee on Rules is packed again.... I hope that at least those Members who voted against the packing before will see fit to do the same thing again, because I believe *it is vital to the interests of their States*....[44] [Emphasis added.]

The Chairman also addressed the new members of the 88th Congress. He warned them that unwise fiscal legislation would soon be introduced.

> Are you going to yield up every little leverage or every little weapon you may have to defeat measures so unsound? Are you going to yield some of your prerogatives and privileges here today that are going to adversely affect your people for the next 20 years? If you do, *that is your business and none of mine*.[45] [Emphasis added.]

---

[42] *Ibid.*, p. 1580.

[43] Particularly noted was the defeat of the federal aid to education bill in the Committee in 1961. Though a bargain had been struck between pro- and anti-parochial school aid members, the parochial aid proponents were not convinced that they would get what they wanted. Thus, a liberal, Democratic, Catholic member of the Committee on Rules, James Delaney of New York, voted with the conservatives to kill the bill. See H. Douglas Price, "Race, Religion, and the Rules Committee," in Alan F. Westin, ed., *The Uses of Power* (New York: Harcourt, Brace & World, Inc., 1962) ; and Robert Bendiner, *Obstacle Course on Capitol Hill* (New York: McGraw-Hill Book Company, 1964).

[44] *Congressional Record,* 88th Cong., 1st sess., January 9, 1963, p. 18.

[45] *Loc. cit.*

Howard W. Smith proved himself to be an unintentioned prophet. By a margin of 39 votes (see Table 1), the House did make an attempt to clarify the distinction between its business and that of Judge Smith. Thus occurred the second important increment in the decline of the chairmanship of the Committee on Rules.

The third increment came in 1965. With very little debate, the House re-invoked the 21-day rule[46] and took away the Committee on Rules' power, when any member of the House objected, to grant rules to send a bill to conference (or to agree to the Senate version). In both instances, the powers of the Speaker were increased. To Clarence Brown (R-Ohio) this raised the spectre of the all-powerful Speaker before 1910. In a colloquy with Speaker McCormack, he observed:

> You are too nice a fellow. But I am thinking about some dirty dog that might come along some other time and say here is a nice little wrinkle in the rule which we can use to block this legislation.
>
> In other words, should we give that power to every Speaker in the future? We gave that power to "Uncle Joe" Cannon and Tom Reed as the gentleman recalls. We gave them too much power.[47]

Ironically, Brown failed to perceive that his colleague, Howard W. Smith, also had been given more power than was compatible with the structure, organization, and composition of the House of Representatives. Smith developed independence from those who ultimately had provided him with this position of authority. Smith's refusal to heed the warning signals of substantive shifts in his procedural majority resulted in changes which forced him to be more dependent on this majority or face a serious loss of influence in the process of building substantive majorities.

Conclusions

In 1910 and 1961 the House of Representatives acted to curb the power of two generally well-loved and admired leaders—Joseph G. Cannon and Howard W. Smith. These men had realized the full potential of the authority inherent in their respective positions in the House. Though in different ways, they both had become virtually independent of their procedural majorities. Defeating them would not have solved the problems raised by their exercise of power. Thus, the House took the more drastic action of making procedural changes to guarantee the predominance of the condition of relatively free bargaining, with leaders acting as "middle-men."

---

[46] The 21-day rule had been implemented during the 81st Congress and abandoned in the 82nd Congress. It has since been abandoned in the 90th Congress.

[47] *Congressional Record,* 89th Cong., 1st January 4, 1965, p. 22.

Though it is not possible as a result of this inquiry to set forth a handbook for successful leadership in the House, it is possible to draw some inferences concerning the limits which must be observed by the "middle-man" type of leader. First, the procedural majority is of major significance for House leaders since the sanctions it allows determine the limits on leaders in forming or thwarting substantive majorities. In order to protect his position, the House leader must be exceptionally protective of this procedural majority —developing techniques which will inform him as to substantive changes which have occurred within various segments of the majority, and making a requisite number of adaptations.

Second, there are cases, as noted here, where leaders have developed, over a period of time, the authority of the position to the extent that they seemingly are independent of the procedural majority. Their exercise of power eventually leads some members to the conclusion that procedural changes are necessary to prevent a recurrence of such independent action. If there are enough members of the majority who perceive violations of bargaining behavior on the part of leaders over a period of time, they may take extreme action to force compliance with their expectations. These instances are of major significance for the study of the House since they provide important clues as to how that body defines leadership for itself.

Third, all House leaders have considerable latitude in using the sanctions provided by procedural majorities in building substantive majorities. In the short run, therefore, leaders thwart the emergence of new majorities. Furthermore, leaders are normally given ample warning of dissatisfaction before action is taken. If the leader persists in ignoring these signs (or in simply failing to read them properly), he will be defeated. If, in addition, he has assumed so much power that he is protected from his procedural majority, the reform condition is set and changes will be made eventually.

Fourth, both cases cited here suggest that leadership positions of great, absolute authority in the House of Representatives are contextually inappropriate. Congressional political parties are coalitions of members, each of whom has some bargaining power. Thus, conditions in the House are not conducive to the exercise of power with such limited accountability to major segments of the procedural majority, as in the two cases cited here.

Fifth, one is inevitably led to inquire whether Speaker Cannon and Chairman Smith could have avoided the consequences which ultimately developed. If the analysis of this essay is accurate, the answer must be "yes." They could have avoided the reforms by accepting the conditions of leadership in the House and behaving accordingly. Had they been more flexible, they would likely have not only avoided being "reformed" but also have preserved more power for themselves in the long run. Speaker Sam Rayburn, the model "middle-man," could have counseled them both on such matters.

VI

Lobbying

No aspect of Congress excites more moral passions than lobbying—that is, attempts by groups to get Congress to do what they want it to. According to one durable political outlook, this practice plumbs the depths of evil. In reaction to this hypermoralism, another perspective has arisen: Once upon a time lobbyists may have behaved badly, but now they merely "communicate" with Congress. This second viewpoint is as misleading in its own bland way as the excited moral condemnation of muckrakers is in the opposite direction.

Lobbying is guaranteed by the Constitution, which gives every citizen the right of petition. Moreover, in the absence of lobbying government officials would be trying to make decisions without information as to how those decisions would be received by the people whom they affect. From a practical point of view, politicians can hardly be expected to stake their futures on measures whose popularity has not been measured by some test, and lobbying, in addition to its other functions, does let congressmen know the strength of forces pro and con. Lobbying is not something done exclusively by big business. In fact, probably the most formidable and ubiquitous lobbying organization on Capitol Hill is maintained by the labor movement; the AFL-CIO and each of the major unions maintain their own force of legislative representatives, who are able to influence congressmen by campaign contributions, by the command of well-trained campaign workers, and by their links to local unions in many states and congressional districts.

On the other hand, lobbying presents plenty of raw material for reporters trying to expose bribery and other forms of the illicit exercise of influence in Congress. One important consideration in this connection is that such unethical lobbying efforts are generally concerned not with the great issues that excite public debate and draw most attention from the press, but rather with relatively minor questions of contracts, specialized provisions in obscure laws, and similar matters which are important chiefly to individuals or to very restricted groups.

The first reading in this section, by Lewis Anthony Dexter, examines the problem of lobbying from the standpoint of organizations which have interests affected or potentially affected by what the government may or may not do. Like Dexter's previous article (Chapter 5), this essay is an attempt to understand the practical problems encountered by people with a job to do, in this case lobbyists rather than congressmen. Dexter is concerned with the specific types of goals pursued by lobbyists, the techniques they can use to attain their goals, and the varied points of access that the government offers them. An important theme of his article is the highly complicated character of modern American government, which offers to any questing petitioner a variety of paths, some of which may turn out to be exceedingly rocky, if not impassable, while others lead quickly to satisfaction. This theme illustrates the importance of skill and knowledge in lobbying, since a premium is placed on knowing which channels to use to get what one wants.

Clem Miller's account comparing effective and ineffective lobbying by different groups, while written from the opposite perspective—the congressman's—nicely illustrates Dexter's emphasis on information and skill as factors affecting the success of lobbyists. Miller compares the professional, highly organized effort made by walnut growers to obtain government help when they were in distress with the disorganized and ineffectual attempts made by chicken farmers facing a similar problem. His selection demonstrates in a specific and highly knowledgeable way at least one reason why lobbying works or does not work.

The same can be said of the third selection, an attempt by a tax expert to explain the success of vested interests in obtaining special tax provisions. Stanley S. Surrey's article brings together a series of important themes about American government: (1) Quite often, all the interest groups active on an issue are on one side, unopposed by any organized or articulate private forces. In other words, there are no "countervailing" powers, and the only people paying attention to the issue are those who seek to gain by certain provisions, while those people who would lose—that is, all the rest of the taxpayers—have such a diffuse interest and are individually so little affected that they are politically inconsequential. In these circumstances, the principal force resisting requests for special treatment is the Treasury Department, whose officials come to feel that they cannot be consistently effective without some political help. (2) The power of committee members tends to increase when the issues they consider are specialized and obscure. In such cases, the committees are not only the first but the last effective court of appeals, and therefore the point at which pressure is to be exerted is the committee, and not the House and Senate as a whole. (3) Surrey's article illustrates how the *process* of American politics varies with the nature of the *issue* being decided; compare his account with Ripley's description of leadership influence in Chapter 13.

On some legislative measures lobbying consists in good measure of mobilizing campaigns of pressure and publicity from thousands or hundreds of thousands of constituents. For example, the vigorous opposition to gun control bills by the National Rifle Association in 1968 was based upon nationwide letter writing stimulated by local branches of that organization. Here the issue was rather simple, emotional, and easily understood by large numbers of people. On issues such as civil rights, medical care, and other important, visible, and widely relevant measures, the public which is concerned with the issue is huge and lobbying consists largely of orchestrating manifestations of publicity and public opinion. On such issues, when the political stakes are high, the White House and its formidable, well-organized congressional liaison staff enter the picture, lobbying with a mixture of threats, bargaining, promises, and negotiating skill. On the other hand, on issues such as tax exemptions, the political stakes are important only to a very few people.

17

LEWIS ANTHONY DEXTER

When the Job Is Chiefly Lobbying

A theme of this book is, "It isn't just lobbying." But, for some Washington representatives, the main job *is* lobbying; and for others at some times and periods, lobbying is major. This chapter covers (1) some sorts of situations when lobbying is or ought to be the procedure of choice in government relations; (2) considerations which effective lobbyists keep in mind—for instance, how to talk with congressmen and the emphasis on the soft sell; and (3) some *illustrations* of the technique of lobbying—such as "feeding questions" and establishing a legislative history.

Another topic which is suggested by the chapter is (4) that it is always worthwhile to look out and see whether lobbying may be counterproductive or wasteful. Much of it is one or the other.

I

Lobbying is the choice when:

a. there is a reasonable likelihood that the Congress will take action which affects policy in the preferred direction; and

b. there are enough resources available to the organization so that it can afford to invest time, energy, money, and good will in lobbying; and

c. lobbying or its results do *not* run a great risk of becoming counterproductive.

Reprinted from *How Organizations Are Represented in Washington* (Indianapolis and New York: The Bobbs-Merrill Co., Inc., 1969), pp. 55–60, 62–63, 85–95, 97–101, by permission of the publisher.

334   When the Job Is Chiefly Lobbying

I use the general phrase "take action," rather than the more specific "legislate," in order to include all the areas on which lobbyists might wish to approach congressmen or congressional employees. In the working vocabulary of American legislatures, legislation applies to statutes of a certain generality, but not always to appropriations, investigations, etc. But "nonlegislative" actions of Congress do in fact affect general policy. For instance, an investigation—sometimes even the threat of an investigation—can change, reinforce, or influence practices almost as much as a law. For instance, it appears that the real effect of the Kefauver, Humphrey, and Fountain investigations of pharmaceutical practices was not predominantly on specific legislation. Rather, they influenced relevant agencies—and also pharmaceutical companies[1]—to change policies. So, too, the investigations directed by Senator Joseph McCarthy had a considerable effect for some years on the treatment of male homosexuals in government and working on defense contracts, and perhaps in the entire society.

Equally clear and even more far-reaching is the effect of appropriations and funding on policy.[2] If the Congress increases or cuts money, it may affect policy. A notable example of where policy was influenced through the appropriations process was provided by the House subcommittee concerned with health budgets, under the late Representative John Fogarty. It consistently raised appropriations for Health Institutes beyond presidential requests, often accompanying a raise with a directive.

And confirmation of appointments—or failure to confirm them—certainly may have an effect on policy. Any systematic emphasis by several senators on the kinds of appointments they will disapprove, or on the kinds of patronage they will demand, could influence policy. After all, men influence measures.[3]

---

[1] See Morton Mintz, *By Prescription Only* (Boston: Little, Brown & Co., 1967).

[2] See Richard Fenno, *The Power of the Purse: Appropriations Politics in Congress* (Boston: Little, Brown & Co., 1966).

[3] It is said that the late Senator McCarran had considerable influence over the Immigration and Naturalization Service, and other units in the Department of Justice, precisely because he was able as a sort of patronage to determine middle-level appointments as well as some at higher levels. It does not matter, for our present purposes, whether this was true or not. The point is that it could be true of any able, aggressive, astute senator, over a period of years (and probably also of a senior House member). In a sense, of course, helping or persuading a senator or congressman to use such influence is not "lobbying" but "congressional interference in administration," to use Kenneth Gray's term. Also, the Senate does have a definite, constitutional responsibility for confirming judicial appointments; and it seems almost certain that the influence of several southern senators during the Kennedy administration did tend to discourage the appointment of circuit and district judges who might have quickly implemented the Supreme Court's position on civil rights—not even so much by holding up or insisting on specific appointments, but because, when calculating the chances for potential nominees, the administration itself ruled out those who would run into real trouble with the Judiciary Committee of the Senate, which must first approve nominations to judgeships, and which has several southern members.

In order to find out whether there is a reasonable prospect of the Congress's taking action in some preferred direction, a lobbyist needs to have accurate information about the committees, the leadership, and the schedule, and, of course, about demands from the executive branch, influential groups in the country, and constituencies. A great many bills are introduced each year. The Washington representative who can afford the time will keep track of any which may be relevant. He should find out why the member who introduced them did so; and he will see if anything can usefully be said, *and by whom,* to the member or to the people at whose request the bill was introduced.

A great many bills are *introduced* each year—but few are *chosen* for serious consideration by a committee. Limitations on time and attention mean that only a few measures can be considered by a given committee in a given session. Accordingly, if the preferences of the *active* members of the committee are known, if the priorities of the executive departments are evident, and if some reflection is given to what is likely to be urged from outside the Congress or by the leadership and referred to a given committee,[4] the schedule for a particular year can be more or less foreseen. Since most measures which are introduced will not be taken up seriously in committee, there is little reason to do a great deal about them, unless:

a. Organizing sentiment for them serves to publicize the proposal (or its dangerousness) and make one's supporters enthusiastic. A good many measures have been introduced chiefly in the hope of such publicity, even though there is little or no prospect of enactment or even committee consideration.

b. Trying to do something about them serves as a way to get congressmen and staffs to pay attention to a problem and a proposal—so that in some future year, even if not in this one, they might take up the matter seriously.

There is a third reason why it makes sense for some Washington representatives to do something about proposals that have only a slight chance of being enacted, although such activities do not help the "cause":

c. Activity—introducing a measure, sending out the alarm about another, and so on —may make some clients and supporters feel that the Washington representative really is doing something, that he's on the ball, that there is need to keep him

4 With very rare exceptions, any measure will have to be considered by a committee before it goes to the floor of the Congress. There is some leeway—but not by any means an unlimited amount—in determining which measure goes to which committee. Knowledge of history and procedure helps to determine when such leeway exists; emphasis and key words can be juggled in order to lead to reference to committee X rather than committee Y—or, occasionally, with subcommittees who are sympathetic, some of the purposes of legislation may be achieved by recasting a proposed policy change in terms of a resolution so that it leads to an investigation; or some actions may be initiated without going to the floor in the committee. On all such matters, see Bertram Gross, *The Legislative Struggle* (New York: McGraw-Hill Book Company, 1953).

there. "Going through the motions"—as part of what sociologists call "maintenance functions"—is a large part of all politics—for that matter, of most work. To the extent that an organization relies upon the support of what may be called unsophisticated consumers, no doubt a Washington representative has to engage in this sort of make-believe. There have been, for instance, occasions when a bill or resolution was introduced by a member, when both he and the lobbyist who wrote it knew for certain that it would never get anywhere. A cheap way for a congressman to do a favor for a lobbyist is to introduce such a bill; it gives the lobbyist a talking point with his "constituents," members of his organization. *And congressmen, who after all must spend a lot of time "going through the motions" for electoral purposes, deeply sympathize.*

For a group like the prewar National Council for the Prevention of War (Fred Libby, Jeanette Rankin, *et al.*), the introduction of hopeless measures could be a consequence of the politically unsophisticated character of their support—and also of their own feeling that they must push forward hard for the cause, regardless of practicalities. But a sophisticated government relations program—one run by a business firm or on behalf of most professional associations—presumably will minimize mere gestures. An astute client will certainly want to find out whether his Washington representative really has calculated the score and is best employed in pushing for hopeless measures. Of course, there are times when a Washington representative would never himself introduce a given measure; but some of his allies do so, and in order not to lose their cooperation he has to do something in a battle which he knows can never be won. You can protect yourself, perhaps, from your enemies; *but* your friends inevitably waste your time.

II

The important consideration, of course, is what alternative courses of non-lobbying action are open to the Washington representative which may further the organization's cause—where the chances of success are better. He must also know accurately what resources he has! One of the general statements that can be made most emphatically about Washington representation is this: Most creative and imaginative Washington representatives do not have nearly enough resources to do all that might be conceived of. There are just too many access routes, too many ways in which the Federal government impinges or could impinge upon the organization. . . .

Probably, in terms of total manpower—certainly in terms of total *business* lobbying manpower—most lobbying is "defensive." That is, when some legislative proposal threatens to upset the established order, then lobbyists, professional and amateur, descend on Capitol Hill. This is natural enough; it is much easier to get successful people (the kind who finance and initiate most lobbies) excited about having a favorable situation disturbed than to stir them up (at least in American society) about a contingent benefit.

It has often, although not always, tended since 1933 to be the case that the administration has proposed changes which would disturb some established interest. So, then, established interests have looked to the Congress to prevent the change or modify its harmful effects on them. Consequently, in Congress, to some extent, among lobbyists to a very great degree, the defensive point of view is common.

The generally more conservative cast of Congress, at least on economic matters, means that it often is the last, best hope of endangered interests. More often than not, to be sure, the damage feared by some interest is not so great as apprehensions suggest; and/or the rhetoric about the threat is vastly exaggerated. (Think, for instance, of generally respectable and even "liberal" congressmen, who preached in 1954 that a minor expansion of reciprocal trade was the product of the Communist conspiracy, first hatched by Harry Dexter White, in order to undermine the whole economic strength of the United States!)

Such exaggerations often inhibit discussion of administrative routes and mechanisms by which damage can be avoided. It is quite possible that, if medical interests had tried to prevent some of the real administrative difficulties Medicare and Medicaid would create for them, they could have done so; but the focus of attention was such that administrative considerations could only be really entered into after the legislation was put into effect. Rhetoric obscured consideration of reality. Right now, one of the arguments—which sounds valid—of some pharmaceutical firms against the careful testing now demanded by Federal agencies for new drugs, is that this slows down dreadfully the introduction of drugs which are essential for some people's lives or comfort. But, if this really is true, there are obvious enough administrative ways of making the harm less serious than it would be without planning.

Now, of course, no one should expect an endangered interest to admit that there are ways of modifying the dangers it fears, so long as it believes it can win an all-out victory. But a careful assessment of situations by the government relations department certainly should suggest possibilities of and reactions to partial defeat. I have been told that one of the big auto companies was pretty sure in advance it could live with most auto safety legislation and regulations (bitterly as it resisted them) because it felt it could establish a working relationship with any possible administrator. In this case, the company had probably thought through how much additional investment of effort was justified in fighting the whole movement. . . .

III

Some senators and congressmen—for instance, Senator McCarran of Nevada, Chairman of Judiciary for some years—acquire great power over a department. It was often said that Senator McCarran had more power over the Immigration and Naturalization Service of the Department of Justice than any Attorney General. To the extent that this was true, one reason was that he had utilized the opportunity for special treatment and special favors, arising from his committee post. In securing or prohibiting specific exemptions from general immigration acts, the constant flow of requests made him a man whose goodwill was significant to many persons, including notably many of his fellow senators. For most of them had articulate constituents who wanted a chance to get a relative or friend or technically skilled employee into the United States, despite quota restrictions.

Yet, it took an unusual kind of skill to master such power. Who can imagine Wiley of Wisconsin, or Langer of North Dakota, ranking Republicans on Judiciary during McCarran's Chairmanship, exerting a tenth of the power as Chairman that McCarran held?

Another example of a man who did much for his constituents, chiefly because of his position, was John Taber, for many years ranking Republican, and for two sessions, Chairman of House Appropriations. In preparing an article about him,[5] I talked with a number of his constituents. One of them, an attorney and a liberal Democrat in the tradition of Mrs. Roosevelt and Governor Lehman, said to me in 1948, "I despise most of what that man stands for. But I have to support his reelection. It would take me three weeks a year more in Washington if he weren't there; he does so much for me." Considering the nature of the attorney's clients, I suppose these services concerned taxes, accounting on wartime arrangements, hang-overs from price control, information on labor issues, etc.

Friendship with such congressional operators can be worth a great deal to a Washington representative or favor-seeker; the trouble is that it takes years for most men to build up such powerful operations, and, having acquired it, they are not accessible to all and sundry.

[5] Published as "John Taber—Watchdog of the Treasury," in *Zion's Herald* (August 1, 1948), a polemic, not an analytic, article of a sort I would not now be likely to write.

IV

In understanding how congressmen react to Washington representatives and lobbyists, the favor-seeking patterns just described are crucially important. For, *most congressmen*—and, even more, their staffs (for casework is often delegated to assistants)—*are in the business of trying to get favors for people, or, and this is as important, of going through the motions of trying to get favors for people.* Most of the time, their efforts at getting favors, or of appearing to try to get them, involve requests, appeals, demands, the passing-on of information, to some agency or bureau in the executive branch. Sometimes, these efforts at favors involve requests or pleas to other members of the Congress serving on committees which can handle the request (it is rare to *demand* something from fellow congressmen). Not infrequently, efforts at getting favors involve dealings with other levels of government or private organizations. Some senators and congressmen do casework with state or city or even foreign governments or refer cases to private social welfare agencies, veterans' organizations, and the like.

Occasionally the senator or congressman merely has to try to persuade fellow members of his own committee. But it is only on very rare occasions that he has the capacity to confer the favor by his own decision.

The natural tendency of congressmen and senators to do favors (or appear to be doing them) is reenforced by the fact that many of them have a background in state or local politics, or in the politics of, for instance, veterans' or fraternal organizations. Favor-giving is, generally speaking, even more critical to a sense of political competence in these organizations than it is in national politics. Consequently, *any* request to many Capitol Hill offices is likely to be handled as an opportunity to confer a favor. Naturally, each congressman has a definite notion as to what kinds of favors may appropriately be asked of him. For instance, some congressmen are extremely reluctant to do favors for anybody outside their constituency. An extreme example of this: I was trying in 1953–1954 to interview selected members of the Ways and Means Committee, in connection with the study which led to *American Business and Public Policy*. Congressman X's brother told my assistant very emphatically, "If Mr. Dexter is working for Massachusetts Institute of Technology, there are plenty of Massachusetts Congressmen for him to see. He is their business." So, I had a dozen friends of mine in his district write to the congressman, and then I received a personal call from him, early one morning, almost begging me "to come down and see me, anytime, anytime at all."

Some congressmen are ready, willing, and eager to do what they regard as "casework favors," so that they can be free to do what they want on serious, legislative issues. But, again, what is serious to one man is a constituency favor so far as another is concerned. Senator Fulbright, for instance, for obvious enough reasons, has strongly opposed the tendency of exchange scholars to stay in this country and to seek private immigration bills to permit them to do so if necessary; in his view, such exemptions destroy the purposes of the exchange program; they are to him policy issues. Yet, unquestionably, most of his colleagues who introduce such bills regard them as merely favors to the man in question, and even more to the university or research institute or business firm or friend who requests that it be done.

On the other hand, Senator Fulbright's record would suggest that he may regard certain actions as simply favors to the cotton growers, utilities, and textile interests in Arkansas. Whereas some senators regard these very same matters as involving profound issues of far-reaching legislative importance, which they never handle as favors.

The favor-trading, favor-giving orientation of Congress is well illustrated by the following: I asked the knowledgeable assistant to the senator from a certain state why Congressman X in that state had voted against the Speaker and the leadership and the interests of his district and the committee and his own committee on several votes involving foreign trade. "Well, you see, Jack Q is a pal of Jim Y [congressman from an adjoining district but of quite different economic character]; they usually travel home together and everything; and Jack knew that Jim absolutely *had* to vote against the leadership on these matters; all those rubber-workers and textile-makers in his home district are yelling like hell about Japanese imports. And Jim did not like to be left alone, out there, naked, for everybody to see, voting against the Speaker and the committee report and everything. So, Jack voted with Jim to make Jim look better." And, of course, some day, if other issues of more importance to Jack develop, he can count on Jim's voting alongside him, regardless of anybody.

In dealing with most congressmen, most Washington representatives will be well-advised to present their position, where possible, as a request for a favor, in the form in which that congressman and his staff like requests to be made, backed up by the kind of support which that congressman appreciates. I suspect one reason for the unpopularity of some serious-minded lobbyists who stress the public interest is that they do not ask for favors; they come to *tell* congressmen what the latter *ought* to be thinking. Many congressmen, that is, do not concede that anybody else knows more than they do about the public interest; but they are willing and eager to do favors.

On almost any matter, if the congressman is going to get anywhere with it, he is going to have to ask a favor from someone else. This means he may have to expend some of his capital, his stock in trade, his ability to be listened to.

So, the best thing of all for a Washington representative is to be able to approach a congressman or senator with something that will somehow enable the latter to increase his political capital—to increase his prestige, his publicity value, his ability to get campaign contributions or speaking dates, his respect from his colleagues, his influence downtown in the bureaus or back home. As a practical matter, some approaches to congressmen by Washington representatives do involve a net credit potential in prestige and power. For instance, when Dorothy Detzer of the Women's International League for Peace and Freedom and her associates persuaded Senator Gerald Nye of North Dakota to sponsor the inquiry which became the investigation of the "merchants of death," he became (to be sure, reportedly, contrary to his own expectations), as an outcome, one of the best-known members of the Senate, more in demand on college campuses than any other Republican at that time. Or it is widely believed that the tie-in between the late Senator Bridges of New Hampshire and the so-called "(Free) China lobby" was beneficial to the former in several ways. And, whoever (perhaps the National Association of Retired Persons) persuaded Senator Winston Prouty of Vermont to sponsor, and carry against administration and committee objections, the payment of $35 a month to older people not receiving other government checks, did not hurt Senator Prouty; the latter was not at the time as well known as many of his colleagues, but this amendment spread his name among some people inside and outside of Vermont.

But congressmen are like most people nowadays, they have learned to be cautious. Too many of the people who come in and see them (*even quite experienced people*) try to sell them on something which will not basically help the congressman's career or reelection. So, like housewives dealing with a door-to-door salesman, or publishers listening to an author with a book which "will make a million dollars," they are skeptical. An idea should, if possible, be presented in such a way that it obviously helps the congressman; but the congressman should be led to sell himself on its advantages to him.

V

One story illustrates the nature of favors, the advantages of having a skilled Washington representative, the tendency of members of Congress just to go through the motions, and a typical relationship between congressmen and the executive branch. I was questioning an industrialist in a medium-sized city,[6] who (1) since there was no trade association in his rather small industry, and, since he was, unlike his competitors, independently wealthy, acted from time to time as the industry's "action agent" in Washington, and (2) was really as much or more interested in the missionary activities of his denomination as in his industry.

He explained that the industry was harassed by competition from foreign-made goods. So, he went to his senator, whom he had known all his life, and to whose campaigns, I suspect, he had always contributed. He explained the issue to the senator and the latter's personal secretary, whom he had also known most of his life. He had a file of correspondence about the matter, which amounted to the senator having raised it with, as I now recollect, the State Department and the Tariff Commission. The latter agencies sent gobbledygookish replies, referring to statutes and regulations by number, which seemingly amounted to a statement: "We will look into the matter; we cannot be too encouraging." At that time, it was the obvious general policy of State (and probably of the Tariff Commission) to procrastinate about demands for action to restrict imports.

Later, the interview with the industrialist went on to his missionary interests. He told me in rather vivid detail how the government of India was making it difficult for the denomination's missionaries to bring in and use trucks, moving picture equipment, and school supplies. Naively, I asked: "And did you talk to the senator and his secretary about that, too?" Immediately and firmly, he replied: "No, what the dickens business is that of the senator's! That is the responsibility of Tom so-and-so in such-and-such a section of" either State or the organization for foreign aid, a section of which I personally never heard before or since. He told me all about it.

Now, he was quite right that negotiations with the Indian government on this issue was the responsibility of this particular section (perhaps, also, of other branches of the executive, but not of the Congress). He was absolutely right that, constitutionally speaking, it was none of his senator's business. And, too, practically speaking, his senator would not have been a good source of referral and guidance on the matter.

But these things were also true of the foreign import issue with which he was concerned. Action on this matter was not, due to numerous laws passed in the preceding twenty years, any longer the direct responsibility of Congress. Help would have to come first from the executive branches.

[6] Called New Zanzuel in Raymond A. Bauer, Ithiel de Sola Pool, and Lewis Anthony Dexter, *American Business and Public Policy* (New York: Atherton Press, 1963), pp. 310–11.

The senator's office, of course, recognized this fact by referring the matter to the Department of State and the Tariff Commission. This is, typically, what senators and congressmen do with most requests for favors. They refer them to some branch of the executive. Very often, all they ask for is information—how should this thing be handled? What procedures should the aggrieved person follow?

But, note that in this instance two things did not happen: (1) the issue was not sharply explained by the senator's office to the administrative agencies—all the letters from the senator really said were "here is a problem," and (2) the issue was not presented to all the administrative agencies which might have been able to take helpful action.

There are, for instance, provisions administered by the Treasury to make difficult certain kinds of selling below cost, "dumping." There are "Buy American" provisions which might apply to some branches of Defense and Interior which probably bought the product in question. There was nothing in the correspondence—or in my subsequent conversation with the senator's staff—to indicate that anyone there had thought that either of these routes might be helpful. It was clear that the senator's office was not prepared for the work of turning the complaint into a form with which the bureaucrats could grapple, and it was even clearer that the bureaucrats who replied to the senator's letters had no interest in figuring out how the issue could best be handled from the standpoint of the industry.

Now, there is no necessary reason why any senatorial or congressional staff assistant should be competent at such specification of issues. In general, in many instances, they get along about as well—and with considerably less bother—if they only "go through the motions." This particular senator was distinguished for a different kind of case service; he would, for instance, personally buy fashionable clothes in Washington stores for people who lived in rural parts of his constituency.

There are senatorial and congressional offices where my manufacturer interviewee would have got better referral than he did in this particular instance; or had the constituent known what precisely to ask for, this senator would have been more helpful.

But the case basically illustrates the importance of having a Washington representative. To be sure, so far as the particular matter of foreign imports is concerned, it may have been more of a nuisance, at the time, than a crisis, to the industry. But there were, the manufacturer said, other problems—problems, of course, on tax policy, and problems with scarce materials (this was just after the Korean War), and problems on labor, which both he and others in the industry faced. Apparently, he handled them as the industry's substitute for a trade association in much the same way; they had been sent through the office of Senator Personal Service. It must have been chance if helpful handling was given any of them. .

A skillful Washington representative would have found out, in the case of taxes or foreign imports or labor or scarce materials, what the issues were, and which should have priority. The senator's office, after all, had no way of knowing whether any of these issues were particularly critical (materials, actually, probably had been really most critical). *It would, ordinarily, be impolite for a congressional office to ask the kind of searching questions which a good Washington representative might ask.* And, too, a senator is unlikely to be in a situation where he would look foolish, if he did not know a good deal about the case. The Washington representative, to protect himself, has to find out the facts. For, only by finding out the facts, will he be prepared to defend his case, if he has to do so.

And a Washington representative, worthy of that name, would have formulated and reformulated the problem, so that it would fit into the right bureaucratic categories. Could it be a matter of anti-dumping? Is there some obscure provision of the Reciprocal Trade Act which would permit defensive action, and, if so, what facts are needed? Would any kind of "escape clause" action be feasible? Would there be any way in which the Buy American Act could be invoked? The plant was, as it happens, unionized; the president of the company, and his immediate assistants, knew nothing whatever about the international union, but just assumed it would be hostile—their experiences with unions were not unusually encouraging. But, in fact, in the particular case, there was a good chance that the international union would have cooperated with the industry. Would its help have been useful? Even if it would not have actually helped, nevertheless, on some aspects of the matter, such as those to be suggested in the next paragraph, its advice would have been valuable; and that advice could have been obtained just as easily as the senator's. In fact, the international union probably would have welcomed a chance to build a bridge to such employers as this one.

A really skillful Washington representative—one who saw his job in fullest perspective, as affecting policy outcomes, *however* they can be affected—would have seen, I believe, in the particular situation, a promising way out. Most consumers of this product (an extremely durable, expensive good) were, as it happened, professional groups. It also happened that, on the face of the facts as reported to me by the manufacturer, it would seem that the conditions of labor in the plants which were producing the foreign competing goods were such as to horrify most United States purchasers. A public relations campaign could have been organized, without any great expense, directed to the responsible officers of purchasing organizations. In

the then dominant state of opinion in these organizations, such a campaign
—reenforced presumably by salesmen for the U.S. industry—would have,
almost certainly, led many buyers to be willing to pay somewhat more for
the United States-made product. . . .

There is a familiar saying that "a man who has himself for a client has a
fool for a lawyer." Like all folk generalizations, this is occasionally untrue;
but it is true where the man in question does not know in detail the professional and legal issues involved, and where the issue is important. So, also,
with Washington representation. An unsophisticated, untrained man—manufacturer, county official, or whatever he may be—should either acquire expertise about government relations, or he should hire somebody who has it,
if his relationships with the government are important to his organization.
He cannot rely on Congress!

The characteristic point in this case was that the manufacturer suspected
that government policy in at least four matters was actually or potentially
of great moment to his firm, and to the entire industry, for which he was
acting. But he did not know. I suspect that careful study would perhaps
have shown that foreign imports were not a problem of moment, and that
the effort I have suggested would not be worthwhile; but, before approaching the Senator, it would have been helpful to find how much effort it was
worth! I suspect that tax policy and materials allocation regulations were of
considerable importance, in ways which the manufacturer did not understand as well as in ways which he did. I suspect that a skillful Washington
representative could have found helpful, unexpected allies (for instance, in
the particular case, among church and professional organizations) on the
materials allocation matter. But, again, this should have been checked out.
If it turned out that these two issues mattered, and the other two, relatively,
did not, a sophisticated client would have cooperated with the Washington
representative in asking the Senator's help in specific ways on the two which
mattered—and not wasted the Senator's time on the other two, foreign
imports and labor.

The ironic twist to the situation is that, at least in large measure, the
manufacturer in his other role as chairman of a denominational missionary
committee, had become fairly sophisticated about Washington representation. He knew who, actually, could take the relevant action and how to
approach him. In this regard, he had been briefed and educated by his
predecessor as chairman, and by the full-time paid staff of the denomination
and possibly of the National Council of Churches. But there had been no
such briefing, no such education, in his business capacity, so he handled
that whole relationship amateurishly and ineffectively. Who says business is
necessarily more politically sophisticated than "naive" churchmen?

VI

Put in general terms, the point of the story is: *referral to obvious sources can and will be made by a congressman or senator. Guidance in using the full range of government resources is more than most senators or congressmen give, or can be expected to give. Such guidance has to come from elsewhere. Hence, Washington representation.* What use then are senators or congressmen? Basically, senators and congressmen can often:

a. Get information more quickly and fully than the constituent or the representative. Government agencies are generally supposed to attach priority to congressional requests, and many of them do so. Many of them will go to great trouble to answer a request from a congressman.

For instance, a congressional request to appropriate branches in Commerce, Labor, and State might have produced full documentation on the labor practices of the industry's major foreign competitor. It would have been important, however, to know which sections of the State, Commerce, and Labor Departments might be able *and willing* to find the relevant information. Some people in the State Department, including some who were at the time engaged in legislative liaison, would have interpreted the request as a threat to United States relations with the foreign country involved; others would have inquired willingly from international agencies as to pertinent information.

b. Congressional staffs can help check and add to the inquirer's notions as to agencies which should be asked for information or action; there are congressional offices which on a given topic are as good as a Washington representative (for instance, on anything relevant to the major manufacturing industries of New England, Senator Saltonstall's office would have been nearly as good as a competent Washington representative), and, of course, there is a lot of exchange between congressional offices. But, usually, once the inquirer has some idea of where to go and why, he can profitably discuss the matter with the staff of congressional offices, to see if they have something additional to suggest, or some experience which will help shape his questions.

c. Congressmen can provide access—often quickly—to most agencies or bureaus. Sometimes this can be a disadvantage; if the decision is actually going to be made at a section chief level, and a senator or congressman makes a big issue of the favor, the first interview may be with an undersecretary, who does not know the facts and who simply wastes time. But more often it is an advantage.

d. Congressmen and their staffs can in a good many instances, but by no means all, add to the likelihood that a matter will be considered favorably by the department or section handling it.

Members of relevant committees, who have established a friendly relationship with the agencies with which they deal, or who seriously frighten these agencies, are perhaps most likely to influence a favorable response. If, in addition, the member has a staff assistant or supervises a committee clerk who thoroughly understands the procedures of the agencies in question, then he can be extremely influential in a few cases. Even so, there is little he can achieve in regard to most requests, simply because to do anything about them would involve altering a set of procedures or traditions, or run counter to the agencies' notion of what is permissible and safe. For instance, a shrewd bureaucrat will foresee that if one change is made, in the seemingly reasonable general direction requested by Member X, at the moment, then other organizations and interests will come in, perhaps sent over by Member X himself, a year or two hence, bitter about the effects of the change upon them, and insisting on a return to previous practice.

At the opposite extreme from the influential members just described is a member who has been in Congress for a few years, long enough to make an impression, who is serving on an unimportant and irrelevant committee, who has attracted attention in the bureaucracy because he sends over a number of people with impossible and improper requests, who is not at all specific about what he wants done for the petitioner, and who is in the habit of "throwing his weight around" even in circumstances where he has no leverage.

Most members, of course, fall somewhere between these two extremes. And a member who may be influential with one agency, say the Office of Economic Opportunity—simply because he is regarded as their sort of person—may have a negative impact in some old-line bureau in an established department. A skillful Washington representative will try to determine which congressional ally will be useful where; he would hardly expect, for instance, a request from Eugene McCarthy, at the present moment, to be especially well-regarded by some bureaus in the Department of Defense, whereas it might be attended to favorably in an agency staffed with intellectual "liberals." Most reputations are not as clear and easy to judge as his, of course, and take more specialized knowledge of how the member is regarded by whom.

e. Sometimes, if he is sufficiently interested, or becomes so, a congressman can aid in a publicity campaign, which helps achieve the purposes of the client or employer—even though no direct governmental action is involved. Senator Personal Service was not, by temperament or affiliation, likely to be of help himself on the kind of publicity campaign suggested as worth considering in our story above. But his executive secretary was in close and continuing contact with prominent leaders of the party in the senator's state; at least one of these leaders might have been glad to lend himself to any such campaign. And, had the matter come up under the senator's successor, the latter might well have been delighted to participate in such an effort.

There is, of course, one other thing which often makes it useful to consult a member or his staff fairly early:

f. It may turn out, ultimately, that some kind of legislative action is called for. If the senator's office has been in touch with the development of the situation, it is more likely to take an interest and of its own volition suggest appropriate legislative action. But, against this, must be traded off the effort and bother involved in dealing with the congressional office, if it turns out not to be necessary, if otherwise the whole matter could have been more easily handled directly with the relevant section of the executive, which is often the case. Intermediaries usually take time and often misinterpret situations—even congressional intermediaries.

18

CLEM MILLER

*The Walnut Growers and
the Chicken Farmers*

In today's world most people are ready to admit that, as much as they
dislike the word "lobbying," the function carried on under this name
is essential to government. (In fact, the right to lobby is protected by
the First Amendment.) In recent months there has been a graphic contrast
here in effectiveness of lobbying activity between two segments of
agriculture important to the economic health of our district: walnut growers
and poultrymen. Both groups are in economic trouble because of
abundance.

The walnut growers have a large carry-over from last year which,
if placed on top of this year's record production, would break the market.
The growers wanted the government to buy walnuts for diversion into the
school lunch program, to be financed from existing tariffs on foreign
walnut imports.

In the poultry industry, overproduction led by huge combines of
bankers and feed companies, with million-hen farms, has broken the
egg and meat-bird markets wide open. Independent poultrymen are
losing six to eight cents per dozen eggs and four to eight cents per pound
of meat, and are going bankrupt in droves.

The walnut industry is well organized. They have been proud that they

Reprinted from John W. Baker, ed., *Member of the House: Letters of a
Congressman* (New York: Charles Scribner's Sons, 1962), pp. 137–40, by
permission of the publisher. Copyright © 1962 by Charles Scribner's Sons.
Clem Miller was a United States Representative from California from 1958 until
1962, when he was killed in an airplane crash while campaigning for reelection.

don't have supports and don't ask the government for "handouts." This is easy to understand. One marketing cooperative controls 70 per cent of the state's production. So, when the industry got in trouble and came to Washington, they came well prepared. Each California congressman received a personal, carefully reasoned, five-page letter. It was followed up by another, shorter letter. Then, a telegram called attention to the letters. Finally, there was a telephone call, asking for comments on the letters. By this time, we were fairly wide awake. Quite properly, the group worked through the congressman in whose district the association offices and many growers are located. We received several calls from the congressman's staff, alerting us, keeping us posted, offering help in answering questions.

After this preliminary barrage, the walnut growers' representative was ready to come to town. He set up headquarters at a nearby hotel. He called on congressmen several times, accompanied by a gentleman from the packing and canning section of the industry. He talked to my legislative assistant. Then we were all invited to a luncheon at the hotel, where the plight of the industry was laid before us and it was announced that a meeting was set up with the Secretary of Agriculture. Meticulous care was taken to be sure that all congressmen and senators who represent walnut growers would be there. In a large Department of Agriculture conference room with numerous department officials present, a skillful "presentation" for the industry was made. Immediately afterward, the walnut congressmen jumped up to demand action. One was self-contained but bitter about department inaction. Another pointed out the illogical Administration position in caustic terms. In turn, each congressman added his bit to the complaint. The Administration was bland and quite self-righteous ("We have more confidence in the walnut grower than he has in himself."). The exasperation of the Republican congressmen toward the Republican Secretary of Agriculture mounted. "Would a 'shaded' market price have to become a rout before the government moved?" they wanted to know. Administration officials were apparently unshaken.

However, two weeks later, the Administration did act. The industry was delighted. The work of the lobby had been effective.

Let's contrast this with the way things are developing in the egg industry. Some time ago I received a long letter from a constituent asking what congressional action was expected in poultry. A check revealed that nothing was contemplated in Congress. Of the seven thousand bills in Congress, there was not one on poultry or eggs. No hearings were scheduled. My interest piqued, I discussed the situation with House Agriculture Committee staff members and with the acting chairman of the subcommittee. The prevailing view was that since there was no leadership in the industry, and no agreement on policy, hearings would serve no purpose. I urged that hearings be scheduled to see if policy might materialize. A day or so later, I heard that a group of distressed poultrymen from New Jersey were asking to meet with their government. The Georgia and Alabama broiler people also asked to be heard.

All of a sudden, we learned that there was to be a hearing. Citizens were petitioning their government for a redress of grievances. At the hearing a crowd of two hundred poultrymen swarmed into the Agriculture Committee room which had been designed for about seventy-five people. Poultrymen-witnesses testified that the lowest prices in eighteen years for eggs and chickens were bankrupting an industry. As one witness said, in 1957 we were separating the men from the boys; in 1959 it was the men from the giants. One poultryman gave a stark, moving account of his town's plight. He gestured to his friends, sitting somberly at his side. They had been against federal help until a month or so previously, he said. "We called the people who were down here in 1957 looking for handouts 'radicals.' Now, we are here ourselves."

Throughout two days the same depressing story was recounted as the farmer-witnesses, speaking for themselves and other small producers, took their turn. Technological advances, together with banker-feed company-grower integration, were destroying the independent poultryman. Then the Department of Agriculture spokesman told its story. He confirmed the growers' story but indicated that nothing could be done. It was the inexorable law of supply and demand. Significantly absent were representatives of the larger organized farm groups. At nightfall, the poultrymen had to return to their farms.

What was the next step? It is up to the interested congressmen, they told us. How come, we asked? What are we to do? The leader of the poultrymen said that we had been told the problem. Yes, was the response, but he and his friends should go to see the Secretary of Agriculture. Testimony had indicated that Congress had already given the Secretary all of the authority he needed to act. It would do no good to pass more laws, particularly since they would certainly end with Presidential vetoes.

All of the men were active poultrymen who had to get back to their flocks. They were leaving that night. Who was to carry the ball for them here in Washington during the next critical weeks? Who was going to do the telephoning? Who was going to coordinate policy between New Jersey, California, Alabama, Wisconsin, Georgia, and Kansas? The answer from them was, "No one." We had been given a problem. It was ours now. The result to date: a resolution of the Agriculture Committee urging the Secretary to "implement such programs of purchase, diversion, and export of poultry products as will lead toward improvement of the present critical situation." Results for the poultrymen: nothing.

19

STANLEY S. SURREY

How Special Tax Provisions
Get Enacted

Recently there has been considerable criticism directed against the existence in our tax laws of provisions granting special treatment to certain groups or individuals. The purpose of this article is to consider the question of why the Congress enacts these special tax provisions.

Some Major Factors

High Rates of Tax

The high rates of the individual income tax, and of the estate and gift taxes, are probably the major factor in producing special tax legislation. This is, in a sense, a truism, for without something to be relieved of, there would be no need to press for relief. The point is that the average congressman does not basically believe in the present rates of income tax in the upper brackets. When he sees them applied to individual cases, he thinks them too high and therefore unfair. Any argument for

Reprinted from Randall B. Ripley, ed., *Public Policies and Their Politics* (New York: W. W. Norton & Company, Inc., 1966), pp. 51–60, by permission of the author, The Harvard Law Review Association, and W. W. Norton & Company, Inc. Copyright © 1957 by The Harvard Law Review Association [in an earlier version: "How Special Tax Provisions Get Enacted," *Harvard Law Review*, 70 (1957), 1145–82]; copyright © 1966 by W. W. Norton & Company, Inc. Mr. Surrey is Jeremiah Smith, Jr. Professor of Law at the Harvard Law School and was Assistant Secretary of the Treasury for Tax Policy during the Kennedy and Johnson Administrations.

relief which starts off by stating that these high rates are working a "special hardship" in a particular case or are "penalizing" a particular taxpayer— to use some words from the tax lobbyist's approved list of effective phrases— has the initial advantage of having a sympathetic listener.

Tax Polarity

The existence of two rate structures in the income tax and of two types of taxes on the transfer of wealth permits a congressman to favor a special group by placing its situation under the lower rate structure or the less effective tax. Thus, the presence of the 25 per cent capital-gains rate enables Congress to shift an executive stock option from the high rates applying to executive compensation to the lower capital-gains rate. If there were no special capital-gains rate, or if we did not tax capital gains at all, this shift could not be made, since a congressman would not completely exempt the stock option. Similarly, the presence of a gift tax permits certain transfers of wealth, such as transferred life insurance, to be shifted from the higher estate tax to the lower gift tax. As a consequence, given this congressional tendency, we reach the paradox that having a gift tax as well as an estate tax may, given the present lack of proper co-ordination of the two taxes, result in less effective taxation of certain transfers of wealth than if we relied only on an estate tax.

Technical Complexity

The high rates of tax, the complexities of modern business, the desires of the wealthy and middle-income groups for clear tax charts to guide their family planning, the Government's need for protection against tax avoidance, the claims of tax equity, and various other factors have combined to make the income, estate, and gift taxes exceedingly complex in technical detail. These technicalities involve the drawing of countless dividing lines. Consequently, a case on the high-tax side of a line may closely resemble the cases on the other side receiving more favorable tax treatment. The result is a fertile ground for assertions of inequity and hardship as particular taxpayers desire legislation to bend the dividing lines and thereby extend the favorable treatment to their situations. Also, faulty tax planning, ill-advised legal steps, or transactions concluded in ignorance of tax law can produce severe tax consequences. These "tax penalties" could have been averted under an informed tax guidance that would have taken the taxpayer safely through the technical tax maze. In these circumstances, the taxpayer facing severe monetary hurt because of a "mere technicality" (to use the phrase that will be pressed on the congressman) is quite likely to evoke considerable sympathy for his plight.

History and Politics

The accidents of tax history also play a major role in the existence of special provisions. Tax-exempt securities in large part achieved their favored status through the vagaries of constitutional interpretation and not through any special desire to relieve the wealthy. Percentage depletion for oil and gas and the deduction of intangible drilling expenses have their roots in legislative compromises and administrative interpretation which for the most part do not appear to have been planned as special-interest relief. It is only later that the extent of the tax generosity inherent in such provisions is comprehended. But by then they are in the law, the problem of the group benefited is one of defense rather than attack, and the strategic advantages are all with that group. This is especially so when the area involved touches on major political matters, as in the case of percentage depletion and tax-exempt securities.

Political considerations naturally overhang this whole area, for taxation is a sensitive and volatile matter. Any major congressional action represents the compromises of the legislator as he weighs and balances the strong forces constantly focused on him by the pressure groups of the country. Many special provisions—capital gains, for one—are caught in these swirling pressures.

Separation of Executive and Legislative Branches of Government

But many of the tax provisions we are considering do not lie at this political level. They are simply a part of the technical tax law. They are not of major importance in their revenue impact. But they are of major importance to the group or individual benefited and they are glaring in their departure from tax fairness. The inquiry, therefore, must here be directed toward some of the institutional features in the tax-legislation process which may be responsible for special provisions of this technical variety.

Congress occupies the role of mediator between the tax views of the executive and the demands of the pressure groups. This is so whether the tax issue involved is a major political matter or a minor technical point. The Congress is zealous in maintaining this position in the tax field.

The Congress regards the shaping of a revenue bill as very much its prerogative. It will seek the views of the executive, for there is a respect for the sustained labors of those in the executive departments and also a recognition, varying with the times, of the importance of presidential programs. But control over the legislation itself, both as to broad policies and as to details, rests with the Congress. Hence a congressman, and especially a member of the tax committees, is in a position to make the tax laws bend in favor of a particular individual or group despite strong objection from the executive branch. Under such a governmental system the importance to the tax structure of the institutional factors that influence a congressman's decision is obvious.

Some Institutional Factors

The Congressman's Desire To Be Helpful

A congressman's instincts are to be helpful and friendly. If it were otherwise, he would not be in Congress. When a constituent, or some other person who is in a position to claim attention, seeks legislative action, the congressman likes to respond within reason. If the proposal presented to him is at all rational he will, in all probability, at least introduce it in bill form so as not to offend the constituent. If the congressman is not a member of one of the tax committees, that may end the matter—but it may not, for the proposal has been launched and lies ready to be pushed ahead by whatever pressures may be generated in its behalf.

Lack of Congressional Appreciation of Departure from Fairness

In many cases the congressman considering a special tax provision may not realize that tax fairness is at all involved. He sees only the problem of the particular constituent or group concerned. The case in this focus may be very appealing, for human beings are involved with human problems. The income tax, always an impersonal, severe, monetary burden, becomes an oppressive force bearing down on men in difficulty. The congressman may therefore not even appreciate that arguments of over-all fairness and equity have any relation to the question, or may very well think them too intangible and remote. Provisions for the relief of the blind and the aged are perhaps illustrations. Or the congressman, moved simply by a desire to help a constituent, may not understand the ramifications of the proposal. He is not a tax technician and he may view the proposal in isolation rather than perceive its relationship to the intricate technical structure of the revenue code. The proposal, so viewed, becomes merely a "little old amendment" which helps a constituent and does no harm. His brother congressmen are quite willing to be good fellows and go along, especially if the congressman urging the proposal is well-liked. After all, they too from time to time will have "little old amendments" to propose. Thus, in 1955 the Ways and

Means Committee decided that in the initial consideration of members' bills dealing with technical matters it would allow each member one bill to be considered and then reported by the full committee if the bill met with unanimous agreement.

The Treasury Department's Presentation

The congressman's failure to recognize that tax fairness is at all involved may often be due to the inadequacy of the Treasury Department's presentation of the issues. This is not said critically, but by way of explanation. The problem facing the Treasury in these matters is formidable. The interested constituents or groups are generally skillful in presenting their cases in appealing form. Their energies are concentrated on one matter; they have time and money to devote to it; they may have the advantage of personal acquaintance, directly or through intermediaries, with the congressman; they can obtain skilled counsel informed on the ways of the Congress. The Treasury's tax staff must tackle all of these problems; its members are usually not chosen for skill in the presentation of issues or in handling congressmen; although on the whole remarkably good, considering the compensation, they are rarely among the ablest in the tax field, nor do they usually have the needed experience.

Lack of Omniscience on the Part of the Treasury

The treasury tax staff is not omniscient. Yet understanding approaching omniscience is needed to do its job. A lack of knowledge on any particular matter, a failure of skill at any moment, can be fatal. The approach of the average congressman is to hear the private group, find out in general what it wants, react sympathetically for a variety of reasons, and then ask the Treasury whether there is any objection to the proposal. If the Treasury is off its guard and acquiesces, the proposal becomes law. If the Treasury is unprepared and presents a weak case, the proposal becomes law. Equally serious is the in-between situation in which the Treasury acknowledges that some hardship is present in the particular situation, but points out that the dfficulty is but a phase of a general problem and that it has not yet been able fully to analyze the general area. It therefore urges that the partciular proposal be postponed until further study is given to the whole matter. But recognition of some hardship and of some merit in his particular proposal is all that the congressman needs. His constituent wants relief from that admitted hardship now, and not years later when the whole matter has been thought through and his case fitted into a solution appropriate for many cases. Hence the congressman will seek approval of the proposal in the limited form necessary to solve the particular problem presented to him— and a special tax provision is thereby born.

Lack of Opposition Apart from the Treasury Department to Proponents of Special Tax Provisions

The critical importance that attaches to the level of treasury competence and the fatal consequences of any slip on its part derive from its unique position in tax legislation. The question, "Who speaks for tax equity and tax fairness?" is answered today largely in terms of only the Treasury Department. If that department fails to respond, then tax fairness has no champion before the Congress. Moreover, it must respond with vigor and determination, and after a full explanation of the matter it must take a forthright stand on the issues. A Treasury Department that contents itself with explaining the issues and then solemnly declaring the matter to be one for the policy determination of Congress abdicates its responsibility. The congressman understands aggressiveness and a firm position. He is often in the position of the small boy inwardly seeking parental bounds for his conduct while outwardly declaiming against them. He may not accept policy guidance from the treasury policy spokesman, but he wants it presented. He will invariably interpret a treasury statement that the matter is one for his own policy decision as a victory for the seeker of the special provision.

Thus, in the tax bouts that a congressman witnesses the Treasury is invariably in one corner of the ring. Assuming the Treasury decides to do battle, which is hardly a safe assumption at all times, it is the Treasury versus percentage depletion, the Treasury versus capital gains, the Treasury versus this constituent, the Treasury versus that private group. The effect on the congressman as referee is inevitable. He simply cannot let every battle be won by the Treasury, and hence every so often he gives the victory to the sponsors of a special provision. Moreover, the Treasury is not an impersonal antagonist—it is represented before the Congress by individuals. These individuals are constantly forced to say that enactment of this proposal will be unfair, and the same of the next, and the next. The congressman, being only human, is bound from time to time to look upon these individuals as the Cassandras of the tax world. To avoid this dilemma, the Treasury in a close case will sometimes concede the issue if the proposal can be narrowly confined. It feels compelled to say "yes" once in a while simply to demonstrate that it maintains a balanced judgment and possesses a sense of fairness. A special provision is thus enacted simply because it happens to have somewhat more merit than the numerous other special proposals before the committees and because an affirmative answer here by the Treasury will protect negative responses to the other proposals.

The Congressional Tax Staff

The description of the Treasury as the principal and often the sole defender of tax fairness calls for a consideration of the role of the congressional tax staff. Most of the congressional tax technicians are members of the staff of the Joint Committee on Internal Revenue Taxation and as such serve both the House Ways and Means Committee and the Senate Finance Committee. There are a few technicians attached to the separate committees, and the clerks of the committees can play a very important role if they are personally so inclined. But institutionally the chief guidance given to Congress by its own employees comes from this joint committee staff.

The members of this staff work closely with the treasury tax technicians. Their work on the details of proposals and drafts is highly important, but the task of policy formulation and policy guidance to the congressmen appears to be reserved exclusively to the chief of that staff. His role is a difficult and unenviable one. Many congressmen pass along to him the tax proposals that they are constantly receiving from their constituents. Undoubtedly, the Chief of Staff discreetly but effectively blocks many of these proposals from proceeding further. But he also, whatever his inclinations may be, cannot in his situation always say "no." Perhaps inevitably on the crucial issues his role tends to be that of the advocate of the congressman advancing a particular proposal on behalf of a special group. The special-interest groups cannot appear in the executive sessions of the committees, and the congressman sympathetic to their point of view is not technically equipped to present their case; he tends to look to the Chief of Staff to assume that task. Further, he looks to the Chief of Staff to formulate the technical compromises which will resolve the dispute between the special-interest group and the Treasury. The Chief of Staff must therefore work closely with the congressmen and be "brilliantly sensitive to their views." He must necessarily be able to gauge the degree of interest that a congressman may have in a proposal and weigh that in the consideration of the guidance he will give.

Because of these institutional pressures the Chief of Staff is very often the opponent of the Treasury Department before the tax committees. As a result, the difficulties for the average congressman on the tax committees become even greater. The issues get more and more complex as the "experts" disagree, and the congressman can hardly follow the technical exchanges. He is quite often content to fall back on the comfortable thought that, since the congressional expert appears to disagree with the treasury experts, there is adequate technical justification for voting either way. Hence the congressman is free to be guided by his own sympathies and instincts. Since generally these sympathies are in favor of the private groups, their proposals obtain his vote.

Unfortunately agreement between the congressional Chief of Staff and the Treasury can sometimes present just as difficult a problem. When the two disagree, at least the congressman who is seeking to discover the real issues may find them exposed at some time through this disagreement of experts. But if the experts agree, the effect is often to foreclose any real committee consideration of the issues. The congressman may be lulled into thinking that no significant issues are involved, and the proposal therefore becomes law. But if the government experts have erred, or if they have incorrectly gauged the congressional sentiment, special benefits may well result which the congressman would not have sanctioned had he understood what was involved.

Lack of Effective Aid from the Tax Bar

The lack of any pressure-group allies for the Treasury in its representation of the tax-paying public could have been remedied in part by effective aid from the tax bar. Yet for a good many years the vocal tax bar not only withheld any aid but very often conducted itself as an ally of the special pressure groups. Many a lawyer representing a client seeking a special provision could without much difficulty obtain American Bar Association or local bar association endorsement for his proposal. He could then appear before Congress and solemnly exhibit the blessing of the legal profession. In fact, the activity of the Bar Association in this respect became so obvious that it seemingly boomeranged—many a congressman began instinctively to smell mischief when presented with a Bar Association tax proposal or endorsement.

Lack of Public Knowledge of Special Tax Provisions

Perhaps the most significant aspect of the consideration of special tax provisions by the Congress is that it usually takes place without any awareness of these events by the general public. Almost entirely, these matters lie outside of the public's gaze, outside of the voter's knowledge. The special provisions which are enacted lie protected in the mysterious complex statutory jargon of the tax law. This technical curtain is impenetrable to the newspapers and other information media. The public hears of debate over tax reduction or tax increase and it may learn something about the general rate structure. But it seldom learns that the high rates have no applicability to much of the income of certain wealthy groups. Nor does it understand how this special taxpayer or that special group is relieved of a good part of its tax burden. All of these matters are largely fought out behind this technical curtain. Hence the congressman favoring these special provisions has for the most part no accounting to make to the voters for his action. He is thereby much freer to lend a helping hand here and there to a group which has won his sympathy or which is pressing him for results.

The Relationship of Special Tax Provisions to Private-Relief Bills

Some of these special provisions represent simply private-relief claims for the particular individual benefited. While phrased as amendments to the tax law, they are only money claims against the Government based on the equities asserted to exist. Thus, it is said of a senator skilled in congressional ways that he would ask the legislative draftsman preparing the draft of a particular tax provision to make the amendment as general in language and as specific in application as was possible. The tax committees and the Treasury have not solved the problem of how to handle these special bills. Curiously enough, some tax situations do come through the judiciary committees as private-relief bills along with other private-relief bills involving claims against the Government. These bills may involve, for example, a removal of the barrier of the statute of limitations in cases thought equitable, or the recovery of funds spent for revenue stamps lost in some fashion. Here they are subject to the criteria developed over the decades by those committees in the handling of private-claims bills. These criteria are reasonably strict, and few of the bills pass the Congress. Of those that do succeed, a number are vetoed, and a veto is customarily regarded as a final disposition of the bill.

Many situations come before the tax committees that are quite comparable, in that the tax proposal is equivalent to a money claim against the Government, equal to the tax to be saved, sought for a specific taxpayer on equitable grounds. This is especially true in the case of proposals of a retroactive character. In the tax committees these special proposals tend to take on the coloration of an amendment to the tax code of the same character as all the various substantive tax matters before these committees. In essence, all amendments to the tax laws that private groups push on their own behalf are designed to lower taxes for the proponents and thereby relieve them from a tax burden to which they are subject. The special proposals thus become simply one more amendment in the long list of changes to be considered. The proponents of these special proposals are thereby able to cloak the fact that they are presenting private-relief claims against the Government. This is especially so when the proposal is considered as merely one more item in a general revenue bill. Here is is also protected from the threat—and fate—of a presidential veto. Even when the proposal is considered as a separate bill, the fact that it is merely one of the bills before a tax committee that is considering a great many substantive bills involving amendments to the tax code generally produces the same result. The committee will tend to focus on the proposal as curing a substantive defect in the law and lose sight of the fact that the special proposal is essentially a private-relief bill.

VII

Congress and
the Executive Branch

There is a tendency when thinking about dealings between the Legislative
and Executive Branches to dwell on "presidential-congressional relations."
What is known about relations between the White House and Congress
is fairly well summarized in textbooks, is implicit in much of the foregoing
material, and can be stated briefly: Since the president has a different
constituency than individual congressmen and senators, particularly
the most influential ones, he is likely to respond to different political
stimuli, to have different political needs and goals than Congress.
This is true when the president's party has a congressional majority and
is even more obvious when the two branches are controlled by
different parties.

The president does, of course, have resources that he can use against
recalcitrant congressmen, particularly those in his own party: federal
contracts, influence with prominent constituents, the advantages of
the White House as a source of information and publicity, and his
position as the leader of his party. But these are only marginal weapons;
they seldom if ever can make a congressman do something that he thinks
would make him unpopular with his constituents. On the other hand,
there are certain forces which induce cooperation between the president
and congressional members of his party. For one thing, they generally
want to support their party if this does not conflict with their local
political interests. The parties are, after all, the principal way that
American politics is organized, they are the basis of competition and
identification, and they provide important bonds and channels between

the White House and Congress. The president's national popularity has an important impact on the political fortunes of congressmen from competitive districts and states. For this reason, opposition congressmen generally try to frustrate proposed legislation that will enhance the president's standing. Moreover, the administration has enormous advantages—in some cases approaching a monopoly—in its possession of certain kinds of information. Finally, the president is the steward of the national interest, a fact which gives him particularly great influence in the conduct of foreign relations and military affairs, although even here he is not omnipotent.

But the president is by no means the totality of the Executive Branch; on many kinds of issues, including some extremely important ones, the various departments and agencies of government are in the forefront of the political struggle and the president is in the background, often by his own choice. The kinds of relationships between Congress and its subcommittees and committees, on the one hand, and various component parts of the executive branch on the other are therefore quite diverse.

The first two readings in this section illustrate this diversity. In the first we see Congress absolutely refusing to yield its influence over "pork barrel projects," i.e., rivers and harbors work done by the Army Corps of Engineers. For many years the Engineers' public works projects have been a notorious instance of collaboration between bureaucrats, interest groups, and Congress. But in the middle 1960s the Engineers began to accept the notion that more rigorous criteria of economic feasibility should be applied to their proposed activities, that more care should be given to figuring out whether individual projects would really provide enough benefits to justify their cost. But, as Chapter 20 shows, keeping such a sharp eye on the merits of individual projects was thought by many congressmen to be so undesirable that they prevented the Engineers from adopting more stringent standards that might disqualify some congressional proposals.

In Chapter 21 the shoe is completely on the other foot. Here Lewis Anthony Dexter describes the extent to which congressmen have abdicated any important role in making military policy. As Dexter shows, congressmen, even those on the Armed Services Committees, often do not concern themselves with the important policy implications of their decisions, and instead give the military a remarkable amount of autonomy with respect to the policies they pursue, the uses to which appropriations are put, and so on. In large measure this abdication is a result of a fairly widespread feeling among congressmen that they lack the information and expertise to make sensible decisions about military policy. The biggest exception seems to be in the area of "real estate": questions having to do with the location of military bases and other topics which are related to how much spending will be done in individual congressional districts. Research done within the past year reveals that, despite all the recent sound and fury about greater congressional involvement in military affairs, there has been little actual change in Congress' role since Dexter's study. Weldon Barton found that the most important activity of the House Armed Services Committee is its "appellate function" of restoring cuts in the individual services' budget requests that are made by the Department of Defense or the Bureau of the Budget. (See his "The Procurement, Research, and Development Process in the House Armed Services Committee," a paper given at the 1970 Annual Meeting of the American Political Science Association.) This is another example of alliances between congressmen and career officials at the expense of the administration.

The last pair of readings is concerned essentially with the appropriations process. The first of these, by Aaron Wildavsky, is something of a companion piece to Fenno's article on the Appropriations Committee. Fenno showed how that committee is almost obsessed with cutting the budgets submitted to it. Wildavsky looks at how administrative officials respond to the committee's preoccupation. Like several other articles in this book, it illustrates the complicated interactions between private interest groups, political ambitions, and problems of making rational calculations when issues are complex and time is short. Wildavsky finds that two of the principal methods used by administrators trying to get generous decisions from the Appropriations Committee are their ability to support their requests with testimonials from private interests, and their ability to help committee members make what the members think are valid decisions. The latter consideration explains the importance of mutual trust and alliances between bureaucrats and congressmen. It also illustrates another recurring theme in this book: the importance of personal relationships and perceptions in getting things done, even in a government as large and specialized as ours.

These themes are also found in the final reading, in which Seymour Scher examines the circumstances in which congressional committees are likely to be vigilant overseers of activities in the executive branch, and those in which they are likely to let the administrators alone. Here again, we see congressmen confronted with an almost infinite variety of things to do, things to learn, and possibilities for influence. Scher describes many of the same problems of calculation and control, many of the same problems of how congressmen deal with the shortage of information, that have appeared in the other readings. We can also see in this article how congressmen "sample" from the panorama of opportunities, hoping thereby to get some valid indication of how well the Executive Branch is performing. These attempts at oversight are, of course, heavily constrained and promoted by both partisan and individual political considerations.

20

ROBERT HAVEMAN / PAULA STEPHAN

The Domestic Program Congress Won't Cut

In its drive to cut Federal spending for domestic programs, Congress
has shown little enthusiasm for paring from the pork barrel the inefficient
navigation, flood-control, and hydroelectric projects in the various states
that are planned and executed by the Army Corps of Engineers.
Last year, Congress appropriated more than $1 billion for the construction
of some 450 water-resource projects. Earlier it had overturned the Corps'
own commendable efforts at benefit-cost criteria reforms that would
have saved the taxpayers money and had written into law a set of
evaluation standards so loose that nearly every stream big enough to
require a bridge may qualify for large Federal appropriations.

Even Representative Wilbur Mills, the Arkansas Democrat who more
than any other man in Congress symbolizes the budget-cutting mood,
loses his passion for economy when it comes to eliminating some of the
most inefficient of these expenditures. While Mills isn't satisfied with
the depth of the cuts in President Johnson's new budget, there is no
evidence that he will push for decreases in the Corps of Engineers'
share. This will be no surprise. When the Eighty-ninth Congress acted
to nullify the Corps' improved project evaluation standards, Mills, far
from objecting, voted with the majority.

Indeed, one of the largest and most inefficient Corps undertakings is

Reprinted from *The Reporter* (February 22, 1968), 36–37, by permission of
the authors and the publisher. Copyright © 1968 by The Reporter Magazine
Company. Mr. Haveman is Professor of Economics at Grinnell College. Miss Stephan
is a doctoral candidate in economics at the University of Michigan.

the $1.2-billion Arkansas River Project for the creation of a 516-mile barge channel from the Mississippi to Tulsa, Oklahoma. After this was approved, Mills praised "our good neighbor," Representative Ed Edmondson (D., Oklahoma), for pushing it through when Arkansas had no member on the Public Works Committee. Under the Corps' improved criteria, that project might never have come into being. Some economists expect the channel to generate so little traffic that it will be better not to use it after it is constructed, so as to save the cost of maintenance and upkeep. Another proposed Corps of Engineers job, the Trinity River Project linking Fort Worth with the Gulf of Mexico, has such uneconomical aspects that some Texans have suggested that it might be cheaper to move the city to the ocean.

The short, unhappy history of the Corps' attempt to improve its benefit-cost criteria provides a clear picture of Congressional unwillingness to assure efficiency in the public-works program.

Since the 1930's, appropriations for inland navigation projects have been made by Congress after it has the Corps' statement that the economic benefits to the nation are expected to be at least equal to project costs—a computation reached by comparing the value of the labor, capital, and other resources required to provide transportation on the waterway with the value of the resources needed to provide transportation by another means, usually rail.

In estimating the benefit to the entire nation of a proposed waterway, there are a number of ways to exaggerate its real worth. One is to measure the savings in terms of the difference between rail and waterway *rates* instead of in terms of the difference in transport *costs*, which more accurately reflect the possible national benefit. Since ineffective regulation by the Interstate Commerce Commission has permitted rates to exceed costs on railroads by more than waterway rates exceed costs, this practice yields a bloated estimate. A second means of exaggerating benefits is to overestimate the amount of traffic that will use the waterway by ignoring the probability that rail rates will fall because of the waterway's competition and improved rail technology. Both of these practices lead to the inclusion in the benefit estimate of gains to barge users—mainly oil, steel, and coal companies. But since these gains are offset by losses to other shippers, they are not real benefits. When they are added to the benefit estimate, the total clearly overstates the waterway's true worth.

Until 1960, the procedures employed by the Corps for calculating waterway benefits incorporated both of these practices. That year, the Corps undertook a major revision of its procedures. Real national benefits were to be measured by using cost reductions (in terms of national resources saved) to estimate transportation savings, and future rates reflecting the competition of the waterway to estimate traffic.

However, under pressure from Congress to approve more projects, the Corps was unable on short notice to develop a reliable method of estimating future rail costs. So as not to sacrifice all its improvements, the Corps in 1964 formulated an interim procedure to be used "until acceptable data for consistent application of the cost basis" could be developed. This allowed for use of rates if cost estimates were not obtainable. While obviously a political compromise, the interim procedure was based on the proposition that true benefits had to be defined in terms of savings of the nation's resources. Consequently, it did assure that the traffic and benefit estimates would not be arbitrarily bloated.

But even this compromise met a most unfavorable reception on Capitol Hill. Representative Edmondson described it as a "danger" to which "every American who is interested in the continual development and improvement of our rivers and inland waterways should be alerted at once." Representative Kenneth Gray (D., Illinois) was "appalled" by "such stringent criteria." Others defended the old procedure by noting that easily measurable data on current rail rates, even if wrong, are preferable to data more difficult to secure, even if correct.

Finally, some Congressmen argued that an objective of waterway construction was to lower railroad rates by providing more competition and that the use of current rates would help to attain this objective by justifying the construction of more projects. No one bothered to ask whether there might not be a cheaper way of regulating the railroads than by the construction of billions of dollars' worth of half-used waterways.

In 1966, when the administration submitted a bill creating the new Department of Transportation, a further attempt was made to ensure the application of sound economic criteria to transportation projects. Section 7 of the bill would have required the Secretary of the new department to develop "standards and criteria consistent with national transportation policies, for the formulation and economic evaluation of all proposals for the investment of Federal funds in transportation facilities. . . ." This provision was consistent with the President's 1965 executive order calling on all executive agencies to develop program planning and budgeting systems of the type pioneered by Secretary McNamara in the Defense Department.

Hearings were held by the Senate Committee on Government Operations under the chairmanship of John McClellan (D., Arkansas). From the outset, the Senator mounted an attack on Section 7, and its amendment virtually came to be McClellan's price for allowing the Transportation Department to be formed. He badgered the acting chief of the Corps of

Engineers, who testified in support of the administration version; he took testimony from a formidable array of waterway lobbyists who decried the evils of the new Secretary's anticipated support of the improved Corps procedures; he ignored the recommendations of the Corps, the Bureau of the Budget, the Comptroller General, and independent transportation authorities in support of the proposed Section 7.

The result of these hearings was a revised section, which forced the Corps to revert to the arbitrary pre-1960 evaluation procedures, and which McClellan referred to as "my amendment." In fact, it was a word-for-word adoption of a suggested amendment introduced into the Senate hearings by the waterway lobbies and barge-line interest groups. These groups were led by the National Rivers and Harbors Congress (of which Senator McClellan was at one time president and Representative Edmondson is a director) and included, among others, the Mississippi Valley Association, the Arkansas Basin Development Association, Inc., the Coosa-Alabama River Improvement Association, Inc., the Florida Waterways Association, the Trinity Improvement Association, and the American Waterways Operators, Inc.

On the floor of the Senate, only William Proxmire (D., Wisconsin) supported the improved procedures. He stated: "Now that the Corps has implemented a system which more accurately measures future benefits it is only natural that it should come under fire from legislators who are threatened with the loss of multi-million-dollar projects. . . . I believe it is high time someone spoke out in support of the Corps efforts to spend our tax dollars wisely. . . . The very purpose of benefit-cost analysis is to eliminate those projects which imply a waste of the society's resources. To plead for a return to an erroneous measurement technique because it yields a greater public works program is, quite frankly, to plead for an increase in uneconomic and wasteful government expenditures."

Proxmire's defense had little impact. On October 13, 1966, Congress passed the Transportation Act containing the amended Section 7. Senator Karl Mundt (R., South Dakota) called that amendment "one of the most important changes which we made."

Since then, there has been little action to divert resources from the wasteful dredging of nine-foot channels to nowhere. Indeed, in the fiscal year 1969 budget submitted last month by an administration acutely aware of the Congressional mood, the proposed Corps appropriation is about three per cent below its 1968 level while the budget for the Office of Education, for example, has been cut by over seven per cent. Having opened the gate for a procession of monumental white elephants by passing Section 7, Congress shows no inclination to close it.

21

LEWIS ANTHONY DEXTER

Congressmen and the
Making of Military Policy

Role Conceptions of Congressmen

This report is concerned with the way in which congressmen, especially those on committees dealing with military matters, interpret their role and status concerning their exercise of influence over military policy. Although Congress's traditional friendliness for the Pentagon seemed to cool a bit in 1969, the basic importance of the factors described in this study is as great as when the research was done.[1]

The conceptions held by a group of men about their role, status, responsibility, and influence presumably have some sort of relationship

[1] This paper was based on 100 interviews, chiefly with members of congressional committees having military responsibility, and other leading congressmen, a few committee staff members, administrative assistants, and legislative liaison personnel from the Department of Defense. The majority of these interviews were done under contract with the Center for International Studies of Massachusetts Institute of Technology, under a Carnegie Corporation grant; others were for the Advisory Committee on Civil Defense of the National Research Council. I had previously conducted 400 interviews with congressmen, lobbyists, and prominent constituents on foreign trade issues, often touching on military questions. This other study is reported in part in Raymond A. Bauer, Ithiel de Sola Pool, and Lewis Anthony Dexter, *American Business and Public Policy* (New York: Atherton Press, 1963). See also my "The Representative and His District," reprinted as Chapter 8 of my *The Sociology and Politics of Congress* (Chicago: Rand McNally & Co., 1970).

Revised in 1969 by the author; originally published in Robert L. Peabody and Nelson W. Polsby, eds., *New Perspectives on the House of Representatives* (Chicago: Rand McNally & Company, 1963), pp. 305–24. Reprinted by permission of the author and publisher. Copyright © 1963 by Lewis Anthony Dexter.

to what they actually do—but there is no reason for supposing that the relationship is direct and unequivocal.[2] Men may, consciously or unconsciously, emphasize or underemphasize their influence and importance; they may emphasize one aspect of their activity and underemphasize another. Tentatively, it seems reasonable to suppose that the way in which men define situations has some effect on how they behave in those situations; this point (that men's definitions of situations tend to have real and significant consequences) presumably is just as important in studying congressional work-roles as in studying any other social behavior.

Military Policy Is Not Considered

Congressmen interviewed generally indicated that they were not inclined to raise or consider questions of military policy *in terms of its meaning for some national or international political objective or goal.* By military policy I mean decisions dealing with the relationship of weapons, personnel, organization, and administration to foreign policy, national interests and purposes, and societal values and objectives. In fact, during the 1946–57 period, few examples could be found where congressional committees gave any impression of seriously evaluating decisions about weapons, appropriations, personnel, missions, organization, or administration in terms of national or international goals or objectives. The great difficulty in making this statement is the obvious fact that here, as elsewhere in politics, there is a rhetoric of justification which purports to explain what was decided in terms of high and serious considerations quite regardless of the relevance of these considerations to the decision-making process. I have not come across any major example where the rhetoric of justification seems to reflect much predecision policy analysis; nor have I found any other evidence during the 1946–57 period where there seems to have been much congressional concern with the over-all policy implications of military decisions.

On the other hand, instances where Congress *appeared* to concern itself with over-all military policy seem generally to fall into one of the following

---

[2] This point probably ought to be a perfectly obvious one, but I was delayed in interpreting the results of interviews conducted in 1955–57 because it took me five years fully to see that I was not reporting on how congressmen affect military policy but simply on *how congressmen define* their role and responsibility in regard to military policy.

Were this simply a personal error of my own, it would hardly be worth commenting upon, but I suspect that whether relying upon documents or interviews, a good many reports about politics, especially about Congress, fall into a similar error—role definition, attitude, or orientation, is interpreted as though it threw *direct* light on the substantive exercise of influence or formation of policy. An extreme, but obvious, parallel is this: a whole series of interviews with quarrelling husbands and wives would not necessarily tell us what happens when spouses disagree. What it would tell us—and an extremely important thing to know—is how husbands and wives of certain sorts interpret their roles, responsibilities, etc. But it is important to know, too, what such sources do not *by themselves* yield.

categories: (1) Those where Congressmen felt able to judge between clamoring claimants—usually different military services—and gave one or another of them a larger slice of the available pie. (2) Where congressmen were concerned with some local situation, usually an employment situation. Congressional support, especially support in the House of Representatives, of what Huntington has called "strategic monism,"[3] consisted largely of the congressional assumption of a judicial role, tempered by the pressure of various local contractor and employment interests—all within a framework of verbal "toughness." This is a stance rather than a policy.

Congressmen also occasionally wish to mollify widespread personnel complaints (*e.g.,* those emanating from the National Guard mobilization in 1961). And, of course, congressmen have personal concerns of their own (*e.g.,* personal loyalty to the Marine Corps). And, naturally, they always have straight constituent interests to defend (*e.g.,* preserving specific military installations in local areas).[4]

3 Samuel P. Huntington, "Radicalism and Conservatism in National Defense Policy," *Journal of International Affairs,* VIII (1954), 206–33. This exceptionally brilliant analysis of the politics of national defense differs from the present report in one significant respect—it works back from the consequences of significant decisions to presumed ideologies and therefore takes seriously the justifications given in more or less formal statements for the record as to the reasons why a position has been taken. This may be a perfectly valid approach to political behavior, but in the instant case, at least, it seems to the writer that it misleads, much as the effort to categorize office-holders in terms of what they happen to say on some particular issue such as "home rule" would mislead. Unfortunately, in terms of the available data and the present state of political science knowledge, there is no clear reason for choosing between Huntington's approach and others.

4 R. H. Dawson, "Congressional Innovation and Intervention in Defense Policy: Legislative Authorization of Weapons Systems," *American Political Science Review,* LXVI (1962), 42–57, reports a congressional effort (in 1959 and following years) to assume more systematic responsibility. Unfortunately, my study and interviews were entirely confined to the pre-1959 period; however, I strongly suspect that what Dawson reports could be interpreted more precisely in terms of the role which Congress from time to time does assume as an arbiter between technologists, discussed below; in the absence of such arbitrament and of such local pressures (as to which congressmen typically do regard themselves as experts) the episode would not have occurred.

I suspect, also, that Dawson in a sense is dealing with the congressmen's public and overt picture of themselves—the kind of picture which is likely to be presented in reports and speeches—whereas I am dealing with the private picture (the covert culture) of Congress. There is nothing which of necessity makes a man's private picture of himself or a covert culture "truer" than the public picture; both must be taken into account, and, if they are different, may suggest further investigation. The sociological analysis suggested here becomes particularly interesting in view of the signs of congressional dissatisfaction with military spending and procurement displayed in 1969.

However, it is possibly relevant that in 1955–56, a distinguished scholar, familiar with congressional action on military matters in recent years, initially challenged emphatically my point that Congress in fact had very little influence on military policy. He stated that he had a list of some fourteen areas in which Congress had been influential. But after he reconsidered the point, he stated he had to agree that Congress had either given a little more or a little less than the Department of Defense asked or decided between competing technologists, but had not, in fact, undertaken any initiative.

Policy Analysis: Military Versus Civilian

The attitudes and responses to military policy-making of members of the congressional committees concerned with military policy contrasted with those of members of committees concerned with foreign economic policy. Also, members not on key committees in either field showed a similar differentiation between these fields. In general, the broad aspects of military policy are not considered. In the tax field, members of Ways and Means often consider the presumptive effect of particular tax legislation upon national economic policy, but military decisions are generally treated by the relevant committees as independent of broader policy decisions.

This need not be the case, for it has not always been the case. In the 1930's, available evidence suggests, Ross Collins of Mississippi, for many years a member, sometime chairman, of the Subcommittee on Military Appropriations of the House Appropriations Committee, did in fact stimulate research and development in tank warfare—and he did a great deal to keep the possibilities of tank warfare before the informed public.[5] In fact, Collins' impact in the United States may be compared with that of the military critics Fuller and Liddell-Hart in Britain and the military officer, de Gaulle, in France. (It may now be largely forgotten that de Gaulle's first claim to fame was as a theorist of mobile warfare.)

In addition, in two particular areas, the Subcommittee on Military Operations of the House Government Operations Committee during the 1950's played a similar part. For a number of years, serious thinking about *civil* defense, its mission, purpose, and meaning, was kept alive by that subcommittee, especially by its chairman, Chet Holifield (D.-Calif.); it is probably no exaggeration to say that if it were not for the pressure of the Holifield subcommittee on the administration, the whole subject of civil defense would have lapsed into a patronage "boondoggle." Despite the word "civil," "civil defense" is in fact an item in military policy[6]—but it is quite possible that it was very psychologically important for congressional activity that civil defense was called "civil" and until 1961 had a "civil" administration. If so, this would be crucial in terms of the rest of our

---

[5] On Collins, see Frank C. Hanaghen, "The U.S. Army," *Harper's Magazine* (December 1940), esp. pp. 9–13, and Ross A. Collins, "Do We Want a Mass Army?" *Reader's Digest* (June 1941), pp. 1–9. It is greatly to be hoped that, with the present emphasis on oral history and on congressional behavior, some foundation will have the imagination and initiative, while some of the participants are still alive, to undertake interviews which would permit testing more accurately such matters as the assertions made in the text about Collins.

[6] The well-known writings of Herman Kahn make this point from one standpoint. From another—emphasis on "Defense Means Protection"—I make the same point in an article by that title, published in the *American Scholar,* XXIV (Summer, 1955), 299–308.

argument.[7] Other congressmen were probably more willing to accept Congressman Holifield's leadership here because civil defense seemed civilian; they did not think that they were infringing on military technology.[8]

Particularly under the chairmanship of Congressman Riehlman (R.-N.Y.), but during the entire decade of the fifties, the same subcommittee also was actively concerned with, and probably stimulated, intelligent action about the optimal use of scientists in defense research, a matter which is at least on the fringes of military policy.

The Armed Services Committee
"Is Primarily a Real Estate Committee"

In general, it was necessary to avoid the phrase "policy" in interviews on military policy; it was too ambiguous, although it was not too ambiguous in 1953–56 interviews with congressmen on foreign economic "policy." At that time, it was rarely necessary to explain to congressmen what was meant when we came to discuss policy implications; congressional thinking about the tariff and reciprocal trade have been structured in terms of policy by a history of discussion and communications within and outside Congress.[9]

One congressman, who was probably more concerned about the apparent absence of concern with military policy in the Congress than any other member of a relevant committee with whom I talked, said:

If I were talking to a new member of [my committee], I'd say that the main problem is to pinpoint responsibility at the White House and the boards [the various councils and committees concerned with national security] for policy determination. You can't really tell who does determine it; it moves into DOD [Department of Defense] and each of the three services, and you have a feeling [that], as relates to appropriations, there is not any unity. The capable men in each area are just trying to push for more for their services which is natural, but

7 The argument that congressmen are timid about invading the area of the military specialist; see below.

8 Of course, this fact has been by no means an unalloyed benefit to civil defense. Some of those who advocated the action which actually took place in 1961—the transfer of civil defense to the Department of Defense—supported it partly because they thought a military identification would provide it with more prestige. However, part of the objective which advocates of the transfer had in mind was not achieved when the Subcommittee on Independent Offices of the House Appropriations Committee, which was accustomed to deal very harshly with civil defense budget requests, succeeded in keeping responsibility for the civil defense budget. Supporters of civil defense had hoped that the responsibility would be transferred to the Military Appropriations Subcommittee, which is inclined to be much more generous and less critical.

9 In fact, in these interviews, because I was chiefly (though not exclusively) interested in communications, I often found it necessary to steer informants away (sometimes quite sharply as with the late Senator George of Georgia) from discussion of policy toward consideration of communications.

it means they think more in terms of how to spend more and more money than they do in terms of really thinking out a strategy that would more successfully justify these great appropriations.

In our hearings, I tried for purposes of communication to do some research to determine this matter of policy. What were they thinking of? Did they anticipate [this or that]...? What had they in mind to accomplish?

Then, of course, you wonder about what actually the policy of the Congress is.... It's never been clear to me what direction there is in the matter.... Policy is supposed to be wrapped up [by the Joint Chiefs] under certain restrictions, but you wonder sometimes if the chairman of the Joint Chiefs knows what is going on in the minds of other chiefs....

After our lengthy hearings, I wonder to what extent members of Congress... bring together sufficient staff to get a real perspective. *Most questions even in what are called policy hearings are directed really towards production. This is true equally of off-the-record hearings.* People are asked questions about specific manpower requirements, et cetera, not about general policy.

It does look as though the congressional committees operate in a vacuum. It comes right back to the tragic lack of time for reflection and study on the part of members of the Congress. *So maybe they don't get clear in their minds what policy is.*

...I believe there should be some serious policy thinking on the ideological side. It should relate the military to State and USIA....

So far as I know you are the only person in my [more than eight years of] *service in Congress, or outside, who has been making any effort to delve into these problems.* I called on several people in various government departments, DOD, the committee staff, et cetera, to try to help me to frame questions to get at these policy issues [but did not get much help]. Symington's subcommittee is concerned with program and production—not too much with big policy issues.

I can see enormous possibilities in a very careful study of the problem. Could we move into new types of weapons and a future type of defense? How can we become more potent ideologically? [The military] lack direction. We [the Congress] must assume responsibility for policy determination.

More typical was the response of a much more influential member of the House Committee on Armed Services—who, when I tried to explain that I was trying to find out what Congress did do or could do on policy said:

What the hell is the point of that? What would you do with it? I don't see that any public service could be performed by it. You can't find anything particular to say. In fact, how do we [members] know what should be considered? We mostly reflect what the military people recommend; military policy is made by the Department of Defense.

Our comittee is a real estate committee.

How do we check the military recommendations? I don't know. We just ask a lot of questions—questions that are not resolved. It's most difficult to make inquiries. Take bases. DOD says we need such-and-such bases. Well, we want to know why such-and-such a size. But we don't mostly know how to evaluate the answers; we aren't equipped to do so. So 95 per cent of the legislation is what DOD recommends. It's only when you come to personnel problems, size of army, that sort of thing, that you find us doing more—and that's naturally because that affects the lives of every voter.

And perhaps the most experienced staff man on military matters on the Hill, when I told him I was studying the Armed Services Committee, repeated again and again, to be sure the idea was properly communicated, "Our committee is a real estate committee. Don't forget that. *If you study our committee, you are studying real estate transactions.*" By that, he meant that the *location of installations and related transfer, purchase, and sale of properties is the main concern of the House Armed Services Committee.*

One of the major reasons why the congressional committees involved concern themselves with accountable and avoidable waste, marginal issues in the appropriations field, personnel problems, and other such peripheral matters is the fear of lack of competence.[10]

The Tyranny of Information and Ideas: "Who Are We to Say 'No'?"

Congress is today better equipped to evaluate, assay, and sometimes develop and integrate ideas than it is to invent them or stimulate their invention. But if Congress is to function smoothly, there must *somewhere* be people who invent and transmit competing ideas. That is to say, generally speaking, Congress can readily check and balance when there are within the politically alert public, sets of ideas and interests which check and balance each other, thus creating a situation within which the Congress is able to *sift, winnow, and judge.*

But if there is no check and balance *outside* the Congress, then the Congress will find it difficult to perform the legislative functions of investigation, inquiry, check, and balance. So far as congressmen are aware (or were aware in 1955–57), there is no such climate of controversy, opinion, and interest pertaining to military policy as such—outside the armed services themselves. The people for the most part certainly believe in a "strong National Defense," but beyond that, the members of Congress receive little or no articulate information on military policy from them. Most congress-

10 I discuss the general phenomenon of the increasing fear by the non-expert of the expert as a function of our schooling and university systems in *Tyranny of Schooling* (New York: Basic Books, 1964). See also my "Check and Balance Today: What Does It Mean for Congress and the Congressmen?" in Alfred de Grazia, ed., *Congress: The First Branch of Government* (New York: Anchor Books, 1967).

men on relevant committees reported in interviews that, so far as constituent views and attitudes on military policy are concerned, there were none! This situation contrasts more or less sharply with other policy fields regarding which congressmen may hear a good deal from constituents; the members are well aware of the difference.

In regard to other matters of legislative concern, there are persons known to congressmen who have articulate views and to whom the congressmen can turn for ideas, suggestions, ammunition, and moral backing. The latter point is very important; few congressmen want to challenge the experts in a highly specialized field without first having their own experts to back them.[11]

In any case, members of Congress share the views which they generally attribute to their constituents: they hesitate to question the *basic* proposals of the military; that is, they regard the military as *experts,* not only on matters of organization and command, but on types of war plans, etc. Said one member of a relevant committee, better prepared by previous experience than most committee members, "The whole problem is that we are not military experts, and we have to rely upon what the military people tell us. We try to get them to cut out the window dressing, but it's hard."[12] He repeated several times in the course of our talks the rhetorical question: "Who are we to say 'no' to the military people?" Members do not feel this respect for foreign policy experts from the State Department or for tax experts from the Treasury or for economists from relevant agencies.

Military Specialists Exercise a Monopoly on the Presentation of Alternatives

In terms of the feeling just described, most congressmen and members of the relevant committees usually, if not always, *did* follow the recommenda-

---

[11] The point is not so much to be guided by the specific advice of a particular expert; it is, rather, not to stick one's neck out by finding oneself opposed to all those who are "respectable" and "informed." A few seeming experts who take a minority view are all that are sometimes needed to embolden those who latently sympathize with them. See works cited in note 10, above.

[12] Significantly, in the course of these interviews, no members said anything (except for reference to civil defense theorists) which indicated an awareness that there is within the scientific community considerable controversy about war plans. However, I know that three or four of the members I talked with do have some knowledge of the sort of argument one would find in the *Bulletin of Atomic Scientists,* but only one of them mentioned the matter in the framework of our interviews. In terms of the orientation of this article—*the social psychology of the occupational interfaces between congressmen and military specialists*—the omission did not need to be challenged; it would be interesting to replicate my interviews today to see if there is more spontaneous mention of the scientific discussion.

tions of the military when these were clearly and explicitly propounded. However, members of Congress did not, in fact, want to know the military's specific war plans for security reasons,[13] and in many cases, they were not at all concerned with the nature of the war plans. In general, they seemed to be assuming that there are only two possible kinds of war—either (1) a thermonuclear war, or (2) a Korean-type war. They appeared to have no idea that other possibilities (of other kinds of war) are worth investigating.

The military exercises a monopoly or quasi-monopoly on presentation of alternatives, with the result that congressmen have no reason to be aware of the gamut of possibilities open to them. When the generals very largely determine the explanations they hear, and the choices they are forced to make, congressmen have little opportunity to move into an area of reflection broader than that of the generals—unless they have the time and ability to innovate.[14]

The problem for congressmen is, then, to get alternatives posed for them. The issue is not confined to the military field; it is, impressionistically speaking, probably true in all areas in which the legislative branch is faced with specialists whose occupational prestige is such that members of the legislature are apt to feel that they are sticking their necks out by contradicting them. In other words, military men often belong to a category of technological specialists who can to a considerable degree get their own way by posing the questions for the legislature; public health specialists are another such category.[15]

"How the Hell Do We Know What Should Be Considered?"

How do the members of the relevant committees reach their decisions and evaluate the proposals made by the military? The answer seems to be that usually no such evaluation is made. In answer to the question, "Aside

---

13 That is, they are afraid they will be inhibited and restrained and embarrassed by having access to more confidential security information than they desire to know.

14 In an area not one of military policy as we have defined the term, but closely related thereto, Congressman John W. McCormack (D.-Mass.) has, according to members of his staff, manifested such innovative tendencies: He has, they report, played a creative part in pressuring the Department of Defense to rationalize purchasing procedures. Congressional influence in this area may increase in the 1970s.

15 Of course, this is a report from the standpoint of the legislature; most military men and public health experts will probably feel that they do not get their own way; and sometimes the legislature may say "no" to them, or say more often "a little less" or "a little later," but generally the legislature does concede to them the formulation of the issues. On this point see my *How Organizations Are Represented in Washington* (Indianapolis: Bobbs-Merrill Company, Inc., 1969).

from your common sense and whatever help the staff can supply you, is there any way to check on the military experts?" members said:

No. The most effective way is for a congressman to have a good knowledge of the installations in his district which unfortunately I do not have.

The problem as I see it is that even if we put into effect policy legislation, the executive department can circumvent it if it wants to. [This member stated that he probably attends more committee and subcommittee meetings than any other member; he was referred to by several committee colleagues as "an expert."]

Lord knows we need some help; I hope you can find something which tells us what to listen to.

How the hell do we know what should be considered anyway? We mostly reflect what the military men tell us. [This was from a member widely regarded as one of the two or three ablest men on the relevant committees.]

Such acceptance of the leadership of the military, so far as the House is concerned, seems to be more characteristic of the Armed Services Committee than of the Appropriations Subcommittee on Defense. Almost all members agreed with the following point:

We don't have a hell of a lot before our [Armed Services] committee. There's really much scarcity of policy legislation.... Maybe we have given too much authority to the Secretary of Defense and the Joint Chiefs of Staff. Congress itself has promulgated legislation which says to them "use your own judgment."... So policy is found in Appropriations more than anywhere else. Yes, the question of jurisdiction on these matters keeps people sore. Vinson stays at loggerheads with Cannon about it [Vinson (D.-Ga.), Chairman, Armed Services; Cannon (D.-Mo.), Chairman, Appropriations].

And, from another member of Armed Services:

Our committee accepts reports of the Department of Defense more completely than does Appropriations. We never question opinions about personnel, et cetera. [This is not absolutely correct, but more or less so.] We kid Appropriations members about this, say we aren't military experts, but they are, et cetera.

The foregoing comments apply to the House rather than the Senate. Although there are differences in the personalities of the members of the two House committees, the significant contrast seems to arise out of the functional differences between them. Armed Services is a *legislative* committee, and, as such, deals chiefly with the basic issues only once—when they are enacted into legislation. The Appropriations Committee, on the other hand, considers issues *annually,* and, as one member of Armed Services said:

Right. Appropriations *is* more important. We are over-all men and deal with the over-all things. Now, you must qualify that to this extent; this may not be true from the standpoint of the armed services themselves. We do deal with things that might not seem very important to civilians but are tremendously important to the military—like how many general officers can there be? [A Senate committee staff member indicated that they have more personal visits on personnel matters, promotions, pensions, etc., than on any other matter.[16]]

But in the conventional course of events, the Appropriations Committee is concerned mainly not so much with *legislation* as with avoiding *accountable waste*. As to getting into the *policy* field, there its members have no clear viewpoint of whether they should or should not. Thus, by and large, when Appropriations Committee members do get into a policy question, it is either by accident or because some external event has attracted attention to it, or because of the personal interest of particular members.[17]

"We Need More Interservice Squabbling"

Several fairly senior members, when asked, "What are the major characteristics of a good committee member?" replied, in effect, "Be suspicious of the military! We need guys who won't let them put anything over on us." For instance, one member said:

Well, now, I'm sure you can supply [better] words to what I'm saying. . . . There's no way on earth to prevent military leaders from pulling the wool over our eyes. But we should keep check. . . . You have to watch their requests; many times they're made for political expedience. You've got to trust what military leaders tell you, but you can't turn them loose on things. . . .I'm not one of those who think the military are all bad, but we need a close check on them. Unfortunately you cannot have such a check unless you have well-staffed standing committees with tremendous expenditures.

Another, one of the two most impressive members of the relevant committees in 1956:

Congress can preserve a republican form of government and avoid a dictator by this sort of control [which Appropriations supplies]. . . . They frequently forget

16 The parallel with school committees in cities and towns—which in some instances spend more time discussing routes and who is entitled to bus rides than considering educational matters—is interesting.

17 But the tremendous workload of the committee, plus the quite inadequate staff assistance, means that, at present, its most conscientious and penetrating members would have to make a very conscious decision to let millions of dollars of avoidable, accountable, or quasi-accountable waste go unchecked, if they were to allow themselves the time to think through military policy problems! For anyone, and particularly for the kind of man who is likely to gravitate to the Appropriations Committee, this would be a most difficult decision.

man is a human being; [yet] they're always talking about morale until I'm sick of the word.... A very important ability [on Appropriations] is to resist the blandishments and glitter of stars and rank. I make a rule never to accept any social invitation involving a top-ranking military man.... [Then you have] to be thick-skinned. It's hard to say "no." The services may not attack you directly, but indirectly....

But since the military is supposed to be "trying to put something over on us" (the Congress and the people), what then? Again and again, the members said, in effect: "What we need is more interservice squabbling. *When the military falls out, then and only then can the Congress find out.*"

One of the more influential staff men, a trusted advisor of one of the most influential men on the Hill, said, for example:

Looking at these things, as I must, from the big end of the funnel, it seems to me that if everything goes smoothly, nobody ever knows what's going on, neither Congress nor anybody else. But when some one of the forces gets into trouble or gets riled up, then we hear about it and learn a lot. [Of course] we don't know whether the roots are in the military services themselves or start with the DOD civilians or with the military contractors; I just don't know and I wouldn't want to be quoted, but I'd like to know whether Boeing has stirred things up chiefly on these B-52s. Naturally, Senator Jackson [D.- Wash.] openly says . . . he'd like to see some more jobs there.

I would say there is no secret that [in 1956] SAC has priority in people and things—*all over.* And the big squabbles arise when it [or somebody else] gets hurt.... But if nobody gets badly hurt, all the services will sit there as calm as can be, and Congress will hear nothing about it....

This old stuff of roles and missions is the central thing in our investigations, and always there you're cutting or threatening to cut flesh, nerve, muscle; and everybody wants to be seated at the table where such a threat is made. The reason for all the sensitivity is the simple possibility of a change in roles and missions.

Fights gets to Congress and lead Congress to know what's going on....

If somebody comes to you and wants you to investigate such-and-such a condition, you'll learn only what they in the services want you to learn, *unless there is interservice rivalry.* Then you can find out from the Air Force or vice versa and from Strategic Air Command about Air Defense or vice versa. That is, each service, then [when there's a fight], is ready to say "those dirty dogs are doing so-and-so" and you learn something.

A staff member is quoted here because he expressed, as it happened, more articulately and systematically what many members clearly indicated or implied. Said a member who had actually campaigned on the basis of membership on a committee related to the armed services:

The thing I was least aware of before my service [here on the committee] was the interservice rivalry. Of course, my community tends towards one particular service; I'm not objecting to this [interservice rivalry]. I think a spirited competition is a very healthy thing.

This emphasis on competition and on the healthiness of it seems to imply what the staff member just quoted actually said; in a couple of instances, it came very close to the old saying, "When thieves fall out, honest men have their day." The atmosphere of not trusting the armed services was widespread in the Congress. Not that they think the military witnesses and leaders are thieves, of course, but in the words of another member:

I suppose I'm unique among congressmen; I have a strong native bias against the military, as witness that word "garbage" which I just used as applied to what I hear from the Pentagon, but for refined intellectual reasons I'm more convinced than most that we have to have an intelligent defense policy and defend it, so I refrain from criticism except on special points. I find myself, that is, a strong supporter of an institution which I distrust profoundly.[18]

The belief that other members have a higher opinion than oneself has of the military seems fairly common, so I raised the question, "Do you really think that's unique? It seems to me to be standard."

Oh, well, I think a lot of 'em would say "We've got to have the ——s but we hate 'em"; mine is a more refined, permanent, philosophical distrust!

"The Military Is the Real Corruptor of Congress"

The late E. L. Bartlett, then Delegate from Alaska and later a Senator, recalling the excitement in the late 1950's about attempts by oil and gas interests to bribe a senator, said:

Relatively, if they were really to study "corruption," all that [oil business] is peanuts in my judgment; the people who are really trying to bribe and pressure Congress are from the Department of Defense. They learn you want to go somewhere, and they call you up and say, "How about travelling on one of our planes?" And it just so happens there is riding along with you a pleasant, agreeable officer from the service which gives you the ride; he does not argue with you at all, but he does call your attention to things from their standpoint.

Bartlett then pointed out that this kind of contact is designed to give the armed services the opportunity to determine what issues the congress-

---

[18] This member shared with several others the illusion that his was a unique point of view; in fact, it was the commonest one.

man thinks about. He averred that, collectively, such contacts are far more "corrupting" than oil industry efforts because they do more to shape the way Congress looks at military questions than any mere bribe. His kind of awareness, however—that all the military services *may share* a common set of assumptions or views which it would be profitable to question, or *may omit* from consideration some important point which, in terms of over-all national interest, should be taken into account—is not commonly found among members of the committees directly concerned with military issues.

In fact, congressmen frequently assume the validity of *the terms* in which interservice disputes are raised because they know of no other way of getting at the issues. In any event, it is a common enough human tendency to accept the framework within which an argument is conducted; but in the Congress this tendency is considerably enhanced by the feeling that the Armed Services Committee is a *"quasi-judicial* committee."[19] Perhaps the judicial role is often a desirable model for congressmen to adopt; it might in fact increase impartiality and a readiness to change one's mind on due cause being presented. On the Armed Services Committee, it leads to the notion that that committee has two chief responsibilities: (1) to listen to the requests of the various services and say "yes" or "no"; or (2) in more complex issues, to decide which of the "litigants"—Army, Navy, Air Force, Marines, or subservices—shall get the most of what is wanted in the way of missions, money, prestige, and power.[20]

But this notion appears to have the grave weakness that it assumes that through the operation of some form of invisible hand, the "litigants" will necessarily present the basic issues of public policy with which the Congress ought to be concerned. It also assumes that the interservice hostility, thus not diminished, will not interfere with genuine cooperation between the armed forces where this is desirable.

---

[19] This notion of being engaged in a judicial process is common enough on congressional committes, naturally so in a body which contains many lawyers, some would-be judges, and some would-be members of regulatory commissions. Committee chairmen may operate on the notion that they conduct hearings with the neutrality which a judge shows in court. At the time of this investigation such chairmen as former Senator Millikin (R.-Colo., Senate Finance) or the former chairman of the House Interior Committee, now Senator Engle (D.-Calif.), who had clearly-known views on controversial legislation, endeavored to portray themselves as impartially engaged in a judicial activity while conducting hearings on such legislation.

[20] Of course, on many matters, the committees could have great importance because of their latent power (the degree to which the executive branch calculates upon their acceptance or rejection of proposals may be as important as the actual approval or disapproval they articulate) rather than because of what they actually do. Hypothetically, it should be pointed out that committees would "rubber-stamp" all suggestions from a department if the department always guessed correctly what the committees would approve and submitted no other suggestions.

What Is "Technical" and What Is "Non-technical"?

*"You Have to Gnaw and Gnaw to Get Anything
Out of the Service"*

Even more basic, possibly, than the points already made in explaining
or "justifying" congressional reluctance to tackle military policy problems
is the little word technical. Congressmen tend to regard as "technical" such
questions for "professional" military men as the nature of war plans. But
they regard as "non-technical" and fit subjects for their consideration such
matters as the way in which oil is stored at overseas installations or how
service credit shall be allocated for ROTC or military academy training—
problems of the type which at some universities would be thankfully left as
a "technical" matter for registrars to decide.[21] Similarly, Congress will
evaluate or try to evaluate the efficiency of given types of rifles or waste in
the procurement of military overcoats. However—with the partial exceptions
of the Subcommittee on Military Operations when Riehlman (R.-N.Y.)
was chairman and the Senate Foreign Relations Committee in 1959–60—
they have recently shown little interest in stimulating the invention and
development of newer types of weapons or innovations in "grand strategy."[22]
The historic distinction between *grand* strategy—war plans involving, for
instance, such matters as the desirability and feasibility of *massive* retaliation
versus *measured* retaliation—and *specific* strategies is quite unfamiliar in
the Congress. This explains in part why questions about military policy are
often regarded as suggesting that congressmen concern themselves with
technical military issues. In other words, many congressmen assume that
there is some sort of over-all approach to military policy which need not be
questioned, or which is axiomatic. In any case, questions of over-all policy
are not raised by many witnesses or "litigants" (in general, it would be
against the interest of *most* of the vociferous litigants who approach Congress to query prevailing assumptions). But a contrast is provided by congressmen who have recently been able and eager to consider basic policy in

---

21 Officers might or might not receive longevity pay credit for their years in the
military academies or in the ROTC; Congress in this case has tended to support
reservists against the claims to special considerations from West Pointers, etc.

22 The Foreign Relations Committee may seem an unlikely candidate here, but
the truth was well-expressed by a sophisticated and experienced staff member of
another committee who said, "I think you'll find out that jurisdiction is nine-tenths
assertion" among congressional committees. If several influential members of the
Interior Committee desired to do so, no doubt they could study basic military policy
because of their responsibilities for public lands, conservation, etc., which provides
an entering wedge; the only difficulty would be that, if they did this, they would
not have time to do something else which they might wish to do.

fields such as full employment or international trade, and *may* have begun in 1969 with respect to military policy.

A number of members made the point that the Constitution gives the President special authority over military matters because he is designated as Commander-in-Chief. This, again, seems to assume that questions about military policy must necessarily deal with specific war plans and to ignore the area of grand strategy. In any case, it might equally well be argued that the American constitutional system is supposed to operate through competition between the branches of government, that is to say, check-and-balance, and that there is also constitutional warrant for assumption by Congress of responsibility in military matters.

One reason cited by several congressmen for hesitation about "interfering" with the executive branch on military matters is that efforts to do so during the Civil War resulted (actually or supposedly) in difficulty and trouble. Southern members, who are, of course, in senior positions when the Democratic party is in the majority, seem to be particularly influenced by this contention. Perhaps Senator Truman of Missouri, through his establishment of and leadership in a committee concerned with investigating defense mobilization, contracting difficulties, etc., and because of his own intense historical sense, called attention to or enhanced the importance of this point of view.

The question is, could Congress learn to think about military policy without getting into the war plans area? This is, of course, a standard problem of legislative-executive relationship, generalist-specialist tension, and, for that matter, top administrator-middle administrator difficulty. The president of a university, and the board of trustees under some circumstances, may properly be concerned with the curriculum but not with the content of the comprehensive examination; they may set policy within which future comprehensive examinations may be established, but they should never handle complaints about current comprehensives. Senator Truman's position (which he probably saw no reason to change when he became President) was that the Congress could not, psychologically, make the judicious sort of distinction here described, and therefore should stay out of the field altogether.[23]

Under present practice, it is probably true to say, as one active and influential congressman did, that "On these matters, you have to be a____ bulldog and gnaw and gnaw and gnaw to get any [information out] of the

[23] The Congress does not ordinarily get into specific administration; however, I have several times heard the assertion that under Senator McCarran's chairmanship, the Judiciary Committee did get into specifics of immigration administration. In some state legislatures, ways and means committees deal on a continuing basis with administrative matters, although of course state governments do not anticipate the same military crises the Congress must envisage.

services." (He added, "the whole damn trouble with Congress is they let people file things.") "You've got to be a policeman and keep hounding and hounding...to get a job done."

Power-seeking Politicians versus Technologists?

One commonly held conception about politics is that politicians seek power actively and aggressively. Whatever other conclusions may be derived from the present report, it seems apparent that congressmen on relevant committees could readily enough have reached for greater power in military affairs with a reasonable chance of obtaining it. *In fact, they have thought that the satisfactions they obtain by not seeking power are greater than those they would get by trying to maximize it.* Among the factors which may explain such "restraint" are (1) traditions of institutional organization including "separation of powers"; and (2) the notion in Congress that professional and technical matters should be left to professional and technical men. On the basis of the present study we cannot say whether these traditions and notions are "rationalizations" of some other motivation (such as the discomfort conceivably involved in systematic thinking about the potentialities of modern war—former Civil Defense Administrator Petersen, also a politician, spoke of himself as one "who [has] been looking into hell for three years") or are independent causal factors. The writer's best guess is that they are, to a considerable extent, causal factors, the weight and significance of which are very much increased by other motivations, such as the one just mentioned, and by simple fear that a civilian who fights a technical man will be made to look ridiculous before his public.[24] It must of course be left to future research to see if the signs of congressional independence displayed in 1969 (largely in the Senate) were a flash in the pan or the beginning of a new assertiveness vis-à-vis the Pentagon. In any event, the reasons for congressional abstention from consideration of basic policy questions are by no means limited to military issues.

24 For another discussion of self-restraint where some interpretations would predict an aggressive seeking of power, see Lewis A. Dexter, "Where the Elephant Fears to Dance Among the Chickens. Business in Politics? The Case of Delaware," *Human Organization,* XIX (1960–61), 188–94, republished with some modifications in Bauer, Pool, and Dexter, *op. cit.*

22

AARON B. WILDAVSKY

Budgetary Strategies
of Administrative Agencies

Budgetary strategies are actions by governmental agencies intended to maintain or increase the amount of money available to them. Not every move in the budgetary arena is necessarily aimed at getting funds in a conscious way. Yet administrators can hardly help being aware that nothing can be done without funds, and that they must normally do things to retain or increase rather than decrease their income.

Our major purpose in this chapter is to describe in an orderly manner the major budgetary strategies currently being employed and to relate them to the environment from which they spring. In this way we can, for the first time, describe the behavior of officials engaged in budgeting as they seek to relate their requirements and powers to the needs and powers of others. Strategies are the links between the intentions and perceptions of budget officials and the political system that imposes restraints and creates opportunities for them. When we know about strategies we are not only made aware of important kinds of behavior, we also learn about the political world in which they take place.

Strategic moves take place in a rapidly changing environment in which no one is quite certain how things will turn out and new goals constantly emerge in response to experience. In this context of uncertainty,

Reprinted from *The Politics of the Budgetary Process* (Boston: Little, Brown and Company, 1964), pp. 63–84, by permission of the publisher. Copyright © 1964 by Little, Brown and Company. Mr. Wildavsky is Professor of Political Science and Dean of the Graduate School of Public Affairs of the University of California at Berkeley.

choice among existing strategies must be based on intuition and hunch, on an "educated guess," as well as on firm knowledge. Assuming a normal capacity to learn, however, experience should eventually provide a more reliable guide than sheer guesswork. When we discover strategies that are practiced throughout the entire administrative apparatus, we suspect that officials have discovered paths to success which may not be wholly reliable but which have proved to be more advantageous than the available alternatives.

Ubiquitous and Contingent Strategies

What really counts in helping an agency get the appropriations it desires? Long service in Washington has convinced high agency officials that some things count a great deal and others only a little. Although they are well aware of the desirability of having technical data to support their requests, budget officials commonly derogate the importance of the formal aspects of their work as a means of securing appropriations. Budget estimates that are well prepared may be useful for internal purposes—deciding among competing programs, maintaining control of the agency's operations, giving the participants the feeling they know what they are doing, finding the cost of complex items. The estimates also provide a respectable backstop for the agency's demands. But, as several informants put it in almost identical words, "It's not what's in your estimates but how good a politician you are that matters."

Being a good politician, these officials say, requires essentially three things: cultivation of an active clientele, the development of confidence among other governmental officials, and skill in following strategies that exploit one's opportunities to the maximum. Doing good work is viewed as part of being a good politician.

Strategies designed to gain confidence and clientele are ubiquitous; they are found everywhere and at all times in the budgetary system. The need for obtaining support is so firmly fixed a star in the budgetary firmament that it is perceived by everyone and uniformly taken into account in making the calculations upon which strategies depend.

"Contingent" strategies are particular; they depend upon conditions of time and place and circumstance; they are especially dependent upon an agency's attitude toward the opportunities the budgetary system provides for. Arising out of these attitudes, we may distinguish three basic orientations toward budgeting in increasing order of ambition. First, defending the agency's base by guarding against cuts in old programs. Second, increasing the size of the base by moving ahead with old programs. Third, expanding the base by adding new programs. These types of strategies differ considerably from one another. An agency might cut popular programs to promote a restoration of funds; it would be unlikely to follow this strategy in adding new programs. We shall take up ubiquitous and contingent strategies in turn.

Clientele

Find a Clientele

For most agencies locating a clientele is no problem at all; the groups interested in their activities are all too present. But for some agencies the problem is a difficult one and they have to take extraordinary measures to solve it. Men and women incarcerated in federal prisons, for instance, are hardly an ideal clientele. And the rest of society cares only to the extent of keeping these people locked up. So the Bureau of Prisons tries to create special interest in its activities on the part of Congressmen who are invited to see what is going on. "I wish, Mr. Bow, you would come and visit us at one of these prison places when you have the time. . . . I am sure you would enjoy it." The United States Information Agency faces a similar problem—partly explaining its mendicant status—because it serves people abroad rather than directly benefiting them at home. Things got so bad that the USIA sought to organize the country's ambassadors to foreign nations to vouch for the good job it said it was doing.

Serve Your Clientele

For an agency that has a large and strategically placed clientele, the most effective strategy is service to those who are in a position to help them. "If we deliver this kind of service," an administrator declared, "other things are secondary and automatic." His agency made a point of organizing clientele groups in various localities, priming them to engage in approved projects, serving them well, and encouraging them to inform their Congressmen of their reaction. Informing one's clientele of the full extent of the benefits they receive may increase the intensity with which they support the agency's request.

Expand Your Clientele

In order to secure substantial funds from Congress for domestic purposes, it is ordinarily necessary to develop fairly wide interest in the program. This is what Representative Whitten did when he became a member of the Appropriations Committee and discovered that soil conservation in various watersheds had been authorized but little money had been forthcoming: "Living in the watersheds...I began to check...and I found that all these watersheds were in a particular region, which meant there was no general interest in the Congress in this type of program.... It led me to go before the Democratic platform committee in 1952 and urge them to write into the platform a plank on watershed protection. And they did." As a result, Whitten was able to call on more general support from Democrats and increase appropriations for the Soil Conservation Service watersheds.

Concentrate on Individual Constituencies

After the Census Bureau had made an unsuccessful bid to establish a national housing survey, Representative Yates gave it a useful hint. The proposed survey "is so general," Yates said, "as to be almost useless to the people of a particular community.... This would help someone like Armstrong Cork, who can sell its product anywhere in the country...but will it help the construction industry in a particular area to know whether or not it faces a shortage of customers?" Later, the Bureau submitted a new program that called for a detailed enumeration of metropolitan districts with a sample survey of other areas to get a national total. Endorsed by mortage holding associations, the construction material industry, and federal and state housing agencies, the new National Housing Inventory received enthusiastic support in Congress where Representative Preston exclaimed, "This certainly represents a lot of imaginative thinking on your part...." In another case the National Science Foundation made headway with a program of summer mathematics institutes not only because the idea was excellent but also because the institutes were spread around the country, where they became part of a constituency interest Congressmen are supposed to protect.

Secure Feedback

Almost everyone claims that his projects are immensely popular and benefit lots of people. But how do elected officials know? They can only be made aware by hearing from constituents. The agency can do a lot to ensure that its clientele responds by informing them that contacting Congressmen is necessary and by telling them how to go about it if they do not already know. In fact, the agency may organize the clientele in the first place. The agency may then offer to fulfill the demand it has helped to create. Indeed, Congressmen often urge administrators to make a show of their clientele.

SENATOR WHERRY: Do you have letters or evidence from small operators ... that need your service that you can introduce into the record? ... Is that not the test on how much demand there is for your services?

RALSTON [Bureau of Mines]: Yes. ... If it is important, as a rule they come to talk.

When feedback is absent or limited, Congressmen tend to assume no one cares and they need not bother with the appropriation. "... A dozen or more complaints do not impress me very much. ... We cut this out last spring and we did not hear any wild howls of distress. ..." When feedback is present it can work wonders, as happened with the Soil Conservation Service's Small Watershed program. Representative Andersen waxed enthusiastic:

... Will you point again to Chippewa-Shakopee? I know that project well because it is in my district. I wish the members of this subcommittee could see that Shakopee Creek watershed as it is today. The farmers in that neighborhood were very doubtful when we started that project. Now many of them tell us, Mr. Williams, that the additional crops they have obtained ... have more than repaid their entire assessment. ...

Guarding the treasury may be all right but it becomes uncomfortable when cuts return to haunt a Congressman. This is made clear in Representative Clevenger's tale of woe.

CLEVENGER: I do not want to economize on the Weather Bureau. I never did. I do want an economical administration. ... I have been blamed for hurricane Hazel. My neighbor, who lived across the road from me for 30 years, printed in his paper that I was to blame for $500 millions in damage and 200 lives. ... His kids grew up on my porch and yet he prints that on the first page and it is not "maybe." I just "am." He goes back to stories that related to cuts that I made when I was chairman of the Committee.

Most agencies maintain publicity offices (under a variety of titles) whose job is to inform interested parties and the general public of the good things the agency is doing, creating a favorable climate of opinion. There may be objections to this practice on the part of Congressmen who do not like an agency and/or its programs, but those who favor the agency consider it desirable. House subcommittee Chairman Kirwan urged this course on the Bureau of Indian Affairs in connection with its Alaskan Native Service, a worthy but not overly popular program. "Why don't you make some arrangement to tell the Americans every year," Kirwan suggested, "instead of telling this committee what is going on? If you write a letter when you go back to Alaska ... I will guarantee you the press will get it." The Weather

Bureau was urged to put out some publicity of its own by Representative Flood, who observed that

> ... forecasts ... were obviously, literally, and figuratively all wet. Somebody pointed out in this [*New York Times*] editorial where this ... forecast has been "a little cold, a little wet, a little snow, but not bad." ... But something took place which ... dumped the whole wagonload of snow on Broadway and made them very unhappy. This happened repeatedly over a period of 30 days, which did not make you look very good, if I can understate it. ... All right. Why do you not prepare a statement for the many newspaper readers in the area and point out to them that you know the problem is there, and that this is what you want to do about it. ...

A final example comes from a student who wrote away for a summer job and received in reply a letter from an administrator refusing him on account of budgetary limitations. "Because of our inadequate funds at this critical time," the official wrote, "many students, like yourself, who would otherwise receive the professional training that this work provides, will be deprived of that opportunity. ... Only prompt action by Congress in increasing these funds can make the success of our mission possible."

Divided We Stand

The structure of administrative units may be so arranged as to obtain greater support from clientele. It may be advantageous for a department to create more bureaus or subunits so that there are more claimants for funds who can attract support. "We have had the rather disillusioning experience that too often when we create a new agency of Government or divide up an existing agency," a Representative concluded, "that we wind up with more people on the payroll than we ever had before. ...." There can be little doubt the division of the NIH into separate institutes for heart research, cancer research, and so on has helped mobilize more support than lumping them together under a general title with which it would be more difficult for individuals to identify.

United We Fall

The Weather Bureau is an example of an agency that did rather poorly until it took the many suggestions offered by its supporters in Congress and established a separate appropriation for research and development. The new category was the glamorous one and it was easier to attract support alone; being lumped in with the others hurt its appeal. Indeed, putting projects under the same category may be a way of holding down the expenditures for some so that others will not suffer. One of the imposing difficulties faced in building up the Polaris missile program was the fear that it would deprive traditional Navy activities of resources.

Advisory Committees Always Ask for More

Get a group of people together who are professionally interested in a subject, no matter how conservative or frugal they might otherwise be, and they are certain to find additional ways in which money could be spent. This apparently invariable law was stated by Representative Thomas when he observed that "All architects [doctors, lawyers, scientists, Indian chiefs] are for more and bigger projects, regardless of type. I have not seen one yet that did not come into that classification."

Advisors may be used to gather support for a program or agency in various ways. They may directly lobby with Congress or the President. "I happened to have lunch with Dr. Farber [a member of the quasi-governmental advisory committee of the NIH] the other day," Congressman Fogarty reveals, "and I learned there is considerable sentiment for these [clinical research] centers." Congressman Cederberg did not know of "anyone who would in any way want to hamper these programs, because I had lunch with Dr. Farber. . . ." Advisors may provide a focus of respectability and apparent disinterest to take the onus of self-seeking from the proponents of greater spending. They may work with interest groups and, indeed, may actually represent them. They may direct their attempts to the public media of information as anyone can see by reading the many columns written by Howard Rusk, M.D., a writer on medical subjects for the *New York Times,* requesting greater funds for the NIH.

Do Not Admit Giving in to "Pressure"

CIVIL AERONAUTICS BOARD OFFICIAL: . . . One of the reasons there has been such substantial expansion in local airline service, believe it or not, is largely due to the members of Congress.

REPRESENTATIVE FLOOD: I hope you are talking about Hazleton, Pa.

CAB OFFICIAL: I am talking about Pennsylvania as well as every other state. I do not want to leave the impression here that there has been undue pressure or that we have been unduly influenced by members of Congress, but we have tried to cooperate with them.

REPRESENTATIVE FLOOD: I do not care what the distinction is.

But If They Press Make Them Pay

CAB OFFICIAL: . . . Senator . . . if there are any members of Congress apprehensive about the increasing level of subsidy, this has not been evident to the Board. . . . I cannot think of any local service case in which we have not had at least

15, 20, or 25 members of Congress each one urging an extension of the local service to the communities in his constituency as being needed in the public interest.... We felt that they, if anyone, knew what the public interest required ... as to local service ... with full knowledge that this would require additional subsidy.

Avoid Being Captured

The danger always exists that the tail will wag the dog and the agency must exercise care to avoid being captured. Rival interests and Congressmen may be played against each other. New clientele may be recruited to replace the old. The President and influential Congressmen may be persuaded to help out. Or the agency may just decide to say "no" and take the consequences. Dependence upon the support of clientele, however, implies some degree of obligation and the agency may have to make some compromises. The interests involved may also have to compromise because they are dependent upon the administrators for access to decisions, and they may have many irons in the fire with the agency so that it is not worth jeopardizing all of them by an uncompromising stand on one.

Spending and Cutting Moods

Unfortunately, no studies have been made about how cutting and spending moods are generated. Yet changes in the climate of opinion do have an impact on appropriations. Possibly a great many groups and individuals, working without much direct coordination but with common purpose, seize upon events like reaction to World War II controls and spending to create a climate adverse to additional appropriations, or upon a recession to create an environment favorable for greater expenditures.

Budget Balancing and End-runs

It is clear that the slogan of the balanced budget has become a weapon in the political wars as well as an article of belief. This is not the place to inquire whether the idea has merit; this is the place to observe that as a belief or slogan budget balancing is one determinant of strategies.

When the idea of a balanced budget becomes imbued with political significance, the Administration may seek appropriations policies that minimize the short-run impact on the budget although total expense may be greater over a period of years. In the Dixon-Yates case a proposed TVA power plant was rejected partly because it involved large immediate capital outlays. The private power plant that was accepted involved much larger expenditures over a 25-year period, but they would have had comparatively little impact during the Eisenhower Administration's term of office.[1]

---

[1] See the author's *Dixon-Yates: A Study in Power Politics* (New Haven: Yale University Press, 1962).

396 Budgetary Strategies of Administrative Agencies

When clientele are absent or weak there are some techniques for making expenditures that either do not appear in the budget or appear much later on. The International Monetary Fund may be given a Treasury note that it can use at some future date when it needs money. Public buildings may be constructed by private organizations so that the rent paid is much lower in the short run than an initial capital expenditure. The Federal Government may guarantee local bond flotations. An agency and its supporters who fear hostile committee action may also seek out ways to avoid direct encounter with the normal budgetary process. This action is bitterly opposed, especially in the House Appropriations Committee, as back-door spending.

I do not mean to suggest that getting constituency support is all that counts. On the contrary, many agencies lay down tough criteria that projects must meet before they are accepted. The point is that there are ordinarily so many programs that can be truly judged worthwhile by the agency's standards that its major task appears to be that of gaining political support. Priorities may then be assigned on the basis of the ability of the program and its sponsors to garner the necessary support.

Confidence

The sheer complexity of budgetary matters means that some people need to trust others because they can check up on them only a fraction of the time. "It is impossible for any person to understand in detail the purposes for which $70 billion are requested," Senator Thomas declared in regard to the defense budget. "The Committee must take some things on faith." If we add to this the idea of budgeting by increments, where large areas of the budget are not subject to serious questions each year, committee members will treat an agency much better if they feel that its officials will not deceive them. Thus the ways in which the participants in budgeting try to solve their staggering burden of calculation constrain and guide them in their choice of means to secure budgetary ends.

Administrative officials are unanimously agreed that they must, as a bare minimum, enjoy the confidence of the Appropriations Committee members and their staff. "If you have the confidence of your subcommittee your life is much easier and you can do your department good; if you don't have confidence you can't accomplish much and you are always in trouble over this or that." How do agency personnel seek to establish this confidence?

Be What They Think They Are

Confidence is achieved by gearing one's behavior to fit in with the expectations of committee people. Essentially, the desired qualities appear to be projections of the committee members' images of themselves. Bureaucrats are expected to be masters of detail, hard-working, concise, frank, self-effacing fellows who are devoted to their work, tight with the taxpayers' money, recognize a political necessity when they see one, and keep the Congressmen informed. Where Representative Clevenger speaks dourly of how "fewer trips to the coffee shop...help make money in most of the departments...." Rooney demonstrates the other side of the coin by speaking favorably of calling the Census Bureau late at night and finding its employees "on the job far later than usual closing hours." An administrator is highly praised because "he always knows his detail and his work. He is short, concise, and to the point. He does not waste any words. I hope when it comes to the economy in your laundry soap it is as great as his economy in words."

To be considered aboveboard, a fair and square shooter, a frank man, is highly desirable. After an official admitted that an item had been so far down on the priority list that it had not been discussed with him, Senator Cordon remarked, "All right, I can understand that. Your frankness is refreshing." An administrator like Val Peterson, head of the Federal Civil Defense Agency, will take pains to stress that, "There is nothing introduced here that is in the field of legerdemain at all.... I want... to throw the cards on the table...."

The budget official needs to show that he is also a guardian of the treasury: sound, responsible, not a wastrel; he needs to be able to defend his presentations with convincing evidence and to at least appear to be concerned with protecting the taxpayer. Like the lady who gets a "bargain" and tells her husband how much she has saved, so the administrator is expected to speak of economies. Not only is there no fat in his budget, there is almost no lean. Witness Dewey Short, a former Congressman, speaking on behalf of the Army: "We think we are almost down to the bone. It is a modest request...a meager request...." Agency people soon catch on to the economy motif: "I have already been under attack...for being too tight with this money...," Petersen said. "I went through it [a field hospital] very carefully myself to be sure there were no plush items in it, nothing gold-plated or fancy."

If and when a subcommittee drops the most prevalent role and becomes converted into an outright advocate of a program, as with the Polaris missile system, the budget official is expected to shoot for the moon and he will be criticised if he emphasizes petty economies instead of pushing his projects. Democratic Subcommittee Chairman Kirwan and ranking Republican Jensen complained that the Bureau of Land Management did not ask for enough money for soil conservation. "It is only a drop in the bucket," Kirwan said, "they are afraid to come in." "This committee has pounded for the seven years I know of," Jensen responded, "trying to get them to come in with greater amounts for soil conservation and they pay no attention to it." The norm against waste may even be invoked for spending, as when Kirwan proclaimed that, "It is a big waste and loss of money for the U.S. Government when only 6 million is requested for the management of fish and wildlife." In 1948 the head of the Cancer Institute was told in no uncertain terms, "The sky is the limit...and you come in with a little amount of $5,500,000...." It is not so much what administrators do but how they meet the particular subcommittee's or chairman's expectations that counts.

Play It Straight!

Everyone agrees that the most important requirement of confidence, at least in a negative sense, is to be aboveboard. As Rooney once said, "There's only two things that get me mad. One is hare-brained schemes; the other is when they don't play it straight." A lie, an attempt to blatantly cover up some misdeed, a tricky move of any kind, can lead to an irreparable loss of confidence. A typical comment by an administrator states, "It doesn't pay to try to put something over on them [committee members] because if you get caught, you might as well pack your bags and leave Washington." And the chances of getting caught (as the examples that follow illustrate) are considerable because interested committeemen and their staffs have much experience and many sources of information.

Administrators invariably mention first things that should not be done. They believe that there are more people who can harm them than can help and that punishments for failure to establish confidence are greater than the rewards for achieving it. But at times they slip up and then the roof falls in. When Congress limited the amount of funds that could be spent on personnel, a bureau apparently evaded this limitation in 1952 by subcontracting out a plan to private investors. The House subcommittee was furious:

REPRESENTATIVE JENSEN: It certainly is going to take a housecleaning...of ...all people who are responsible for this kind of business.

OFFICIAL: We are going to do it, Mr. Chairman.

REPRESENTATIVE JENSEN: I do not mean "maybe." That is the most disgraceful showing that I have seen of any department.

OFFICIAL: I am awfully sorry.

If a committee feels that it has been misled, there is no end to the punitive actions it can take. Senator Hayden spoke of the time when a bureau was given a lump-sum appropriation as an experiment. "Next year...the Committee felt outraged that certain actions had been taken, not indicated in the hearings before them. Then we proceeded to earmark the bill from one end to the other. We just tied it up in knots to show that it was the Congress, after all, that dictated policy."

Four months after a House subcommittee had recommended funds for a new prison, a supplemental appropriation request appeared for the purchase of an institution on the West Coast that the Army was willing to sell. Rooney went up in smoke. "Never mentioned it at all, did you?" "Well," the Director replied, "negotiations were very nebulous at that time, Mr. Rooney." "Was that," Rooney asked, "because of the fact that this is a first-rate penal institution...and would accommodate almost 1,500 prisoners?" It developed that Rooney, catching sight of the proposed supplemental, had sent a man out to investigate the institution. The supplemental did not go through.

Integrity

The positive side of the confidence relationship is to develop the opinion that the agency official is a man of high integrity who can be trusted. He must not only give but must also appear to give reliable information. He must keep confidences and not get a Congressman into trouble by what he says or does. He must be willing to take blame but never credit. Like a brand name, a budget official's reputation comes to be worth a good deal in negotiation. (This is called "Ivory soap value," that is, 99 and 44/100% pure.) The crucial test may come when an official chooses to act contrary to his presumed immediate interests by accepting a cutback or taking the blame in order to maintain his integrity with his appropriations subcommittee. It must not be forgotten that the budget official often has a long-term perspective and may be correct in trying to maximize his appropriations over the years rather than on every single item.

If you are believed to have integrity, then you can get by more easily.

ROONEY: Mr. Andretta [Justice Department], this is strictly a crystal ball operation; is it?
ANDRETTA: That is right.
ROONEY. Matter of an expert guess?
ANDRETTA: An expert guess....
ROONEY: We have come to depend upon your guesswork and it is better than some other guesswork I have seen.

A good index of confidence is ability to secure emergency funds on short notice with skimpy hearings. No doubt Andretta's achievement was related to his frequent informal contact with Rooney.

ROONEY: I am one who believes we should keep in close contact with one another so we understand one another's problems.

ANDRETTA: I agree.

ROONEY: You very often get in touch with us during the course of the year when you do not have a budget pending, to keep us acquainted with what is going on.

ANDRETTA: Exactly....

Make Friends: The Visit

Parallel in importance to the need for maintaining integrity is developing close personal relationships with members of the agency's appropriations subcommittee, particularly the chairman. The most obvious way is to seek them out and get to know them. One official reports that he visited every member of his subcommittee asking merely that they call on him if they wanted assistance. Later, as relationships developed, he was able to bring up budgetary matters. Appropriations hearings reveal numerous instances of personal visitation. A few examples should suggest how these matters work. Representative Jensen: "Mr. Clawson [head of the Bureau of Land Management] came in my office the other day to visit with me. I don't know whether he came in purposely or whether he was just going by and dropped in, and he told me that he was asking for considerably more money for...administrative expenses and we had quite a visit...." A subordinate employee of that bureau showed that he had caught the proper spirit when he told Representative Stockman, "If you would like some up-to-date information from the firing line, I shall be glad to call at your office and discuss the matter; will you like for me to do that?"

When columnist Peter Edson editorially asked why the Peace Corps did so well in appropriations compared to the difficult times had by the State Department and the Agency for International Development, he concluded that Sargent Shriver, head of the Corps, "has tried to establish congressional confidence in him and his agency. Of the 537 members of Congress, he has called on at least 450 in their offices."

The Pay-off

Wherever possible, the administrators seek to accommodate the Congressman and impress him with their interest and friendliness. This attitude comes through in an exchange between a man in the Fish and Wildlife Service and Senator Mundt.

OFFICIAL: Last year at the hearings...you were quite interested in the aquarium there [the Senator's state], particularly in view of the centennial coming up in 1961.

MUNDT: That is right.

OFFICIAL: Rest assured we will try our best to have everything in order for the opening of that centennial.

The administrator recognizes and tries to avoid certain disagreeable consequences of establishing relationships with Congressmen. The Congressman who talks too much and quotes you is to be avoided. The administrator who receives a favor may get caught unable to return one the following year and may find that he is dealing with an enemy, not just a neutral.

I'd Love to Help You But...

Where the administrator's notion of what is proper conflicts with that of a Congressman with whom it is desirable to maintain friendly relations, there is no perfect way out of the difficulty. Most officials try to turn the Congressman down by suggesting that their hands are tied, that something may be done in the future, or by stressing some other project on which they are agreed. After Representative Natcher spoke for the second time of his desire for a project in his district, Don Williams of the Soil Conservation Service complimented him for his interest in watershed activity in Kentucky but was "sorry that some of the projects that were proposed would not qualify under the...law...but...they are highly desirable."

The "it can't be done" line was also taken by the Weather Bureau in an altercation with Representative Yates.

WEATHER BUREAU OFFICIAL: We cannot serve the public by telephone...because we cannot put enough telephone lines or the operators to do the job.... We expect them [the public] to get it through the medium of newspapers, radio, television. If you have six telephones you have to have six people to deal with them. You have no idea....

YATES: Yes; I do have an idea, because I have been getting calls from them. What I want to do is have such calls transferred to you.... But as long as you have only one phone, I shall get the calls and you will not....

WEATHER BUREAU OFFICIAL: We find we must do it on the basis of mass distribution.

Sometimes, action may be delayed to see if the committee member will protest. The Weather Bureau tried for a while to cut off weather reports from Savannah to the northern communities that constitute its major source of tourists despite the fact that the Bureau's House subcommittee chairman represented that city.

REPRESENTATIVE PRESTON: I wrote you gentlemen...a polite letter about it thinking that maybe you would [restore it]...and no action was taken on it. Now, Savannah may be unimportant to the Weather Bureau but it is important to me....

WEATHER BUREAU OFFICIAL: I can almost commit ourselves to seeing to it that the Savannah weather report gets distribution in the northeastern United States.

Give and Take

At other times some compromise may be sought. Secretary of Commerce Averell Harriman was faced with the unpalatable task of deciding which field offices to eliminate. He first used internal Department criteria to find the lower one-third of offices in point of usefulness. Then he decided which to drop or curtail by checking with the affected Congressmen, trying to determine the intensity of their reactions, making his own estimate of whom he could and could not afford to hurt. Harriman's solution was a nice mixture of internal and political criteria designed to meet as many goals as possible or at least to hold the Department's losses down.[2]

Truth and Consequences

In the end, the administrator may just have to face the consequences of opposing Congressmen whose support he needs. Even if he were disposed to accommodate himself to their desires at times, he may find that other influential members are in disagreement. He may play them off against one another or he may find that nothing he can do will help. The best he may be able to do is to ride out the storm without compounding his difficulties by adding suspicions of his integrity to disagreements over his policies. He hopes, particularly if he is a career man, that the Congressmen will rest content to damn the deed without damning the man.

Emphasis

The administrator's perception of congressional knowledge and motivation helps determine the kind of relationships he seeks to establish. The administrator who feels that the members of his appropriations subcommittees are not too well informed on specifics and that they evaluate the agency's program on the basis of feedback from constituents, stresses the role of supporting interests in maintaining good relations with Congressmen. He may not feel the need to be too careful with his estimates. The administrator who believes that the Congressmen are well informed and fairly autonomous is likely to stress personal relationships and demonstrations of good work as well as clientele support. Certain objective conditions may be important here. Some subcommittees deal with much smaller areas than others and their members are likely to be better informed than they otherwise would be. Practices of appointment to subcommittees differ between House and Senate and with passing time. Where Congressmen are appointed who have direct and important constituency interests at stake, the information they

2 Kathryn Smul Arnow, *The Department of Commerce Field Offices,* The Inter-University Case Program, ICP Case Series, No. 21, February, 1954.

get from back home becomes more important. If the composition of the committee changes and there are many members without substantial background in the agency's work, and if the staff does not take up the slack, the agency need not be so meticulous about the information it presents. This situation is reflected in the hearings in which much time is spent on presenting general background information and relatively little on specifics.

Subcommittee and Other Staff

Relationships of confidence between agency personnel and subcommittee staff are also vital and are eagerly sought after. Contacts between subcommittee staff and budget officers are often frequent, intensive, and close. Frequency of contacts runs to several times a day when hearings are in progress, once a day when the bill is before the committee, and several times a month during other seasons. This is the principal contact the committee staff has with the Executive Branch. Even when the staff seeks information directly from another official in the agency, the budget officer is generally apprised of the contact and it is channeled through him. Relationships between ordinary committee staff members and Budget Bureau personnel are infrequent, although the people involved know one another. The top-ranking staff members and the Budget Bureau liaison man, however, do get together frequently to discuss problems of coordination (such as scheduling of deficiency appropriations) and format of budget presentation. At times, the BOB uses this opportunity to sound out the senior staff on how the committee might react to changes in presentation and policy. The staff members respond without speaking for the committee in any way. There also may be extensive contact between committee staff and the staff attached to individual Congressmen, but there is not a stable pattern of consultations. House and Senate Appropriations Committee staff may check with one another; also, the staff attached to the substantive committees sometimes may go into the financial implications of new bills with appropriations staff.

When an agency has good relations with subcommittee staff it has an easier time in Congress than it might otherwise. The agency finds that more reliance is placed on its figures, more credence is given to its claims, and more opportunities are provided to secure its demands. Thus one budget officer received information that a million-dollar item had been casually dropped from a bill and was able to arrange with his source of information on the staff to have the item put back for reconsideration. On the other hand, a staff man can do great harm to an agency by expressing distrust of its competence or integrity. Asked if they would consider refusing to talk to committee staff, agency officials uniformly declared that this refusal would be tantamount to cutting their own throats.

23

SEYMOUR SCHER

Conditions for Legislative Control

Democratic ideology requires control of administrative action by elected representatives of the people. As the scope of public in relation to private decisions expands, the tendency is to expand the area of administrative in relation to legislative policy. With this tendency the control of administrative agencies becomes a pressing issue.[1] A good deal has been said about the merits of control centered in legislatures as compared with elected executives.[2] The antagonists typically argue not for control located in one elective institution to the exclusion of any other but about the amount and kind of oversight that is appropriate for

[1] See, for example, L. D. White, "Congressional Control of the Public Service," *American Political Science Review,* 39 (1945), 1–11; Herman Finer, "Administrative Responsibility in Democratic Government," *Public Administration Review,* 1 (1941), 335–50; Charles S. Hyneman, *Bureaucracy in a Democracy* (New York, 1950), esp. chaps. i–iii. For a somewhat different view of the adequacy of political control of administration see Carl J. Friedrich, "Public Policy and the Nature of Administrative Responsibility," in C. J. Friedrich and E. S. Mason, eds., *Public Policy, 1940* (Cambridge, 1940), pp. 3–24.

[2] For the best recent examples see Charles S. Hyneman, *op. cit.;* also Emmette S. Redford, *Administration of National Economic Control* (New York, 1952); Marver Bernstein, *Regulating Business by Independent Commission* (Princeton, 1955), pp. 150–54. But according to Hyneman, "writers about public administration differ sharply as to what the President can do best and what Congress can do best in the direction and control of administration, and their differences stem largely out of states of mind that are not derived from objective examination and evaluation of evidence." Hyneman, p. 66.

Reprinted from *The Journal of Politics,* 25 (August 1963), 526–51, by permission of the author and publisher. Mr. Scher is City Manager of Rochester, New York.

legislatures in relation to executives.[3] Legislators, understandably, see themselves as the community's primary agents for the job of reviewing administrative performance. In 1946 this conviction was formalized by the Congress of the United States when it charged its standing committees and their staffs with responsibility for continuous oversight of the federal agencies. Relatively little has been said, however, about the way in which this responsibility is managed.[4]

This paper is an attempt at identifying the conditions under which committee review is likely to occur and, conversely, the factors which explain why frequently it does not occur at all. The character of agency review, when it is undertaken, is not of primary concern. What is offered are some propositions that emerge from a review of hearings and reports for the period 1938 to 1961 of two House committees and one Senate committee within whose oversight jurisdiction fall seven of the regulatory commissions[5] and from interviews with members of these House and Senate committees and with members of the committee staffs.[6] Since these proposi-

---

[3] Emmette Redford, for example, calls for an effort to provide "more effective congressional oversight of administration." But, "irrespective...of success in this effort, it appears that congressional control is too remote, divisive and sporadic to compensate for the absence of a clearly recognized executive authority of coordination and direction. The tendencies in modern congressional control strongly confirm the judgment of the framers of the Constitution on the need for unity in the executive branch of the government." Redford, *op. cit.*, p. 306; see also pp. 354*ff*; and in the same vein see Pendleton Herring, "Executive-Legislative Responsibilities" *American Political Science Review*, 38 (1944), 1153–65; but *cf.* Hyneman, *op. cit.*, esp. pp. 168–72.

[4] But see V. O. Key, "Legislative Control" in F. Morstein-Marx, ed., *Elements of Public Administration* (Englewood Cliffs, N.J., 1949), pp. 312–33; Arthur W. Macmahon, "Congressional Oversight of Administration: The Power of the Purse," *Political Science Quarterly*, 58 (1943), 161–90, 380–414; Hyneman, *op. cit.*, chap. ix; Bernard Schwartz, *The Professor and the Commissions* (New York, 1959); Seymour Scher, "Congressional Committee Members as Independent Agency Overseers: A Case Study," *American Political Science Review*, 54 (1960), 911–20; George B. Galloway, "The Operation of the Legislative Reorganization Act of 1946," *American Political Science Review*, 45 (1951), 59–62.

[5] The House Committee on Interstate and Foreign Commerce has oversight jurisdiction over the Civil Aeronautics Board, the Federal Communications Commission, the Federal Power Commission, the Federal Trade Commission, the Interstate Commerce Commission, and the Securities and Exchange Commission. The House Committee on Education and Labor and the Senate Committee on Labor and Public Welfare deal with the National Labor Relations Board. For the purposes of this paper, it is these seven agencies that are meant by the term "independent regulatory commission."

[6] Interviews were conducted in 1954, 1955, 1961, and 1962 with, among others, 58 Senators, Representatives, and committee staff men. These interviews contributed to a larger study by the writer on legislative control to be published shortly. The interviews were semi-structured and ranged in duration from fifteen minutes to six hours, in one, two, and three installments. Although the bulk of the data relates to House attitudes and performance, the evidence, documentary and interview, that related to Senate committee behavior suggests few differences in the two houses in the conditions under which agency review occurs.

tions are derived from data that apply to one kind of committee—the substantive legislative committee—as it deals with a particular variety of agency—the independent regulatory commission—they must be considered hypotheses. Because of space limitations, only some of the pertinent data is included here. These findings invite further investigation to determine what may be of more general applicability. Without pursuing the similarities and differences here, it is supposed that oversight through the appropriations committees, for example, is subject in some ways to influences other than those stated in this paper. Similarly the conditions for and the character of committee review of the executive service-type agency as compared with the independent regulatory agency are presumed to offer some contrasts. But this is a matter for investigation.[7]

I

It is useful to consider the conditions under which committees become involved in agency oversight[8] as ones in which Congressmen make rational decisions about the allocation of their scarce personal resources (energy, time, etc.) so as to maximize gains to themselves in things which they value and minimize losses in those things.[9] Some prime legislator values are sup-

[7] Cf. Arthur W. Macmahon, *op. cit.;* Lucius Wilmerding, *The Spending Power,* (New Haven, 1943); J. Leiper Freeman, *The Political Process: Executive Bureau-Legislative Committee Relations* (New York, 1955); James A. Robinson, *Congress and Foreign Policy-Making* (Homewood, Ill., 1962); Robert R. Wallace, *Congressional Control of Federal Spending* (Detroit, 1960).

[8] The terms "oversight," "control," and "review" are all used here with the meaning of the 1946 Reorganization Act which gave to the standing committee the responsibility of maintaining "continuous watchfulness of the execution by the administrative agencies concerned of any laws the subject matter of which falls within the jurisdiction of such committee." This "watchfulness" may take the form of special committee investigations of agency activity or of inquiry into agency policies and procedures which occurs in the course of a committee's performance of its legislative function.

[9] This framework of the rational (in the sense of efficient) estimate of loss and gain in political decision-making is a crude application of concepts familiar in economic theory, and employed particularly in game theory. This kind of analysis is used with interesting results by Anthony Downs in the analysis of democratic voting and government decision-making. See his "An Economic Theory of Political Action in a Democracy," *Journal of Political Economy,* 65 (1957), 135–50; also his *An Economic Theory of Democracy* (New York, 1957). See also the collection of articles on game theory in Martin Shubik, *Readings in Game Theory and Political Behavior,* (New York, 1954), and particularly the foreword by Richard C. Snyder, pp. v–x. For an application by political scientists of a decision-making analysis using concepts of costs and gains in national values which result from the choice among a range of alternatives, but choice in which rationality is not assumed, see Richard C. Snyder and Glenn D. Paige, "The United States Decision to Resist Aggression in Korea: The Application of an Analytical Scheme," *Administrative Science Quarterly,* 3 (1958), 341–78.

port, influence, and prestige. In a setting in which there are innumerable claims upon his time, both from those within his immediate group environment (his Congressional and committee colleagues) and those outside (his local party, the President, groups in and outside of his constituency),[10] the Congressman must early choose those that will occupy him. He realizes that how he accommodates these demands is likely to be crucial to the success of his efforts to maintain and if possible improve his legislative and electoral position. Although each Congressman necessarily makes his own appraisal of his situation and the manner in which he must deal with it, common to all is the necessity for such an appraisal. In making this estimate, which is subjected to continuing review, he will allocate his scarce time and energies on something very much like a cost and return basis. Considering what is expected of him within his immediate Congressional-committee setting and in the parts of his external environment which can affect his survival, he arranges his priorities. What will be the likely cost to him in support, influence, and prestige measured against the likely gain in these same valued things of pursuing one course of action rather than another? What profit and what loss can be anticipated from satisfying committee and party leadership expectations if this means rejecting, even though momentarily, constituent or interest group demands which he considers important? What price will he have to pay in order to reap the psychic rewards of following his own ideological predispositions—or in his language "his conscience" —when these run counter to the position expected of him by committee or party colleagues whose good will and support he values? This is not to suggest that he typically confronts a stark either-or situation in deciding what he will do, but his earliest experience with conflicting demands is likely to stimulate a determination of priorities which will prepare him for the times when he is forced to choose a course where gains can be had only at a price.

II

These theoretical observations have an empirical basis in attitudes expressed by Congressmen. Among twenty-three interviewed for this purpose,[11] a reccurrent theme was the concern with spending scarce time "well." All did not agree on what this required but each agreed that he established some kind of priority system which indicated his estimate of things that were important. And the standard of importance tended to be a highly personal

10 See J. Leiper Freeman, *op. cit.;* David Easton, "An Approach to the Analysis of Political Systems" *World Politics,* 9 (April 1957), 383–400; David Truman, *The Congressional Party* (New York, 1959), pp. 279*f.*

11 All of these were members of subject matter committees with oversight jurisdiction over the regulatory agencies.

one—"what would do *me* the most good." The concept of costs and gains was always implicit, at least, in the descriptions of their choice-making processes.[12]

The Congressman formally recognizes and guards his obligation not only to participate in the legislative process but to "keep an eye" on how legislative policy fares after it is turned over to an administrative agency to interpret and apply. Particularly among members whose committee responsibility involves review of regulatory agency performance, the ideology of the maintainance of Congressional prerogatives is forcefully asserted. Whatever the situation with Executive departments and bureaus, the regulatory commissions are considered "arms of Congress" and how those agencies read legislative policy is seen as primarily the business of Congress. But the Congressional norm requiring oversight from the legislature is of limited use in explaining the frequency of the oversight. In practice committee review is a spasmodic affair marked by years in which the agencies are virtually ignored followed by spurts of committee interest in agency activity.[13] The committee member who has an opportunity to choose between devoting his

---

[12] These were some of the phrases used to suggest this concept: "I know what I need to do, and if I can, I do it"; "we always keep an ear out for reaction at home"; "most of us don't want any part of that—it's too hot"; "I want to know where this will leave me with the [committee, house] leadership"; "that isn't as pressing as ———; it can wait"; "something has to be done about ———, and the people expect us to do it"; "there just isn't time for everything"; "if I only had a larger staff..."; "you can easily spend lots of time chasing up a blind alley and get nowhere"; "nobody really wants to get involved in ———; there's just not enough in it"; "maybe some people here don't have to worry about it but I have an election this year"; "we all know why Congressman X got on to that: there was good mileage in it"; "normally none of us would touch it, but if we thought it would make a big bang..." The rational estimate of costs and gains is an abstraction from what is an everyday reality to legislators.

[13] See Robert E. Cushman, *The Independent Regulatory Commission* (New York, 1951, pp. 678*f*., Bernstein, *op. cit.*, p. 83; Hyneman, *op. cit.*, p. 166; also the report by James M. Landis on regulatory agencies in U. S. Senate, *Report on the Regulatory Agencies to the President-Elect* [Committee Print], Committee on the Judiciary, 85th Cong. 2nd Sess. (Washington, 1960), p. 35. In the case, for example, of the NLRB, which was established in 1935, the agency's policies or procedures were the object of a substantial amount of attention from the House and Senate labor committees in 1939, 1946, 1947, 1949, 1953, 1959, and 1961. Except for 1961, notice of the agency by these committees was coincidental with committee consideration of proposals for legislative revision. The 1961 House (Pucinski) Subcommittee on the NLRB was intended and functioned primarily for agency review. Of course the NLRB's performance figured prominently in the activity of committees other than labor: for example, the 1941 House Special (Smith) Committee to Investigate the NLRB, which was designed to by-pass the House labor committee; the 1948–1949 Joint "Watchdog" Committee to observe the Board's implementation of the new Taft-Hartley Act; and House and Senate committees in 1950 and 1961 that considered Presidential reorganization plans for the agency. What the bulk of this committee activity represents is not regular or routine committee review of agency performance but responses by committees to periodic demands from dissatisfied private groups for an opportunity to air grievances against the agency, revision of the regulatory statute, or both.

own and committee time to a review of agency procedures and policies or to new legislative activity can be expected to ask himself "what's in it for me?" Although typically it is the chairman who decides what his committee will do, all members may propose committee action to him, albeit with varying results. And once action is initiated, members tend to make their own determinations of the extent of their participation in the committee's work. For the committee leader as well as the member the allocation of time and energy is determined in terms of expected pay-offs—to party, constituent, group, and through these, to the Congressman himself.

The years during which the agencies, except for the yearly defense of appropriations and occasional confirmation of appointments, escape Congressional notice are probably explained by the decision of committee leaders or individual committee members that their energies are likely to be better spent elsewhere. This decision, in turn, might be explained by the presence of any or a combination of the following circumstances.

1. *Congressmen tend to see opportunities for greater rewards in the things they value from involvement in legislative and constituent-service activity than from participation in oversight activity.* Of course, this estimate is likely to change if the legislator believes that important constituent and group purposes can be served by committee rather than exclusively personal contact with an agency. But without this incentive, the committee man would rather be associated with popular, district-serving legislation and individual constituent services than with what he sees as typically unnoticed hearings on agency performance. This is made clear when Congressmen explain the amount of time and work they devote to each of their committee assignments. In cases where they attend commitee hearings at which regulatory agency officials are being examined on agency policies or procedures the members frequently view their participation with a "somebody has to do it" attitude. If he can choose between attendance at such meetings and others dealing with proposed legislation which the legislator believes is important for his district, he chooses the latter. One committee chairman put it this way: "There is always so much the committee has to do with important legislation, we just can't take the time to worry about what an agency is doing with something we drafted five or ten years ago. The agency's going to be on its own for the most part because nobody wants to do the job of checking on it." According to another Congressman on the same committee: "There's always an election around the corner and what we do between times has to have something in it that we can sell back home." But this same standard explains the successful pressure by a member of one committee for the creation of a special subcommittee to review the performance of a regulatory agency. A barrage of complaints from powerful groups in his district about ill-treatment at the hands of the agency convinced him that an investigation, particularly one which he headed, was necessary. This

subcommittee chairman then insisted, somewhat formally, that "it is the responsibility of Congress through its committees to police these agencies. The 1946 Reorganization Act requires it." From among twenty-three Congressmen interviewed on this issue all but three indicated they considered committee review of agency activity a time-expensive, low priority concern except when there was likely to be something "big" in it.

2. *Committee members tend to view the agencies as impenetrable mazes and to believe that any serious effort at penetrating them poses hazards for the inexpert Congressman which outweigh any conceivable gain to him.* New committee members are more likely to admit this than their senior colleagues but it is a common committee attitude to see agency procedures and decisions as snarled in unnecessary complexities, with many Congressmen believing that this situation exists as part of a bureaucratic design to conceal agency activity from Congressional and public view. In spite of this, the committee member is likely to avoid heavy involvement with these agencies in public hearings, believing, first, that they are immovable objects and second, that attempts at moving them might show to disadvantage the Congressman who typically has only a superficial familiarity with the statute or the agency's policies and procedures. This was put well by one Senator as follows:

Even when we [on the committee] suspect something's not right [in the agencies] what can we do about it? It would take forever to really get into the thing. First we'd get a long run-around in and out of the statute. There's always some little provision that nobody knew was there, except the bureaucrat who pulls it out of the hat—"but, Senator, the law does require that we do such and such." Before we finish they have us thinking it's all because of the terrible law we wrote and nothing at all to do with how they treated it.

A member of a House committee put it more simply: "The [regulatory] agencies' work is pretty technical. Most of us just don't know enough about it to even begin to ask intelligent questions."

This reluctance to engage in committee review of agency activity is mitigated to a limited extent by the availability of sometimes expert committee staff upon whom would fall the bulk of the detailed work of examining the agencies. The role of the committee staff man in the committee's work is itself a subject for much needed investigation. In the committees dealing with the seven regulatory agencies the staff men tend to be involved in the many things other than agency oversight that occupy their Congressmen employers. In recent years, however, the Senate Labor and Public Welfare Committee has assigned a majority and a minority staff person to concentrate on NLRB and Labor Department activity for the information of the committee members. However, in a situation in which the committee, as a committee, only rarely examines agency behavior, these staff men find themselves well supplied with expertise on agency affairs but with little demand from the committee members for their information. This condition seemed to prevail even in the House Subcommittee on Regulatory Agencies, a subcommittee intended especially for agency oversight. The relative quiescence of the subcommittee after the busy investigative years from 1958 to 1960 left a few staff men digesting agency decisions and reports and then sharing their information primarily with other staff men rather than with the subcommittee leadership.

3. *Congressmen who have established mutually rewarding relationships with agency people tend to be reluctant to initiate or become actively engaged in a close review of that agency's affairs.* In spite of the common legislator's suspicion of the bureaucracy, this feeling does not keep the Congressman from forming close ties with agency people in order to serve group or constituent needs or for other reasons. Even without friendly personal links to the agencies, the committee member's concern for promoting and protecting interests that are subject to agency regulation will incline him to leave the agency alone if those interests are not faring badly. As one Congressman put it: "Unless I get a lot of noise from people back home, I hardly give a thought to what they're [the regulatory agencies] doing. There are just too many other things to do." In committees that deal with regulatory policy the committee chairman and senior members who have worked in the area over a long period of time tend to develop personal associations with both regulatory commissioners and parts of the agency clientele. Whether based on personal regard or on shared ideological or group sympathies, these ties serve to prolong the periods in which the agencies escape careful Congressional scrutiny. This, naturally, is difficult to document but it is at least unlikely that a committee leader who counts as friends leaders in the natural gas industry or in radio and television broadcasting or in labor unions will be much inclined to put the agencies regulating in these areas under a committee light if the regulated themselves are not unhappy. And it is of some interest that Congressmen have this impression of one another: "You can't really expect Congressman ———— to push the FCC into tougher regulation of broadcasters considering his own interests in a television channel back home." Or, "When you consider how much we [in Congress] depend on our local [radio and television] stations for free time to report to our constituents and for air time during the campaigns, we're going to do what we can to help them [station owners], too." Or, "Everybody knows [Congressman] Z is a natural gas man. As a matter of fact, he helped get [FPC commissioner] A his job. He won't go upsetting any apple

carts." Congressmen who are friends of an agency or of group interests that are promoted rather than regulated by an agency do not normally make aggressive overseers.

4. *Congressmen tend to view their personal contacts with the agencies as more efficient than committee investigations for serving constituent and group needs.* From the perspective of the Congressman the characteristic legislator-to-regulatory commissioner telephone calls, which range from inquiries on the scheduling of constituents' cases to overt efforts at influencing an agency's determination in a particular case, afford generally satisfactory communication between the two. This is not to say that Congressmen invariably get what they want through this procedure, but it works well enough so that they normally prefer their own direct dealings with agency people to committee activity over which individual Congressmen obviously have less control. In interviews with twenty-three members of committees with jurisdiction over regulatory agencies fourteen indicated that their personal efforts with agencies in behalf of constituents involved in adjudicatory or licensing proceedings consumed "some" amount of their own or their staff's time. Of these, eight stated they would inquire only about the status of cases, while six indicated an "I do what I can" approach in their agency communications. Of this group of fourteen, eleven believed that direct personal contacts with the agency generally were adequate for their local needs. Three indicated that committee hearings were necessary when they believed "nothing else would do any good." Of the twenty-three respondents, three said they did not personally ask anything of regulatory agency officials in behalf of groups in or out of their districts—that instead, their committee was the place for the regulated to bring their grievances. Six indicated that "a lot" of their own or their staff's time was occupied with inquiries to the agencies in response to outside requests for help. Of these, all indicated a belief that the route of individual Congressman-to-agency official generally told them what they needed to know about the agencies' activities. Thus, a total of seventeen of twenty-three members seemed to be satisfied that their individual relations with the agencies were adequate to deal with their requests for help from "outside." And committee oversight might very well make the useful personal communications between Congressman and agency official more difficult and thus less rewarding. As stated by one member of a committee with jurisdiction over regulatory agencies: "Why should [Congressman] Y bite the hand that feeds him—they [agency officials] 'cooperate' with him now. What hearings might do is just dry up his [agency] channels." Although *ex parte* contacts between Congressman and regulatory agency are not often subjects for Congressional scrutiny, investigations, once begun, often take unpredicted courses with sometimes unintended consequences. It is probably true, for example, that the publicity resulting from

disclosures by the House Legislative Oversight Subcommittee of off-record contacts between agency adjudicators and their regulated clientele made similar contacts initiated thereafter by Congressmen more self-conscious and less frequent. But at least one Senator publicly declared that these disclosures would have little effect on his unrestricted communications with agency officials in behalf of constituents. Witness this statement by Illinois Senator Everett Dirksen:

> Ever since 1933, when I came here as a freshman Congressman, I have been calling every agency in Government in the interest of my constituents. I expect I am going to continue to do it whether this becomes law or not, and I am afraid this bill [to bar *ex parte* communications by "any person" in adjudicatory proceedings] is not going to become law with my sanction, because I don't go that far.
>
> I make the case just as clear as crystal, so the whole world may know. But now let's get the specific examples. There is an airline, let us say X, based in Chicago. I know the president and all the personnel and a good many of the pilots. There is another airline based in Missouri, my neighboring State. I don't know very much about it. But there is a petition or an application pending before CAB, and they both want to be certified for a stop in Iowa, so I call up this Chairman of the CAB and I say: "Look, Mr. ———, X Airlines has an application pending. I know these people, they are good, reliable operators; they are good, solid citizens. I just want to know what the status of the matter is." . . .
>
> These people get lost down here in this baffling, bewildering labyrinthine Government. Even we Senators get lost in it. I sometimes wonder what the average citizen would do if he didn't have the opportunity to come down here and talk with us and see what his rights are, and where he has to go, and whether we can't do a little something for him. . . .
>
> I went way beyond the trial examiner; I didn't even bother with him; he is just an intermediary, I went where the decision is to be made. The Commissioner I talked to would have a vote. If it is a five-man commission and I get three votes on that commission for my constituent, everything is hunky-dory. So I went right to the point where the decision is made.[14]

5. *Committee members will tend to avoid agency review if they expect it will provoke costly reprisals from powerful economic interests regulated by the agencies.* There is ample testimony from Congressmen of the political hazards they had incurred as a result of participating too vigorously in investigations which, for example, betrayed improper relations between an agency and its regulated clientele. A primary fight for renomination, financial support for an opponent, clandestine organized campaign activity against

[14] In U.S. Senate, *Administrative Procedure Legislation,* Hearings before the Subcommittee on Administrative Practice and Procedure of the Committee on the Judiciary, 86th Cong., 1st Sess. (Washington, 1959), pp. 92 *f.*

his reelection remind the aggressive Congressman-investigator of the far-reaching implications of his oversight vigor. The Congressman is likely, therefore, to take careful stock of his reserves of support from other sources before becoming too deeply involved with groups subject to agency regulation, particularly if they are strongly represented in his own district. In more cases than not, this estimate is likely to convince him that engaging in committee activity which antagonizes these groups is not economical. It obviously is difficult for public officials to admit to anyone (sometimes including themselves) that they fear retaliation for their public acts. But in talks with committee members whose legislative and oversight responsibilities involved the sensitive areas handled by the regulatory agencies, frequent references were made by them to the "influence" of particular regulated industries or groups which they thought inhibited *their colleagues* from vigorous committee action! One member of the House Legislative Oversight Subcommittee who was noted for his vigor in pressing for disclosures of links between some regulatory agencies and their clientele told of his conviction that political retribution had been visited upon him as a result. As he described it, there occurred a procession of people from his district in the industries involved who suggested to him that the regulatory commissioners were, after all, "good fellows" and there was thus no reason to cause them any embarrassment. But the Congressman's persistence thereafter led, he believed, to campaign support for an opponent which otherwise would not have developed. That this kind of pressure can be effective was suggested when this Congressman later indicated his belief that the oversight subcommittee had probably done its job—he, at least, wouldn't press for its continuance.

6. *Congressmen who perceive that gains to themselves can be had by loyalty to the President can be expected to avoid close examination of the performance of agency officials appointed by the Executive.* For example, whatever inclination the Democratic members of the House commerce committee had from 1957 to 1960 to examine the performance of Eisenhower-appointed regulatory commissioners had been largely exhausted by 1961 as the Democratic leadership in Congress confronted appointees of President Kennedy in the agencies. In interviews held in 1961 and 1962 members of both parties on the committee were agreed that the prospect was remote of a Democratic majority continuing its inquiry into agency relations with their regulated clientele once the new administration's appointees began to appear in the agencies' top positions. Similarly, Democratic Congressman Roman Pucinski who, for primarily local reasons, chaired an investigation of the National Labor Relations Board in 1961 by a House labor subcommittee, was urged by fellow partisans in and out of Congress not to prolong his inquiry unnecessarily. The agency by then was being populated by Kennedy appointees and the Congressman was reminded that any criticism of

the pre-1961 NLRB would probably make more difficult the work of the new agency officials. According to a variety of informants who were intimately concerned with the NLRB investigation, the subcommittee chairman was directly and indirectly advised by spokesmen for the AFL-CIO, the President, the agency itself, and by many administration supporters among his colleagues in the House that his critical study of the "Eisenhower" NLRB could easily be misinterpreted by many as an attack on the "new Kennedy" Board members. The Congressman, according to these reports, was further advised that the "new" Board ought to be given a chance to function without the distractions of a Congressional investigation led by members of the administration's own party in Congress.

In spite of the typical Congressional insistence that the regulatory agencies are "arms of Congress" and thus not part of the President's administration, in a more realistic mood the legislator is likely to admit that the successes or failures of the "independent" as well as of the executive agencies will be publicly credited to or blamed on the President. Thus, the President's allies in Congress tend to assume a posture of support and protectiveness toward his appointees in whatever agency. Witness, for example, the attitude of minority (Republican) members of the 1957–60 House Oversight Subcommittee toward the majority report. The Republican members argued that the Harris Committee Democrats unfairly emphasized improper conduct between Eisenhower officials (Sherman Adams) and Eisenhower agency appointees, but ignored or treated gingerly efforts by prominent Democrats (Thomas Corcoran) to get off-the-record favors from the agencies.[15] Only the most unusual circumstances in agency conduct will justify violating that elementary rule of party politics which requires that the opposition be denied any good targets at which to shoot. Such circumstances apparently did confront Republican members of the House Legislative Oversight Subcommittee and, indeed, President Eisenhower himself in 1958. The disclosures by subcommittee counsel Bernard Schwartz of off-the-record influence directed at FCC Commissioner Richard A. Mack, an Eisenhower appointee, in allocating the Miami Television Channel 10 caused Republi-

[15] In U.S. House of Representatives, *Independent Regulatory Commissions,* Report of the Special Subcommittee on Legislative Oversight of the Committee on Interstate and Foreign Commerce, 86th Cong., 2nd Sess. (Washington, 1961), pp. 85*f.* On the other hand there obviously are occasions when even administration supporters in Congress break with the White House; see, *e.g.,* the alignment in the Senate in 1961 on President Kennedy's nomination of Lawrence J. O'Connor to the F.P.C. After a lengthy criticism of the nomination by Democratic Senator Proxmire, the nomination was confirmed. But nay votes came in this case not primarily from the Republican opposition but from such regular Kennedy supporters in addition to Proxmire as Senators Church, Douglas, Gruening, Hart, Kefauver, McNamara, Morse, and Young of Ohio. 107 *Daily Congressional Record* (1961), 14183. These people apparently found in O'Connor's prior ties to the natural gas industry justification for opposing his nomination to a position which involved regulating that industry.

can committee members as well as the Eisenhower Administration some embarrassment. Considering the subcommittee staff's case against Mack, the Congressmen apparently had little choice but to join belatedly in the criticism of the Commissioner. The President eventually called for and received his resignation from the FCC.[16]

7. *As committee routines become fixed, for all of the foregoing reasons, in ways that make no regular provision for agency oversight,*[17] *in the absence of powerful external stimuli they tend to resist change.* Unless there are compelling reasons, such as those that are considered below, to alter normal committee life by "taking on" the agencies, committee members are likely to consider it easier and less costly not to. One Senate and three House chairmen whose committees are concerned with regulatory policy were in agreement, in interviews, on the low priority which they gave to committee reviews of agency performance. All considered such reviews to be outside of their committees' routines. "The pressure of current legislative business" and the absence for long periods of time of what they considered any urgent need to lay aside that business for the sake of an examination of agency activity were cited as explanations. But several other members of these committees expressed the belief that while legislative oversight is likely to be occasional and irregular, they were satisfied nonetheless that agency people are kept "on their toes" for not knowing "where and when lightening will strike." According to this view, uncertainty over when a committee will focus its attention on an agency is sufficient to keep the agency "honest" in much the same way as would regular and frequent surveillance.[18]

III

The typical pattern of committee review of the regulatory agencies is, then, one of no review at all for long periods of time. But these occasionally are interrupted. The years between 1958 and 1961, for example, saw a progression of committees—standing, special, and *ad hoc*—deal with the agencies. The House Legislative Oversight Subcommittee, an *ad hoc* subcommittee

[16] See Report of the Special Subcommittee on Legislative Oversight, 1959, *op. cit.,* pp. 24–26, 93–98; Bernard Schwartz, *op. cit.,* pp. 101*ff.,* 110*ff.*

[17] This, of course, does not apply to a committee like the House Oversight Subcommittee which was created especially for agency surveillance, although as a special committee, with a limited life. It was succeeded in the 87th Congress by a Subcommittee on Regulatory Agencies of the House Commerce Committee. At this writing, it is too early to determine the extent and character of agency review by this new committee.

[18] These Congressmen appeared sensitive to the apparent gap between their expressions of support for the norm of continuous legislative watchfulness and their own unwillingness to act according to the norm.

on the National Labor Relations Board, Senate subcommittees on agency organization and procedure, plus standing committees of the two houses that considered Presidential reorganization plans for half a dozen independent commissions suggest a mass of oversight activity in apparent contradiction of the propositions stated above. What all this seems to represent, however, is a series of oversight bursts.[19] When and why do they occur? Again a profit-cost kind of analysis is relevant. *Committee leaders can be expected to involve committee resources in studies of agency performance if and when the likely gain in things valued by Congressmen is gauged as greater than any prospective loss in those things.* This situation may prevail under these possible conditions.

1. *When the leadership of the majority party in Congress believes it can cause sufficient embarrassment, with accompanying profit for itself, to a past or current opposition President who is held responsible for the performance of his agency appointees, committee oversight tends to be used for this purpose.* This accounts in part at least for the probe by the Democratic (Pucinski) subcommittee, immediately following the 1960 Kennedy election victory, of the NLRB's performance in the Eisenhower years. In another situation a Democratic Congressman who in 1958 pressed for a close look at the six other regulatory agencies by the House Legislative Oversight Subcommittee summed up the basis for his enthusiasm in what he saw as Republican President Eisenhower's "holier than thou" attitude. "We [Democrats] knew damn well that there were things [improper influence] going on between people in the White House and agency officials that shouldn't have gone on. We might not have bothered with it if it hadn't been for that pious business of Eisenhower's before he was elected about keeping his administration 'as clean as a hound's tooth.' " Other Democrats on the subcommittee admitted that the communications between Eisenhower assistant Sherman Adams and regulatory agency officials normally would have aroused no more than a mild flurry in Congress. What helped mobilize at least these Congressmen to expose this influence situation was the irresistible urge to tarnish a popular Republican's administration plus an opportunity to topple his disliked and resented assistant from his position of power.

The estimate of the prospects for party gain to be had from oversight activity is made in light of several limiting circumstances. First, among all the possible ways of embarrassing an administration, there must be enough of sufficient dramatic quality that can emerge from probing the regulatory

---

19 Some striking evidence of these alternating periods of committee oversight activity and inactivity can be found in the sharp reduction of staff between 1960 and 1961 when the House Commerce Committee's oversight subcommittee went out of existence and was replaced by the Subcommittee on Regulatory Agencies. A professional staff of eighteen dwindled to a staff of three with responsibility for maintaining surveillance over six commissions.

agencies to justify utilizing that procedure rather than other politically profitable techniques, assuming a choice among techniques to be made. The possibility is always present that a committee investigation of these agencies will get lost in the morass of agency decisions and procedures so that the moral of presidential failure cannot be strongly driven home. According to one senior committee member: "Getting involved with those agencies can be a trap. We start out with what is a good case of hanky-panky and by the time we finish clearing away the smokescreen they [the agency] send up, the point's lost." And from another member: "Before our hearings [on agency performance in an opposition President's administration] we sent a couple of our staff people over to the agency to go through their files of decisions and intra-agency memoranda. They were snowed under. It would have taken an army of staff men a year to begin to make sense out of what's going on over there. We just did what we could." Secondly, the fixing of responsibility for agency action or inaction is likely to be difficult in circumstances where appointees carried over from an earlier friendly administration concurred in the very agency decisions and practices which are considered ripe for partisan committee attack. Unless there is good reason to believe that investigation of an agency will produce vivid, easily grasped conclusions it is more likely that other routes to partisan advantage will be exploited instead.

2. *When the committee leadership or powerful committee members believe that constituent or group interests important to them cannot be satisfied by the routine personal intercessions between Congressman and agency, committee review tends to be used as a substitute.* When a Congressman perceives a pattern of unfriendly agency decisions or the thwarting of friendly decisions because of an agency's strangulation in its procedures, or both, the mobilization of committee in place of individual Congressman's weapons may be considered necessary. The committee member becomes aware of these agency tendencies as a result of incessant and anxious communications over a period of time from economic groups in or out of his district whose interests he shares. In the NLRB's history, for example, the 1940 House special investigation resulted from both AFL and employer pressure for an exposure of what each viewed as discriminatory agency action. Similarly, the 1947 and 1953 labor committee hearings, especially those in the House, gave primarily disgruntled employers an opportunity to air grievances against the agency. And in 1961 another House special investigative subcommittee was organized in response to urgings from particular unions which suffered injury that was attributed to agency action or inaction. In each case some segment of the agency's clientele had communicated for years to friendly Congressmen its dissatisfaction with agency performance

and had urged committee exposure and remedy. The employer pressure that preceded the 1940 and 1947 hearings originated immediately after the agency began to function effectively in 1937. The 1961 investigation was the culmination of union discontent that had simmered all through the Eisenhower years until ultimately a committee leader was persuaded to undertake the investigative job.

Those whose dissatisfaction initially brought the agency's activities to the Congressman's attention will need to be convinced that the committee's efforts were worthwhile. When committee review of agency performance occurs under these circumstances, it is likely to be directed at those features of agency conduct that are expected to produce maximum returns in favorable publicity to the committee members.

Congressmen are prone to admit that a primary source of the ailment plaguing the regulatory agencies is their intricate, delay-serving-procedures. Yet these Congressmen also agree that legislative studies of agency procedure are seriously lacking in political appeal and are usually embarked upon by committee members with great reluctance and a sense of self-sacrifice.[20] Clearly preferable in terms of potential constituent and group payoffs is a committee inquiry which might substantiate group allegations of agency bias or of improper links between agency officials and some of their clientele. A 1961 House investigation with some of these characteristics was directed, under liberal Democratic auspices, at the National Labor Relations Board. House labor committee chairman Adam Clayton Powell designated Congressman Roman C. Pucinski of Illinois to direct a special subcommittee's investigation of the Board's performance in the Eisenhower years. Considerable attention was given to the organizing difficulties of the Texitile Workers' Union in the South, difficulties attributed, in part, to alleged appeals by employers, without challenge by the NLRB, to employees' racial feelings. A Chicago Democratic Congressman, such as Pucinski, concerned with the status of minorities and with the movement of industry from northern unionized cities to non-unionized low-wage areas in the South, could be expected to seek and work hard at an agency investigation in which such

[20] According to Senator John Carroll, who chaired a 1959 Senate Judiciary Subcommittee on Administrative Practice and Procedure which considered proposed legislation directed at curbing *ex parte* contacts, including those by Congressmen, with the regulatory agencies: "Now by the same token, as I understand this legislation, or my purpose in being here as a chairman, or I wouldn't have taken on this difficult task—it is a task on which we will be here for a long time [*sic*]. I was not sent here by the people of Colorado to come into this jungle that has grown up here for 25 years. I have other important work to do. But I see the tremendous importance of this issue..." In U.S. Senate, *Administrative Procedure Legislation,* Hearings before the Subcommittee on Administrative Practice and Procedure of the Committee on the Judiciary, 86th Cong., 1st Sess. (Washington, 1959), p. 96.

issues were raised.[21] In short, the Congressman tends to become interested, and will try to interest committee and house colleagues, in a committee probe of agency activity when he believes that his own intervention with the agency in behalf of groups with whom he identifies is not enough and that the heavier weapon of committee action is required. He will press for this committee action with the conviction that the support it will generate from these groups is more important to him than is the loss of support from others who may be disadvantaged by a close committee look at the agency. Among seventeen Congressmen interviewed who participated actively in two sets of committee hearings involving agency review, in all but three cases there appeared a clear orientation to one or another of the private group interests which were subject to agency regulation. In each of these fourteen cases, the respondent was not only willing to associate himself with the regulated but also judged the need for and the results of the committee's work in part, at least, in terms of its effects on them.

3. *When Congressmen perceive a threat, particularly from the President, to their traditional prerogatives of primacy in relation to the regulatory agencies, committee interest in the agencies is a likely response.* The concern for guarding these prerogatives is based only in part on an abstract attachment to a Constitutionally prescribed separation of Executive and Legislature. The designation of the regulatory agencies as "arms of Congress" originates basically in a determination by Congressmen that the policy areas

---

[21] The following statements made at the subcommittee hearings by Congressman Pucinski and an aggrieved union witness are suggestive:

MR. PUCINSKI. It rather disturbs me to see a great deal of industry leaving nothern industrial centers, including Chicago, going down to these areas where the atmosphere of hostility to any efforts of organizing the workers is so pronounced, and then apparently if your testimony stands unrefuted, getting the blessing of the National Labor Relations Board to conduct this kind of tactics and condone such situations.

I think this is extremely disturbing to someone like myself who does represent an area where the workers are highly organized and do get a reasonably decent standard of living. . . .

MR. PUCINSKI. I must say myself I am very surprised to hear testimony today to know that the Board would condone this almost barbaric appeal to racial prejudice to frustrate the efforts of organizing these people in the South.

UNION WITNESS. Mr. Chairman, the only difference between you and me is that you are apparently learning about it today and we have been suffering it now for many, many years.

MR. PUCINSKI. This is one purpose for these hearings.
See U.S. House of Representatives, *Administration of the Labor Management Relations Act of the NLRB,* Hearings of the Subcommittee on National Labor Relations Board of the Committee on Education and Labor, 87th Cong., 1st Sess. (Washington, 1961), pp. 576ff., also pp. 147–349. An NLRB investigation with some similar characteristics occurred in 1953 as Republican and conservative Democratic members of the House labor committee conducted a review of the allegedly anti-employer tendencies in the Truman-appointed agency. See Seymour Scher, *op. cit.,* esp. pp. 913ff.

administered by these agencies should be subject to direct and primary influence by the Congress. Despite the fact that long periods of time elapse during which Congress as a body takes no notice of the agencies, and that when interest in them occurs it tends to be expressed through individual legislators or committees largely uncontrolled by the parent body, the defense by Congressmen of legislative supremacy in relation to these agencies is no less vigorous. The Congressman's recognition that the regulatory commissions affect private interests whose fate is or may be important to him contributes to his commitment to preserve the agencies' status within Congress's primary sphere of influence. As one member of a committee that deals with the regulatory agencies put it:

> With [President] Kennedy and his boy Landis [James Landis, special assistant for regulatory agencies to President Kennedy] calling signals at the FCC the [broadcasting] industry is in for a hard time. We [in Congress] have to constantly remind them [the regulatory agencies] that they're arms of the Congress and not of the President. If somebody needs to tell them what to do, we'll do it.

Or, from a Democratic committee chairman from a gas-producing state:

> The President [Eisenhower] left them [the FPC] pretty much alone and everybody got along just fine. Once he appointed a group of honest people to the commission there was no need for him to keep looking over their shoulders. People like ——— [a Congressman from a Northern natural gas-consuming area] will always be screaming that the agency's working for the gas producers but there's no call for any of that. They're [agency officials] hardworking folk doing their best. And our committee has been a pretty good watchdog.

Moves, real or imagined, to expand Presidential direction over the agencies can be expected to be met by Congressmen, regardless of party, with a burst of interest in what these "arms of Congress" are doing. The 1961 Presidential reorganization plans, for example, preceded as they were by a Kennedy assistant's indictment of what he saw as the agencies' ineffectiveness and by suggestions for expanding Presidential direction over them, prompted committee examination of agency procedures which probably would not have occurred otherwise.[22] A vivid illustration of Congressmen's feelings about Presidential "interference" with these agencies is found in the following colloquy between James Landis, President Kennedy's special

22 See the Landis report on the regulatory agencies in U.S. Senate, Committee on the Judiciary, *Report on the Regulatory Agencies to the President-Elect* [Committee Print], 86th Cong., 2nd Sess. (Washington, 1960); and see the committee hearings on FCC organization following the defeat in the House of the Presidential reorganization plan for that agency, in U.S. House of Representatives, *Federal Communications Commission Reorganization,* Hearings before a Subcommittee of the Committee on Interstate and Foreign Commerce, 87th Cong., 1st Sess. (Washington, 1961).

assisant for regulatory agencies, and members of a House Commerce subcommittee to consider Presidential reorganization plans:

MR. YOUNGER. Were the reports in the newspaper correct when they said that you had recommended a czar to be established in the executive department overseeing the regulatory agencies?

MR. LANDIS. No, they were not correct. They were far from correct.

MR. YOUNGER. To what extent were they not correct?

MR. LANDIS. They were not correct because my recommendations were simply a recommendation to establish in the Office of the President an individual, an office, which would oversee—I think the word was chosen wrongly on my part—which would oversee the operations of these administrative agencies and bring to their attention or to the attention of the appropriate authorities, Congress or otherwise, lags in the process, the logjams that were occurring, and suggestions as to how to deal with these....

MR. YOUNGER ... but as I understand in your answer before to questions by Mr. Springer, you held that these regulatory agencies were arms of Congress.

MR. LANDIS. That is right.

MR. YOUNGER. Then if they are arms of Congress, how can you put somebody in the executive branch to oversee them? ...

MR. YOUNGER. Well, it seems to me, just as a layman, that what you are trying to get is a control of the regulatory agencies and you were not able to get in your plan of having somebody in the executive office. Apparently that idea died or was abandoned for some reason and the reorganization plan was substituted. But I am rather convinced by your testimony and the reorganization act that you are attempting to accomplish exactly the same thing by putting all the power in the Chairman of these Commissions with the Chairman designated by the President and the executive would accomplish exactly the same thing as you originally had in mind by putting a so-called czar in the executive branch. I cannot get away from that idea, Dean. I am not a lawyer and I cannot see through all of these ramifications, but I think I can see and follow a line of direct authority, and I am sure in my own mind that you still have that idea of a czar in mind and this reorganization plan has that same thought, but in a more subtle and roundabout way.

MR. LANDIS. I will deny that ...

CHAIRMAN [Oren Harris]. ... The concern that we have, and it has always been my concern during the entire time, is the independence of these agencies. I do not think that there is any great area of disagreement that these are agencies that were established by the Congress and they are independent branches of our Government, set up to act for and instead of the Congress and in some way to legislate on behalf of the Congress.

It is our feeling, and certainly mine, and I think it is the feeling generally of this subcommittee, that that independence shall not in any way be interfered with. There is grave concern on behalf of the committee that there might be an unwarranted interference on behalf of the Executive and not necessarily because this administration happens to be in office now, but with reference to any administration. I am very glad, as has been expressed by others here, that with all deference to you, that your recommendation of the so-called czar, which you said you did not intend, and you did not claim that characterization of it, but an overseer just the same—I am very glad that that recommendation has not been carried out, and I think that that would probably be an unwarranted invasion of authority and influence and interference of these agencies as an independent branch of the Government, designed to perform a particular purpose.[23]

4. *When, periodically, interest builds in Congress for revising regulatory policy, committee attention to the regulatory agency tends to occur as a by-product.* Agency oversight, when it occurs, is frequently incidental to the primary committee purpose of considering and drafting substantive legislation. Group demands for the revision of regulatory statutes are likely to include demands for a review of agency administration of existing law. In fact, proposals in Congress for new legislation are often stimulated by regulated groups conveying to Congress their dissatisfaction with agency handling of legislative policy. In the 79th and 80th Congresses, for example, the irritation with what was considered overly aggressive and irresponsible labor union activity transferred naturally to the Wagner Act, which was written to protect union organization, and the National Labor Relations Board which, in applying the legislative policy, was viewed as a union captive. In the course of proposing new legislative restraints on unions, the Republican-controlled House labor committee directed vigorous criticism at the agency's performance and wrote into the amended labor-management statute a major organizational overhaul designed in large part to prevent agency scuttling of the new policy.

The process by which private groups and committee members build their case for new legislation often includes critical examination of the performance of the agency which applied the old. (Bad legislation, administered with necessarily bad effects, justifies new legislation.) Sometimes support for an old policy is circumvented by a committee determination that while there is nothing wrong with that policy, its vagueness gives the administering agency an opportunity to distort its original good purpose; therefore, to prevent agency sabotage, more precise (typically meaning *new*) legislative standards need to be enacted.[24] An examination of agency conduct frequently is used, in such cases, as a screen behind which new legislation is built.

[23] In U.S. *House Reorganization Plans 1 and 2 of 1961,* Hearings before a Subcommittee of the Committee on Interstate and Foreign Commerce, 87th Cong., 1st Sess. (Washington, 1961), pp. 37*ff.*, 49.
[24] This argument, among others, was used with some success in 1947 by the Republican leadership of the labor committees in order to win bipartisan committee and floor support for the Taft-Hartley amendments to the Wagner Act.

5. *When the committee leadership becomes convinced that interests to which it is opposed can be substantially advanced by the exposure of dramatic evidence of agency failure, it can be expected to move first to neutralize or minimize these gains by initiating its own inquiry.* Those leader identifications which prompt such "preventive oversight" often are those of the individual leader rather than those of a cohesive legislative party for whom he acts. A review of agency activity in these circumstances is undertaken with an expectation that it can be kept under careful leadership control. Only selected aspects of agency performance are likely to be examined and with only such intensity as will satisfy interested observers of the honesty of the investigation. Witness, for example, the perfunctory hearings in 1939 by Democratic Congresswoman Mary Norton's House labor committee in grudging response to the pressure from an unusual alliance of employer associations, the American Federation of Labor, and their respective Congressional supporters for drastic revision of the Wagner Act and for judicializing its administering agency. The Chairman and a committee majority, supported by the Congress of Industrial Organizations, had little intention of disturbing the status quo and managed only to stimulate bipartisan moves to bypass that committee. A year later a still Democratic House with Republican help and over Chairman Norton's bitter objections created a special committee under Democrat Howard W. Smith of Virginia that produced a devastating indictment of the NLRB and the Wagner Act.[25]

The importance of group orientations as compared with loyalty to a Congressional party as a determinant of committee behavior has been suggested, too, in the performance of the House Legislative Oversight Subcommittee from 1958 to 1960. Since these hearings were conducted by a Democratic committee during a Republican President's administration, one might have expected, assuming a cohesive legislative party, vigorous committee action for partisan advantage. Yet, according to the subcommittee's first counsel[26] and some dissident Democratic subcommittee members,[27] such was not the case. According to this minority Democratic view the committee leadership and some Democratic committee members behaved in a fashion that would have been expected of a Republican committee doing its best under opposition party pressure to protect a Republican administration. It was suggested that the ties of Congressmen in both parties to personnel in some of the agencies and to parts of the agencies' clienteles led to a "mini-

[25] See U.S. House of Representatives, *Proposed Amendments to the National Labor Relations Act,* Hearings before the Committee on Labor, 76th Cong., 1st Sess. (Washington, 1939); and U.S. House of Representatives, *To Investigate the National Labor Relations Board,* Hearings before the Special Committee to Investigate the National Labor Relations Board, 76th Cong., 3rd Sess. (Washington, 1940).
[26] See Bernard Schwartz, *op. cit.,* esp. pp. 82–90.
[27] In interviews.

mum" inquiry that could not be avoided rather than to a partisan no-holds-barred examination of agency-clientele-White House relations.[28] As one Democrat on the subcommittee phrased this:

> This [special oversight subcommittee] was a good case of a shotgun marriage. The [Democratic commerce committee] leadership didn't want much of an investigation of the agencies and the [Eisenhower] administration certainly didn't want one. But once the staff started turning up all those interesting things the leadership either had to slam the lid down tight and risk getting clobbered for it, or lift it just a little to let out some of the steam. As far as I'm concerned, a real job still needs to be done—it certainly can't hurt me any. But I suppose it's not likely to happen very soon.[29]

There is much to suggest that the decision of committee leaders and members to initiate and participate in a review of agency policies and practices often results from an unenthusiastic determination that a limited examination of an agency by its friends may cost less than an uncontrolled one by its enemies.[30]

Summary

What has been proposed here are statements of general tendencies. They are offered as hypotheses that are supported by some evidence but which invite further testing. They are not intended to be exclusive. No doubt there are other explanations for committee oversight of administrative agencies or the absence of it. From the documents produced by a limited number and a particular kind of Congressional committee and from interviews with committee members and staff, these propositions appear to be major ones. As suggestions of tendencies they might be useful in alerting us to the contrasts between prescribed Congressional conduct—the "continuous watchfulness" called for in the 1946 Reorganization Act—and real attitudes and

[28] This tends to be a somewhat different picture of the relevance to a Congressman's behavior of his legislative party, particularly for members of the majority party, than that presented by David Truman in his examination of roll call votes in the 81st Congress. See his *The Congressional Party,* esp. pp. 280*ff.* This contrary evidence is inconclusive, however, since there are occasions in which the inclinations of majority as well as minority members to engage in agency review are closely related to their loyalty to a President of their party. See, *e.g.,* hypothesis 6 above, section II.

[29] The new situation which in 1961 made even less likely than before such an intensive examination of agency performance by a Democratic committee was the filling of top agency positions with appointees of a new Democratic President. See hypothesis 6 above.

[30] This language—"better by friends than by enemies"—was in fact used by several committee members to explain their willingness in a given case to review agency programs.

behavior. But these propositions are offered also to suggest some theoretical unity which links them to one another. Congressional committee leaders and members are viewed as people who act on the basis of rational estimates of their situation. The decision to initiate, participate actively in, or avoid committee inquiry into agency performance is understood by the Congressman as one involving costs and gains. The political environment in which he lives—one requiring that he decide which among multiple and often conflicting demands he will try to satisfy in exchange for rewards he can expect in return—explains his frequent preference for leaving the agencies alone as well as his periodic willingness to examine them closely. In a decentralized party system in which his loyalty to Congressional and Presidential parties is sporadic, the Congressman's decision tends to result most often from his generally closer identification with constituent, local-party, and interest-group needs.